The Political Economy
of Transition in Eurasia

The Political Economy of Transition in Eurasia

DEMOCRATIZATION AND ECONOMIC LIBERALIZATION IN A GLOBAL ECONOMY

Edited by Norman A. Graham and Folke Lindahl

Michigan State University Press • *East Lansing*

Michigan State University Press
East Lansing, Michigan 48823-5245
www.msupress.msu.edu

Printed and bound in the United States of America.

12 11 10 09 08 07 06   1 2 3 4 5 6 7 8 9 10

LIBRARY OF CONGRESS CATALOGING-IN-PUBLICATION DATA
The political economy of transition in Eurasia : democratization and
economic liberalization in a global economy / edited by Norman A.
Graham and Folke Lindahl.
p. cm. — (Eurasian political economy and public policy studies series)
Includes bibliographical references.
ISBN 0-87013-766-2 (pbk. : alk. paper)
1. Democratization—Europe, Eastern. 2. Democratization—Europe,
Central. 3. Democratization—Former Soviet republics. 4. Europe,
Eastern—Economic policy—1989– 5. Europe, Central—Economic
policy—1989– 6. Former Soviet republics—Economic policy.
I. Graham, Norman A. II. Lindahl, Folke. III. Series.
JN96.A91P643 2006
320.947—dc22
2006005193

Cover design by Erin Kirk New
Book design by Sharp Des!gns, Inc., Lansing, MI

g **green** Michigan State University Press is a member of the Green
press Press Initiative and is committed to developing and en-
INITIATIVE couraging ecologically responsible publishing practices. For more information about the Green Press Initiative and the use of recycled paper in
book publishing, please visit *www.greenpressinitiative.com*.

Contents

1

Introduction and Overview

Norman A. Graham

The 27 new "republics" of Eurasia[1]—basically the successor states to the Soviet Union and the former members of the Warsaw Pact—present a wide range of progress in democratization and economic liberalization. Some, like Belarus, Tajikistan, Turkmenistan, and Uzbekistan, must still be regarded as authoritarian regimes with only limited departures from the old, centrally planned command economies. Others, like Hungary, Poland, the Czech Republic, Slovenia, and the three Baltic States, seem to have "consolidated" vibrant and competitive (but still young) democracies, and—on the surface at least—appear to be well on their way in progress toward working market economies. Is it now possible to assess this varied performance systematically? Are there important lessons learned and patterns evident? What determines the variance?

This chapter provides a cross-national overview assessment of the transition of the post-communist[2] regimes and economies of Eurasia—hereafter referred to as ECA (European and Central Asian) transition countries. A primary goal will be to uncover the interactions between the economic and the political. It will also seek to introduce the remaining chapters in this volume, which explore these interactions in more detail for select cases.

Strategies of Economic Liberalization

It is not possible here to provide great detail on the strategies of economic liberalization that have been "offered" to the transition governments of Europe and Central Asia, beset with the unusual challenge of finding an effective way of moving from a centrally planned state socialist economy to a Western-style market economy. There are numerous discussions of the range of policy packages available, often adapted from the "Washington Consensus" that undergirds the structural adjustment and "conditionality" policies of the International Monetary Fund and the World Bank (see, for example, Bhaduri and Nayyar 1996, 1–122, and Stiglitz 2002; for specific discussions of the ECA context, see Andor and Summers 1998, and Lavigne 1999). An attempt to summarize the common package may be useful, however.

In general, the focus is on adopting "orthodox" market reforms under the guidance of neoclassical economics, bringing the discipline of the market into the economy with a pricing structure that responds to supply and demand, reducing the size of the public sector through privatization, encouraging free trade, attracting foreign capital, and devaluing local currencies to the world market values. The size and power of government is a common target, with some emphasis placed on decentralization—following the advice of the "reinventing government" movement, popular for a time in the United States and Western Europe. The specific measures proposed include:

▶ Privatization (selling state enterprises to the private sector); this often involves foreign investment, but it can include a voucher program with shares distributed in various ways to the public.
▶ Raising producer prices for agricultural goods in particular, but pricing according to market forces more generally (removing state subsidies).
▶ Devaluing local currencies to the world market value (the Soviet ruble used to trade officially (in the USSR only) at about a 1 to 1 ratio with the US$; by 1993 it was down to < 0.2 cents in value).
▶ Reducing government deficits (including cuts in subsidies, but also cuts in social welfare, health, and free higher-education programs)—again privatizing and bringing "market" discipline in; this obviously was quite painful for much of the population, particularly those who also found themselves suddenly unemployed.

An important part of the policy debates on economic liberalization involved "tactical choices" over sequencing and the pace of transition. What should come first—price liberalization, foreign-trade and capital-movement liberalization, banking and financial reforms, privatization, etc.? These involved important tradeoffs, obviously, and were decided sometimes with a rational calculus of what made the most economic sense in a given situation. But there was also a tendency to follow the path of least political resistance, avoiding entrenched bureaucratic interests or powerful independent opponents. Voucher privatization of large public-sector firms often found limited opposition, as opposed to the tough work of establishing a new system of property rights and protection, commercial law reform, foreign-investment regulation, or cuts in public expenditures and subsidies.

The speed and depth of the liberalization process raised larger and more controversial questions. The usual depiction was a choice between a "big bang"/ "shock therapy" approach, as one might characterize the general advice of liberalization gurus like Jeffrey Sachs (and employed most seriously in the GDR, though Poland is normally offered as the best example of a stand-alone shock-therapy approach), versus a more gradual or incremental approach like that adopted by Hungary. The debate largely centered on the question of political feasibility. Sachs and his sympathizers argued that the change required was massive (and essential—all of it), and that one should institute as many of the elements of the Washington Consensus as possible, swiftly and in a concentrated time frame, while the euphoria from the collapse of the communist regimes was still strongly felt by much of the population that would feel the shock. By the time the euphoria wore off, the public would begin to see the positive effects of the therapy. Anders Åslund added to these arguments the view that swift and comprehensive reform was necessary because the continuation of large and unregulated state apparatuses live on corruption (Åslund 2002). One can look to Russia, the Ukraine, and Central Asia for support of this view to different degrees.

Gradualism or incrementalism was preferred by those not entirely confident of the correct mix of medicine required, given the weakness of the economies, the size of the task of restructuring, and the challenge of promoting fundamentally different economic behavior in the East from that which had been common under state socialism. Moreover, some argued that small bites of reform and pain would be easier to swallow politically. Indeed, some analysts have argued that a more gradual approach allowed for policy refinement and more effective choice among policy alternatives, perhaps insulating state agencies from particularistic claims, as well as providing benefits in building true support behind difficult (but promising) options (see Orenstein 2001 for a comparison of Poland and the Czech Republic in this respect, and Bartlett 1997 for an analysis of the Hungary case).

There were certainly ambiguous mixed cases, like the reforms in Russia that seemed to start out with a "shock therapy" approach, but backed off rather quickly. A common charge was that there was often plenty of shock, but too little therapy in some reform packages. Moreover, a number of transition countries did very little in the way of economic reform in the initial years (e.g., Romania), and some might still be characterized today as waiting on serious reform (e.g., Belarus, where the wait may yet be a long one).

David Bartlett argues that this debate is misguided in that the key for transition regimes is the ability to construct appropriate institutions (banks, legal framework for bankruptcy and accounting, tax collection, etc.), which cannot be done swiftly. Rapid liberalization of prices, foreign trade, and investment is important (cf. the Polish case), but it is not determinative of ultimate success (Bartlett 1997, 265). Table 1.1 presents a "scorecard" of economic-transition progress, derived from assessments by the European Bank for Reconstruction and Development (2001) and Freedom House (Karatnycky et al. 2002).

The 27 transition countries are ranked by perceived "progress" on economic liberalization as measured by the average Freedom House ratings in the three categories of privatization, macroeconomic reform, and microeconomic reform in 2002. The EBRD rankings for 2001 are indicated in parentheses. There is evidence of recent progress in Russia and Southeastern Europe, but in large measure the successor republics to the former Soviet Union in Europe and Central Asia remain very modest in their progress on each of the key dimensions of economic liberalization.

Moreover, as suggested below, there is considerable argument for the need to examine models well beyond the scope of the Washington Consensus on economic liberalization for transition countries. Proponents of the "Third Way" are relevant here of course (see, for example, Giddens 1998, 2000, and 2001), as are those who point to the merits of the "East Asian development model" as a viable alternative (see, for example, the World Bank assessment in World Bank 1993).

The Consolidation of New Democracies

There is, of course, a long tradition of scholarship on the appropriate strategies and ingredients of democratization. The work of Lipset and Lijphart on the socioeconomic bases, or at least the correlates of democracies is widely familiar, and has stimulated considerable empirical work on the requisites of democracy and the explanation of patterns of political-party formation, voting behavior, and political conflict (Lipset 1963; Lipset and Rokkan 1967; and Lijphart 1984). This is complemented by substantial work on political culture and the cultural influences on political behavior and the effectiveness of democracy (see the early conceptions and surveys of Almond and Verba in *The Civic Culture* [1963], as well as the more recent studies of specific cases, such as the study of Italy led by Robert Putnam in *Making Democracy Work* [1993]; and Larry Diamond's collection of studies of *Political Culture and Democracy in Developing Countries* [1994; see especially Christine Sadowski's essay on Eastern Europe in that collection]).

Putnam and his colleagues examine the effectiveness of democratic institutions based on three broad models of explaining performance: effective

TABLE 1.1 Progress of Economic Reform in Eurasia

RANK	COUNTRY	PRIVATIZATION		MACRO-ECONOMIC REFORM		MICRO-ECONOMIC REFORM		AVERAGE[a]
		1998	2002	1998	2002	1998	2002	2002
1.	Poland (3)[b]	2.25	2.25	1.75	2.0	1.75	1.5	1.92
2.	Estonia (2)	2.0	1.75	2.0	2.0	2.0	2.0	1.92
3.	Hungary (1)	1.5	1.5	1.75	2.5	1.75	2.0	2.00
4.	Czech Rep. (4)	2.0	1.75	2.0	2.25	2.0	2.25	2.08
5.	Slovenia (5)	2.5	2.5	2.0	2.0	2.0	2.0	2.17
6.	Latvia (7)	2.5	2.5	2.5	2.25	2.5	2.25	2.33
7.	Slovakia (9)	3.25	2.0	3.75	2.5	3.75	2.5	2.33
8.	Lithuania (6)	2.25	2.25	2.75	2.75	2.75	2.25	2.42
9.	Bulgaria (11)	4.0	3.0	4.0	3.0	4.25	3.75	3.25
10.	Croatia (10)	4.0	3.25	3.75	3.5	3.75	3.75	3.50
11.	Armenia (18)	3.75	3.25	4.25	3.5	4.25	4.0	3.58
12.	Kyrgyzstan (20)	4.25	4.25	3.5	3.5	3.5	3.5	3.75
13.	Albania (19)	4.0	3.25	5.0	4.0	4.5	4.0	3.75
14.	Georgia (12)	4.0	3.25	4.0	4.0	4.0	4.0	3.75
15.	Romania (8)	4.5	3.75	4.5	3.75	4.5	4.25	3.92
16.	Russia (16)	3.0	3.5	4.25	3.75	4.25	4.5	3.92
17.	Moldova (14)	4.0	4.0	4.25	4.5	4.25	4.25	4.25
18.	Kazakhstan (13)	4.25	4.0	4.5	4.25	4.75	4.5	4.25
19.	Ukraine (15)	4.5	4.25	4.5	4.5	5.25	4.5	4.42
20.	Azerbaijan (21)	5.0	4.25	5.0	4.5	5.0	4.5	4.42
21.	Macedonia (17)	4.0	4.25	5.0	4.75	5.0	5.0	4.67
22.	Serbia/Mont. (24)	4.5	4.75	5.0	5.25	5.0	5.0	5.0
23.	Tajikistan (25)	6.25	5.5	6.0	5.5	5.75	5.25	5.08
24.	Bosnia-Herz. (22)	5.5	5.0	6.0	5.5	6.0	5.5	5.33
25.	Uzbekistan (23)	6.25	6.0	6.25	6.0	6.25	6.0	6.0
26.	Belarus (26)	6.0	6.0	6.25	6.25	6.5	6.5	6.25
27.	Turkmenistan (27)	6.75	6.75	6.25	6.25	6.25	6.5	6.5

SOURCES: Freedom House Ratings 2003 and European Bank for Reconstruction and Development 2001.

(a.) This column represents the average 2002 rating of all 3 dimensions. Ratings are based on the normal Freedom House system where essentially 1 = maximum "progress" and 7 = no progress. (b.) The number in parentheses summarizes and ranks the reform progress reported by the EBRD on a range of specific measures of economic liberalization in 2001.

institutional design, socioeconomic factors, and sociocultural factors, with clear focus on the third. They find striking, though not uncontroversial, differences in the effectiveness of regional political institutions, which they largely attribute to differences in the political cultures of Northern and Southern Italy. Putnam followed up this work with his equally controversial examination of the United

States in *Bowling Alone*, which argued that a decline in social organization and political communication among its citizens had detracted dramatically from the quality of American democracy (Putnam 2000).

"Models" of institutional design and efforts to measure and assess the effectiveness of democratization are clearly an important thrust of scholarship. Here the work of scholars like David Held (1987, 1993) and Samuel P. Huntington (1991) represent important dimensions and efforts to synthesize the various models or types and the historical patterns or "waves" of democratization.

David Held categorizes a variety of models of democracy. Modern models include *competitive elitism*—a parliamentary government with a strong executive (the focus here is on a method for selection of a skilled and imaginative political elite capable of making necessary legislative and administrative decisions in a technocratic world); *pluralism*, which secures government by minorities and hence political liberty (the goal is to avoid both excessively powerful factions and an unresponsive state); *legal democracy*, which stipulates that majority rule must be circumscribed by the rule of law; *participatory democracy*, which posits that the equal right to self-development can only be achieved in a participatory society, stressing the need for a sense of political efficacy, and the formation of a knowledgeable citizenry capable of taking a sustained interest in the governing process; and *democratic autonomy*, which stresses that individuals should be free and equal in the determination of the conditions of their own lives, but that one cannot deploy this framework to negate the rights of others.

Samuel P. Huntington has been long known for his interest in strong political institutions as a key ingredient of political stability (see Huntington 1968). In *The Third Wave: Democratization in the Late Twentieth Century*, he provides a masterful synthesis of practice and progress in sources of authority, purposes, and procedures of democratic government of nation-states since the seventeenth century. He occasionally offers some "guidelines for democratizers" and warns that one must look beyond the mere existence of elections to assessments about such qualities as openness, honesty, effective citizen control over policy, and rational deliberation. He stresses the need to determine if elected officials exercise real power, and he returns to his previous focus on stability and institutionalization, as he addresses the question of the fragility of democratic political systems.

Larry Diamond (1999) uses the Freedom House ratings and his own independent judgments to categorize states into four main categories: (1) *liberal democracies*, (2) *non-liberal electoral democracies*, (3) *pseudo-democracies*, and (4) *authoritarian regimes*. Table 1.2 summarizes his categorization for Eurasia, based on 1997 data.

TABLE 1.2 Diamond's Classification of Regimes in 1997 (as applied to Eurasian post-state-socialist cases)

Liberal democracies				
1.0[a]	(United States; Sweden)		4.0	Albania
1.5	Czech Republic			Croatia
	Estonia			Kyrgyz Republic
	Hungary		4.5	(Turkey)
	Latvia		5.0	Bosnia-Herzegovina
	Lithuania			
	Poland		**Pseudo-democracies**	
1.5	Slovenia		4.5	Armenia
	(United Kingdom; France)		5.0	Azerbaijan
2.0	Romania		5.5	Kazakhstan
	(Republic of Korea)		6.0	Belarus
2.5	Bulgaria			Yugoslavia (Serbia and Montenegro)
Non-liberal electoral democracies			**Authoritarian regimes (one-party or no-party)**	
3.0	Slovakia		6.0	Tajikistan
3.5	Georgia		6.5	Uzbekistan
	Macedonia		7.0	Turkmenistan
	Moldova			(China)
	Russia			
	Ukraine			

SOURCE: Diamond 1999.

(a.) These numbers represent the average of the Freedom House ratings on political rights and civil liberties as of the end of 1997, where 1 = highest rights/liberties and 7 = lowest. Diamond supplements these ratings with his own judgments to classify states into pseudo-democracies vs. authoritarian regimes.

We shall return to this classification later in the chapter to see if any of the Eurasian post-state-socialist regimes might be "upgraded," as we try to assess democratic consolidation in 2003.

Adam Przeworski and his colleagues offer an alternative classification of democracies and dictatorships in *Democracy and Development* (2000) into (1) *autocracy*, (2) *bureaucracy*, (3) *presidentialism*, (4) *parliamentarism*, and (5) *mixed*. At this stage in my work, at least, I find it less helpful than Diamond's, but the Przeworski-led team does offer some interesting arguments on why a state should not really be termed a democracy until a ruling party has lost an election. Quoting a definition offered by Przeworski in 1991, they note: "Democracy is a system in which parties lose elections" (Przeworski et al. 2000, 16). Japan might not be considered democratic for much of the post–World War II period as a consequence, and the elections and interparty competition in

Botswana do not qualify, because one party has ruled since independence. This "rule" for the classification and comparison of new republics in Eurasia may be problematic, but it offers an interesting way to distinguish among democracies in terms of quality or degree of consolidation. Alternatively, Diamond adopts the view offered by Dankwart Rustow that consolidation encompasses "'habituation,' in which the norms, procedures, and expectations of democracy become so internalized that actors routinely, instinctively conform to the written (and unwritten) rules of the game, even when they conflict and compete intensely" (Diamond 1999, 65). How one clearly "operationalizes" this definition may be a serious challenge, however.

In an earlier work, Diamond argues:

> The consolidation of democracy is not civil society but political institutionalization. Consolidation is the process by which democracy becomes so broadly and profoundly legitimate among its citizens that it is very unlikely to break down. It involves behavioral and institutional changes that normalize democratic politics and narrow its uncertainty. . . . Robust political institutions are needed to accomplish economic reform under democratic conditions. Strong, well-structured executives buttressed by experts at least somewhat insulated from the day-to-day pressures of politics, make possible the implementation of painful and disruptive reform measures. Settled and aggregative (as opposed to volatile and fragmented) party systems—in which one or two broadly based, centrist parties consistently obtain electoral majorities or near-majorities—are better positioned to resist narrow class and sectoral interests and to maintain the continuity of economic reforms across successive administrations. (Diamond and Plattner, eds. 1996, 238–39)

According to this definition, as noted below, few of the post-Soviet republics could be termed consolidated democracies.

The Challenge of Simultaneous Democratization and Economic Liberalization

A set of questions that remain yet to be thoroughly addressed center on the challenges associated with efforts to achieve simultaneous economic liberalization and political democratization. This "dual transition" was adopted very seriously by several Central European countries, with some measure of success, but also with considerable pain and political uncertainty.

For those who study the connection between economic systems and democracy, Joseph Schumpeter is likely the pioneer. His *Capitalism, Socialism, and Democracy* focused on effective democracy, in a procedural sense, as the institutional arrangements for acquiring power "by means of a competitive struggle for the people's vote" (1947, 269).

Adam Przeworski and his colleagues have produced a masterful examination of democracy and development for the period 1950–90. The timing of their analyses precludes serious treatment of the post-communist states and limits their ability to analyze the experiences of Korea and Taiwan, unfortunately. They tend not to examine cases in detail to uncover the relevance of political culture and distinctive economic policies. But they offer substantial quantitative information and systematic treatment of the relationships between regime types, economic development, economic growth, political stability, and population dynamics. They conclude that economic development does not tend to generate democracy; indeed, they make a strong argument that there is no clear trade-off between democracy and development, despite the common arguments made by modernization theorists and the oft-cited experiences of the "miracles" of East and Southeast Asia, most notably the Republic of Korea and Taiwan (Przeworski et al. 2000).

Some radical political economists have extended the focus on procedure to promote "economic democracy," in which all forms of power are brought to popular accountability (see, for example, Bowles and Gintis 1986). The more general question of the proper role for the state in "national" economies is, of course, relevant here. This debate remains intense and includes those who argue for a more coherent industrial policy and a focus on educational reform to meet the needs of twenty-first-century capitalism (Reich 1991; see also Yergin 2002), versus those who argue that the state has largely become obsolete as an effective instrument of economic prosperity (Ohmae 1995).

Linda Weiss, in *The Myth of the Powerless State* (1998), points to the evolving nature of the state's role in the economy, drawing on the cases of Germany, Japan, and Sweden to suggest that proclamations of "the end of the nation-state" are premature at best. Richard Rosecrance (1999) adds a new level of uncertainty by arguing that the state will not disappear, but will change dramatically in its character. He argues that a new type of state is emerging—the virtual state—in a global environment in which land and military power are less important than a state's share of world economic output. Small states with managerial, financial, and creative skills may dominate through their ability to control assets elsewhere.

What, then, are the special challenges faced by political economies undergoing political democratization and economic liberalization in roughly the same time frame? What is the appropriate sequencing of economic and political reform for transition and newly industrializing countries? What is the appropriate role of the state? What has worked best among our 27 transition countries of Eastern Europe and Central Asia?

One way to confront this is to seek a verdict on "the Lee hypothesis" (advocated by Lee Kuan Yew of Singapore), which stresses the need for discipline and centralized state power for effective economic development. Singapore, the Republic of Korea, Taiwan, and Chile are often cited as effective examples of this model in practice, and a long tradition of political and economic-development scholars have struggled with this question. (As noted above, see the arguments made in the 1960s by scholars such as Samuel P. Huntington, who posited that the causes of instability in emerging countries derived from the lag in the development of viable political institutions behind social and economic change). There is some compatibility here with the critics of initial reform efforts in Russia (as opposed to the "shock therapy" approach of Poland and the "economic reform first" strategy of the authoritarian political regime in China).

Alternatively, the approach advocated by Nobel laureate Amartya Sen stresses the "instrumental" and "constructive" values of democracy in the economic-development process. In the July 1999 issue of the *Journal of Democracy*, Sen wrote that democracy plays a crucial role in avoiding famine because "a responsive government intervenes to help alleviate hunger." He went on to stress that the economies worst hit by the Asian financial crisis, particularly South Korea, Thailand, and Indonesia, suffered "the penalties of undemocratic governance." Here he pointed to the "lack of transparency in business, in particular the lack of public participation in reviewing financial arrangements." At minimum, Sen argues that the data do not support any particular negative or positive connection between economic development and democracy. Nicolas Van de Walle made a similar set of arguments in connection with political liberalization and economic reform in Africa (Van de Walle 1994).

David Bartlett took this line a step further, concluding from his study of the Hungarian case that success in the dual transformation of democratization and economic liberalization is certainly possible. Hungary offers a case where state agencies were insulated from the opponents of economic reforms by democracy and the creation of democratic institutions; political reform can, in fact, promote economic reform (Bartlett 1997, 3).

A number of scholars point to the structure of competition in the emerging global economy as an important influence on both economic development and democratization. Those that see this impact as inevitable, and the engine of global economic efficiency stress the evident drive (and need) among large manufacturers for new markets in the face of intense competition. This in turn leads to rationalization, consolidation, simplifying the range of component and material suppliers, cutting costs and increasing leverage for discounts, shifting production overseas in order to reach new markets and cut labor costs, engaging in strategic (interfirm) alliances—often with former competitors—in order to share research-and-development costs and avoid costly and inflexible production expansion, forging increased use of communication networks and information technology, and the rise of global media and marketing (see Wendt 1993; Ohmae 1995; and Ohmae, ed. 1995). Globalization to them is the wave of the future, and is both irresistible and desirable. Micklethwait and Wooldridge (2000) are a bit more measured, arguing that globalization can be an important tool for incipient entrepreneurs in developing countries if the governments in question provide access and policy support. Joseph Stiglitz (2002) is rather more skeptical, despite his role in government and at the World Bank as a "promoter."

Critics stress the contradictions that dominate globalization, such as social polarization within and among societies, the loss of regulatory power by states, and the tendency toward decomposition of civil society (see Cox 1987, 26–27; Gill 1995; Mittelman, ed. 1996). Add to this those that speak of the impact of globalization on state authority—weakening a government's ability to manage a "domestic" economy or perform desirable social-welfare functions (Habermas 1991; Korten 1995; Lasch 1995; Grieder 1997; and Andor and Summers 1998). To what extent is globalization transforming the conditions under which liberal democracy operates?

Philippe Schmitter (1996, 91–92) warns of the disillusionment that flows from the economic performance of neodemocracies; he fears that disaffected actors will revive old authoritarian themes or invent new ones, and he argues that even if there is no revival of authoritarianism, democracies may stumble on without consolidating an acceptable and predictable set of rules for political competition and cooperation. The posture of the West has been to place overwhelming priority on market reform, while only providing lip service to the formation of the necessary institutions of liberal democracy. Political apathy and disillusionment result from institutional weakness. Feelings of powerlessness to effect change and skepticism about the competency of politicians, together with suspicion of corruption, encourage a willingness to contemplate a return to the security of the dominant public sector of the past in state-socialist regimes of Eastern Europe and the former Soviet Union. See also the similar warning offered by Claus Offe, stressing that "Only a developed market economy produces the social structural conditions for stable democracy and makes it possible to form compromises within the framework of what is perceived as a positive-sum" (Offe 1991, 881). These arguments can be connected to what is commonly referred to as the "voting function"—alternating regimes that stay in office only long enough for the disaffected electorate to toss the incumbents out for lack of suitable economic and social progress. One might argue that this phenomenon is alive and well in Central Europe. On the one hand, this can be seen as evidence of strengthening institutions that provide new accountability. On the other hand, it is easy to imagine that precipitous change in ruling administrations may disrupt medium- to long-term economic-transition programs. One should be most concerned, of course, if viable policies are abandoned prematurely under political pressure without adequate substitutes. Can new governors from the Left, with campaign goals for change toward a stronger social conscience, find a way to overcome the harsh realities of budget constraint and limited "wiggle room" that also faced their more conservative predecessors?

Finally, theorists ask, what are the most important international linkages that affect the prospects for economic progress and democratization in transition countries? How have economic progress and democratization been helped or hindered by the multilateral institutions that have been most involved in providing loans and other financial assistance to these countries? The current tidal wave of public criticism directed toward the IMF, World Bank, and World Trade Organization is not matched by systematic analysis of the roles of those institutions in the experience of transition political economies since 1989, although some preliminary accounts have emerged (see Wedel 1998).

As we turn now to the measurement of economic progress and democratic consolidation in transition countries since 1989, how might we examine these various theoretical strains? To what extent are they interrelated? Have the various elements of globalization helped or hindered economic progress and the democratization process in transition countries? Theoretical development here is in some respects in its infancy, but it certainly draws on a long tradition of debate between proponents of neoclassical economics and economic nationalism/neomercantilism on the one hand, and an equally long tradition of democratic theorists on the other. Examining the impact of the context of these efforts, in the post-cold-war international system and in the institutional framework of fragile democratic reform, is particularly interesting and potentially exciting theoretically. As we speak of the emergence of fragile democratic states in transition economies, how have the challenges inherent in their situation been raised or perturbed by globalization and international institutions?

Measuring Economic Progress and Challenges

Measuring economic progress in the European and Central Asian transition countries is a complex task. The relevant data are available to a greater extent now than ever in the past, but there remain important uncertainties and limitations. This section of the introduction will make some hard choices, focusing largely on international sources that enhance the comparability and objectivity of the potential assessments. It may well be useful to explore the prospects for constructing composite indices of progress and rank, in the spirit of previous efforts along these lines (see, for example, Estes 1998). But this will have to wait for a subsequent iteration. At this stage, we shall simply compare data on economic growth, income distribution, and poverty, and the degree to which each country has become integrated into the global economy, after years of isolation and autarky.

ECONOMIC GROWTH

One pattern is abundantly clear from a review of the data on economic growth since 1989. The restructuring accomplished during the early period of liberalization meant that economic output had to fall. Some of the depths reached by several countries in the region were much worse than others. But all ECA countries experienced an initial drop in GDP growth and industrial production. Tables 1.3 and 1.4 show the initial dip in GDP growth, comparing the period 1980–90 with 1990–2002, and point to the return to positive growth in nearly all cases by 2002. The weakest GDP growth percentages (2001–02) were experienced by Kyrgyzstan, Macedonia, and Poland. Several other countries (e.g., Georgia, Moldova, Romania, Slovakia, Tajikistan, and the Ukraine) still have not reached their pre-1990 industrial production levels.

Tables 1.5 and 1.6 present the unemployment and inflation-rate figures for European and Central Asian transition countries, along with the GDP growth rates for 2000–03. Romania, Belarus, Moldova, the Ukraine, Tajikistan, and Uzbekistan all suffer from inflation rates in excess of 15 percent. The highest

TABLE 1.3 Growth in Gross Domestic Product in Central and Eastern Europe

	1980–1990[a]	1990–1998[a]	1995–2000[b]	1990–2002[c]	2001–2002[a]
Albania	1.5%	1.8%	4.3%	5.4%	4.7%
Bulgaria	3.4%	–3.3%	–1.0%	–0.7%	4.3%
Czech Republic	1.7%	–0.2%	0.4%	1.3%	2.0%
Hungary	1.3%	–0.2%	4.2%	2.2%	3.3%
Poland	1.8%	4.5%	5.1%	4.3%	1.2%
Romania	0.5%	–0.6%	–2.4%	–0.2%	4.3%
Slovakia	2.0%	0.6%	4.1%	2.3%	4.4%
Bosnia/Herz.					3.9%
Croatia			3.5%	1.3%	5.2%
Macedonia					0.3%
Serbia/Mont.					3.0%[d]
Slovenia			4.4%	4.1%	2.9%

SOURCES: (a) World Bank, *World Development Report*, 2000–2004; (b) UNCTAD, *Handbook of Statistics*, 2002; (c) World Bank, *World Development Indicators*, 2004; and (d) International Monetary Fund, *World Economic Outlook*, 2004.

TABLE 1.4   Growth in Gross Domestic Product in the Former Soviet Union

	1980–1990[a]	1990–1998[a]	1995–2000[b]	1990–2002[c]	2001–2002[a]
Europe and Russia					
Belarus	n.a.	–6.1%	6.7%	–0.01%	4.7%
Estonia	2.2%	–2.1%	4.8%	0.1%	5.8%
Latvia	3.5%	–8.5%	4.6%	–0.1%	6.1%
Lithuania	n.a.	–5.2%	3.2%	–0.9%	6.7%
Moldova	3.0	–14.1%	–2.7%	–7.1%	7.2%
Russia	(1.6)	–7.0%	0.8%	–2.7%	4.3%
Ukraine	n.a.	–13.1%	–1.9%	–6.6%	4.5%
Caucasus and Central Asia					
Armenia	n.a.	–10.3%	5.1%	0.4%	12.9%
Azerbaijan	n.a.	–10.3%	7.3%	1.2%	10.6%
Georgia	0.4%	–16.3%	5.5%	–4.3%	5.4%
Kazakhstan	n.a.	–6.9%	1.9%	–1.6%	9.5%
Kyrgyzstan	n.a.	–7.3%	5.3%	–2.2%	–0.5%
Tajikistan	n.a.	–16.4%	1.1%	–6.8%	9.1%
Turkmenistan	n.a.	–9.4%	4.0%	–1.0%	14.9%
Uzbekistan	n.a.	–1.9%	3.5%	0.08%	4.2%

SOURCES: (a) World Bank, *World Development Report*, 2000–2004; (b) UNCTAD, *Handbook of Statistics*, 2002; and (c) World Bank, *World Development Indicators*, 2004.

TABLE 1.5. GDP Growth, Unemployment, and Inflation in Central and Eastern Europe

	GDP GROWTH		UNEMPLOYMENT			INFLATION	
	2000	2002	2000[a]	2001[b]	1998–2001[b]	2000	2003
Albania	7.8%	4.7%	18%		18.0%	0.4%	2.4%
Bulgaria	5.8%	4.3%	14%	19%	14.1%	9.0%	2.3%
Czech Rep.	2.9%	2.0%	9%	8%	8.8%	4.0%	0.1%
Hungary	5.2%	3.3%	7%	6%	6.5%	9.5%	4.7%
Poland	4.0%	1.2%	17%	18 %	16.7%	10.0%	0.8%
Romania	1.6%	4.3%	11%	7%	10.8%	43.0%	15.3%
Slovakia	2.2%	4.4%	19%	19%	18.9%	12.0%	8.5%
Bosnia/Herz.		3.9%			n.a.		0.2%
Croatia	3.7%	5.2%	21%	16%	20.6%		1.5%
Macedonia		0.3%			34.5%		1.2%
Serbia/Mont.		3.0%			n.a.		11.3%
Slovenia	4.6%	2.9%	8%	6%	7.5%		5.6%

SOURCES: World Bank, *World Development Report*, 2000–2004; (a) UNCTAD, *Handbook of Statistics*; and (b) *World Economic Outlook*, September 2004.

TABLE 1.6 GDP Growth, Unemployment, and Inflation in the Former Soviet Union

	GDP GROWTH		UNEMPLOYMENT			INFLATION	
	2000	2002	2000[a]	2001[b]	1998–2001[b]	2000	2003
Europe and Russia							
Belarus	5.8%	4.7%	2%	2%	2.0%	183.0%	28.4%
Estonia	6.4%	5.8%	15%	13%	14.8%	4.0%	1.3%
Latvia	6.6%	6.1%	8%	13%	8.4%	3.5%	2.9%
Lithuania	3.9%	6.7%	11%	17%	16.6%	1.0%	−1.2%
Moldova	1.9%	7.2%	11%	7%	11.1%	32.0%	11.7%
Russia	8.3%	4.3%	11%	n.a.	11.4%	20.0%	13.7%
Ukraine	5.8%	4.5%	12%	11%	11.9%	70.0%	5.2%
Caucasus and Central Asia							
Armenia	6.0%	12.9%	9%	n.a.	9.3%	-0.4%	4.8%
Azerbaijan	11.1%	10.6%	1%	1%	1.2%	2.0%	2.2%
Georgia	1.9%	5.4%	14%	11%	n.a.	4.0%	4.8%
Kazakhstan	9.6%	9.5%	14%	n.a.	13.7%	13.0%	6.4%
Kyrgyzstan	5.0%	−0.5%	5%	n.a.	n.a.[a]	19.0%	3.1%
Tajikistan	8.3%	9.1%	3%	n.a.	n.a.[a]	25.0%	16.4%
Turkmenistan	17.6%	14.9%	n.a.	n.a.	n.a.	7.0%	5.6%
Uzbekistan	4.0%	4.2%	1%	n.a.	4%?[a]	23.9%	14.8%

SOURCES: World Bank, *World Development Report*, 2000–2004; (a) UNCTAD, *Handbook of Statistics*; and (b) *World Economic Outlook*, September 2004.

(a.) Reliable data are not available; informal employment activity range above 30% for all Central Asian countries now except perhaps Turkmenistan. The 4% estimate for unemployment in Uzbekistan is based on a labor market survey performed recently by the government. Most analysts believe the actual rate is much higher.

current unemployment rates are reported by Albania, Bulgaria, Georgia, Kazakhstan, Slovakia, and the Baltics—all 12 percent or more. Data on unemployment in Central Asia are spotty and unreliable, but the combination of real unemployment and underemployment, particularly in the informal sector, appear quite large, except perhaps in Turkmenistan. In some cases, for example, Kazakhstan and Russia, relatively high unemployment and inflation rates are accompanied by a high rate of economic growth. On the other hand, Romania, Slovakia, Moldova, Tajikistan, and Uzbekistan unfortunately experienced rather low GDP growth accompanied by high unemployment and inflation rates.

EQUITY AND POVERTY

As noted previously, virtually all of the ECA transition countries experienced a collapse in economic output in the initial years of economic liberalization. There was substantial variance in the severity of this drop and in the pace of

TABLE 1.7 Income Per Capita and PPP in Central and Eastern Europe

	GROSS NATIONAL INCOME	PURCHASING POWER PARITY	
	Per Capita (2002)	1996	2002
Albania	$1,380	$2,864	$4,040
Bulgaria	$1,790	$4,683	$6,840
CzechRepublic	$5,560	$12,197	$14,500
Hungary	$5,280	$9,832	$12,810
Poland	$4,570	$7,543	$10,130
Romania	$1,850	$5,571	$6,290
Slovakia	$3,950	$9,624	$12,190
Bosnia/Herz.	$1,270		$5,800
Croatia	$4,640	$6,698	$9,760
Macedonia	$1,700		$6,210
Serbia/Mont.	$1,400		n.a.
Slovenia	$9,810	$14,399	$17,690
UnitedStates	$30,600	$30,600	$35,060
Canada	$19,200	$23,725	$28,070
India	$450	$2,149	$2,570

SOURCE: World Bank, *World Development Report*, 2000–2004.

recovery. This variance is undoubtedly explained by a complex mix of factors, including the alternative tactical choices noted above and the points of emphasis in the liberalization policies, but also involving the problems of bureaucratic corruption and resistance, simply incomplete or incompetent implementation, and the undue influence or even "capture" of the government by new but powerful business elites. Business elites have emerged in most of the countries, and in general it is clear that the growth that has occurred in the ECA transition countries has favored some sectors of the societies more than others.

Tables 1.7 and 1.8 point to considerable variance in gross national income per capita and average purchasing power parity among ECA countries. Clearly, the countries of Central and Eastern Europe enjoy the highest average national-income levels in relation to the size of their populations. Using the World Bank's approach to relate these data to the actual purchasing power that such an income would mean in local currencies, the numbers rise substantially in relation to the average figures for the United States. Slovenia heads the list, with the Czech Republic close behind. Armenia, Azerbaijan, Georgia, Moldova, Kyrgyzstan, Tajikistan, and Uzbekistan all have national-income-per-capita levels below $1,000 and purchasing-power-parity averages below 3,500 in 2002. Russia, Belarus, Georgia, Kazakhstan, and the Ukraine enjoy higher

TABLE 1.8 Income Per Capita and PPP in the Former Soviet Union

	GROSS NATIONAL INCOME	PURCHASING POWER PARITY	
	Per Capita (2002)	1996	2002
Europe and Russia			
Belarus	$1,360	$6,318	$5,330
Estonia	$4,130	$7,563	$11,120
Latvia	$3,480	$5,777	$8,940
Lithuania	$3,660	$6,283	$9,880
Moldova	$460	$1,995	$1,560
Russia	$2,140	$6,186	$7,820
Ukraine	$770	$3,130	$4,650
Causcasus and Central Asia			
Armenia	$790	$2,074	$3,060
Azerbaijan	$710	$2,168	$2,920
Georgia	$650	$3,429	$2,210
Kazakhstan	$1,510	$4,317	$5,480
Kyrgyzstan	$290	$2,247	$1,520
Tajikistan	$180	$1,040	$900
Turkmenistan	$1,200	$2,875	$4,570
Uzbekistan	$450	n.a.	$1,590

SOURCE: World Bank, *World Development Report*, 2000–2004.

levels, but the star economic performers per capita of the former Soviet Union are the Baltic republics of Estonia, Latvia, and Lithuania.

Tables 1.9 and 1.10 depict a substantial gap between the rich and poor within the countries. This, of course, reflects a substantial change from the relative equity of the previous state socialist societies. Russia is not a promising case in this respect, accounting for 60 percent of those living in absolute poverty in the region in the late 1990s. (Absolute poverty is defined by the World Bank in its income surveys of the transition countries of Europe and Central Asia as incomes of less than $2.15 per day [World Bank, *Poverty and Inequality*, 2000]). But the highest percentages of the populations living in absolute poverty exist in Armenia, Azerbaijan, Moldova, Kyrgyzstan, and Tajikistan, with levels in excess of 20 percent. Belarus, Croatia, the Czech Republic, Hungary, Poland, and Slovenia all have levels less than 2 percent. For Belarus, this is likely due to the fact that little economic reform has been implemented, with much of the equity of the old system retained (low national income per capita, but relatively evenly distributed); for the other five, all of which have implemented substantial measures of economic liberalization and have experienced substantial growth in

TABLE 1.9 Poverty and Inequality in Central and Eastern Europe

	% of population in absolute poverty[a]	% of population below national poverty line[d]	Gini Index[b,c]
Albania	11.5%	25.4%	23.0
Bulgaria	3.1%	12.8% (2001)	31.9
Czech Rep.	0		25.4
Hungary	1.3%	17.3% (1997)	24.4
Poland	1.2%	23.8% (1993)	31.6
Romania	6.8%	21.5% (1994)	30.3
Slovakia	2.6%		25.8
Bosnia/Herz.		19.5% (2002)	n.a.
Croatia	0.2%		29.0
Macedonia			28.2
Serbia/Mont.			n.a.
Slovenia	0		25.8

SOURCES: (a) World Bank, *Making Transition Work for Everyone: Poverty and Inequality in Europe and Central Asia*, 2000; (b) World Bank, *World Development Report*, 2000–2004; (c) UNDP, *Human Development Report*, 2003; and (d) UN Statistics Division, *Millennium Indicators*, 2002.

GDP, these data seem to reflect more successful transition economic policies. Similar differences are evident if one compares the percentages of the populations living below the national poverty line as reported in United Nations data. The Belarus survey completed in 2000, however, indicated a large proportion of the population living below the national poverty line.

The Gini Index figures offer another way of measuring income distribution, and suggest similar patterns. A score of 0 essentially would constitute perfect equality, while a score of 100 would represent perfect inequality. The countries of Eastern and Central Europe all have Gini scores in the range of 20–32, while most of the rest have substantially higher scores, with Russia measured as the ECA transition economy with the most inequitable income distribution at nearly 46.

The World Bank *Poverty and Inequality* report (2000) clearly argues that there has been a substantial increase in poverty and inequality in the region since the onset of economic-liberalization policies. Anders Åslund examines this argument with some vigor in his book *Building Capitalism* (2003). Indeed, while granting deterioration in some countries, he argues that "we cannot establish that average living standards have actually fallen during transition. . . . We know little but that Poland has seen a substantial improvement in average living standards, and that official statistics grossly exaggerate human hardship" (Åslund

TABLE 1.10 Poverty and Inequality in the Former Soviet Union

	% of population in absolute poverty[a]	% of population below national poverty line[d]	Gini Index[b,c]
Europe and Russia			
Belarus	1.0%	41.9% (2000)	30.4
Estonia	2.1%	8.9% (1995)	37.6
Latvia	6.6%		32.4
Lithuania	3.1%		36.3
Moldova	55.4%		36.2
Russia	18.8%	30.9% (1994)	45.6
Ukraine	3.0%	31.7% (1995)	29.0
Causcasus and Central Asia			
Armenia	43.5%	53.7% (1999)	37.9
Azerbaijan	23.5%	49.6% (2001)	36.5
Georgia	18.9%	11.1% (1997)	38.9
Kazakhstan	5.7%	34.6% (1996)	31.2
Kyrgyzstan	49.1%	64.1% (1999)	29.0
Tajikistan	68.3%		34.7
Turkmenistan	7.0%		40.8
Uzbekistan	n.a.	27.5% (2000)	26.8

SOURCES: (a) World Bank, *Making Transition Work for Everyone: Poverty and Inequality in Europe and Central Asia*, 2000; (b) World Bank, *World Development Report*, 2000–2004; (c) UNDP, *Human Development Report*, 2003; and (d) UN Statistics Division, *Millennium Indicators*, 2002.

2002, 309). His argument should give us pause, but it would be more convincing if his treatment of the World Bank survey data on poverty levels had been more complete (i.e., not just focused on the absolute poverty-level results).

Reduced public expenditure on health, education, and social-welfare programs makes the dislocation from high unemployment and inflation levels more painful, particularly given the increased need for informal supplementary payments in order to get adequate health care. Differential impact based on ethnicity is a severe complication in several countries, where groups like the Roma find themselves in even more desperate conditions in many cases. Life expectancy has actually deteriorated substantially in many countries. There was a drop of four years in life expectancy of males by the mid-1990s in the Baltic countries, and a drop of five years in Russia, the Ukraine, and Kazakhstan (World Bank, *Poverty and Inequality*, 2000, 29–106). A common refrain is that the politicians have become captured by special interests during the liberalization process, and have little incentive to advocate policies in the interest of the

TABLE 1.11 Foreign Direct Investment Flows in Eurasia (millions of US$)

	1990	1995	2000	2001	2002	2003
Poland	89	3,659	9,341	5,713	4,131	4,225
Azerbaijan	0	330	130	227	1,392	3,285
CzechRepublic	72	2,568	4,984	5,639	8,483	2,583
Hungary	311	5,103	2,764	3,936	2,845	2,470
Kazakhstan	0	964	1,283	2,835	2,590	2,068
Croatia	0	114	1,089	1,561	1,124	1,713
Romania	0	419	1,037	1,157	1,144	1,566
Ukraine	0	267	595	792	693	1,424
Bulgaria	4	90	1,002	813	905	1,419
Serbia/Mont.	0	45	25	165	475	1,360
Bosnia/Herz.	0	20	376	506	772	1,153
Russia	0	2,065	2,714	2,469	3,461	1,144
Estonia	0	202	387	542	284	891
Slovakia	93	258	1,925	1,584	4,123	571
Latvia	0	180	411	163	384	360
Georgia	0	6	131	110	165	338
Slovenia	4	152	137	369	1,606	181
Albania	0	70	143	207	135	180
Lithuania	0	73	379	446	732	179
Belarus	0	15	119	96	247	171
Armenia	4	25	124	88	150	155
Turkmenistan	0	233	126	170	100	100
Macedonia (TFYR)	0	9	175	442	78	95
Uzbekistan	0	−24	75	83	65	70
Moldova	0	67	134	146	117	58
Tajikistan	0	10	24	9	36	32
Kyrgyzstan	0	96	−2	5	5	25

SOURCE: UNCTAD, *Foreign Direct Investment Database* (www.unctad.org), November 2004.

greater society. This situation is accentuated in some cases by the impact of new ills that seem to accompany the opening of the economies and societies. The rapid spread of illegal drugs and AIDS in Russia, especially Siberia, has caught the weakened health and social-services network largely unprepared.

INTEGRATION AND GLOBALIZATION

Many of the ECA countries have clearly ended their long isolation from the rest of the world. But to what extent have they become integrated into the global economy? A persistent challenge for all countries, except for the former German Democratic Republic (GDR), is the lack of capital infusion for industrial development and restructuring. There clearly are differences in the ability to attract foreign direct investment (FDI). Table 1.11 provides a snapshot of the extent of FDI flows for the period 1990–2003. Poland remains the leader in attracting FDI, with the Czech Republic and Hungary also still quite high in relation to the size of their economies. Azerbaijan and Kazakhstan attract substantial oil-related investment, while Russia ranked number 12 with just over US$1.1 billion in FDI inflows—not very impressive given its size, having suffered some downturn due to uncertainties in the political climate after an initial recovery from the financial crisis of 1999–2001. The annual survey released in 2000 by *Business Central Europe* noted that cumulative FDI in Russia was less than half that enjoyed by the Czech Republic, Hungary, or Poland, while cumulative foreign debt in Russia was more than five times that of any other Central European transition country. Southeastern Europe and Central Asia have generally attracted the least FDI, particularly in non-oil-related sectors.

Much of Central and Eastern Europe has turned its attention to membership in the European Union as the key solution to the paucity of development and restructuring capital. The prospects for generosity here are uncertain at best, even for the new EU members from this region (Czech Republic, Hungary, Poland, Slovakia, Estonia, Latvia, Lithuania, and Slovenia), as the European Union remains beset with stagnation and internal differences over the depth of integration and the prospect for additional enlargement. Integration in subregions of the ECA countries perhaps holds more near-term promise for many of the 27 ECA countries, especially given continued reluctance of key EU members, most notably France, to reform the Common Agricultural Policy seriously. The progress to date, though, has been limited in subregional institution building.

Assessing the Consolidation of Democracy in Eurasia

Tables 1.12 and 1.13 provide a rough summary of the degree of "consolidation" reached in the new democracies of Eurasia. While both tables rely substantially on the judgments offered in the Freedom House annual ratings, table 1.13 tries to update the classification offered by Larry Diamond for 1997 (see table 1.2) while adding judgments on some of the other important dimensions he and others raise as important in reaching democratic consolidation—namely, competitive presidential and/or parliamentary elections, regimes actually being able to lose elections (the voting function), and the maturity of political parties in the system (settled and aggregative, as opposed to volatile and fragmented).

The electoral process has worked quite smoothly in much of Central Europe. This is particularly true in the Czech Republic, after the traumatic but peaceful "Velvet Revolution" and "Velvet Divorce." The initial election involving organized political parties brought a conservative/centrist free-enterprise-oriented government to power. The second election brought a resurgence of the Left, as the realities of economic restructuring and the pain of declines in living standards for a large proportion of the populations were evident.

The parliaments have been active and professional, constitutions were adopted, and working procedures and structures were developed. What is missing to date in Central European parliaments is clear success in exerting legislative influence over the economic policy adopted and implemented by the executive departments. The countries of Central Europe differ in their economic resources and paths to economic development, but they all face substantial distress in their respective electorates, and significant feebleness in parliamentary efforts to frame the appropriate path. This was particularly clear in the Czech Republic, and especially under the Klaus government. The governing margin after the 1996 elections was very narrow. Indeed, a vote of confidence during the first few months was won by only 101–99, thanks to the cooperation of an independent member of parliament. This vote, however, enabled Klaus to attempt his first real austerity measures, including total spending cuts of $1.3 billion—about 8 percent of the budget. The cuts hit welfare and social services substantially, and unfortunately followed increases in utility prices. The public reaction was not warm, particularly given the general unease among much of the working class, long used to full employment and a substantial state-supported social safety net.

The question is often whether social consensus can be developed in support of the sacrifice planned. What is the government's side of the bargain? Government commitment to respond to public concern about crime, corruption, legal reform, and privatization reform is a partial answer. Unfortunately, there is little evidence that a consensus was built. There remain few opportunities for intensive public discussion, interest aggregation, and the development of broad-based support around clear long-term plans and policies. The political side of civil society remains weak, and its mobilization sporadic. Indeed, what was most remarkable during periods of unpopular austerity in the region was the apparent lack of organized and effective action by interest groups and nongovernmental organizations (NGOs). Governments often seemed rather isolated from effective public pressure. The policy and political side of civil society remains underdeveloped. Indeed, the executive departments of the administration seem insulated from parliamentary pressure as well.

TABLE 1.12 Freedom House Political Rights and Civil Liberties Ratings

	1991–95 average		1995–99 average		1999–2000			2003–2004		
	PR	CL	PR	CL	PR	CL		PR	CL	
Central and Eastern Europe										
Albania	3.25	3.75	3.75	4.25	4	5	PF	3	3	PF
Bulgaria	2	2.5	2	2.75	2	3	F	1	2	F
Czech Republic	1.5[a]	2[a]	1	2	1	2	F	1	2	F
Hungary	1.5	2	1	2	1	2	F	1	2	F
Poland	2	2	1	2	1	2	F	1	2	F
Romania	4.25	4	2.5	2.5	2	2	F	2	2	F
Slovakia	2.25[a]	2.75[a]	2	3.25	1	2	F	1	2	F
Former Yugoslavia										
Bosnia/Herz.	6	6	5.25	5.25	5	5	PF	4	4	PF
Croatia	3.75	4	4	4	4	4	F	2	2	F
Macedonia	3.33	3.33	3.75	3	3	3	PF	3	3	PF
Serbia/Mont.	6	5.5	6	6	5	5	F	3	2	F
Slovenia	1.5	2.25	1	2	1	2	F	1	1	F
Former Soviet Union: Europe and Russia										
Armenia	3.75	4	4.5	4	4	4	PF	4	4	PF
Azerbaijan	5.5	5.5	6	4.75	6	4	NF	6	5	NF
Belarus	5.5	3.75	5.75	5.75	6	6	NF	6	6	NF
Estonia	2.75	2.5	1.25	2	1	2	F	1	2	F
Georgia	5	5	3.5	4.25	3	4	PF	4	4	PF
Latvia	2.75	2.75	1.5	2	1	2	F	1	2	F
Lithuania	1.5	3	1	2	1	2	F	1	2	F
Moldova	4.75	4.5	3	4	2	4	PF	3	4	PF
Russia	3	3.75	3.25	4	4	5	PF	5	5	PF
Ukraine	3.25	3.5	3	4	3	4	PF	4	4	PF
Former Soviet Union: Central Asia										
Kazakhstan	5.5	4.5	6	5	6	5	NF	6	5	NF
Kyrgyzstan	4.5	3	4.25	4.25	5	5	NF	6	5	NF
Tajikistan	5.75	5.75	6.5	6.5	6	6	NF	6	5	NF
Turkmenistan	6.75	6.25	7	7	7	7	NF	7	7	NF
Uzbekistan	6.5	6.25	7	6.25	7	6	NF	7	6	NF

SOURCE: Freedom House Annual Surveys ().

KEY: PR = Political Rights Rating, PF = Partly Free, CL = Civil Liberties Rating, NF = Not Free, F = Free. 1 = highest rights/liberties

(a.) "Velvet Divorce" in 1993

TABLE 1.13 Classifiying the Democratization of States in Eurasia

	Freedom House Ratings (2003)			Competitive Pres.	Elections Parl.	Regime Change?	Maturity of Pol. Party Syst.
	PR	CL	T				
Liberal Democracies							
Czech Rep.	1	2	F		Y	Y	Y?
Estonia	1	2	F		Y	Y	N?
Hungary	1	2	F		Y	Y	Y?
Latvia	1	2	F		Y	Y	N?
Lithuania	1	2	F	Y	Y	Y	N?
Poland	1	2	F		Y	Y	Y?
Slovenia	1	1	F	Y?	Y	N?	Y?
Romania	2	2	F	Y?	Y	Y	Y?
Bulgaria	1	2	F	Y?	Y	Y	N
Slovakia	1	2	F	Y?	Y?	Y	N
Non-Liberal Electoral Democracies							
Serbia/Mont.	3	2	F	Y?	Y?	Y?	N
Croatia	2	2	F	Y	Y	Y?	N?
Albania	3	3	PF		Y?	Y?	N
Georgia	4	4	PF	Y?	Y	Y?	N
Macedonia	3	3	PF	Y	Y	N?	N
Moldova	3	4	PF	?	Y	Y?	N?
Russia	5	5	PF	Y?	Y	Y*	N
Ukraine	4	4	PF	Y?	Y	Y ?	N
Bosnia Herz.	5	5	PF	Y?	Y?	N?	N
Pseudo-Democracies							
Armenia	4	4	PF	Y?	Y?	N	N?
Azerbaijan	6	5	NF	N?	N?	N	N
Kazakhstan	6	5	NF	N	N	N	N
Kyrgystan	6	5	NF	Y?	Y?	Y?	N
Tajikistan	6	5	NF	N	Y?	N	N
Belarus	6	6	NF	N	N	N	N
Authoritarian Regimes							
Uzbekistan	7	6	NF	N	N	N	N
Turkmenistan	7	7	NF	N	N	N	N

SOURCES: Classification scheme is an update/adaptation of the appendix in Diamond 1999. The first three columns are taken from Freedom House Annual Surveys (www.Freedomhouse.org/ratings/). The remaining columns are the author's current judgments on the competitiveness of the relevant presidential and parliamentary elections, the question of whether or not meaningful regime change has in fact occurred through elections (the voting function), and the degree to which a mature political party system is operative.

KEY: PR = Political Rights Rating, PF = Partly Free, CL = Civil Liberties Rating, NF = Not Free, F = Free. 1 = highest rights/liberties

*PM esp.

There is little argument that important elements of civil society were largely destroyed in Central Europe under the state socialist regimes in power until 1989. Spontaneously developing civil associations were either prohibited, or controlled and monitored. Religious communities were almost alone in being able to preserve a measure of autonomy and independence from the state, and this varied substantially from state to state.

New NGOs include some quite vibrant regional "local enterprise agencies" that have been very effective in promoting entrepreneurial activity with financial support from Western governments, the European Union, and Western foundations. Political organizations remain somewhat embryonic, though the principal political parties have roots in social movements and civic associations in several cases. Government policy has been ambiguous. The legal framework is not complete, but there is considerable emphasis on the constitution and on legislation respecting individual political rights, including freedom of assembly. Statements in support of a strengthening of civil society are common, but concrete action is less evident. Indeed, there have been several legislative proposals aimed at restricting nonprofit-organization activity by less-advantageous tax treatment, and prohibition from business activity and from service provision.

In the Czech Republic, the path of evolution was tortured. A legal framework for foundations and nonprofit organizations has now been established, but the government of Prime Minister Václav Klaus was openly hostile to facilitating the growth of civic associations. His argument was that nothing should interfere with the direct relationship he sought between the government and the "people." One should keep in mind, however, that the Czech Republic is the home of what might be the single most exemplary instance of a nongovernmental political association with far-reaching impacts on the drive to democracy. This, of course, is Charter 77, which essentially engineered the "Velvet Revolution" and the rise of Václav Havel to president of the republic.[3] Havel spoke of the importance of nonprofit organizations and nongovernmental organizations as the crucial "third sector" in a democracy in his 1994 New Year speech. Prime Minister Klaus immediately counterattacked, asking why Czechs should look for a third way and a retreat to corporativism and collectivism (Pajas 1996).

Civil society as expressed in political or policy-oriented organizations is growing, but still weak in Central European countries. Certainly there is little concrete positive effort in any of the regimes to reach out to NGOs for consultation, advice, or consensus building. Proposals for advisory/consultative committees to serve this end for parliament have been made in Hungary, for example, but they have gone nowhere to date. Such consultation does seem to take place in city and county governments in some areas. NGOs are largely seen as potential irritants, or as service providers that can help implement independently derived government policy, or help fill in the gaps left by discontinued social-welfare programming.

Central European countries seem mired in a stage of limited political civil society, in part due to the designs of the ruling administrations. Consensus building on key policy issues takes place through the media, rather than through associational activity. Average citizens feel cut off, alienated, even betrayed, as they become the objects of policy and austerity, with little say until the next parliamentary election—elections that have become media events of image building/destroying rather than searching debate—much in the pattern of the campaigns in mature Western political systems. The criticisms that Habermas and others pile on Western democracies seem to apply more and more to the East. (See the chapters by Hunt and Lindahl in this volume for extended discussions of this issue, both theoretically and empirically. See also Graham 1999, 150–51, for more discussion of the "stages" of the political side of civil society in East Central Europe.)[4]

Nonetheless, this is occurring at the same time that apolitical voluntary associations and economic organizations seem to be flourishing. This economic activity is not entirely encouraged by Central European governments, but legal frameworks have been established, particularly for nonprofits and foundations. If the economic associational activity continues to grow, we may have reason for optimism. But this, of course, assumes that Central European citizens can continue to remain patient in their economic sacrifice.

Hungary developed its own approach to using scarce economic resources for economic development (not many tools were available), but it quickly faced substantial distress in the electorate and significant feebleness in parliamentary efforts to frame the appropriate path. Certainly, this is not the "economic democracy" that utopians like Bowles and Gintis (1986) proposed.

In Hungary, a key continuing question is whether social consensus can be developed in support of the sacrifice demanded. The first three political regimes, with different ruling parties, faced this question, and with only limited success. The 2002 parliamentary elections ushered in yet another new government, suggesting that the voting public had not lost its appetite for punishing elected officials for performance that was less than ideal (but that could compare quite favorably with other post-communist regimes).

The second parliamentary election in Hungary resulted in a government dominated by the Socialist Party, made up of former communists, as the public showed convincingly the extent of impatience over economic reform and austerity measures. The government dithered for some months under Prime Minister Gyula Horn, but put together a set of reform proposals by mid-1995 that appeared rather more austere than that of the previous Conservative regime! The reforms—popularly known as the "Bokros Package" after Lajos

Bokros, the finance minister, who along with central-bank governor Gyorgy Suranyi crafted the package—included a serious effort to reduce Hungary's large welfare state (the annual expenditures of which amounted to perhaps 27 percent of GDP). Austerity was a major emphasis, as was a renewed effort to move forward with privatization. Key targets were the free child-care and higher-education systems, generous maternity benefits, and substantial numbers of the public-sector jobs. Not surprisingly, the public was outraged; strikes and protests were organized, especially in the educational sector, and several ministers resigned (including Bokros).

The government held firm, though, thanks to its large parliamentary majority, in the view that tough medicine was indicated if the Hungarian economy was to recover in the face of its exposure to global competition. After years of belt-tightening, amounting to a 15 percent cut in living standards, one could begin to see results. To be sure, an important portion of the success was owed to the performance of its export sector, which was led by transnational corporations, especially in the automobile industry. Hungary has often led the region, with as much as 35 percent of the total foreign direct investment attracted to the former communist countries of Eastern Europe. Anticipating the parliamentary elections, social-service spending cuts were eased.

The 1998 parliamentary elections brought another change, with the conservative Alliance of Young Democrats (FIDESZ) managing a governing coalition with the Hungarian Democratic Forum and the Independent Smallholders Party. Viktor Orban of FIDESZ was named prime minister, with promises of serving the middle class and turning out the entrenched elites. A campaign to crack down on crime and corruption was launched, and the Postabank (post office savings bank) scandal that had hounded the previous administration was cleaned up. The new government also scrapped tuition fees for higher education, reintroduced universal child benefits, and put tax reform on hold. Progress on pension and health reform appears uncertain at present. Prime Minister Orban attacked the "independent" central-bank governor, Gyorgy Suranyi, publicly for losses incurred at the bank's Austrian subsidiary, but there may be some connection to a previous report by the bank, criticizing the FIDESZ economic program during the election campaign. Political motivations may also explain the regime's reform of the local-government funding system, apparently favoring councils controlled by FIDESZ.

Opposition leaders criticized Orban's authoritarian disposition, and worried about his diffident attitude toward parliament, which met only once every three weeks, in violation of rules requiring weekly meetings. The anti-crime campaign led to charges of civil-liberties violations, but the Freedom House survey rates Hungary as among the most free of the ECA transition countries. FIDESZ was created as a dissident youth party, but critics suggest that it has become a party of the nationalist and authoritarian right. In any case, the 2002 parliamentary elections narrowly turned out the Orban government in favor of the Left. The "voting function" is clearly alive in the Hungarian political system. (See the chapter on Hungary by András Lánczi in this volume for an interesting discussion of the implications of this political turn.)

Prices were deregulated and subsidies cut in much of the region. The Soviet Union (and COMECON generally) disappeared as a market. Initial efforts to substitute with a push on Western European markets looked promising, but largely collapsed after two years, and have been slow to develop since.

Land was privatized substantially in Central Europe, with an important impact on agricultural production, given the value of the past record of cooperation between large state cooperative farms and small household plots. Some basic food items had to be imported for the first time. The political priority attached to this privatization overwhelmed the cautious advice of indigenous economists. An important pillar of the economy was damaged abruptly, again without a clear strategy for agricultural reform and market penetration. Given that Central Europe would seem to be well placed to penetrate EU markets (assuming the Common Agricultural Policy of subsidies and protection is in fact reformed) with its traditional agricultural productivity, this was potentially a very shortsighted development.

Large commercial, industrial, and agricultural organizations were broken up, and a policy of self-management was introduced, with directors elected by workers. Workers were given freedom to take on other jobs after hours. This improved wage earnings, but harmed productivity and did little to promote real industrial development (Bossanyi 1995, 93; and Bakos 1994, 1198).

As noted earlier (see table 1.1), the European Bank for Reconstruction and Development (EBRD) cited Hungary as the most successful of the Eastern European and former Soviet Union successor republics on a range of measures of transition progress in its 1999 Transition Report. The World Bank cited Hungary's reform efforts as incomplete, but a promising model for other transition countries in its *World Development Report 2000*. Hungary became a member of the Organization for Economic Cooperation and Development (OECD) in May 1996, and in December 1997, the EU invited it to begin the accession process.

The region's strategy for integration into the European Union has promise as one of its few tools—but also serious pitfalls, some of which are not entirely within its own control. The European Union's Common Agricultural Policy, though under reform, was dearly unfriendly, at French insistence.

Evaluated in the light of the theoretical writing on the challenges of simultaneous economic and democratic reform, the Czech Republic and Hungary are mixed cases. By some measures, they are models of both democratization and economic liberalization. A smooth transition to competitive parliamentary democracy has been achieved, with peaceful elections that have led to significant political change on several separate fronts. The quality of this democracy remains underdeveloped and problematic in important respects, particularly with regard to the question of effective legislative oversight and the existence of a vibrant political interaction between government and civil society. The warnings of both Schmitter and Huntington noted above seem relevant. But David Bartlett argues that Hungary is perhaps unique in the way in which it has developed key institutions for economic liberalization. Moreover, democratization has been an important tool in this development, not a constraint. In his view,

> the decisive factor in Eastern Europe's transition is not the sheer magnitude of the social costs of economic transformation but the institutional environment in which distributional conflicts occur. The opponents of Hungary's economic reforms enjoyed greater influence under the communist regime, whose institutional structure afforded local agents multiple access points to negotiate individual exceptions to market rules. The demise of communism disrupted the political channels through which vulnerable actors secured compensation for the socioeconomic fallout of adjustment. Democratization facilitated marketization by insulating state agencies from particularistic claims and channeling distributional politics into the electoral arena, where the "losers" of reform operated at a disadvantage in the early post-communist period. Hungary's experience thus demonstrates not only that political liberalization and economic transformation are compatible but that the former promotes the latter. (Bartlett 1997, 2–3)

It is largely now unthinkable to return to anything close to the pre-1989 political systems in Central Europe, though Schmitter's concerns about the authoritarian impulse of populations distressed by the lack of real and broad-based economic gains should be remembered (Schmitter 1996). It is not entirely clear that the present political systems are seen by most of the citizens as more responsive to the demands of society than other possible alternatives. More broadly, the compromised elections and political tightening in Azerbaijan, Ukraine, Kazakhstan, and Russia between 2000 and 2005 are worrisome. The "color" revolutions of Georgia, Ukraine, and Kyrgyzstan provided a strong dose of optimism. Whether the apparent democratization will be sustained or spread to resistant authoritarian regimes in the region remains a big question.

In Central and Eastern Europe, it does appear that there is enough confidence in the vitality of the new political systems that necessary adjustments may yet be made without a resort to unconstitutional measures. The EU enlargement in 2004 added some promise for both the new members and those still on the candidate list.

Hungary's banking-reform efforts are regarded by the proponents of the "Washington Consensus" as a promising model for other transition countries. Skeptics abound, however, on this and other dimensions of privatization and liberalization efforts. Reform and privatization that lead to a banking sector largely owned by foreign interests must raise questions.

Generally, indigenous industrial development remains decidedly weak, and there is little clear evidence of a viable strategy or policy beyond privatization and attracting FDI. Hungary has few independent tools, and limited "clout" for sustained economic development and competitiveness. Hungary has attracted substantially more foreign direct investment than has its neighbors, but what seems clear from an initial review is that the Hungarian economy faces considerable challenge in finding a viable path in the face of global industrial competition. Efforts at restructuring and privatizing the old industrial infrastructure have thus far been disappointing. The competitive challenges of globalization appear to be making these efforts less promising, while the attendant growth in consumerism and media manipulation are at the same time corrupting the spirit and patience of the citizenry. The taste for democracy and free enterprise may be souring too rapidly to survive the sacrifice necessary to achieve system-wide prosperity and a healthy civil society.

Polarities within society have been accentuated, given the rise of a wealthy entrepreneurial elite and the decline in living standards and social security thus far experienced by the masses. One might argue that Hungary now constitutes a case somewhere between the poles of the Lee hypothesis of discipline and centralized state power, and the instrumental or constructive values of democracy advocated by Amartya Sen (1999). Hungary is not an authoritarian regime, but there are clearly enough central authority and insulation from democratic pressures evident to permit painful economic and social-austerity policies. That fact that several different constellations of elected political power have found it necessary to make such policies may be a reflection of the imperatives of globalization as much as anything. But the organized resistance to those measures specifically, and to globalization generally, has thus far been limited. The political regimes seem able to operate without the threat of political instability that Huntington most fears in the development context.

Turning away from Central Europe, most of the successor republics to the former Soviet Union, excluding the Baltics, present a much more problematic picture. It is hard to argue that the "consolidation" of democracy has taken place in almost any of the cases, though there is clear progress and considerable variance (see the summary in table 1.13). Georgia and Russia have some promise among the European republics, though neither has a settled or aggregative political-party system, and the transfer of power would not measure up to the strict standards proposed by Przeworski and his colleagues in *Democracy and Development* (2000). Russia's 150-plus political parties (and perhaps 26 significant ones) suggest a steep uphill climb before one might call democracy consolidated. (See the chapters by Hadenius and Herron in this volume for extended discussion of the challenges of developing mature political parties and electoral systems throughout the post-Soviet space.) Moreover, the moves by President Putin against the Russian media and his potential political opposition in 2003–5 may stimulate memories of past political authoritarianism, while his efforts to strengthen economic institutions have reassured foreign investors and trading partners.

The November 2004 presidential elections in the Ukraine were widely condemned by international observers—including the United States, the European Union, the OSCE, and local domestic officials—as full of irregularities and media bias, with the opposition calling for defiance and a campaign of civil disobedience. Supporters of Prime Minister Viktor Yanukovych in turn charged the opposition with moves toward a coup. Corruption and anti-opposition bias are not new features of the struggle for democratization and economic reform in the Ukraine, of course. The situation was complicated by Russian concerns about undue U.S. influence on its "borders" in an effort to obtain a pro-U.S. regime. At this writing, it appears that the campaign of internal protest and international condemnation has yielded a rather more democratic system—perhaps ending the record of post-Soviet "transition" regimes.

Among the Central Asian republics, Kyrgyzstan normally has the nod as the strongest case of democratization and economic liberalization, but the 2000 elections raised questions of manipulation and fairness. The 2005 regime change left the Kyrgyz situation unsettled but not without promise.

Kazakhstan, Tajikistan, Turkmenistan, and Uzbekistan have new constitutions and electoral systems, but opposition is either not tolerated or clearly discouraged. Efforts to contain Islamic fundamentalist violence and destabilizing activity, some of it directed or at least inspired externally, provide ample motivation and common justification for political repression. But international agencies and Western governments have been openly critical in recent years. Uzbekistan's violent reaction to protestors in 2005 led to aid suspension by the United States and European Union.

One might raise the question of whether there are instances of "enlightened" centralized rule or authoritarianism with a clear developmental purpose—following the Lee hypothesis, perhaps. But there is very little evidence that Lee's Singapore or even Park's South Korea is serving as an important model here. Kazakhstan, in particular, is blessed with enormous natural resources that could be important ingredients in a statist development effort. But even here, one would not conclude easily that the regime is postponing democratization with this strategy in mind. Table 1.14 might well lead one to question the viability of the Lee hypothesis in any case. Amartya Sen is more likely to appreciate the evident trends and apparent correlations more than would Lee Kuan Yew or the modernization theorists of old. But there remains considerable complexity to unravel. Drawing from the sources of tables presented earlier in this chapter, these limited data do seem to suggest that those regimes that have the higher Freedom House ratings also largely have the strongest GDP growth and income-per-capita/PPP figures. Anders Åslund provides related evidence for the "correlation between democracy and successful economic reform," with some emphasis on his call for a radical versus a gradual reform strategy (2003).

Plan of Presentation

The 27 new states in Eurasia do present a wide range of progress in democratization and economic liberalization. Belarus, Tajikistan, Turkmenistan, and Uzbekistan must still be regarded as authoritarian regimes that have made only tentative moves toward political accountability, and only limited effort to privatize or invigorate the old, centrally planned command economies. Hungary, Poland, the Czech Republic, Slovenia, and the three Baltic States, on the other hand, clearly have competitive democracies with effective political institutions and processes. Each has made substantial progress in the transition to market economies. More limited but promising reforms have been introduced now in Bulgaria, Croatia, Romania, and Slovakia. Armenia, Azerbaijan, Georgia, Kazakhstan, Kyrgyzstan, Moldova, Ukraine, and the rest of the former Yugoslavia raise more questions about progress and promise. "Two steps forward and three steps back" may be an apt description, as the challenges of accommodating political unrest and widespread unemployment and poverty remain largely unmet. This chapter reflects some preliminary progress toward assessing this varied performance systematically. The data compiled by the European Bank for Reconstruction and Development, Freedom House, UNCTAD, and the World Bank offer a useful basis for comparative analysis, but there is a clear need for intensive exploration of the individual cases.

It is clear that the "dual transition" of democratization and economic liberalization has been a challenge for all the regimes that have seriously attempted it. Even the most successful ones in Central Europe and the Baltics find themselves in search of more rewarding strategies for managing tough economic and social measures in an environment of financial constraint and political stress. The chapters to follow in this volume should help to shed some light on the complexities at work.

TABLE 1.14 Income / PPP Per Capita, GDP Growth, and Political Transition

	Per Capita Nat. Income (2002)	PPP (2002)	GDP Growth (2001-2002)	Freedom House Rating (2003-2004)
Slovenia	$9,810	$17,690	2.9%	1,1F
CzechRepublic	$5,560	$14,500	2.0%	1,2F
Hungary	$5,280	$12,810	3.3%	1,2F
Poland	$4,570	$10,130	1.2%	1,2F
Estonia	$4,130	$11,120	5.8%	1,2F
Slovakia	$3,950	$12,190	4.4%	1,2F
Lithuania	$3,660	$9,880	6.7%	1,2F
Latvia	$3,480	$8,940	6.1%	1,2F
Bulgaria	$1,790	$6,840	4.3%	1,2F
Croatia	$4,640	$9,760	5.2%	2,2F
Romania	$1,850	$6,290	4.3%	2,2F
Serbia/Montenegro	$1,400	n.a.	3.0%	3,2F
Albania	$1,380	$4,040	4.7%	3,3PF
Macedonia	$1,700	$6,210	0.3%	3,3PF
Moldova	$460	$1,560	7.2%	3,4PF
Bosnia/Herzegov.	$1,270	$5,800	3.9%	4,4PF
Armenia	$790	$3,060	12.9%	4,4PF
Ukraine	$770	$4,650	4.5%	4,4PF
Georgia	$650	$2,210	5.4%	4,4PF
Russia	$2,140	$7,820	4.3%	5,5PF
Kazakhstan	$1,510	$5,480	9.5%	6,5NF
Azerbaijan	$710	$2,920	10.6%	6,5PF
Kyrgyzstan	$290	$1,520	−0.5%	6,5PF
Tajikistan	$180	$900	9.1%	6,5NF
Belarus	$1,360	$5,330	4.7%	6,6NF
Uzbekistan	$450	$1,590	4.3%	7,6NF
Turkmenistan	$1,200	$4,570	14.9%	7,7NF

SOURCES: World Bank, *World Development Report*, 2000–2004; Freedom House Annual Surveys (www.Freedomhouse.org/ratings/).

KEY: PF = Partly free, NF = Not free, F = Free

We begin this effort with Erik Herron's analysis of "Too Few or Too Many Parties? The Implications of Electoral Engineering in Post-Communist States." This nicely complements the more general survey provided above and offers insight on challenges of institutional design in emerging democracies. It is commonly argued that the large number of political parties in transition systems is problematic, particularly if there are no large and mature ones among them. Herron finds that electoral rules do influence the size of the party system and could mitigate the level of multipartism. Noting that some post-communist states suffer more from the lack of strong, independent parties, he stresses that the key in such cases is less the character of electoral laws in existence (now in all 27 states) than the progress toward more effective democratization and rule of law more generally. Herron concludes with a list of reform proposals based on his comparative research—flowing from his concern that "the presence of 'too few' or 'too many' parties may undermine democratic stability."

Two theoretical discussions of the relevance and condition of civil society are offered in Louis Hunt's "Hegel's Institutionalist Liberalism: Political Economy and Civil Society in the *Philosophy of Right*," and Folke Lindahl's "The Dissidents and the Antipolitical Ideology of Civil Society." Hunt examines the writings of Hegel on the relation between civil society and political economy, noting important insights on the role of the state and its relation to the family and civil society. He concludes that the most enduring contribution of Hegel's political philosophy is the clear connection between the health of these moral and political institutions and the prospects of transition to a market economy. Lindahl focuses his discussion on the ideology of civil society as it was developed by three well-known dissidents in the pre-1989 period, and then critically evaluates to what extent this ideology can be viewed as relevant for the transition period and the furthering of liberal democracy.

Kathleen Dowley addresses the challenges of subnational pluralism and ethnic polarization in transition societies in "Nation-Building in East Central Europe: Civic or Ethnic Majorities?" Avoiding another Yugoslavia lurks in the background of this challenge, of course, and Dowley examines a range of survey data to determine the extent to which minority interests are promoted or demoted/assimilated in recent public policies. She provides an inventory of cross-national differences, while noting that even in Central Europe, where legislation is more commonly developed to be consistent with the minority-rights positions proffered by the European Union, "mass attitudes have not kept apace these efforts."

We turn to individual transition case studies first with "Party Development in Russia" by Axel Hadenius. Stressing the crucial connection between democracy and the existence of parties, Hadenius explores the character of political parties in Russia in three of their roles: in government, in the citizenry, and as organizations. He finds weakness in all three areas, noting the low degree of cohesiveness even in the Duma, the instability more generally, and the challenges they face in formal membership, finance, and personalism.

Jiří Lach analyzes "The Political Elite in Hungary Through Transition," tracing its roots to 1956 and noting concern about the polarization of the leadership today, and the attendant "discrepancy between action and propaganda, particularly in the economic sphere." András Lánczi provides a different slant of critical evaluation of Hungary and its neighboring transition states in "A Post-Communist Landscape: Social and Moral Costs of the Regime Change in Post-Communist Hungary." In some respects, he picks up on the polarization concerns expressed by Lach and warns of complacency about the widely perceived "progress" of democratization and economic liberalization in Central Europe. Here he criticizes the policy of self-preservation of Prime Minister Péter Medgyessy, and in particular, the extent to which the (orchestrated?) indifference evident in Hungarian media and civil society is symptomatic of longer-term dangers.

Mircea Maniu asks "Why is Romania Different?" as he explores the impact today of the economic and political precursors to the onset of transition. Here, he seeks to account for the "slower" transition in Romania, compared with most of its neighbors, outlining the lingering effects of repression under Ceausescu and the lack of previous experience with democratic reform and economic liberalization. He remains hopeful, particularly on the political side, and looks to the drive toward eventual membership in the European Union as the engine to reduce the lag. Marius Jucan provides a more cultural and philosophical interpretation, "On the Question of European-ness in Romania." His argument has much to say about the crucial question of the extent to which Romania can be integrated fully into the new Europe, and offers a more sociocultural explanation for the lag that Maniu describes economically and politically.

Graham and Lindahl provide a concluding chapter that seeks to summarize the key issues raised, and provide a map for future empirical research and theoretical development.

NOTES

1. Eurasia is a category not without ambiguity and intellectual baggage. Indeed, it has a range of political meetings well steeped in the history of the Russian and Soviet empires. Here we use the term largely to encompass the geographical region that includes the countries of Europe, and West and Central Asia. Our primary focus, however, is on the new republics formed in the wake of the collapse of the Soviet Union and the Warsaw Treaty Organization.

2. Our preference normally is to refer to these regimes as "post-state socialist" rather than post-communist, given that none of them ever approximated the dreams of Marx for a communist society. Post-communist is decidedly less awkward and more commonly used, however, so we shall submit to this label.

3. Havel speaks of this period and the general pattern of state "persecution" during most of his adult life in an extended interview published after the "Velvet Revolution" (Havel 1990).

4. Briefly, the stages of the political side of civil society might include (1) individual or small-group dissidence and informal political discussion groups; (2) developing a forum for debate on alternative structures and policy proposals, pressuring the authoritarian regime (often bringing together disparate groups and individuals, unified only in their opposition to that regime); (3) negotiating terms of transfer/elections with an outgoing regime; (4) forming political parties and organizations to contest elections. (Subsequent stages perhaps remain to be defined.)

REFERENCES

Agh, Attila, ed. 1994. *The emergence of East Central European parliaments: The first steps.* Budapest: Hungarian Centre of Democracy Studies.

Agh, Attila, and Gabriella Ilonszki, eds. 1996. *Parliaments and organised interests: The second steps.* Budapest: Hungarian Centre of Democracy Studies.

Agh, Attila, and Sandor Kurtan, eds. 1995. *Democratization and Europeanization in Hungary: The first parliament, 1990–1994.* Budapest: Hungarian Centre of Democracy Studies.

Almond, Gabriel A., and Sidney Verba. 1963. *The civic culture.* Princeton, NJ: Princeton University Press.

Andor, Laszlo, and Martin Summers. 1998. *Market failure: Eastern Europe's "economic miracle."* London: Pluto Press.

Andorka, Rudolf. 1993. Cultural norms and values: The role of the intellectuals in the creation of a new democratic culture in Hungary. *Society and Economy* 15(5): 1–17.

Ash, Timothy Garton. 1999. *The magic lantern: The revolution of '89 witnessed in Warsaw, Budapest, Berlin, and Prague.* New York: Random House/Vintage Books.

Åslund, Anders. 2002. *Building capitalism: The transformation of the former Soviet Bloc.* Cambridge: Cambridge University Press.

Bakos, Gabor. 1994. Hungarian transition after three years. *Europe-Asia Studies* 46(7).

Bartlett, David L. 1997. *The political economy of dual transformations: Market reform and democratization in Hungary.* Ann Arbor: University of Michigan Press.

Berglund, Sten, and Jan Ake Dellenbrant, eds. 1994. *The new democracies in Eastern Europe: Party systems and political cleavages.* 2nd ed. Aldershot: Edward Elgar.

Bhaduri, Amit, and Deepak Nayyar. 1996. *The intelligent person's guide to liberalization.* New Delhi: Penguin Books.

Blanchard, Olivier Jean, Kenneth A. Froot, and Jeffrey D. Sachs. 1994. *The transition in Eastern Europe.* Vol. 1, *Country studies.* Chicago: University of Chicago Press.

Bossanyi, Katalin. 1995. Taking stock of the economic transition. *Hungarian Quarterly* 36.

Bowles, Samuel, and Herbert Gintis. 1986. *Democracy and capitalism: Property, community, and the contradictions of modern social thought.* New York: Basic Books.

Bromley, Simon. 1996. Feature review. *New Political Economy* 1(1).

Bryant, Christopher G. A., and Edmund Mokrzycki, eds. 1994. *The new great transformation? Change and continuity in East-Central Europe.* London: Routledge.

Carson, Richard L. 1990. *Comparative economic systems: Part II—Socialist alternatives.* Armonk, NY: M. E. Sharpe, Inc.

Cerny, Philip G. 1996. Globalization and other stories: The search for a new paradigm for international relations. *International Journal* 51(4): 617–37.

Csepeli, Gyorgy, Daniel German, Laszlo Keri, and Istvan Stumpf, eds. 1994. *From subject to citizen.* Budapest: Hungarian Center for Political Education.

Csepeli, Gyorgy, Laszlo Keri, and Istvan Stumpf, eds. 1993. *State and citizen: Studies on political socialization in post-communist Eastern Europe.* Budapest: Hungarian Center for Political Education.

Diamond, Larry. 1999. *Developing democracy: Toward consolidation.* Baltimore: Johns Hopkins University Press.

———. 1996. Toward democratic consolidation. In Larry Diamond and Marc F. Plattner, eds. *The global resurgence of democracy.* 2nd ed. Baltimore: Johns Hopkins University Press.

———, ed. 1994. *Political culture and democracy in developing countries.* Boulder, CO: Lynne Rienner Publishers.

Diamond, Larry, and Marc F. Plattner, eds. 1996. *The global resurgence of democracy.* 2nd ed. Baltimore: Johns Hopkins University Press.

———, eds. 1995. *Economic reform and democracy.* Baltimore: Johns Hopkins University Press.

Estes, Richard J. 1998. Social development trends in transition economies, 1970–1995: The search for a new paradigm. Paper presented to the Conference on China, India, and Russia: Progress and Challenges of Economic Transition, Michigan State University, 23–25 October.

European Bank for Reconstruction and Development. 1999–2001. *Transition report.*

Fuller, Graham E. 1991. *The democracy trap: Perils of the post–cold war world.* New York: Penguin Books.

Giddens, Anthony. 1998. *The third way: The renewal of Social Democracy.* Cambridge: Polity Press.

———. 2000. *The third way and its critics.* Cambridge: Polity Press.

———, ed. 2001. *The global third way debate.* Cambridge: Polity Press.

Gill, Stephen. 1995. Globalisation, market civilisation, and disciplinary neoliberalism. *Millennium* 24(3): 399–424.

Gills, Barry K., ed. 1997. Special issue: Globalisation and the politics of resistance. *New Political Economy* 2(1).

Graham, Norman A. 1999. Globalization and civil society in Hungary and the Czech Republic. In *The revival of civil society,* ed. Michael G. Schechter. London: Macmillan.

Gray, John. 1998. *False dawn: The delusions of global capitalism.* New York: New Press.

Grieder, William. 1997. *One world, ready or not: The manic logic of global capitalism.* New York: Simon and Schuster.

Habermas, Jürgen. 1991. *The structural transformation of the public sphere: An inquiry into a category of bourgeois society.* Cambridge, MA: MIT Press.

Havel, Václav. 1990. *Disturbing the peace: A conversation with Karel Hvizdala*. New York: Vintage Books.

Held, David. 1987. *Models of democracy*. Stanford, CA: Stanford University Press.

———, ed. 1993. *Prospects for democracy: North, South, East, West*. Stanford, CA: Stanford University Press.

Hunt, Louis. 2000. Civil society and the idea of a commercial republic. In *The revival of civil society: Comparative and international cases*, ed. Michael G. Schechter. London: Macmillan.

Huntington, Samuel P. 1968. *Political order in changing societies*. New Haven: Yale University Press.

———. 1991. *The third wave: Democratization in the late twentieth century*. Norman: University of Oklahoma Press.

Jones, R. J. Barry. 1995. *Globalisation and interdependence in the international political economy*. London: Pinter.

Karatnycky, Adrian, Alexander Motyl, and Amanda Schnetzer, eds. 2002. *Nations in transit 2002: Civil society, democracy, and markets in East Central Europe and the newly independent states*. New Brunswick, NJ: Transaction Publishers/Freedom House.

———. 2003. *Nations in transit 2003: Democratization in East Central Europe and Eurasia*. New York: Rowman and Littlefield Publishers, Inc./Freedom House.

Keane, John. 1988. *Democracy and civil society: On the predicaments of European socialism, the prospects for democracy and the problem of controlling social and political power*. London: Verso.

Kettle, Steve. 1996. The development of the Czech media since the fall of communism. *Journal of Communist Studies and Transition Politics* 12(4): 42–60.

Kofman, Eleonore, and Gillian Youngs. 1996. *Globalization: Theory and practice*. London: Pinter.

Korten, David C. 1995. *When corporations rule the world*. West Hartford, CT: Kumarian Press.

Kornberg, Allan, and Harold D. Clarke. 1992. *Citizens and community: Political support in a representative democracy*. New York: Cambridge University Press.

Kuti, Eva. 1996. *The nonprofit sector in Hungary*. Manchester, UK: Manchester University Press.

Laakso, Liisa. 1996. Relationship between the state and civil society in the Zimbabwean Elections 1995. *Journal of Commonwealth and Comparative Politics* 34(3): 218–34.

Lánczi, András, and Patrick H. O'Neil. 1996. Pluralization and the politics of media change in Hungary. *Journal of Communist Studies and Transition Politics* 12(4): 82–101.

Lasch, Christopher. 1995. *The revolt of the elites and the betrayal of democracy*. New York: W. W. Norton.

Lavigne, Marie. 1999. *The economics of transition: From socialist economy to market economy*. 2nd ed. New York: St. Martin's Press.

LeDuc, Lawrence, Richard G. Niemi, and Pippa Norris, eds. 1996. *Comparing democracies: Elections and voting in global perspective*. Thousand Oaks, CA: Sage Publications.

Lewis, Paul G. 1997. Theories of democratization and patterns of regime change in Eastern Europe. *Journal of Communist Studies and Transition Politics* 13(1): 4–26.

Lijphart, Arend. 1984. *Democracies: Patterns of majoritarian and consensus government in twenty-one countries*. New Haven: Yale University Press.

———. 1994. *Electoral systems and party systems: A study of twenty-seven democracies, 1945–1990*. Oxford: Oxford University Press.

———. 1999. *Patterns of democracy: Government forms and performance in thirty-six countries*. New Haven: Yale University Press.

Lipset, Seymour Martin. 1963. *Political man: The social bases of politics*. Garden City, NY: Anchor Books.

Lipset, Seymour Martin, and Stein Rokkan. 1967. *Party systems and voter alignments: Cross-national perspectives*. New York: Free Press.

Lomax, Bill. 1997. The strange death of "civil society" in post-communist Hungary. *Journal of Communist Studies and Transition Politics* 13(1): 41–63.

Lord, Christopher, ed. 2000. *Central Europe: Core or periphery?* Copenhagen: Copenhagen Business School Press.

Magyari-Beck, Istvan. 1993. Culture and the market. *Society and Economy* 15(5): 21–107.

McGrew, Anthony, ed. 1997. *The transformation of democracy? Globalization and territorial democracy*. London: Polity Press.

Micklethwait, John, and Adrian Wooldridge. 2000. *Future perfect: The challenge and hidden promise of globalization*. New York: Crown.

Milton, Andrew K. 1996. News media reform in Eastern Europe: A cross-national comparison. *Journal of Communist Studies and Transition Politics* 12(4): 7–23.

Mittelman, James H., ed. 1996. *Globalization: Critical reflections*. Boulder, CO: Lynne Rienner.

Miszlivetz, Ferenc. 1997. Participation and transition: Can the civil society project survive in Hungary? *Journal of Communist Studies and Transition Politics* 13(1): 27–40.

Muravchik, Joshua. 1992. *Exporting democracy: Fulfilling America's destiny*. Washington, DC: AEI Press.

Norpoth, Helmut. 1996. The economy. In *Comparing democracies: Elections and voting in global perspective*, ed. Lawrence LeDuc, Richard G. Niemi, and Pippa Norris. Thousand Oaks, CA: Sage Publications.

Offe, Claus. 1991. Capitalism by democratic design? Democratic theory facing the triple transition in east Central Europe. *Social Research* 58(4).

Ohmae, Kenichi. 1987. *Beyond national borders*. Homewood, IL: Dow Jones Irwin.

———. 1990. *The borderless world*. New York: HarperCollins.

———. 1995. *The end of the nation state: The rise of regional economies*. New York: Free Press.

———, ed. 1995. *The evolving global economy: Making sense of the new world order*. Boston: Harvard Business School Press.

Olson, Mancur. 2000. *Power and prosperity: Outgrowing communist and capitalist dictatorships*. New York: Basic Books.

Orenstein, Mitchell A. 2001. *Out of the red: Building capitalism and democracy in postcommunist Europe*. Ann Arbor: University of Michigan Press.

Pajas, Petr. 1996. Czech Republic: The case for a civil society? Unpublished paper. Prague: Centre for Democracy and Free Enterprise.

Pinto, Diana. 1992. The great European sea change. *Daedalus* (Fall): 129–50.

Przeworski, Adam, Susan C. Stokes, and Bernard Manin, eds. 1999. *Democracy, accountability, and representation.* Cambridge: Cambridge University Press.

Przeworski, Adam, Michael E. Alvarez, Jose Antonio Cheibub, and Fernando Limongi. 2000. *Democracy and development: Political institutions and well-being in the world, 1950–1990.* Cambridge: Cambridge University Press.

Putnam, Robert D. 2000. *Bowling alone: The collapse and revival of American community.* New York: Simon and Schuster.

———, et al. 1993. *Making democracy work: Civic traditions in modern Italy.* Princeton: Princeton University Press.

Reich, Robert B. 1991. *The work of nations: Preparing ourselves for twenty-first-century capitalism.* New York: Alfred A. Knopf.

Rosecrance, Richard. 1999. *The rise of the virtual state: Wealth and power in the coming century.* New York: Basic Books.

Sadowski, Christine M. 1994. Autonomous groups as agents of democratic change in communist and post-communist Eastern Europe. In *Political Culture and Democracy in Developing Countries,* ed. Larry Diamond. Boulder, CO: Lynne Rienner.

Sarkozy, Tamas. 1994. *The right of privatization in Hungary (1989–1993).* Budapest: Akademiai Kiado.

Schmitter, Philippe. 1996. Dangers and dilemmas of democracy. In Larry Diamond and Marc F. Plattner, eds. *The global resurgence of democracy.* 2nd ed. Baltimore: Johns Hopkins University Press.

Seligman, Adam B. 1992. *The idea of civil society.* Princeton, NJ: Princeton University Press.

Sen, Amartya. 1999. Democracy as a universal value. *Journal of Democracy* 10(3): 3–17.

Sjolander, Claire Turenne. 1996. The rhetoric of globalization: What's in a wor(l)d? *Millennium* 51(4): 603–16.

Schumpeter, Joseph. 1947. *Capitalism, socialism, and democracy.* New York: Harper.

Sorensen, Georg. 1998. *Democracy and democratization: Processes and prospects in a changing world.* Boulder, CO: Westview.

Spegele, Roger D. 1997. Is robust globalism a mistake? *Review of International Studies* 23: 211–39.

Stiglitz, Joseph E. 2002. *Globalization and its discontents.* New York: W. W. Norton.

Szekely, Istvan, and David Newbery. 1993. *Hungary: An economy in transition.* Cambridge: Cambridge University Press.

Van de Walle, Nicolas. 1994. Political liberalization and economic reform in Africa. *World Development* 22(4): 483–500.

———. 1997. Economic globalization and political stability in developing countries. Paper prepared for the Rockefeller Brothers Fund, delivered at the Pocantico Conference Center, 24–25 April.

Wedel, Janine K. 1998. *Collision and collusion: The strange case of Western Aid to Eastern Europe, 1989–1998*. New York: St. Martin's Press.

Weiss, Linda. 1998. *The myth of the powerless state*. Ithaca, NY: Cornell University Press.

Wendt, George. 1993. Global embrace: Corporate challenges in a transnational world. New York: HarperCollins.

World Bank. 1990–2005. *World development report*. Washington, DC: Oxford University Press.

———. 1993. *The East Asian miracle: Economic growth and public policy*. New York: Oxford University Press.

———. 2000. *Making transition work for everyone: Poverty and inequality in Europe and Central Asia*. Washington, DC: World Bank.

Yergin, Daniel. 2002. *The commanding heights: The battle between government and the marketplace that is remaking the modern world*. New York: Simon and Schuster.

2

Too Few or Too Many Parties?
The Implications of Electoral
Engineering in Post-Communist States

Erik S. Herron

lections and democracy are inseparable. After the collapse of communism in Central and Eastern Europe in 1989 and the Soviet Union in
1991, 27 newly independent states emerged. All of these countries have
held elections; many have met international standards and were considered free and fair. Others were little more than farces marked by substantial
fraud and corruption.

The advent of competitive elections in the post-communist region prompts
many questions about the relationship between institutions and democracy.
Have differences in electoral practices influenced the progress of democracy in
the region? Have some electoral institutions been more conducive to the development of stable political-party systems? How have fraud and corruption
affected election campaigns and outcomes? How have election rules
influenced representation in the legislature? How have elections empowered
or constrained presidents?

This chapter will begin to address these broader questions about the relationship between elections and democracy in post-communist states by focusing on how election rules affect the development of political competition.
Specifically, I explore three questions. First, why is the number of political parties important for new democracies? Second, what factors affect the number of
parties in competition? Third, what influences party-system development?

The number of parties affects the development of democracy in many ways. In some cases, there may be too few parties for viable democracy. When fewer than two effective parties gain legislative seats, or fewer than two effective candidates run for president, citizens' preferences may not be adequately represented in government. While limited competition may be the result of legitimate choices by voters, it is more often caused by disproportionate election rules or restrictions on democratic practices.

In other cases, there may be too many parties. This assertion may seem counterintuitive; multiparty competition is often associated with political diversity, minority representation, and "full" democracy. However, in presidential or semi-presidential states, multiparty competition can undermine political stability. In its extreme manifestations, multipartism can inhibit representation and governance by creating party systems that are fragmented and unstable.

Parliaments with fragmented party systems are less likely to produce coherent policies, because the chief executive may not have majority or near-majority support in the legislature. This is particularly problematic in countries with weak presidents. With limited legislative support and a weak opposition, presidents may be encouraged to rule by decree (if decree power exists). The regular use of decree power chips away at democracy. This is particularly problematic in countries with strong presidents.

Two features of political systems help predict how many parties will emerge in political competition: institutional rules and contextual factors. Election rules for parliament and the presidency, the size of the legislature, and other aspects of the "rules of the game" create the incentives that influence the behavior of political actors. While institutional rules play a significant role in determining the number of parties that compete, the nature of political competition (such as the level of ethnic heterogeneity) also affects the development of political organizations. Using data from 80 countries, I assess what elements of institutional and contextual features generally influence party-system development. Once I evaluate the predictors of political competition, I turn to the implications for post-communist countries.

Institutional designers in post-communist states selected diverse electoral systems after the collapse of communism. Some combinations of rules are more likely to produce a manageable party system; others are more likely to generate political instability. I review the institutional choices of post-communist states and point to troubling aspects of electoral system design.

The chapter consists of three main components. I first discuss the relationship between elections and democracy. After outlining party-system development in the post-communist region, I identify the institutional and contextual determinants of the number of parties using data from 80 countries (including many post-communist states). I assess the state of election rules and partisan competition in post-communist states, noting how post-communist states could adjust their election rules to increase the likelihood of democratic stability.

The Number of Parties and the Development of Democratic Institutions

Two general approaches to defining democracy dominate the political-science literature: procedural, minimalist definitions and substantive, maximalist approaches (Shin 1994). The archetype for the minimalist approach is that democracy is a system "for arriving at political decisions in which individuals acquire the power to decide by means of competitive struggle for the people's vote" (Schumpeter 1947, 269). This approach focuses on the institutional components of regime types, and suggests that the existence of elections that are "competitive" qualify a state to be democratic. Such a simple definition makes empirical distinctions between states easier to obtain. However, one risks including among democracies states that have contested elections, but have limited participation or other restrictions on individual freedoms. Some scholarly work has emphasized the utility of a focus on electoral institutions (Huntington 1991), and other research has refined or expanded the definition (Dahl 1971).

While procedural definitions of democracy permit empirical clarity because they are relatively easy to measure, some scholars contend that elections are intermittent and can restrict choices made by citizens. Consequently, focusing on elections ignores other important factors that should be included in definitions of democracy. Specifically, democracies depend on actors (rulers, representatives, citizens) and procedures (competition and cooperation) (Schmitter and Karl 1991).[1] Because democracies depend upon both actors and procedures, there is variation in the forms of democracy among democratic states. That is, there exists more than one approach to creating "democratic" electoral rules, political institutions, political parties, participation, and access to and accountability of government.

The distinction between minimalist and more substantive definitions of democracy also reflects real differences among newly independent states. Many scholars have noted that some states have elections, but provide limited protection of individual freedoms. These are alternatively called "pseudo" democracies[2] (Diamond 1996), "delegative" democracies[3] (O'Donnell 1994), and "illiberal" democracies[4] (Zakaria 1997). The underlying premise is that the existence of free and fair elections alone is not adequate for a state to qualify as a democracy. The assumption that "free elections equals democracy" has been challenged, particularly in post-communist states. Nevertheless, all definitions of democracy include free and fair elections as a central component. While elections alone are not sufficient for democracy to emerge, they are necessary.

The impact of elections on democracy can be measured in many ways. Because elections influence the growth of political parties, and political parties are viewed as key actors in democratic politics, substantial work has connected election rules to party-system development.

Too Few or Too Many Parties?

Counting the number of parties in a system is a critical aspect of understanding who has power. Giovanni Sartori (1976, 120) noted that "it does matter how many are the parties. For one thing, the number of parties immediately indicates, albeit roughly, an important feature of the political system: the extent to which political power is fragmented or non-fragmented, dispersed or concentrated." Implicit in this statement is the possibility that there can be too few parties for viable democracy (power is concentrated in the hands of a few) or too many parties (power is too fragmented and dispersed to facilitate governance).

A common measure of the party system's size is the Laakso-Taagepera Index.[5] This measure generates an index, weighting the raw number of parties by their electoral performance or level of representation in parliament. Table 2.1 shows the effective number of parties in parliament in all post-communist states (the raw number weighted by representation), and table 2.2 shows the effective number of presidential candidates (weighted by election performance).[6] These measures provide some insight into the degree of competition. If the index is under two, it indicates that fewer than two effective parties or candidates were present. Higher numbers reflect greater fragmentation and dispersion of power.

TOO FEW PARTIES

Table 2.1 shows that political competition is quite restricted in many post-communist countries. In Azerbaijan, Georgia, Moldova, Mongolia, and Tajikistan, the effective number of parliamentary parties is below 2.0. This indicates that parliament is dominated by a single, strong party.[7]

Azerbaijan held parliamentary elections in late 2000 and early 2001. While opposition parties were allowed to participate, their activities were limited and they experienced problems with registration. International observers noted that election officials altered results to improve the seat allocation for the pro-presidential party, the New Azerbaijan Party (YAP). Opposition parties received few seats, and opposition members on the Central Electoral Commission refused to certify the results (OSCE 2001a). The final results provided YAP with a majority (72 out of 125 seats). Some unaffiliated presidential supporters also gained seats (26 independent candidates were elected).

TABLE 2.1 Effective Number of Legislative Parties in Post-Communist Statesa

COUNTRY	1998	1999	2000	2001	2002
Albania				2.53	
Armenia		2.82			
Azerbaijan			1.59		
Belarus			3.76		
Bosnia-Herzegovina			7.21		
Bulgaria				2.92	
Croatia			2.84		
Czech Republic					3.67
Estonia		5.50			
Georgia		1.79			
Hungary					2.21
Kazakhstan		2.58			
Kyrgyzstan			2.49		
Latvia	5.49				
Lithuania			4.04		
Macedonia	2.90				
Moldova				1.85	
Mongolia			1.08		
Poland				3.57	
Romania			3.18		
Russia		4.55			
Slovakia	4.75				
Slovenia			4.65		
Tajikistan			1.89		
Turkmenistan					
Ukraine					4.44
Uzbekistanb		3.71			
Yugoslavia			3.11		

SOURCES: ; OSCE (http://www.osce.org/odihr); http://www.essex.ac.uk/elections/.

(a.) Calculations are based on the most recent elections through August 2002. Independent and appointed candidates are excluded from the effective number of legislative parties. Seats designated for ethnic minorities or residents abroad are also excluded. (b.) A large number of seats (110 of 250) are reserved for local officials and are not included in the calculation. Indirect elections increase the president's influence over parliament and reduce the effective number of parties.

Elections in Tajikistan in February 2000 were also marked by excessive government interference. In some cases, ballots were altered and local election-commission protocols were completed in pencil (permitting others to alter results). Official election protocols did not match copies obtained by international observers, suggesting that votes were manipulated during the tabulation

TABLE 2.2 Effective Number of Presidential Candidates in Post-Communist States

COUNTRY	1997	1998	1999	2000	2001
Armenia		3.64			
Azerbaijan		1.67			
Belarus					1.68
Bosnia-Herzegovina					
Bosniaks		1.31			
Croats		2.53			
Serbs		2.16			
Bulgaria					3.39
Croatia				3.35	
Georgia				1.50	
Kazakhstan			1.53		
Kyrgyzstan				1.73	
Lithuania		3.27			
Macedonia			4.66		
Mongolia					2.13
Poland				2.86	
Romania				4.15	
Russia				2.70	
Slovakia			2.71		
Slovenia	2.78				
Tajikistan			1.06		
Turkmenistan[a]					
Ukraine			4.66		
Uzbekistan				1.18	
Yugoslavia				2.53	

SOURCES: ; OSCE (http://www.osce.org/odihr)

(a.) President Niyazov ran unopposed in 1994. His "term" was later extended indefinitely.

process. The pro-presidential People's Democratic Party (HDKT) received 30 of 63 seats in parliament; 15 nonpartisans who also supported the president were elected (OSCE 2000b).

Although the effective number of parties in other states may suggest the existence of a more vibrant opposition and freer election processes, this impression may not be accurate. Belarus held parliamentary elections in October 2000 that were not considered to be free and fair. Most legislators were unaffiliated (81 of 110) and supported the president. If these legislators are included in the calculation, the effective number of parties would be 1.39. In

Kazakhstan, multiple parties gained positions in parliament, but two parties, Otan (Fatherland) and the Civic Party, supported the president. If these parties are considered as a single pro-presidential party, the number of effective parliamentary parties drops to 1.41. Kyrgyz results are influenced by the high proportion of unclassified independent candidates. If independents are included in calculations, the number of effective parliamentary parties would decline. In Uzbekistan, 110 of the 250 legislators in the lower house are selected by local authorities. Indirectly elected officials are excluded from the calculations, but are highly likely to support the president (reducing the effective number of parties in parliament). In the case of Turkmenistan, no results are available from the initial parliamentary elections, which were not free and fair.

Limited competition in parliamentary elections is generally echoed in presidential elections (table 2.2). The effective number of presidential candidates is below two in Azerbaijan, Georgia, Kazakhstan, Kyrgyzstan, Tajikistan, Turkmenistan, and Uzbekistan. In Belarus, the president extended his term and has not faced a real electoral challenge since 1994. Not surprisingly, these countries also have strong presidents. Executive authority has been transformed into forms of authoritarianism, reflected in ratings for the quality of democracy.[8]

Azerbaijan's 1998 presidential elections were marked by an opposition boycott. Laws governing the elections and the composition of the Central Electoral Commission were disputed, the media provided unbalanced coverage of the campaign, and improper behavior was noted at the polls (OSCE 1998).

Substantial violations of democratic processes in Kazakhstan prompted some international observers to recommend a delay in the elections until the problems could be resolved. The declaration of an election date provided a limited time frame for a campaign to take place (and for opposition candidates to organize effective campaigns). Prominent opposition politicians were denied registration, the media and government clearly supported the incumbent president, and vote tabulations were problematic (OSCE 1999).

Kyrgyzstan's 2000 elections were also criticized for failing to meet international standards. While vote tabulation was more open and transparent than in other post-communist states, preelection decisions undermined the conduct of free and fair elections. The incumbent president was permitted to participate because of a controversial Constitutional Court decision that indicated he had served only one term under the existing constitution (the Kyrgyz president is limited to two terms). Strict registration requirements invalidated the candidacy of 12 potential contenders. The government pressured voters to support the incumbent, and the media provided substantial assistance by focusing attention on the incumbent (OSCE 2001c). In short, political competition was restricted in Kyrgyzstan.

International monitors produced no publicly available reports on the most recent presidential elections in Tajikistan, Turkmenistan, and Uzbekistan. The presidents of Tajikistan and Uzbekistan had minimal opposition, earning 97 percent and 92 percent of the vote, respectively. The president of Turkmenistan was unopposed in the only election, held in 1992. Based on a 1994 referendum, his term was extended until 2002. The Turkmenistan parliament declared him president for life in 1999.

While "too few parties" can be attributed to authoritarian governments, this is not always the case. International observers did not criticize the 2000 presidential elections in Georgia as strongly as elections in other post-communist states. Nevertheless, observers found evidence of fraud in polling stations, and excessive support of the incumbent by the media and government officials. Limited competition in Georgia's elections was due, in large part, to the withdrawal of two major candidates not long before election day (OSCE 2000a).

Moldova's 2001 parliamentary elections produced a small number of parliamentary parties for reasons other than electoral fraud or candidate withdrawal. Elections in Moldova were regarded as free and fair; voters expressed an overwhelming preference for the Moldovan Communist Party, which received almost 50 percent of the vote. Voter support for the Communists was accompanied by a 6 percent electoral threshold that prevented many parties from gaining seats. In fact, 25 percent of the voters supported parties that gained no seats. While the low number of parliamentary parties reflects problems of representation, it does not provide evidence of limited democracy in this case.

Mongolia's 2001 parliamentary elections also generate a puzzle. Mongolia has been touted as a great democratic success story (Fish 1998). Yet, its most recent parliamentary elections suggest a return to the days of communist rule. But public dissatisfaction with a series of unstable governments, scandal, inadequate response to natural disaster, and a single-member district (SMD) system led to a landslide victory for the Communist Party. While the party could, in principle, undermine democratic progress by altering political institutions to ensure that it retains power, the election results themselves do not reflect a leftist takeover that was not supported by the Mongolian people.

Although there are exceptions, the evidence demonstrates that executives in many post-communist states restrict free and fair electoral practices. In these cases, opposition parties are severely constrained or prevented from participating in elections. Although the official election rules suggest that these countries should produce many parties, they produce "too few" for viable democracy.

TOO MANY PARTIES

While it is relatively simple to define cases with too few parties, it is far more difficult to assess when there are too many parties. Moreover, if parties represent legitimate citizen interests, can there be too many parties?

Party systems in young democracies are often inchoate—characterized by the proliferation of constantly changing, personalistic parties that provide limited guidance to voters as labels and minimal benefits to candidates. Party-system institutionalization facilitates democratic success by promoting predictability and order to the process of selecting leaders. Mainwaring and Scully (1995) point out factors that define the level of party-system institutionalization. Party systems are institutionalized when they manifest limited electoral volatility,[9] and contain parties with stable connections to society and solid organizations that are considered to be the main vehicles to positions of authority. Arguably, no post-communist party system is fully institutionalized, although some countries have made greater progress toward institutionalization than others. Extreme multipartism in post-communist states impedes party-system institutionalization by de-emphasizing the strengthening of party organizations and focusing on personalistic appeals.

In institutionalized and inchoate systems, extreme multipartism can lead to various problems. Party systems with high levels of fragmentation undermine government performance, which can cause public dissatisfaction with the regime. As the number of parties increases, discernable differences between the parties decline, reducing the utility of party labels. Further, many parties undermine accountability; it is difficult to determine who is responsible for policies selected by large coalition governments. Multipartism may also undermine the strength of coalition governments, making them more susceptible to failure.

While multipartism can have negative consequences, when do we know if there are too many parties? Proportional representation (PR) systems maximize representation and provide incentives for small parties to participate in elections. Parliamentary institutions are designed to accommodate many parties by facilitating the formation of coalition governments where cabinet portfolios in the executive are shared among those parties. While coalitions with multiple partners are inherently less stable than single-party majority governments, multipartism is better accommodated by parliamentary systems than presidential or semi-presidential systems.

The level of multipartism is not as important a determinant of governmental performance in parliamentary systems as it is in presidential or semi-presidential systems (Jones 1995; Mainwaring and Scully 1995). A strong presidential legislative contingent is considered to be critical for the effectiveness and the successful functioning of democratic presidential government (Lijphart 1994). Further, the combination of presidentialism and a fragmented multiparty system is problematic for stable democracy.

In post-communist presidencies, we are confronted by two potentially problematic scenarios: multiparty parliaments with a weak president, and multiparty parliaments with a strong president. Because multiparty competition may undermine a president's ability to gain legislative support, gridlock may emerge when the president is weak. While gridlock is a feature of many established democracies, it can prevent needed reforms in new democracies. Moreover, in presidential systems, ineffective governments cannot be ousted until the next elections. Semi-presidential systems provide some opportunity to change governments between elections, but regulations vary regarding the effects of no-confidence votes.

If multipartism is combined with a strong president, other problems may emerge. Without coherent parliamentary opposition or support, presidents may be tempted to rule by decree if they cannot pass legislation through parliament. The use of decree power can undermine the legitimacy of presidential rule, and erode representation.

There is no precise way to define when the combination of multipartism and directly elected presidents will be problematic. Among post-communist states with elected chief executives, Bosnia-Herzegovina,[10] Lithuania, Russia, Slovakia, Slovenia, and Ukraine have over 4.00 effective parliamentary parties. We would expect this combination to inhibit effective policymaking.

Slovakia and Slovenia combine relatively weak presidents and multipartism. Anecdotal evidence suggests that they have also encountered recent problems with governance. In Slovakia, the weak presidential office has been occupied by a physically frail president since direct presidential elections were instituted in 1999. Conflict within the coalition leadership combined with the president's condition has contributed to lack of legislative output (EECR 2000a, 2000b). Slovenia's initial failure to pass legislation necessary for accession to the European Union has been attributed to discord in its multiparty parliament (EECR 2000c).

Russia combines a strong president and a multiparty parliament. Russian presidents have resorted to rule by decree when they have been unable to pass legislation through a parliament that has been regularly dominated by the Left. Former president Boris Yeltsin was particularly prone to issue decrees (Huskey 1999). President Vladimir Putin has proposed electoral reform at the national and regional levels to consolidate a presidential majority in parliament and increase the likelihood that his policy initiatives will pass through the legislature.

Ukraine's combination of a strong president and a multiparty parliament has resulted in a struggle for power between the institutions. After the 1998 elections produced a Left-dominated parliament that opposed President Leonid Kuchma, the president called a referendum to alter the legislature. Kuchma's victory in the referendum was followed closely by the revelation of his involvement in scandals, including allegations that he authorized the murder of an opposition journalist. While opposition forces would be expected to rally against the president under these circumstances, the response was weak, even when the popular prime minister was ousted. Multipartism and a strong presidential office have encouraged the president to extend his power, and have undermined opposition to these developments.

While the limited descriptive evidence from these countries is not definitive proof of the link between the number of parties in parliament and effective governance, the anecdotes conform to our expectations. If the number of parties affects governance, can post-communist states influence how many parties compete?

Determinants of the Number of Parties

The literature on party-system development is split over the role of institutional and contextual features in determining the makeup of the party system. Institutionalist approaches, rooted in the work of Maurice Duverger (1954), point to election rules as the primary determinants of the party system. Other scholars point to contextual features, specifically political and social cleavages, as the most important influences. Recent research on the political effects of electoral systems has emphasized the interaction of institutional features and social conditions in determining the shape of partisan conflict. Ordeshook and Shvetsova (1994), and Amorim Neto and Cox (1997) show that ethnic heterogeneity plays an important role in determining the number of parties. This work convincingly demonstrates the effects of both institutional and contextual variables on party systems.

My analysis includes institutional and contextual factors as potential influences on the number of parties. I focus on 80 states that are listed as "free" or "partly free" in Freedom House's rankings,[11] but I include three post-communist states that are considered to be "not free."[12]

Dependent Variable

The dependent variable is the effective number of parliamentary parties; values are assessed using the Laakso-Taagepera Index. The effective number of parliamentary parties (rather than elective parties) is employed for two reasons. First, measuring the effective number of parties in the legislature takes into account how the electoral rules translate votes into seats. Because the analysis focuses on the political implications of institutional rules, and the legislature is the primary forum for policy debate, the dependent variable reflects the distribution of power within parliament. Second, election data at the needed level of aggre-gation are not available to calculate the effective number of elective parties for many countries. However, data about the distribution of seats in parliament are accessible.

Institutional Explanatory Variables

LEGISLATIVE ELECTION RULES

The importance of legislative election rules as an influence on political compe-tition was first noted formally by Maurice Duverger (1954). In his well-known propositions, he indicated that single-member-district systems with plurality rules should lead to two-candidate competition at the district level. By contrast, proportional representation rules should promote multiparty competition.

The analysis assesses the effects of election rules on the number of parties by controlling for four types of election systems: SMD and PR, and two sub-types of mixed electoral systems. Mixed systems that combine SMD and PR rules into a single election have been popular institutional choices, especially in post-communist states. Further, mixed systems produce different incentives for political parties than traditional election rules (Herron and Nishikawa 2001). Mixed systems include two important subtypes: compensatory systems that link seat allocation between the PR and SMD tiers, and non-compensatory systems that do not link the PR and SMD tiers. The effects of both subtypes are evaluated by separate variables.

ASSEMBLY SIZE

Assembly size has been likened to district magnitude and is thought to exert an independent effect on the number of parties (Taagepera and Shugart 1989). Larger assemblies should accommodate a larger number of parties. In district systems, more districts can facilitate greater diversity at the national level. In PR systems, higher district magnitude promotes greater proportionality, encouraging smaller parties to participate in elections.

DIRECTLY ELECTED PRESIDENTS AND PRESIDENTIAL ELECTION RULES

Presidential systems could contribute to the number of parties in two ways.[13] First, the electoral formula could increase the number of parties in competition, indirectly influencing the number of effective parties in the legislature. Second, concurrent presidential elections are thought to decrease the number of parties in competition due to "coattail effects" (Shugart and Carey 1992; Jones 1995).

The majority-runoff system encourages multiple candidates to participate in elections. Because first-round losers can use their supporters as leverage for access to government positions with the competitors in the second round, marginal candidates are expected to compete.[14] The empirical connection between majority-runoff formulas and multipartism in presidential systems has been confirmed recently (Jones 1999). Moreover, because the presidential electoral system has a positive effect on the number of legislative parties, we would expect multipartism in executive contests to increase the number of parties in the legislature (Shugart and Carey 1992; Jones 1995). I control for the electoral formula by including two dummy variables: the first variable measures whether or not the system is presidential; the second is an interactive variable assessing if the formula is majority-runoff.

As I noted above, election timing should also affect the number of parties in competition. When presidential and parliamentary elections are held concurrently, the president benefits from "coattail effects." Legislators associated with the president's party usually gain more seats in parliament when elections are held at the same time. Because I do not have adequate data about election timing for all of the countries in the analysis, I cannot specifically control for this feature. Moreover, presidential and parliamentary elections have been nonconcurrent in most post-communist states.

Contextual Explanatory Variables

CLEAVAGES

The number of issue dimensions can affect partisan competition (Taagepera and Shugart 1989). While many cleavages may be important (i.e., religion, regionalism), I emphasize ethnicity in this analysis. Ethnicity has been the focus of other research, and is at the core of many conflicts in post-communist states.

I control for ethnicity by calculating the effective number of ethnic groups using the Laakso-Taagepera Index mentioned above. While the data I employed are from different years, the variable should provide a rough guide to ethnic heterogeneity in the countries under study.

MONOPOLY OF THE COMMUNIST PARTY

Throughout much of the twentieth century, only one political party was legally sanctioned in post-communist states. Communist Party monopolies were broken in Central and Eastern Europe in 1989.[15] In March 1990, the Central Committee of the Communist Party of the Soviet Union (CPSU) agreed to change the Soviet constitution to accept other political parties and eliminate the Communist Party's vanguard role.

The legacy of one-party rule could have at least two different effects on contemporary partisan competition. Because individual voters have not developed long-term attachments to party organizations (with the possible exception of communist successor parties), many voters may be predisposed to distrust parties (White, Rose, and McAllister 1997, 232). In this environment, independent candidates should fare well in elections, and voters may regularly switch allegiances.[16] A second possibility is that voters, freed from the shackles of one-party rule, would quickly adapt to multiparty competition and support a great diversity of parties. Both possibilities, the distrust of parties and lack of party identification, as well as newfound pluralism, would thus contribute to fragmentation in the party system. I control for the effect of the legacy of one-party rule by adding a variable measuring whether or not the country is a post-communist state.

Results and Discussion

The analysis in table 2.3 shows that both institutional and contextual features help to explain the nature of political competition. Model 1 focuses solely on institutional factors. The results demonstrate that legislative election rules influence the effective number of parties. SMD rules produce the smallest number of political parties. The coefficient is statistically significant and negative in sign; on average, SMD systems produce 2.0 fewer parties than PR systems. The coefficient for mixed non-compensatory systems is significant at the 0.10 level. They produce an intermediate number of parties: 0.8 fewer than PR, but more than SMD.

Model 2 assesses the contextual features independently. The legacy of the Communist Party, represented by the variable *post-communist*, is not statistically or substantively significant in the models. Ethnic heterogeneity, however, is significant at the .10 level. Ethnically divided societies tend to have more parties than more homogenous societies. When we combine institutional and contextual variables into a single model (model 3), the results from the independent models persist. Legislative election rules and ethnic heterogeneity affect the number of parties.

These findings suggest that post-communist states have some control over the kind of competition that develops. While ethnic heterogeneity can be influenced by government policy (i.e., conflict in the former Yugoslavia, ethnic out-migration of Russians in Central Asia), election rules can be more easily altered. Our confirmation of the relationship between institutions and party systems leads to the question: what combinations of election rules have post-communist states adopted and how might these contribute to the development of stable democracy?

TABLE 2.3. OLS Results for Institutional and Contextual Determinants of the Effective Number of Legislative Parties

	MODEL 1	MODEL 2	MODEL 3
Constant	3.642[c]	2.338[c]	2.825[c]
	(0.336)	(0.454)	(0.511)
Institutional Features			
SMD	−2.044[c]		−2.082[c]
	(0.370)		(0.369)
Mixed non-compensatory	−0.826[a]		−0.860[a]
	(0.416)		(0.441)
Mixed compensatory	−0.419		−0.578
	(0.575)		(0.565)
Assembly size	0.001		0.002
	(0.001)		(0.001)
Presidential	−0.664		−0.517
	(0.433)		(0.430)
Presidential + majority – runoff	0.528		0.418
	(0.458)		(0.469)
Contextual Features			
Ethnic heterogeneity		0.395[a]	0.469[b]
		(0.238)	(0.206)
Post-communist state		0.099	−0.150
		(0.382)	(0.392)
Adjusted R^2	0.279	0.010	0.314
SEE	1.302	1.526	1.270
N	80	80	80

NOTE: Dependent variable is the effective number of legislative parties. The excluded category for legislative election rules is proportional representation.

(a.) $p < 0.10$ (b.) $p < 0.05$ (c.) $p < 0.01$

Election Rules in Post-Communist States

The analysis has shown that electoral rules influence the shape of the party system, even when contextual features are included in the analysis. This outcome implies that modification of existing electoral rules could mitigate the level of multipartism that is evidenced in many post-communist states.

Table 2.4 shows the election rules employed in all post-communist states as of August 2002.[17] There is substantial variation in the election rules used for the lower houses of parliament across post-communist states. The most recent elections in three of the countries that officially use single-member districts for lower-house elections—Belarus, Turkmenistan, and Uzbekistan—were not free and fair. Mongolia was an exception. Proportional representation is used in 12 countries: Bosnia-Herzegovina, Bulgaria, Croatia, the Czech Republic, Estonia, Macedonia, Moldova, Poland, Romania, Slovakia, Slovenia, and Yugoslavia.

Two kinds of mixed electoral systems are used in post-communist states.[18] Mixed compensatory systems are employed by Albania and Hungary.[19] In a mixed compensatory system, voters receive one ballot for the party list and one ballot for the local constituency. Although the system uses two allocation mechanisms, PR is used to balance the overall proportionality of the system. For example, if a party won 10 percent of the PR vote and no SMD seats, the party would receive additional PR seats so that its overall allocation would be 10 percent. If the party received 10 percent of the seats through SMD, it would receive no additional PR seats. The overall effect of the mixed compensatory system is to produce a proportional allocation of seats while maximizing voter choice.

Mixed non-compensatory systems are used in Armenia, Azerbaijan, Georgia, Kazakhstan, Kyrgyzstan, Lithuania, Russia, Tajikistan, and Ukraine. These systems do not link seat allocation in PR and SMD. A party's seat acquisition in the SMD component does not affect how seats are allocated in PR (although party strategies in SMD have been shown to exert an indirect effect on a party's performance). Mixed non-compensatory systems produce less proportional results than mixed compensatory or PR systems.

Almost all post-communist states that directly elect presidents use a majority-runoff formula. Majority-runoff rules require a candidate to gain over 50 percent of the vote to win in the first round. If no candidate receives enough votes, a second round is held between the top two candidates, with the plurality winner taking office. The only exceptions to the standard majority-runoff system are found in Azerbaijan, Bosnia-Herzegovina, and Lithuania. Azerbaijan's constitution requires a candidate to win two-thirds of the vote in the first round to be elected.[20] If no candidate wins, the top two finishers from the first round compete in the second round, with the plurality winner taking office. Bosnia-Herzegovina elects a three-member presidium with representation from the major ethnic communities. Lithuania employs a majority-runoff system as long as a majority of voters come to the polls. If under 50 percent of the population votes, a minimum of 33 percent is required to gain office.

The combination of rules is particularly important in countries with elected presidents, as noted above. The "worst-case scenario" from the perspective of

TABLE 2.4 Election Rules in Post-Communist States as of August 2002

COUNTRY	LEGISLATIVE ELECTION RULES: LOWER HOUSE	PRESIDENTIAL ELECTION RULES
Albania	Mixed compensatory	n.a.
Armenia	Mixed non-compensatory	Majority-runoff
Azerbaijan	Mixed non-compensatory[a]	Majority-runoff[b]
Belarus	SMD/majority-runoff	Majority-runoff
Bosnia-Herzegovina	Proportional representation (PR)	Other[c]
Bulgaria	PR	Majority-runoff
Croatia	PR[d]	Majority-runoff
Czech Republic	PR	n.a.
Estonia	PR	n.a.
Georgia	Mixed non-compensatory	Majority-runoff
Hungary	Mixed compensatory	n.a.
Kazakhstan	Mixed non-compensatory	Majority-runoff
Kyrgyzstan	Mixed non-compensatory	Majority-runoff
Latvia	PR	n.a.
Lithuania	Mixed non-compensatory	Majority-runoff[e]
Macedonia	PR[f]	Majority-runoff
Moldova	PR	N/A
Mongolia	SMD/plurality[g]	Majority-runoff
Poland	PR	Majority-runoff
Romania	PR[h]	Majority-runoff
Russia	Mixed non-compensatory	Majority-runoff
Slovakia	PR	Majority-runoff
Slovenia	PR[i]	Majority-runoff[j]
Tajikistan	Mixed non-compensatory	Majority-runoff[k]
Turkmenistan	SMD	n.a.
Ukraine	Mixed non-compensatory	Majority-runoff
Uzbekistan	SMD/majority-runoff and indirect elections	Majority-runoff[l]
Yugoslavia[m]	PR	Majority-runoff

SOURCES: IFES 1995; Reynolds and Reilly 1997; Blais, Massicotte, and Dobrzynska 1997; Shvetsova 1999; Massicotte and Blais 1999; LeDuc, Niemi, and Norris 2002; http://www.electionworld.org; OSCE (http://www.osce.org/odihr); http://www.essex.ac.uk/elections/; various constitutions and statutes.

(a.) A 24 August 2002 referendum approved a change to single-member districts. The results of the referendum were in dispute at the time this chapter was written. (b.) To win in the first round, a candidate must gain a two-thirds majority. A change to this rule was approved in the 24 August 2002 referendum. If the changes are instituted, the system would become a standard majority-runoff system. (c.) The presidency is made up of three elected officials (one Serb, one Croat, and one Bosniak). The candidate winning the plurality of an ethnic group wins a position. (d.) Six seats were occupied by Croatians living abroad. (e.) If turnout is 50% or better. If turnout is lower, the winning candidate needs only 33% of the vote. (f.) Macedonia used a mixed non-compensatory system in earlier elections. A new parliamentary law on 25 June 2002 abandoned the mixed system for PR. (g.) Candidates need at least 33% of the vote to obtain a seat. (h.) Nineteen seats were occupied by ethnic minorities. (i.) Two seats were occupied by ethnic minorities. (j.) The constitution indicates that the winner is elected by a "majority" of valid votes cast. No provisions for a second round are mentioned. However, Kynev (2002, 133) notes that Slovenia employs a runoff system. (k.) The constitution notes that "The person elected to the post of president is the candidate for whom at least one half of the voters, participating in the elections, voted." (see http://unpan1.un.org/intradoc/groups/public/documents/untc/unpan003670.htm). The constitution also states that the details of the elections should be articulated in a statute. By indicating that the winning candidate needs at least one-half of the votes, the constitution implies that a plurality is not adequate. Thus, a runoff would be needed to determine the winner. (l.) Source: "Izbiratelnoe pravo Respubliki Uzbekistana." 1999. *Vestnik Tsentralnoi Izbiratelnoi Komissii*. (m.) The March 2002 agreement between Serbia and Montenegro envisions the establishment of a unicameral parliament, in addition to renaming the state. At the time this chapter was written, the agreement had not yet been fully implemented.

electoral engineering includes majority-runoff electoral rules for president, nonconcurrent elections, high district magnitude, and federalism (Jones 1995). Each element individually encourages parties to participate. In combination, they provide powerful institutional incentives for multipartism and reduce the likelihood of policymaking coherence. This combination is found in Russia. Many other post-communist states have three elements, including Armenia, Azerbaijan, Bulgaria, Croatia, Georgia, Kazakhstan, Kyrgyzstan, Lithuania, Macedonia, Poland, Slovakia, Slovenia, Tajikistan, and Ukraine.

Electoral Engineering and Its Potential Consequences

The problem of too few parties is often intractable. Many post-communist countries with limited electoral competition have not fully emerged from authoritarian rule, despite the collapse of communism in the region. Electoral laws exist in these states, but the rule of law is weak. Thus, electoral laws do not affect party systems in predictable ways. In these cases, electoral reform is less important than the further progress of democratization.

In at least one case, however, the limited number of parliamentary parties was generated by an element of the election rules.[21] In Moldova, the combination of PR, a 6 percent threshold, and many parties produced disproportionate results. Elections were free and fair, but the allocation mechanism wasted the votes of many citizens. Electoral engineering may provide a solution to the problem of "too few parties" in Moldova. Lowering the electoral threshold would reduce the likelihood that parties would narrowly miss receiving seats in the legislature. However, lowering the threshold could also yield a substantial increase in the number of parties in parliament.

Electoral reform could also mitigate the problem of extreme multipartism in other post-communist states. The analysis above demonstrated that election rules have a direct effect on the number of parties in the system, even when social features are considered. Electoral engineering could facilitate governance by helping to create more predictable policymaking environments.

There are several potential remedies to the problematic combination of directly elected presidents and multipartism. In principle, post-communist systems with presidential or semi-presidential forms of governance could adopt parliamentary systems. Parliamentary systems require the emergence of a majority party or coalition to form the executive branch, accommodating multipartism. While states could select parliamentary government in principle, the likelihood of such a substantial institutional change is low. Countries that select presidential or semi-presidential systems rarely convert to parliamentarism. Rather than proposing this change, it is more useful to consider changes in existing laws that could resolve some of the problems associated with multipartism.

First, election timing could be made concurrent or semi-concurrent. While I was not able to control for the effect of election timing with my data, other scholars have found a strong influence of election timing on party systems (Shugart and Carey 1992; Jones 1995). With concurrent elections, presidents are able to benefit from "coattail effects," which generally consolidate support behind a smaller number of parties in legislative elections. Concurrent elections could generate additional benefits. The cost of election administration could be reduced by limiting the number of campaigns. Fewer elections may also generate citizen interest and increased participation. On the other hand, concurrent elections could divert attention from legislative races by focusing attention on the presidential campaign. Nevertheless, altering election timing could reduce multipartism without inhibiting citizens' freedom to express their preferences at the polls.

Second, the presidential formula could be altered to plurality. While I found no statistically significant effect of the presidential formula on multipartism in parliament, other scholars have found an effect. Specifically, plurality rules are expected to facilitate the formation of preelection coalitions and promote a presidential majority or near majority in parliament. Majority-runoff rules, used almost exclusively by post-communist states, are associated with greater political fragmentation (Jones 1999). However, by lowering the effective threshold needed to gain office, plurality rules could facilitate the accession to power of extremist candidates, possibly undermining democratic stability (Herron, Francisco, and Yap 2002).

Third, legislative rules could be changed to discourage extreme multipartism. In PR or mixed systems, the threshold for representation could be increased. Higher thresholds would encourage small parties to coalesce with larger parties. However, thresholds create disproportionality, which can generate concerns about representation. The Moldovan example from above demonstrates how instituting a higher threshold can contribute to problems of representation by reducing the number of parties that gain seats in parliament. Russia's 1995 Duma elections provide another example in which parliamentary seats were disproportionately allocated due largely to the electoral threshold.[22]

Post-communist states could also select SMD with plurality rules for parliament. Plurality rules are generally associated with more restricted partisan competition. However, in the inchoate party systems of post-communist states, two-candidate competition is not guaranteed. Further, some regional politicians have asserted that political parties would not emerge without a party-list element to legislative elections (Sheynis 1999).

Fourth, ancillary rules could be changed to encourage a more coherent party system. Rules on political-party registration could be altered to limit the number of parties in competition. Further, rules governing independent candidates could be changed to limit or exclude non-affiliated candidates. This would force candidates to join parties, and would increase the utility of party names as shortcuts for voters. However, this change would also restrict voter and candidate choice. Many candidates have eschewed party labels because of their potential negative connotations in some post-communist states. Parties have also been unable to provide some candidates with tangible benefits, prompting candidates to remain independent.

Any suggestion for institutional reform must be accompanied by a caveat. Despite the best intentions of constitutional engineers, altering the rules can yield unintended consequences. Institutional designers in post-communist states did not always accurately predict the effects of thresholds (Moraski and Loewenberg 1999) or mixed electoral systems (Herron and Nishikawa 2001). Changing elements of the election system may reduce the problems associated with multipartism while creating new inefficiencies.

Conclusions

Elections are linked to democracy because they are the mechanism for citizens to organize and express policy preferences, they structure the party system, and they influence governance. Election rules measurably affect the number of parties in competition, providing some information about the nature of political competition and the likelihood of a stable policymaking environment.

In this chapter, I argued that the presence of "too few" or "too many" parties may undermine democratic stability. While there is no "correct" number of parties that guarantees effective representation and efficient governance, certain institutional features better accommodate multipartism than others. Post-communist states have combined a wide array of election rules for executive and legislative institutions. In some cases, the rules are complementary: proportional representation generates multiparty competition that is accommodated in parliamentary government. Other rules are not complementary: the combination of directly elected presidents and extreme multipartism in parliament often results in incoherent or incomplete policymaking.

Many post-communist states that elect presidents have adopted electoral rules that inhibit democratic stability. The combination of majority-runoff rules, nonconcurrent elections, high district magnitude, and federalism undermines the emergence of a presidential majority or near majority in parliament. This, in turn, can promote ineffective policymaking or rule by decree—potentially problematic outcomes in countries that are still updating communist-era legislation and are working toward integration with the European Union.

While political actors could alter election timing, presidential and parliamentary election rules, or ancillary election laws, all components of election rules are part of a complete set of institutions that influence party-system development. Electoral engineering may provide a mechanism to adjust the number of political parties, but it may also yield unintended consequences.

NOTES

An early version of this chapter was presented at the Conference on Progress and Challenges in Democratization and Economic Liberalization, Cluj, Romania, June 2001. It was updated in late 2002 and has received minor revisions subsequently. The author thanks Norman Graham and Brian Silver for comments, and Batbold Gankhuu for information about Mongolia. All errors and omissions are the fault of the author.

1. Schmitter and Karl's specific definition of democracy is "a system of governance in which rulers are held accountable for their actions in the public realm by citizens, acting indirectly through the competition and cooperation of their elected representatives" (1991, 76).

2. Like liberal democracies, pseudo-democracies are characterized by the existence of an organized opposition and many civil liberties. However, elections and electoral competition are controlled to prevent the ruling party from losing power (Diamond 1996).

3. In a delegative democracy, elections determine who will rule, but the executive has wide-ranging authority. The underlying premise of a delegative democracy is that "whoever wins election to the presidency is . . . entitled to govern as he or she sees fit" (O'Donnell 1994, 59). While the distribution of power among constituencies and the term of office constrain the executive, the president is generally free to rule without restrictions. Among newly democratizing regimes, Russia and Ukraine have been characterized as delegative democracies (Kubicek 1994).

4. Zakaria (1997) suggests that illiberal democracies are states that have free elections, but do not accept the rule of law or respect the rights of citizens.

5. The Laakso-Taagepera Index indicates the effective number of parties based on the following formula: where p is the proportion of seats obtained (for the legislature) or proportion of the vote obtained (for the president).

6. I use first-round results for presidential data because the second round of a majority-runoff system includes only the top two candidates from the first round.

7. In principle, it is possible to have fewer than two effective parties and retain democratic credentials. For instance, if a country had two parties contesting an election and one gained 60 percent of the seats and the other gained 40 percent, the effective number of legislative parties would be 1.92. The value of 2.00 effective parties should not be viewed

as the lower bound for democratic party systems, but party systems dipping below two warrant special attention.

8. See the discussion of democracy in Norman Graham's chapter in this volume.

9. Electoral volatility is the change in the proportion of votes received by parties from election to election.

10. Bosnia-Herzegovina is a special case. While the executive branch is directly elected, it is plural. Each of the three major ethnic groups elects a member of the presidium. Thus, while the chief executive is elected, Bosnia-Herzegovina diverges from the other countries because a single individual is not selected.

11. See Freedom in the World (http://www.freedomhouse.org) for a complete list.

12. They are Azerbaijan, Kazakhstan, and Tajikistan.

13. Systems with directly elected presidents are included, both pure presidential and semi-presidential. Semi-presidential systems that combine popularly elected chief executives and prime ministers responsible to parliament are common in East Central Europe and Eurasia.

14. Aleksandr Lebed competed in the first round of the 1996 Russian presidential campaign and used his success as leverage to gain a high-ranking post.

15. Communist parties did not have a literal monopoly in some Central and East European states as the CPSU maintained in the Soviet Union. Nevertheless, Communist parties had an effective monopoly on power.

16. However, some research suggests that voters in post-communist states are developing attachments to parties. See Brader and Tucker (2001), and Miller and Klobucar (2000).

17. Many post-communist states are unicameral. States with bicameral parliaments tend to choose representatives to the upper house through indirect elections or appointments. This is the case in Belarus, Bosnia-Herzegovina, Kazakhstan, Russia, Slovenia, Tajikistan, and Turkmenistan. SMD is employed in the Czech Republic and Kyrgyzstan while multi-member districts are used in Poland, Romania, and Yugoslavia.

18. The terminology for subtypes of mixed systems varies from scholar to scholar. Mixed compensatory systems have been called "linked," "compensatory," "Mixed Member Proportional," and "corrective." Mixed non-compensatory systems have been called "unlinked," "non-compensatory," "Mixed Member Majoritarian," and "superposition."

19. Hungary employs a complicated mixed system that includes vote transfers. This approach differs from other systems of compensation that provide seat transfers. I include Hungary among compensatory systems because of the formal linkage between the allocation tiers.

20. A referendum in August 2002 approved a change to standard majority-runoff.

21. Similarly, the use of SMD with a plurality formula facilitated the electoral success of the Revolutionary People's Party in Mongolia.

22. In 1995, only four parties exceeded the 5 percent threshold. However, because Russia employs a mixed system, the overall seat distribution was more proportional than seat distribution in the Moldovan parliament elected in 2001.

REFERENCES

Amorim Neto, Octavio, and Gary W. Cox. 1997. Electoral institutions, cleavage structures, and the number of parties. *American Journal of Political Science* 41: 149–74.

Blais, André, Louis Massicotte, and Agnieszka Dobrzynska. 1997. Direct presidential elections: A world summary. *Electoral Studies* 16: 441–55.

Brader, Ted, and Joshua A. Tucker. 2001. The emergence of mass partisanship in Russia, 1993–1996. *American Journal of Political Science* 45: 69–83.

Cox, Gary W. 1997. *Making votes count.* Cambridge: Cambridge University Press.

Dahl, Robert. 1971. *Polyarchy: Participation and opposition.* New Haven: Yale University Press.

Diamond, Larry. 1996. Is the third wave over? *Journal of Democracy* 7: 20–37.

Duverger, Maurice. 1954. *Political parties: Their organization and activity in the modern state.* New York: Wiley.

EECR 2000a. Slovakia. *East European constitutional review* (Summer 2000).

———. 2000b. Slovakia. *East European constitutional review* (Fall 2000).

———. 2000c. Slovenia. *East European constitutional review* (Fall 2000).

Elster, John, Claus Offe, and Ulrich K. Preuss. 1998. *Institutional design in post-communist societies.* Cambridge: Cambridge University Press.

Fish, M. Steven. 1998. Mongolia: Democracy without prerequisites. *Journal of Democracy* 9: 127–41.

Herron, Erik S., Ronald Francisco, and O. Fiona Yap. 2002. Election rules and social stability. In *Choosing a president: The electoral college and beyond,* ed. Paul Schumaker and Burdett Loomis. New York: Chatham House.

Herron, Erik S., and Misa Nishikawa. 2001. Contamination effects and the number of parties in mixed-superposition electoral systems. *Electoral Studies* 20: 63–86.

Huntington, Samuel P. 1991. *The third wave: Democratization in the late twentieth century.* Norman: University of Oklahoma Press.

Huskey, Eugene. 1999. *Presidential power in Russia.* Armonk, NY: M. E. Sharpe.

IFES. 1995. *Election law compendium of Central and Eastern Europe.* Kyiv: IFES.

Jones, Mark P. 1995. *Electoral laws and the survival of presidential democracies.* Notre Dame: University of Notre Dame Press.

———. 1999. Electoral laws and the effective number of candidates in presidential elections. *Journal of Politics* 61: 171–84.

Kitschelt, Herbert, Zdenka Mansfeldova, Radoslaw Amrkowski, and Gabor Toka. 1999. *Post-communist party systems.* Cambridge: Cambridge University Press.

Kubicek, Paul. 1994. Delegative democracy in Russia and Ukraine. *Communist and Post-Communist Studies* 27: 423–41.

Kynev, A. V. 2002. Institut prezidentstva v strankh tsentralnoi i vostochnoi Yevropy kak indicator protsessa politicheskoi transformatsii. *POLIS* 2: 126–37.

LeDuc, Lawrence, Richard G. Niemi, and Pippa Norris. 2002. *Comparing democracies 2.* Thousand Oaks, CA: Sage.

Lijphart, Arend. 1994. *Electoral systems and party systems.* Oxford: Oxford University Press.

Mainwaring, Scott, and Timothy R. Scully. 1995. *Building democratic institutions.* Stanford, CA: Stanford University Press.

Miller, Arthur H., and Thomas F. Klobucar. 2000. The development of party identification in post-Soviet societies. *American Journal of Political Science* 44: 667–85.

Moraski, Bryon, and Gerhard Loewenberg. 1999. The effect of electoral thresholds on the revival of former communist parties in East-Central Europe. *Journal of Politics* 61: 151–70.

O'Donnell, Guillermo. 1994. Delegative democracy. *Journal of Democracy* 5: 55–69.

Ordeshook, Peter, and Olga Shvetsova. 1994. Ethnic heterogeneity, district magnitude, and the number of parties. *American Journal of Political Science* 38: 100–23.

OSCE. 1998. *Presidential election in the Republic of Azerbaijan.* N.p.: OSCE.

———. 1999. *Republic of Kazakhstan presidential elections.* N.p.: OSCE.

———. 2000a. *Republic of Georgia presidential elections final report.* Warsaw: OSCE

———. 2000b. *Republic of Tajikistan: Elections to parliament final report.* Warsaw: OSCE.

———. 2001a. *Azerbaijan parliamentary elections final report.* Warsaw: OSCE.

———. 2001b. *Belarus parliamentary elections: Technical assessment mission final report.* Warsaw: OSCE.

———. 2001c. *Kyrgyz Republic presidential elections.* Warsaw: OSCE.

Reynolds, Andrew, and Ben Reilly. 1997. *The international IDEA handbook of electoral system design.* Stockholm: International IDEA.

Sartori, Giovanni. 1976. *Parties and party systems.* New York: Cambridge University Press.

Schmitter, Philippe C., and Terry Lynn Karl. 1991. What democracy is . . . and is not. *Journal of Democracy* 2: 75–88.

Schumpeter, Joseph. 1947. *Capitalism, socialism and democracy.* New York: Harper.

Sheynis, Viktor. 1999. *Za chestnye vybory.* Moscow: Center of Economic and Political Research.

Shin, √Doh Chull. 1994. On the third wave of democratization: A synthesis and evaluation of recent theory and research. *World Politics* 47: 135–70.

Shugart, Matthew Soberg, and John M. Carey. 1992. *Presidents and assemblies.* Cambridge: Cambridge University Press.

Taagepera, Rein, and Matthew Soberg Shugart. 1989. *Seats and votes: The seats and determinants of electoral systems.* New Haven, CT: Yale University Press.

White, Stephen, Richard Rose, and Ian McAllister. 1997. *How Russia votes.* Chatham, NJ: Chatham House Publishers.

Zakaria, Fareed. 1997. The rise of illiberal democracy. *Foreign Affairs* 76: 22–43.

3

Hegel's Institutionalist Liberalism: Political Economy and Civil Society in the *Philosophy of Right*

Louis D. Hunt

Introduction

Hegel's account in the *Philosophy of Right* of the relation between civil society and the idea of the market in classical political economy is not only of histori-cal interest as a pioneering attempt to incorporate the new science of political economy into the tradition of political philosophy. It addresses as well the attempts of contemporary political economists to find the proper balance between the market and other social and political institutions. The "old" insti-tutionalist economics of Veblen and Commons had argued that market inter-actions presupposed an institutional framework that could not itself be explained by the logic of the market. In their view, the task of a properly polit-ical economy was to explain how changes in nonmarket institutional struc-tures affected economic processes. By contrast, the "new" institutionalist economics of Coase, Williamson, North, and others sets itself the task of explaining the emergence and functioning of a broad range of social and polit-ical institutions on the basis of the neoclassical model of the market.[1] The debate between the "old" and the "new" institutionalists thus centers on the question of whether the neoclassical model of market exchange, or a more sociological-political account of the development of institutional structures should be given explanatory primacy in accounting for the complex institu-tions of modern market societies.

This theoretical controversy has obvious relevance to the debates about the ongoing task of economic and political transition in former communist countries.[2] The struggle to transform command into market economies in these countries has raised, in a very practical context, the question of the proper balance between encouraging the "spontaneous" forces of the market and developing appropriate institutional structures for guiding and constraining these forces. While proponents of "shock therapy" or "big bang" models of economic transformation argued their case on the basis of neoclassical assumptions, their opponents, the defenders of a "gradualist" or "evolutionary" approach to economic reform, argued for a more institutionalist approach. The widespread disillusionment with socialism, with the failure of command economies to make good on their promise of greater economic efficiency and social welfare, lent plausibility to the initial call for radical implementation of free-market reforms. Practical difficulties in the implementation of such reform, as well as the widespread political backlash in many formerly socialist countries against the immediate economic and social upheaval that followed in the wake of such reforms led to considerable criticisms of this approach.[3]

It is obviously not within the purview of this paper to adjudicate the ongoing debate between these two positions. Its more limited purpose is to argue that Hegel's account of civil society, and its place in the modern social and political order, provides a useful framework for thinking about the relation between the market and other social and political institutions—both in transitional economies, like those of Central Europe and Eurasia, and in developed market economies, like those of the United States and Western Europe.

There are three main points Hegel brings to the current debate about the nature and limits of the market economy. In the first place, Hegel's account of the market anticipates many of the criticisms that the "old" institutionalist economists made of the neoclassical approach to understanding the market. Like the older institutionalists, Hegel is suspicious of the claim (which he knew from his reading of Adam Smith's *Wealth of Nations*) that markets will emerge spontaneously so long as oppressive government does not hinder them. While not denying the spontaneous character of many market transactions, Hegel argues that the modern market economy as a whole presupposes a complex network of social and political institutions (as well as a specific set of moral dispositions) that cannot be fostered by the market alone.[4] In the second place, and as a consequence of the first point, Hegel shows a keen awareness of the need to limit the sphere within which the economic perspective of the market predominates. Precisely if the market itself depends for its flourishing on the existence of nonmarket institutions, it is important to insulate such institutions as far as possible from the potentially corrosive influence of economic rationality. Lastly, Hegel places the discussion about the appropriate place of the market in the modern social and political order in a broader historical and philosophical account of the nature of human freedom. He argues that private property and the market are necessary but not sufficient conditions for the realization of such freedom.

Translated into the context of economic reform in Central Europe and Eurasia, Hegel's account of the social and political presuppositions of a market economy suggests a basic support for privatization of public enterprises and the freeing of markets from state control, accompanied by a cautionary warning about the dangers of ignoring institutions in the process of such reform, as well as a long-term concern about the impact of the unleashed market on the social and political health of these societies. This last point is particularly important, since the process of economic reform in post-communist countries has put considerable strain on precisely those social and political institutions (the family and the state) that Hegel saw as a necessary counter to the market.

Political Economy and Civil Society in the Philosophy of Right

Hegel's account of civil society in the *Philosophy of Right* is related both historically and conceptually to the classical model of the market as a dynamic equilibrium among individuals pursuing their rational self-interest.[5] His depiction of civil society as "a system of all-round interdependence" in which "the subsistence and welfare of the individual are interwoven with, and grounded on, the subsistence, welfare, and rights of all" clearly reflects the influence of Adam Smith's well-known characterization of the market in the *Wealth of Nations* as an "invisible hand" directing individuals' selfish interests to the common good (Hegel 1991a, §183, p. 221).[6] In a striking passage toward the beginning of his discussion of civil society, Hegel makes it clear that he regards the development of an independent science of political economy as an important achievement of the modern world: "'*Political Economy*' is one of the sciences which have originated in the modern age as their element . . . [It is] a science which does credit to thought because it finds the laws underlying a mass of contingent occurrences" (Hegel 1991a, §189, pp. 227–28). Hegel's innovative conception of civil society as a sphere of social interaction distinct from the state presupposes the emancipation of the market from direct moral and political supervision, as well as the development of a coherent theory of how social coordination is possible in the absence of hierarchical authority.[7]

The affinity between Hegel's conception of civil society and the idea of the market in classical political economy does not, however, imply either that he uncritically endorsed the market economy or that he thought civil society could be reduced to its economic basis. In Hegel's account, civil society encompasses not only the market narrowly conceived but also the legal, social, and (in part) political framework within which, and through which, the market operates. Under the rubric of civil society, Hegel includes a range of institutions that serve both to foster the operations of the market economy and to check its excesses. For example, Hegel places in the very center of his account of civil society a section on "The Administration of Justice," in which he argues that the legal system plays a crucial role in facilitating market transaction. Hegel argues in this section both that market transactions require a functioning legal system, and that the habit of engaging in such transactions fosters the rule of law. In his words, "Justice is a major factor in civil society: good laws will cause the state to flourish, and free ownership is a fundamental condition of its success" (1991a, §229, p. 259).

On a more critical note, in the concluding section of his account of civil society, "The Police and the Corporation," Hegel discusses the need for welfare provisions and some form of corporate organization of society to counteract the vicissitudes of the market and to hinder the development of a disaffected underclass. Anticipating later criticisms of laissez-faire capitalism, Hegel argues that left to its own devices, the market tends to generate an impoverished and resentful underclass—he uses the harsher term "rabble" [Pöbel]—unable to enjoy the benefits of civil society. For this reason, Hegel advises against relying entirely on market forces to regulate the economy, noting that "The differing interest of producers and consumers may come into collision with each other, and even if, *on the whole*, their correct relationship re-establishes itself automatically, its adjustment also needs to be consciously regulated by an agency which stands above both sides" (1991a, §236, pp. 261–62).

Hegel's account of the crucial role of legal institutions in fostering market exchange, as well as the need to address the political dangers of economic deprivation, highlights two major difficulties faced by economic reformers in post-communist societies. On the first point: communist regimes did not recognize a right to private property independent of the state, and therefore did not have any reason to develop a set of legal norms for governing market exchanges. Moreover, the judiciary was a highly politicized institution under communism. As Hegel argues, the rule of law [Rechtstaat], which Marxist ideology dismissed as a "bourgeois shibboleth," requires the independence of civil society from the direct control of the state. Both a command economy and a state-controlled judiciary are incompatible with civil society in the Hegelian sense. Economic reform in post-communist regimes is thus necessarily also legal reform. To accomplish this, however, it is necessary both to change an entrenched legal culture and to restore popular trust in a judicial system long seen as nothing more than a tool of state power. The ongoing political struggle in Russia between the Putin government and the so-called "oligarchs" exemplifies the dangers of failing to establish clear-cut and accepted legal norms determining the boundary between legitimate and illegitimate economic activity, and between reasonable and excessive state control over such activity.

The problem of the development of an impoverished and alienated under-class in some former communist regimes—the high unemployment and social anomie in former East Germany is a particularly striking example of this problem—also poses a challenge to economic and political reform. It is worth noting that Hegel's advocacy of some form of welfare state is rooted not so much in a concern for economic justice as in considerations of political legiti-macy and stability. Independently of whether it is just to allow the development of extreme economic inequalities in a society, it is politically dangerous to do so. This is particularly so when the societies in question had enjoyed at least the appearance of economic equality for the majority of the population. (This appearance, of course, was belied by the numerous privileges enjoyed by mem-bers of the *nomenklatura* under communism.) While communist regimes were unable to provide sustained economic growth, or respond efficiently to con-sumer choices, they did satisfy, if in a somewhat "Potemkin village"–like man-ner, the goal of full employment. East Germany is again a good example here. After the initial enthusiasm that greeted the fall of the Berlin Wall and the reunification of Germany, many "Ossies" found themselves adrift in a compet-itive capitalist environment for which they had no survival skills. To be sure, this is in part a generational problem, which will tend to diminish as a younger generation with no memory of the East German past enters the job market. However, despite a massive influx of capital, the eastern region of Germany remains blighted by high unemployment and the social ills, such as political extremism and xenophobia, that it gives rise to.

Hegel's broader account of modern "ethical life" [*Sittlichkeit*]—his term for the normative and institutional basis of social and political order—attempts to address the problematic relation between the market economy and other social-political institutions by situating civil society (and thus the market econ-omy) between the domestic sphere of the family and the political sphere of the state. In this conceptual framework, civil society is the appropriate arena for the contractual and exchange relations typical of a modern commercial society. Hegel argues that the calculative economic rationality proper to civil society must be carefully segregated from the naive emotional solidarity he finds in the family, and the rational (but not calculative) patriotism that animates, in his view, the citizens of the modern state. In civil society, the self-interested indi-vidual is properly liberated from the bonds of both familial love and political loyalty. Civil society presupposes, however, the continued vitality of both the family and the state. Hegel argues that civil society and the market cannot be sustained apart from the support that these encompassing social and political institutions provide. For this reason, Hegel is deeply concerned with the tendency of civil society to "colonize" (in Jürgen Habermas's phrase) both the intimate sphere of the family and the public life of the state—a tendency, of course, that has become even more pronounced in our own time. This tendency is particularly evident in the United States, Great Britain, and, perhaps to a somewhat lesser degree, the EU countries. It will certainly become an increasingly important factor as well in post-communist countries as they move towards a fully functional market economy.

Before turning to Hegel's account of the role of the family and the state in both enabling and limiting the market transactions of civil society, we must examine more closely the structure of civil society itself. Hegel outlines the basic logic of civil society as follows:

> In civil society, each individual is his own end, and all else means nothing to him. But he cannot accomplish the full extent of his ends without reference to others; these others are therefore means to the end of the particular [person]. But through its reference to others, the particular takes on the form of universality, and gains satisfaction by simultaneously satisfying the welfare of others. (1991a, §182, p. 220)

This account of civil society is deliberately paradoxical in that it describes a form of human association whose members do not recognize themselves *as* associated with each other. To complicate matters, Hegel depicts the paradoxical character of civil society in terms borrowed from his speculative logic. Civil society is a form of ethical life [*Sittlichkeit*], a mode of human association, but it is a distorted appearance or manifestation [*Erscheinung*] of ethical life.[8] Civil society is ethical life in an alienated form whose true character is concealed from the members of civil society themselves.

To understand this characterization of civil society, we must have a clearer understanding of what Hegel means by ethical life. He defines ethical life as "the *Idea of Freedom* as the living good which has its knowledge and volition in self-consciousness, and its actuality through self-conscious action" (1991a, §142, p. 189). To put this point in somewhat less opaque terms: Ethical life is the realization of human freedom in actual social and political institutions. Hegel's ethical theory is a self-actualization theory in which the individual realizes his freedom only through participation in social and political institutions that can meet with his rational approval. It is important to keep in mind this last qualification. Hegel is sometimes taxed with the view that he subordinates the moral judgment of the individual to the collective mores of the community.[9] This is a misreading of his argument. Hegel's point is that for an institution to be ethical, it must meet two criteria: First, it must actually realize—i.e., make practically effective in the world—human freedom. It cannot remain at the level of a mere ideal or wish. Secondly, the individual (at least in his truly reflective moments) must be able to recognize the institution as an embodiment of *his* freedom, not simply freedom as an abstraction.

While Hegel clearly does not mean to subordinate the individual to the unreflective standards of his political community, he argues that the realization of individual freedom does require the acceptance of specific social and political institutions. Hegel's starting point in the *Philosophy of Right* is individualistic. He begins his argument with the familiar figure from the liberal social-contract tradition of the isolated individual confronting the natural world and appropriating part of it for his own use. In the course of his argument, however, Hegel gradually reveals the initially hidden normative and institutional conditions of such individualism. The argument of the *Philosophy of Right* provides a conceptual reconstruction of the gradually more adequate embodiment of human freedom from its most abstract form in the institution of private property to its highest manifestation in public service to the state.[10]

Hegel begins from the standpoint of individualism, in other words, because he regards that standpoint as one-sided and in need of correction. His peculiar conception of philosophical dialectic requires that the truth be arrived at through a systematic examination of the false.[11] Apart from its philosophical justification, there are pedagogical advantages to this approach in the *Philosophy of Right*. It enables Hegel to begin his argument from the same ground as that of classical liberalism, the liberalism of Locke and Madison, while avoiding what he regards as the problematic features of their social and political thought. Like these classical liberals, Hegel starts from the assumption that the institution of private property is a necessary condition for the realization of human freedom. In this respect, he agrees with their emphasis on the importance of property rights to the maintenance of freedom. Hegel goes on to show, however, that the institution of private property itself presupposes moral and political institutions that cannot be fully understood or justified in terms of property rights. To use a recurrent formulation: private property is a necessary but far from a sufficient condition for the realization of human freedom. Two conclusions follow from this point: First, even if the existence of private property entails a certain degree of economic and political inequality, property rights cannot be simply abolished, since to do so would be to strike at the very root of freedom. Secondly, property rights cannot be absolute, since their effective exercise requires social and political conditions that may depend on the occasional limitation of such rights.

To put this last point in a somewhat different way: the protection of property rights does not, for Hegel, trump all other moral and political considerations. This is because he does not attempt to deduce other social and political institutions from the primitive right to private property, but rather argues that the existence of private property necessarily presupposes the existence of other, more comprehensive social and political institutions. For this reason, he is not tempted to argue that the purpose of government is *nothing but* the protection of property rights. This gives Hegel's political theory an important advantage over classical liberalism, especially when one considers how difficult it is to justify some of the elementary duties of citizenship, like risking one's life in defense of one's country, in the classical liberal terms of protecting life, liberty, and property.

Ethical life encompasses both moral norms and the effective embodiment of these norms in social and political institutions. Hegel is equally critical of moralistic claims "to construct a *state as it ought to be*" without regard to the constraints that historical conditions and a realistic appraisal of human motivations impose on statecraft, and of historicist and positivistic appeals to the sanctity of historical precedent and the supposed authority of the given, even when this is supported by "the external authority of the state" (Hegel 1991a, preface, 11). (Failure to heed this last point is perhaps the main reason for the misunderstanding of Hegel's thought as an uncritical endorsement of the status quo.) An institution is ethical in Hegel's sense if it provides an objective moral framework for satisfying fundamental human needs. Marriage is a paradigm of what Hegel means by an ethical institution, since the purpose of marriage, in his view, is to give objective and abiding form to the otherwise "transient, capricious, and purely subjective aspects of [sexual] love" (§161, p. 201). The ultimate goal of ethical life—a goal that is fully achieved only through participation in the political institutions of the rational state—is the complete unity of particularity and universality, individual will and social institution.

At the level of civil society, however, particularity and individuality, individual and institution, *appear* to be independent of each other, even though they are in fact dependent on each other. In Hegel's words,

> Although particularity and universality have become separated in civil society, they are nonetheless bound up with and conditioned by each other. Although each appears to do precisely the opposite of the other and imagines that it can exist only by keeping the other at a distance, each nevertheless has the other as its condition. (Hegel 1991a §184, p. 221)

Putting Hegel's point in less abstract terms, the individual in civil society thinks of himself as an independent agent pursuing his own interests without regard to others, while at the same time implicitly relying on the assistance of others in order to achieve his ends. His attitude toward other people is instrumental insofar as he regards them merely as means to the accomplishing of his own ends. In pursuing his own interests, however, the individual in civil society soon discovers that he must accommodate the interests of others. Indeed, since he "acquires [his] means of satisfaction from others," he "must accordingly accept their opinions" (Hegel 1991a §192, p. 230). Ironically, the unfettered pursuit of individual self-interest in civil society leads, in Hegel's view, not to anarchy, but to a kind of social conformity. The more the individual in civil society pursues his selfish interests, the more he becomes entangled in a web of dependency on others. It is not so much the selfishness of civil society that leads Hegel to describe it as an alienated form of ethical life, as the contradiction between the self-understanding of the individual in civil society as an independent agent (a "rugged individualist") and his real situation as a dependent part of a larger whole.

At first glance, Hegel's depiction of the psychology of the individual in civil society recalls nothing so much as the damming portrait of the bourgeois human being in Rousseau's *Emile*: "Always in contradiction with himself, always floating between his inclinations and his duties, he will never be either man or citizen. He will be good neither for himself nor for others" (Rousseau 1997,40). The similarity between Rousseau's and Hegel's accounts of the character of human beings in civil society becomes all the more striking when one notes that the German term for civil society, *Bürgerliche Gesellschaft*, could also be translated as "bourgeois society."[12] Indeed, Hegel calls attention to the bourgeois character of the typical member of civil society by referring to him as "the *citizen* (in the sense of bourgeois)" [*Bürger (als Bourgeois)*] (1991a, §190, p. 228). By resolving the ambiguity in the German term *Bürger* between citizen and bourgeois in favor of the latter, Hegel distances his modern conception of civil society from the classical notion of *societas civilis*. Hegel makes it clear that he is speaking not of the ancient citizen, but of the modern bourgeois. While the ancient citizen's purported dedication to public life rested on the freedom from economic necessity made possible by slave labor, the primary occupation (and preoccupation) of the modern bourgeois is not political deliberation, but the more mundane task of making a living. The inhabitant of modern civil society is the human being as producer and consumer; he is far removed from the heroic image of the ancient citizen invoked by Rousseau.

The similarity of Hegel's conception of *der Bürger* to Rousseau's despised *bourgeois* does not mean, however, that he accepts Rousseau's negative evaluation of modern commercial society. On the contrary, the bourgeois human type whom Rousseau excoriates for his hollowness and hypocrisy turns out to be the unlikely hero of Hegel's account of civil society. Despite the often-critical tenor of Hegel's account of civil society, he regards its development as the principal reason for the superiority of the modern state to its classical and medieval predecessors. Unlike Rousseau, the mature Hegel of the *Philosophy of Right* harbors little nostalgia for the imagined community of the classical polis. He argues that the inability of the classical polis to provide a legitimate outlet for economic acquisitiveness and the other selfish passions was the main reason for its decline. "The self-sufficient development of particularity . . . is the moment which appears in the states of the ancient world as an influx of ethical corruption and as the ultimate reason for their downfall" (Hegel 1991a, §185, p. 222). The virtue of modern civil society is that—unlike the polis as envisaged by classical republican theory—it provides an arena in which human beings can pursue their acquisitive and selfish passions without posing an immediate threat to the social and political order. The existence of civil society as a "sphere of mediation in which all individual characteristics, all aptitudes, and all accidents of birth and fortune are liberated" proves to be a strength rather than a weakness of the modern state (§182, pp. 220–21). Hegel makes this point in an important passage toward the beginning of his discussion of the state:

> The principle of the modern state has enormous strength and depth because it allows the principle of subjectivity to attain self-fulfillment in the *self-sufficient extreme* of personal particularity, while at the same time *bringing it back to substantial unity* and so preserving this unity in the principle of subjectivity itself. (§260, p. 282)

The Functions of Civil Society

The political strength of the modern liberal constitutional state is based on its ability to develop institutional means of incorporating rather than repressing individual freedom. Civil society facilitates this incorporation of individual freedom into the institutions of the political community in two ways. In the first place, an important function of civil society is to provide an institutional framework within which market transactions can take place unhindered by direct moral and political supervision. In this respect, Hegel sides squarely with the liberal critique of the classical and Christian scholastic view that economic acquisition and market transactions should be subject to stringent moral and political control. He also implicitly anticipates and rejects Marx's later proposal to subordinate the "anarchy of the market" to the centralized control of production and exchange within a factory or corporation. His distinction between civil society and the state recognizes the greater independence and centrality of the market in modern social and political life.

Hegel's view of the role of the market in human life is not quite as sanguine, however, as some of its contemporary proponents. By distinguishing between civil society and the state, Hegel intends not only to protect the market from officious moral and political meddling but also to insulate the state and other nonmarket institutions from the undue influence of the market itself. The institutional role of civil society is not only to be a social space for the market but also to be a "preserve" of sorts within which market transactions are to be confined and limited. Hegel is concerned that such important social institutions as marriage and the family, as well as the political obligations of citizenship, be protected from the subversive influence of economic rationality. This aspect of his account of civil society raises the question—a highly pertinent one to proponents of market reform—of whether it is possible to encourage the flourishing of the market economy without having it come to dominate completely the social and political landscape.

A partial answer to this question can be found by looking at the other main function of civil society in Hegel's account. In addition to its role in supplying a legal and political framework for the market, civil society also has a pedagogic function. This latter function is the role played by civil society and the market in the education or cultivation [Bildung] of the bodily desires and needs of human beings into what Hegel calls "social needs" (1991a, §194, p. 230). Civil society is not only the arena in which human beings attempt to satisfy their needs and wants; it is also the medium in which these are first developed and formed. Hegel's account of the market differs from orthodox neoclassical economics not only in incorporating the normative and institutional presuppositions of the market into his analysis but also in treating the formation of preferences and tastes—which orthodox neoclassical economic theory treats as an exogenous factor—as an intrinsic feature of market exchanges.[13]

To understand what this process of education or cultivation of needs implies, we must first be clear about what Hegel means by "social needs." Hegel defines social needs as "a combination of immediate or natural needs and spiritual needs of representational thought, [in which] the spiritual needs, as the universal, predominate" (1991a, §194, p. 230). As is often the case with Hegel, this statement requires some clarification. The phrase "representational thought," Vorstellung in German, is Hegel's usual term for ordinary, nonphilosophical thinking. Such thinking lacks the stringency and inner necessity that Hegel ascribes to "the Concept" [der Begriff]—his term for the logically rigorous mode of thinking developed in his Science of Logic.[14] Nonetheless, "representational thought" still exemplifies what Hegel regards as the uniquely human capacity to abstract from the particular data of the senses and form universal terms. Part of his point in this passage is to emphasize that social needs have a cognitive dimension that transcends their natural bodily origins. In his Philosophy of Mind, Hegel argues that there can be in principle no human needs that are simply bodily in character. Even the most fundamental biological needs, like those for food and sex, are qualitatively different in human beings from their counterparts in nonhuman animals. This is so because there can be, in Hegel's view, no strict separation between the lower (animal) and higher (human) faculties of the mind. The human psyche is a complex whole in which lower and higher faculties reciprocally condition each other (Hegel 1971, §380, pp. 7–8 and passim).

On the basis of Hegel's philosophical psychology, there can be no clear-cut distinction between (bodily) needs and (mental) wants. This point has important consequences for his account of civil society and the market. In the first place, it leads Hegel to reject any normative role for the early modern idea of a state of nature [*Naturzustand*] in constructing his account of civil society. The state of nature is not a possible standard for judging human society, since to be human is to have already to some degree transcended this state. Hegel's most extensive discussion of this point in the *Philosophy of Right* occurs in a long section (1991a, §187) toward the beginning of his account of civil society in which he critically analyzes two prominent views of the role of education [*Bildung*] in modern philosophy. On the one hand, Hegel criticizes a Rousseauian view of "the *innocence* of the state of nature and the ethical simplicity of uncultured [*ungebildeter*] peoples," in which education is portrayed as a corruption of original simplicity. On the other hand, he criticizes a utilitarian view of education as a means to the satisfaction of the "needs . . . pleasures and comforts of individual life," where these are understood to be brute facts about human nature (1991a, §187, pp. 224ff.).

The most striking feature of Hegel's argument in this passage is that he treats these two—apparently antithetical—conceptions of education and of human nature as variants of the same fundamental error. To state this error simply: both views treat education or cultivation as a process extrinsic to the formation of human nature itself. In the case of the Rousseauian model, true human nature is located among primitive and uncultured peoples whose natural simplicity has not yet been corrupted by education. In the case of the utilitarian model, human needs and preferences are regarded as brute natural facts about human beings, and education is treated as a mere means to their satisfaction. In the one case, human nature is portrayed as innocence before the fall; in the other, as the isolated psychic data of empiricist psychology. "Both of these views," Hegel responds, "show a lack of familiarity with the nature of spirit and the end of reason" (1991a, §187, pp. 224ff.). In other words, both of these conceptions of education misunderstand its intrinsic role in the formation of distinctively human needs and preferences. According to Hegel, the primary goal of education or cultivation is "to eliminate *natural simplicity*, whether as passive selflessness [Rousseau] or as barbarism of knowledge and volition [utilitarian]" (1991a, §187, pp. 224ff.). Both of these false conceptions of education fail to grasp that any human nature worth appealing to as a normative standard must already be the product of education or culture. Hegel makes this point with respect to the state of nature in the following passage:

> The notion [*Vorstellung*] that, in relation to his needs, man lived in freedom in a so-called state of nature in which he had only so-called natural needs of a simple kind and in which, to satisfy these, he employed only those means which a contingent nature immediately provided him . . . is mistaken. For a condition in which natural needs as such were immediately satisfied would merely be one in which spirituality was immersed in nature, and hence a condition of savagery and unfreedom. (1991a, §194, pp. 230–31)

Hegel's rejection of the idea that there are simply natural human needs raises, however, the question of whether he has any criteria for distinguishing between various types or levels of needs. It is clear that his position rules out the possibility of uncovering a basic stratum of needs that must first be satisfied before other higher needs, or even mere factitious wants, should be attended to. If no human need is strictly natural, the "naturalness" of a need cannot serve as a meaningful criterion for distinguishing true needs from artificial wants. Hegel's position here can be illuminated by a brief glance at the views of the eighteenth-century Scottish social theorist Adam Ferguson, whose writings almost certainly influenced his treatment of this point. In his major work, *An Essay on the History of Civil Society*, Ferguson rejects the possibility of distinguishing "in the human character, its original qualities, and [pointing] out the limits between nature and art." Against the Rousseauian hypothesis of a pre-social state of nature, Ferguson argues that it is impossible to trace back human history to a period in which "the footsteps of art are unknown" (Ferguson 1980, 8).

> In the condition of the savage, as well as in that of the citizen, are many proofs of human invention. . . . If the palace be unnatural, the cottage is so no less; and the highest refinements of political and moral apprehension, are not more artificial in their kind, than the first operations of sentiment and reason. (Ferguson 1980, 8)

While there is thus no natural "bottom" in either Ferguson's or Hegel's account of human needs—our needs are cultural or artifactual "all the way down," as Richard Rorty would put it—the question remains whether there is any "top." Put less metaphorically, does Hegel follow Ferguson in regarding human needs as infinitely elastic with no intelligible limits to their expansion? Or is there a point at which Hegel thinks more is not necessarily better? The importance of this question is that it determines in part Hegel's attitude toward what has come to be called "consumer society." To put this point in less anachronistic terms: Hegel's attitude toward the question of whether human needs and wants have any intrinsic limits helps to determine where he stands on the eighteenth-century debate about the moral and political effects of luxury, and this in turn influences his evaluation of commercial society. There is a passage early in Hegel's discussion of civil society that strongly suggests he does regard human needs as infinitely expansive.

> What the English call "comfortable" is something utterly inexhaustible; its ramifications are infinite, for every comfort in turn reveals its less comfortable side, and the resulting inventions are endless. (Hegel 1991a, §191, p. 229)

In this passage, Hegel appears to side squarely with the views of David Hume and Adam Smith, among others, who sought to amoralize the idea of luxury, which was associated in both the classical and Christian traditions with moral and political corruption, and demonstrate the economic and political benefits of "luxury spending." The defense of luxury in the writings of Hume and Smith calls attention to the crucial role of custom and social opinion in determining what is to count as a necessity (and thus by implication what is to count as a luxury). Smith makes this point in the following passage from the *Wealth of Nations*: "Under necessities therefore, I comprehend, not only the things which nature, but those things which the established rules of decency have rendered necessary to the lowest rank of people. All other things, I call luxuries; without meaning by this appellation, to throw the smallest degree of reproach upon the temperate use of them."[15]

Hegel's account of the elasticity of human needs and wants is indebted not only to the ideas of the Enlightenment defenders of luxury and commercial society but also to those of perhaps the most powerful critic of the Enlightenment, Jean-Jacques Rousseau. Hegel follows Rousseau in two important respects. First, Hegel adapts to his own purposes Rousseau's account in the *Second Discourse* of human "perfectibility," i.e., human beings' lack of instinctual determination in comparison to other animals. On the basis of this analysis, Hegel argues that the human capacity to multiply and refine needs is a crucial feature that distinguishes human from animal desire. "The animal is a particular entity which has its instincts and the means of satisfying it, means whose bounds cannot be exceeded." Human beings, by contrast, are less bound to a particular ecological niche and have a less immediate relation to the natural world. "The need for food and clothing, the necessity of renouncing raw food and of making it fit to eat and destroying its natural immediacy, means that the human being's life is less comfortable" (Hegel 1991a, §190, pp.

228–29). But this lack of comfort is the mark of our spiritual nature. We are not satisfied with merely eating our food raw, but learn to cook it, and eventually turn the consumption of food into a complex social custom with its own rules and conventions.

Secondly, and still in accordance with Rousseau's analysis, Hegel argues that human beings differ from other animals not only in their comparative freedom from instinctual determination but also in the influence that social norms have on the character of human desires. Unlike animals, human beings desire things not only to satisfy their immediate bodily needs but also because other human beings desire them. Human desires are shaped and formed in the light of what others think. As Hegel writes, "In the end it is no longer need but opinion which has to be satisfied" (1991a, §190, pp. 228–29). But this points to an underlying tension in Hegel's account of civil society. According to Hegel's account of civil society as a pedagogic institution, the market plays a crucial role in both the formation and the social coordination of preferences. Human needs are not simply natural givens, but are in part the creation of the market itself. "A need is therefore created not so much by those who experience it directly as by those who seek to profit from its emergence" (1991a, §191, p. 229). Paradoxically, the very thing that liberates human beings from the bonds of nature seems to increase our dependence on the opinions of others. Unlike Rousseau, however, Hegel does not regard this mutual dependency as deeply problematic. On the contrary, he argues that it plays a crucial role in establishing and maintaining the social conventions on which civilized life rests.

> The fact that I have to fit in with other people brings the form of universality into play at this point. I acquire my means of satisfaction from others and must accordingly accept their opinions. But at the same time, I am compelled to produce means whereby others can be satisfied. Thus, the one plays into the hands of the other and is connected with it. To this extent, everything particular takes on a social character; in the manner of dress and times of meals, there are certain conventions which one must accept, for in such matters it is not worth the trouble to seek to display one's own insight, and it is wisest to act as others do (1991a, §192, p. 230).

The most troubling feature of this argument is that Hegel appears to accept without serious qualms the view that the market is not a neutral mechanism for satisfying independent consumer preferences, but a manipulative force that in part creates the very needs it purports to satisfy. Indeed, unlike critics of the market from Rousseau to Galbraith, who have seen the role of the market in manufacturing needs as evidence of its lack of freedom, Hegel appears to regard this very feature of the market as its most important contribution to the realization of human freedom. Our liberation from the "natural immediacy" of animal life requires the acceptance of a certain degree of conformity to social norms. As Hegel puts this point in a striking phrase, "The rational is the high road which everyone follows and where no one stands out from the rest" (1991a, §15, p. 49).

Hegel is willing to accept such social conformity as the price of market freedom for two reasons. In the first place, he is self-consciously building on the tradition of modern political theory that looked to commerce and the institutions of the market rather than moral and political virtue as a foundation of social and political order. In agreement with this tradition, Hegel argues that the market is a more effective as well as a more decent means of achieving social conformity than older models of social and political control—precisely because it does not rely on moral exhortation or political coercion, but rather on the passions and interests of human beings.[16] In the second place—partly for the reasons suggested above about the incoherence of the idea of a state of nature—Hegel rejects Rousseau's view that human freedom is incompatible with the acceptance of a certain degree of social conformity. On the contrary, he argues that Rousseau's view mistakenly identifies true freedom with a state of independence from others that is either prehuman (his so-called "natural man") or suprahuman (the "solitary walker"). Like Aristotle, Hegel thinks that an individual without a social and political community, and thus dependence on others, must be either a beast or a god, but not a human being.

Beyond Civil Society? The Family, the State, and the Limits of the Market

Hegel's depiction of the social conformity produced by the market does suggest, however, that the model of freedom exemplified in modern civil society is inadequate. There remains a fundamental contradiction between the self-understanding of the individual in civil society as an autonomous agent and his real dependence, both material and psychological, on a complex system of economic exchange. Hegel's depiction of the typical member of civil society seems especially vulnerable to Rousseau's charge that the modern bourgeois is a "selfish conformist" who, lacking any genuine concern for his fellow human beings, is compelled by his own selfishness to conform to the opinions of others. Hegel's attempt to turn this social conformity to the good by arguing that it replaces more invidious forms of social and political control is only partially successful. To be sure, Smith and Hegel were right to argue that one of the virtues of private property and markets is that they help to undermine the power of princes and priests, and thus to liberate human beings from the hierarchical personal dependence characteristic of feudalism. However, this argument is less successful in countering Rousseau's charge that the liberation of the acquisitive passions from traditional moral and political restraints—a liberation accomplished in the name of human freedom—leads to a new and more pernicious (because less obvious) form of dependence on social opinion. As Rousseau puts this point in a note to his *Preface to Narcissus*, "[modern] philosophy loosens the bonds of society formed by mutual esteem and benevolence . . . commerce tighten[s] the bonds of society through self-interest" (Rousseau 1997, 100). If the price of "consumer sovereignty" is inner conformity to the opinions of others, the condition of what Rousseau famously called a "happy slave," and not merely the external observance of socially useful conventions, as Hegel implies, one might well conclude that the modern defenders of the market had made a bad bargain.

Hegel was certainly aware of this difficulty and does not argue that the institutions of civil society and the market alone provide a sufficient basis for social and political life. In his broader account of the structure of ethical life, Hegel locates civil society as a necessary stage between two types of human association—the family and the state—that cannot, in his view, be adequately grasped in terms of the economic rationality of the market. Hegel describes the family "as the *immediate substantiality* of spirit, [which] has as its determination the spirit's *feeling* of its own unity, which is *love*" (1991a, §158, p. 199). In other words, the family is a kind of natural community whose members are bound together not by rational calculation, but by emotional ties. In the family, the individual is able to overcome his selfish isolation and achieve a kind of unity with others that is impossible in civil society, although this unity exists only at the level of prerational feeling. The state, by contrast, is a form of community characterized by the highest degree of rationality, although not the calculative, economic rationality of civil society. In the state, the individual lives what Hegel calls a "universal life," in which participation in the public life of the community is not a means to some other goal—like the protection of property—but an end in itself.[17] If the family represents a state of undivided unity prior to the divisions of civil society, the state represents a return to this unity in a higher, more self-conscious form.

Hegel argues that the family and the state are both forms of human association that transcend the economic logic of civil society. The importance of these institutions is not only that they provide an outlet for fundamental human needs that are not met in civil society, but also that they supply precisely the psychological strengths needed to balance its alienating tendencies. The role of the family, for example, is to provide a locus of emotional solidarity as a balance to the necessarily anonymous and impersonal character of civil society. To borrow a phrase from Christopher Lasch, the family is "a haven in a heartless world." But Hegel's use of this conception of the family is two-edged. First, and most obviously, he is arguing against the view that the "extended order" of the market is an appropriate model for capturing all forms of human sociability.[18] Hegel would agree with Smith's formulation in *The Theory of Moral Sentiments* that the "feeble spark" of benevolence is too weak to serve as a foundation for social life generally (Smith 1976b, III.3.4). For this very reason, however, he thinks such affective motives require some harbor from the cold winds of self-interest. In a commercial society, the family must be the incubator of the emotional solidarity without which human life loses its savor.

Secondly, and this function of the family has been less noted, Hegel wants to *limit* such emotional solidarity to the family, excluding it from the public life of the state. In the *Philosophy of Right*, Hegel engages in a sharp polemic against the Romantic attack on the modern social and political order—an attack made in the name of bringing about a more fraternal social and political order. He accuses the proponents of this position of wanting to "reduce the complex inner articulation of the ethical, i.e., the state, the architectonics of its rationality . . . to a mush of 'heart, friendship, and enthusiasm'" (1991a, pp. 15–16).[19] In Hegel's sober view, the family is the *only* place in the modern social and political order where such emotional solidarity is either possible or desirable. Hegel was prescient in recognizing the threat of totalitarianism implicit in the Romantic longing for an unalienated wholeness at the level of social and political life. His "bourgeois" conception of the family is a necessary corrective against both the unlimited extension of the market and the Romantic communitarian attempt to replace rational self-interest with more affective forms of solidarity.

Like the family, the state is another bulwark against the extension of the market. Hegel begins his discussion of the state with a forceful statement of the impossibility of capturing the nature of political obligation in terms of the economic logic of civil society:

> If the state is confused with civil society and its determination is equated with the security and protection of property and personal freedom, *the interest of individuals as such* become the ultimate end for which they are united; it also follows from this that membership in the state is an optional matter. —But the relationship of the state to the individual is of quite a different kind. Since the state is objective spirit, it is only through being a member of the state that the individual himself has objectivity, truth, and ethical life. *Union* as such is itself the true content and end, and the destiny of individuals is to lead a universal life. (Hegel 1991a, §258, p. 276)

This passage states succinctly what Hegel regards as an inherent contradiction in the liberal social-contract theory of the state: If the state is simply a contract of free and equal persons for the protection of their life, liberty, and property, then citizenship does not have a different status in principle from membership in any other voluntary organization. But this is not how citizenship presents itself, not even to the citizens of a liberal state. This is clear from a brief comparison of citizenship in the state with membership in a modern corporation. No one would call a person who left his firm for a more profitable alliance with a competing firm a traitor—except in a loose, metaphorical sense—but that is precisely how one thinks of a citizen who abandons his country for the embrace of an enemy nation. Conversely, no one would seriously heed an injunction on the part of IBM to "give one's life for Big Blue," and yet citizens of even the most liberal regimes have fought and died for their countries. As with the obligations of family life, the duties of citizenship do not readily lend themselves to the contractual and voluntaristic language of civil society. While the danger of drawing parallels between the family and the state was noted above, they are similar on this crucial point. From the purely "phenomenological" perspective we are adopting here, neither the family nor the state appear to be the product of voluntary choice. Just as no one chooses his parents, so no one chooses his country. In Hegel's view, a theory of the state that cannot account for those features of the state that distinguish it from a voluntary association like a business firm must be considered a failure.

It is important to note that Hegel is not arguing for the absurd thesis that states based on liberal principles will necessarily be unable to act in their own defense. Such a claim would be open to immediate practical rebuttal. On this point, his disagreement with the liberal tradition is theoretical, not practical. As with his account of the social and political presuppositions of private property and the market, Hegel wants to show that liberal theory is insufficient to explain the full range of liberal practice. There would be little point, however, to offering such a theoretical correction—at least in a book with an avowedly practical intention—if he did not think that this theory might be pernicious *in the long run*. Hegel clearly foresaw the possibility of a gradual erosion of habits of citizenship as civil society grew in influence. This prospect underlies the most notorious feature of Hegel's account of the state—his defense of the "ethical" aspect of war. In a critique of Kant's famous essay on *Perpetual Peace*, which argued that the spread of commerce would encourage peaceful relations between nations, Hegel claims that a long peace may lead to a decline in the health of civil society itself:

> In peace, the bounds of civil life are extended, all its spheres become firmly established, and in the long run, people become stuck in their ways. . . . Not only do peoples emerge from wars with added strength, but nations troubled by civil dissension gain internal peace as a result of wars with their external enemies. (Hegel 1991a, §324, p. 362)

The "ethical" purpose of war, in Hegel's view, is to remind the citizens of the modern state that there is more to life than comfortable self-preservation, and that without the occasional willingness to sacrifice the "vanity of temporal things and temporal goods," even comfortable self-preservation may eventually be imperiled. Distasteful as this argument appears to us in the light of the horrific wars of the twentieth century, it is worth noting that Hegel's view is not so far out of the mainstream of liberal thought as some of his critics have alleged. On the point of the possible ill effects of a long peace on the health of a commercial society, Adam Smith, in both of his major works, lists a decline in martial virtue as one of the major consequences of the spread of the commercial spirit. In his famous discussion of the ill effects of the division of labor on the laboring poor in book 5 of the *Wealth of Nations*, Smith offers a qualified defense of militias—even though he recognizes the necessity for a standing army under the conditions of modern government—in order "to prevent that sort of mental mutilation, deformity and wretchedness, which cowardice necessarily involves in it, from spreading themselves through the great body of the people" (Smith 1976a, V.i.f.60). Of course, neither Smith nor Hegel is arguing for the intrinsic goodness of war; both recognize its manifold evils. But they are suggesting that the virtues of heart and mind called upon during war are a corrective of sorts to the tendency of human beings in commercial societies to become excessively preoccupied with their private well-being. In Hegel's view, such preoccupation will lead in the end to an enervation of the energies on which the flourishing of civil society depends. The health of civil society depends on the cultivation of habits of mind that are not automatically produced by civil society itself.

Conclusion: Hegel Today

Despite Hegel's own claim that his account of the modern state is definitive—indeed, the historical realization of the best regime that political philosophers have sought since Plato—it would be fatuous to argue that the Hegelian model of family, civil society, and state can be applied without further ado to our contemporary situation. In particular, the family and the state—the main bulwarks against the expansionary tendency of civil society and the market—seem more imperiled in our age than they were in Hegel's. In examining the case for market reforms in Central Europe and elsewhere, as well as in examining the health of social and political institutions in developed market societies (which parts of Central Europe at least are close to becoming), we must keep in mind the possibility that the institutional resources necessary for the dual task of both enabling and limiting the market may be lacking or seriously depleted. This is not an argument against implementing needed market reforms, but it is a salutary reminder that such reforms are insufficient in themselves to bring about a stable and healthy polity, and that they may well come at a cost to other social and political goods.[20]

Hegel's case for the important role of the family in providing a necessary emotional and moral counterweight to the selfish and competitive atmosphere of civil society and the market still seems theoretically compelling today. Furthermore, Hegel is certainly right to argue that it is important to keep this feeling of emotional solidarity largely confined to the family and out of the public sphere. As the rise of various forms of reactionary nationalism in former communist countries shows, illiberal communitarianism has lost none of its appeal for those who have been marginalized by changing economic and political conditions. Hegel's account of the family loses some of its practical plausibility, however, when one reflects, first, on the changed status of women in the United States and Western Europe during the last 40 years or so, and secondly, on the impact of economic and social reform on families in Central Europe and other former communist countries.

Hegel's conception of the family was patriarchal, although of a relatively liberal variety that was based on a woman's free choice of a husband and permitted a limited right of divorce. Still, the role of the woman, in Hegel's account, is to tend the home fires and provide emotional nurture for her husband and children; it is emphatically not to compete in the market or engage in affairs of state. Women in advanced industrial societies are no longer content (if they ever were) to find their "substantial vocation" simply in pious devotion to the family. Marriage is increasingly thought of as a contractual economic arrangement whose probable dissolution is anticipated by such devices as prenuptial agreements. Moreover, in both the United States and Western Europe (leaving aside some important differences in attitude toward sexual relations), marriage is of declining importance as an institution. With the widespread entrance of women into the work force, even parents who would like to spend more time with their children find themselves forced to look outside of the family for child care. What looks from one perspective like a salutary liberation of women from the drudgery of uncompensated labor in the family, looks from another like the intrusion of the economic rationality of civil society into the most intimate sphere of human life.

The situation is somewhat different in the former communist countries, although here it is even more important to distinguish between different countries and regions. In principle, communist regimes were committed to equality between the sexes, especially in the workplace, and hostile to the "bourgeois family." In practice, communist regimes achieved some genuine equality between the sexes, but did not seriously attack the legitimacy of the bourgeois family. The collapse of communism has led to different results in different countries. In those former communist regimes with large Islamic populations, the abolition of communism has led to a return of far more patriarchal models of the family than would have been acceptable to Hegel. These countries also tend to be resistant to the market insofar as it is a secularizing and "Westernizing" influence. From a Hegelian perspective, one could say they represent a reactionary backsliding from the distinctive achievements of the modern state. In the former East Germany, by contrast, the collapse of communism and reunification with the West introduced a more conservative element into familial relations. For example, abortion as a means of birth control was readily available in officially atheistic East Germany, but not in residually Christian West Germany, where abortion was illegal except in cases of rape or endangerment of the life of the mother. Indeed, this issue was so sensitive that it was left out of the Unification Treaty between the two German states. The compromise finally agreed on was that, while abortion remained technically illegal, the courts would not prosecute if the woman first saw a pregnancy counselor. But what this suggests from the standpoint of Hegel's account of the family is that in Germany, at least, the collapse of communism did nothing to halt—and may even have accelerated—the trend toward the declining importance of marriage and the family. Finally, one should not leave out of account the impact of economic deprivation in those regions of Central Europe and the former Soviet Union hardest hit by the unintended consequences of market reform on marriages and family life generally. Clearly, the bourgeois family can no longer so easily play the role that Hegel ascribes to it in the *Philosophy of Right*.

The idea of the state has also suffered a serious decline in intellectual and moral respectability since Hegel wrote the *Philosophy of Right*. Hegel's account of the public-spirited behavior of the state bureaucracy, his so-called "universal class," seems naive in the light of the actual behavior of state bureaucracies in both capitalist and communist countries. In Central Europe under communism, the idea of civil society was developed largely in opposition to the discredited idea of the state as the central organ of political power. As Lindahl argues in the next chapter, this conception of civil society as wholly opposed to the state led many dissident intellectuals to develop a model of "anti-political politics," which proved to be inadequate and dangerously utopian when they were confronted with the actual task of governing. While certainly oversimplified, Hegel's account of the state reminds us that civil society cannot function in a political void. If the institutions of the state lose their effectiveness and legitimacy, as increasingly appears to be the case in Russia, civil society is threatened as well. The state must be strong enough to enforce the "rules of the game," which enable a modern market economy to function effectively. Moreover, it must be able, at least on occasion, to act and speak effectively as the organ of a common good that transcends economic interests.

This last point, however, is undermined by the economic approach to politics, which dominates contemporary political science in the United States. According to this viewpoint, the "currency" of bureaucrats—power and influence—may be different from that of traders in the stock exchange, but their goal is the same: to maximize their income. As public choice theorists never tire of insisting, there is no reason to suppose that people alter their motives simply because they hold public office.[21] Moreover, Hegel's argument that membership in the state cannot be understood in contractual terms appears to confuse the factual question of the social and psychological sources of obedience with the normative question of the justification of such obedience. Hegel may well be right that looked at "phenomenologically"—i.e., from the perspective of the citizens themselves—the obligations of citizenship do not present themselves as the result of a contract. However, this may be seen as proof not of the superior, noninstrumental rationality of dedication to the public life of the state, but of the irrational character of our traditional notions of citizenship and political obligation. A truly scientific account of the state will necessarily abandon these unscientific notions of citizenship—which reflect no doubt the lingering influence of Hegel's classical education—and explain the institutions of the state as a response to "market failure," or in some other terms derived from contemporary economic theory.[22]

These challenges to the contemporary relevance of the Hegelian model are not easy to answer. It must be conceded that Hegel's elaborate balancing act between the spheres of family, civil society, and the state is no longer tenable in its original form. In many ways, the result that Hegel most feared—the extension of the economic rationality of civil society into the domestic and political spheres—has already come to pass in the advanced industrial democracies of the West. This will probably be the fate as well of those former communist countries that succeed in becoming developed market societies. (For those that fail, of course, the prognosis is far worse: the rise of ethnic nationalism, political authoritarianism, and religious fanaticism.) In the current intellectual and political climate, it is difficult to make a case that there are motives specific to either political life or familial life that are not reducible to those of the economic sphere. The homogeneity of the neoclassical economic model of human behavior reduces the complex heterogeneity of Hegel's account of family, civil society, and the state to "a night in which all cows are black."[23]

It would not be in the spirit of Hegel, however, to conclude on this pessimistic note. It is important to recognize that Hegel is not attached in principle to any particular historical institution. As he notes in his polemic against the conservatives of the German Historical School, to show that a historical institution once played a crucial role in social and political life proves nothing as to its usefulness today. Historical institutions may lose their purpose and survive for a long time as mere husks of their former selves (1991a, §3, pp. 29–30). It would be premature to say that the family and the state as Hegel depicts them have simply outlived their usefulness, but it is important to recognize that what Hegel is defending is not the details of the European family and state circa 1820, but the *functions* these institutions performed in that specific historical context. These functions—to provide a sphere of personal intimacy and an arena for some form of dedication to the public good—are as important today as they were in Hegel's time. Perhaps the most enduring contribution of his political philosophy is to have shown that if we value the benefits of the market economy, we must pay more attention than most of the modern defenders of the market have done to the health of the moral and political institutions on which it depends.

NOTES

1. For a systematic comparison of the old and new institutionalists, see Rutherford (1994). Langlois (1984) is a seminal collection of essays. Eggertsson (1990) provides a good introduction to the connection between neoclassical economics and institutions. Two recent essay collections provide useful overviews of the range of contemporary institutional economics: Drobak and Nye (1997) and Olson and Kähkönen (2000).

2. Lavigne (1999) provides basic data on transition. See also chapter 1 of this volume.

3. A sophisticated statement of the gradualist case can be found in Roland (2000). A strong defense of the shock-therapy approach from the charge of being "institution blind" is given by Åsland (2002). In his "Introduction and Overview" to this volume, Graham provides a synopsis of the stages of this debate. The essay in this volume by Maniu, which examines the course of economic transition in Romania, shows the importance of paying attention to the interplay of economic and institutional factors.

4. To obviate a possible misunderstanding: The "new" institutional economists differentiate themselves from orthodox neo-economists by arguing that institutions must be incorporated into the body of economic theory. But they still accord explanatory primacy to economic models of human behavior. Coase's well-known account of the development of firms as a response to the problem of transaction costs in the market (1990) is representative of this approach. Hegel, like the "old" institutionalists, argues for the role of noneconomic factors in the development of social and political institutions, including those that are indispensable to the functioning of a modern economy.

5. The connection between Hegel's conception of civil society and classical political economy has not gone unnoticed in the scholarly literature. Lukács (1948) is a groundbreaking study of this relationship, although one marred both by Stalinist orthodoxy and lack of familiarity with the original writings of the classical political economists. The essays collected in Riedel (1984) contain much of interest on this relationship—although, like Lukács, Riedel's knowledge of classical political economy seems largely second-hand. The

most thorough and scrupulous scholarly treatment of Hegel's encounter with classical political economy is Waszek (1988).

6. All future references to the *Philosophy of Right* will give the section as well as the page number. Adam Smith, *An Enquiry into the Nature and Causes of the Wealth of Nations* (1976a, IV.ix.51). References to Smith's works will be to the Glasgow edition and use its abbreviations.

7. This argument for the roots of Hegel's conception of civil society in the political economy of the Scottish Enlightenment is developed in Louis Hunt, "Civil Society and the Idea of a Commercial Republic," in Schechter (1999, 11–37). The term "civil society" has come to stand for a variety of different notions, some of them contradictory, and this paper does not mean to suggest that Hegel's conception of civil society is the only legitimate one. For an account of how civil society was understood by the dissidents in Central Europe, who are perhaps most responsible for the revival of the term in contemporary political discourse, see the chapter in this volume by Lindahl.

8. "[Civil society] is the system of ethical life, lost in its extremes, which constitutes the abstract moment of the *reality* of the Idea, which is present here only as the *relative totality* and *inner necessity* of this external *appearance*" (Hegel 1991a, §184, p. 221).

9. For an example of this charge against Hegel, see Ernst Tugendhat (1986, 315–16). Ludwig Siep (1983, 137–55) offers an effective rebuttal of Tugendhat's criticism.

10. Hegel makes it clear that the argument of the *Philosophy of Right* follows a conceptual rather than a historical mode of development: "We wish merely to observe how the concept determines itself. . . . What we obtain in this way, however, is a series of thoughts and another series of existent shapes [social and political institutions], in which it may happen that the temporal sequence of their actual appearance is to some extent different from the conceptual sequence. Thus, we cannot say, for example, that property existed before the family, although property is nevertheless dealt with first" (Hegel, 1991a, §32, p. 61).

11. This methodological point is developed in the preface to Hegel's *Phenomenology of Spirit*.

12. It is striking that the contemporary German term for civil society is *Zivilgesellschaft*, a direct translation from the English.

13. There have been some notable attempts lately to incorporate the formation of tastes and preferences into neoclassical theory. On this literature, see George Messinis (1999). Perhaps the most important contribution to this approach is Gary Becker (1996).

14. There is a relatively clear account of the transition from *Vorstellung* to *Begriff* in Hegel's "Introduction" to *Encyclopedia Logic* (1991b, 24–42).

15. Smith 1976a,II.V.ii.k.3. The editors of the Glasgow edition call attention to Adam Ferguson's comment on this point: "The *necessaries of life* is a vague and a relative term: it is one thing in the opinion of the savage; another in that of the polished citizen: it has a reference to the fancy and to the habits of living" (Ferguson 1980, 142).

16. The inefficacy of moral exhortation in the face of human passions is a central theme of Hegel's philosophy of history.

17. Hegel (1991a, §258, p. 276): "Since the state is objective spirit, it is only through being a member of a state that the individual himself has objectivity, truth and ethical life. *Union as such is itself the true content and end, and the destiny of individuals is to lead a universal life."*

18. The phrase "extended order" is, of course, Hayek's term for the market and its concomitant social and political institutions.

19. Hegel (1991a, 15–16). The particular target of Hegel's criticism here was his bête noire, J. F. Fries.

20. The essay by Lánczi in this volume offers an interesting appraisal of the "social and moral costs" of the transition in Hungary. For an attempt to draw up the balance sheet for the advanced capitalist societies of North America and Western Europe, see the essays in Pharr and Putnam (2000).

21. The *locus classicus* of this approach is Anthony Downs (1957). An up-to-date survey of the field of public choice is provided by Dennis C. Mueller (2003). A more accessible (and shorter) presentation can be found in William C. Mitchell and Randy T. Simmons (1994).

22. For a useful survey of various theories of the origins of the state, from Marxist to rational choice, see Margaret Levi (1988).

23. The phrase, of course, occurs in the preface to Hegel's *Phenomenology of Spirit.*

REFERENCES

Åsland, Anders. 2002. *Building capitalism: The transformation of the former Soviet Bloc.* Cambridge: Cambridge University Press.

Becker, Gary. 1996. *Accounting for tastes.* Cambridge, MA: Harvard University Press.

Coase, Ronald. 1990. *The firm, the market, and the law.* Chicago: University of Chicago Press.

Downs, Anthony. 1957. *An economic theory of democracy.* New York: HarperCollins.

Drobak John N., and John V. C. Nye. 1997. *The frontiers of the new institutional economics.* San Diego, CA: Academic Press.

Eggertsson, Thráinn. 1990. *Economic behavior and institutions.* Cambridge: Cambridge University Press.

Ferguson, Adam. 1980. *An essay on the history of civil society.* New Brunswick, NJ: Transaction Publishers.

Habermas, Jürgen. 1991. *The structural transformation of the public sphere: An inquiry into a category of bourgeois society.* Cambridge, MA: MIT Press.

Hegel, G. W. F. 1971. *Philosophy of mind.* Oxford: Oxford University Press.

———. 1979. *Phenomenology of spirit.* Oxford: Oxford University Press.

———. 1991a. *Elements of the philosophy of right.* Cambridge: Cambridge University Press.

———. 1991b. *The Encyclopedia logic.* Indianapolis: Hackett Press.

Hunt, Louis. 2000. Civil society and the idea of a commercial republic. In *The revival of civil society: Comparative and international cases,* ed. Michael G. Schechter. London: Macmillan.

Langlois, Richard N., ed. 1984. *Economics as a process: Essays in the new institutional economics.* Cambridge: Cambridge University Press.

Lavigne, Marie. 1999. *The economics of transition: From socialist economy to market economy.* 2nd ed. New York: St. Martin's Press.

Levi, Margaret. 1988. *Of rules and revenue.* Berkeley: University of California Press.

Lukács, George. 1948. *Der junge Hegel und die problem der kapitalistichen Gesellschaft.* Zurich, Wien: Europa Verlag.

Messinis, George. 1999. Habit formation and the theory of addiction. *Journal of Economic Surveys* 13(4): 417–42.

Mitchell, William C., and Randy T. Simmons. 1994. *Beyond politics: Markets, welfare, and the failure of bureaucracy.* Boulder, CO: Westview Press.

Mueller, Dennis C. 2003. *Public choice III.* Cambridge: Cambridge University Press.

Olson, Mancur, and Aatu Kähkönen. 2000. *A not-so-dismal science: A broader view of economics and societies.* Oxford: Oxford University Press.

Pharr, Susan J., and Robert D. Putnam. 2000. *Disaffected democracies: What's troubling the trilateral countries?* Princeton, NJ: Princeton University Press.

Riedel, Manfred. 1984. *Between tradition and revolution: The Hegelian transformation of political philosophy.* Cambridge: Cambridge University Press.

Roland, Gérard. 2000. *Transition and economics: Politics, markets, and firms.* Cambridge, MA: MIT Press.

Rousseau, J. J. 1979. *Emile.* Translated by Allan Bloom. New York: Basic Books.

———. 1997. *The discourses and other early political writings.* Translated by Victor Gourevitch. Cambridge: Cambridge University Press.

Rutherford, Malcolm. 1994. *Institutions in economics: The old and the new institutionalism.* Cambridge: Cambridge University Press.

Schechter, Michael. ed. 1999. *The revival of civil society.* New York: St. Martin's Press.

Siep, Ludwig. 1983. The "Aufhebung" of morality in ethical life. In *Hegel's philosophy of action,* ed. Lawrence S. Stepelevich and David Lamb, 137–55. Atlantic Highlands, NJ: Humanities Press.

Smith, Adam. 1976a. *An enquiry into the nature and causes of the wealth of nations.* Oxford: Oxford University Press.

———. 1976b. *The theory of moral sentiments.* Oxford: Oxford University Press.

Tugendhat, Ernst. 1986. *Self-consciousness and self-determination,* trans. Paul Stern. Cambridge, MA: MIT Press.

Waszek, Norbert. 1988. *The Scottish enlightenment and Hegel's account of "civil society."* Dordrecht: M. Nijhoff.

4

The Dissidents and the Antipolitical Ideology of Civil Society

Folke Lindahl

The most important thing the East European experience provides is knowledge that the region's citizens saw and endured radical evil in its pure form. They know much too well the threats involved in any project of compulsory happiness, in the utopias of classless or ethnically "clean" societies. It was also in Eastern Europe that the hope for anti-politics, for an anti-Machiavellian order of public things took shape.

—*Vladimir Tismaneanu (1998, x)*

B efore the dust had settled after the transitional revolutions in Eastern and Central Europe that ended the communist systems throughout the region, an old liberal concept had been resurrected and made its remarkable comeback on the scene of both politics and theory—that of *civil society*. During the 1970s and 1980s, prior to the transitions, the dissident intellectuals had taken great risks in formulating various theories defending the need for and the right to a civil sphere—a "parallel" society, an "antipolitical" realm—independent of the state apparatus controlled by a repressive and cynical Communist Party *nomenklatura*. The writings of the dissidents took different shapes in different contexts, of course, but it became clear over time that the theme of civil society united most of them in a way that makes it plausible to see this particular emphasis as a relatively coherent leitmotif in the opposition to communist rule during the two decades prior to the collapse. Some of these dissident writings, in effect, have become enduring pieces of political thought, and deservedly so. Not only were these writings highly influential in the contexts of oppositional politics against the communist regimes, they were also crucial in stimulating, and arguably even initiating, the renewed interest in and intense debate on civil society in both Western Europe and the Americas—a debate that was reborn around the same time, and that is still with us today. The argument that the revolutions of 1989 did not produce any new big ideas might be true, but they certainly reinvigorated and contributed to the old discussion of the role of civil society in a liberal democracy.[1] "The resurrection of such topics as direct democracy, social capital, and civic trust in Western debates on the preconditions for democracy and democratization cannot be separated from the tribulations of the East European attempts to rehabilitate the ethos of civil society" (Tismaneanu 1998, 142).

The central importance of civil society for a *liberal* democratic regime is now taken for granted by almost all commentators on democracy, whether the concern is the maintenance and health of firmly established democracies, or the consolidation of democratic habits and institutions in the post-communist societies.[2] In the latter countries, the civil-society issue has an added intriguing quality in comparison with the former. In Central and Eastern Europe, the dissidents appealed to and made use of an ideology of civil society in opposition to the established communist power structure; once the transition took place, the same (former) dissidents were faced with the situation of actually having to make the case for creating and sustaining a civil society within a newly democratic society. Not surprisingly, these are two very different roles for a theory to perform. Some of the dissident intellectuals found themselves in the robes of modern-day founding fathers: they had to put their theories to practical tests, and they had to take responsibility for the social and political consequences of both their theories and their political actions. Václav Havel is the most obvious example of this type of dissident intellectual turned politician.

In that radically new and different situation, the civil-society emphasis did not fare particularly well. Already in 1995, Aleksander Smolar argued: "But a civil society whose essence was radical opposition to the communist state could not survive the disappearance of that state." As he also quipped, "Civil society, it turned out, had been a historical costume; its usefulness disappeared with the times that dictated its wearing" (Smolar 2002, 48, 53).

Given this rather extraordinary shift in roles, and arguably the rise and decline of the idea itself in former communist Central Europe, it might be of interest to reflect on some of the theories of the former dissident intellectuals regarding civil society, including some thoughts on the impact of the transition on these theories and on these intellectuals. A critical reflection on what I call here *the ideology of civil society* (prior to the transition), and its subsequent fate once the transition had occurred, might reveal some useful lessons regarding both the complexity of civil society and the ambivalent role of intellectuals in politics. In addition, perhaps, we might begin to discern a curious weakness in the theories of civil society in general—a weakness that is not a necessary part of the theories, but nevertheless a common enough "flaw" that it can be said to involve a tendency within much of the civil-society discourse that has emerged not only in the context of the former communist countries, but in the debate in the West as well. As I will argue below, there is a noticeable—and, given the history under communism, perfectly understandable—skepticism, not to say hostility, towards practical, everyday politics. This antipolitical attitude does, of course, have its origin in the state system controlled by the Communist Party during the long years of oppressive totalitarian rule. As is well known, the term "antipolitics" was often used by the dissidents themselves, and was made particularly famous by George Konrád's book with the same title (1984). In itself, it is an insightful and productive concept that made impressive sense under communism, but, as I will suggest, a potentially deceptive notion if carried too far and if used beyond its historical context. The original critical implication of the term is obvious: it is a turning away from politics, understood as corrupt, unjust, and repressive. The question for us is whether this understandable hostility to communist politics survives the transitions and becomes a more ahistorical and generalized attitude towards all politics, regardless of context. Maybe we can even find this distanced and abstractly negative treatment of politics in some of the Western European and American theorists of civil society. Maybe there is something of a built-in tendency in the very attraction to and preoccupation with civil society that encourages a contempt for, or hostility towards practical politics and the government.

In any case, after more than 15 years of transition politics, it is an appropriate moment to take a critical look at some of the arguments and claims in favor of civil society put forward both before and after the transitions. I will focus my discussion on highly selective writings by three famous dissident intellectuals: George Konrád, Adam Michnik, and Václav Havel. As it turns out, not all the famous dissidents were unable to adjust their thinking to the complex politics of (post-)transition, nor were they all equally hostile to practical politics even under communism. One should not, of course, be surprised—although this is a point often overlooked—that once the target of a dissident opposition is removed, if not before, there is no compelling reason for the now-former dissidents to remain politically or ideologically unified. Why shouldn't dissident intellectuals reveal the same plurality of political positions as one would expect in any typical liberal democratic society? The assumption that there is, or ought to be political consensus among so-called intellectuals strikes me as both misguided and dangerous. Long gone—if they were ever with us—are the days, in both the West and former communist countries, when one could seriously speak of "the responsibility of the intellectuals." Even under the communist regimes—and earlier throughout the region—the unity of the intellectuals was no doubt a romantic myth, but at least a noble-sounding one: "In the 'abnormal' conditions that have actually been normality for much of Central Europe over much of the last two centuries, intellectuals have been called upon, to take roles that they did not take in the West. The conscience of the nation. The voice of the oppressed. The writer as priest, prophet, resistance fighter, and substitute politician" (Ash 2001).[3] (Various versions of this mantra are of course repeated by intellectuals throughout the globe, when circumstances are judged to be appropriate.) For the purpose of this essay, however, (the ideology of) the role of the intellectuals is a background theme, and of relevance only insofar as it illuminates the dissidents' theory of civil society.

George Konrad and Hungary

George Konrád—Hungarian novelist and essayist, and under communism a long-time dissident—defines his notion of "antipolitics" explicitly in terms of civil society: "Antipolitics strives to put politics in its place and make sure it stays there, never overstepping its proper office of defending and refining the rules of the game of civil society. Antipolitics is the ethos of civil society, and civil society is the antithesis of military society." By "military society," Konrád apparently means both the major protagonists of the cold war, and he views antipolitics as the only "radical alternative to the philosophy of a nuclear *ultima ratio*" (1984, 92). (Although most of Konrád's arguments against state power politics are obviously directed against the Soviet Union, he repeatedly also includes Western powers—especially the United States—in his criticism. In fact, a large portion of *Antipolitics* reads as a broadside attack on the superpower politics during the cold war. Most of his comments are by no means without intellectual insights, but to today's reader, the book appears dated and in places overly polemical.) It is not merely communist political power that is Konrád's target of criticism, but political power as such, as in the following sweeping Hobbesian generalization regarding political leaders:

> We see the political leaders of earlier times falling victim to the spell of power, almost as if it were a clinical illness. We see how sane and sober men became paranoiacs, megalomaniacs, possessed beings who would listen to no one. We see how the possession of power turned into a sickness—so much so that we must regard power itself as a pathogenic factor. Those who suffer from power are inclined to suffer from the sickness of self-inflation, the boundless overreaching of the ego.

For that reason political power, as an institution, ought to be surrounded with extraordinary suspicion, with precautionary measures, and with the most stringent vigilance that civil society can muster. For those who possess it are swept by an insatiable passion for more, and are tempted to vie with others who have it, until they come to think of history as only a poker game of kings and presidents in which people are no more than the playing cards. (1984, 100–101)

Although this attitude appears compatible with the type of skepticism classical liberals express towards the exercise of political power, as we will discover, Konrád's argument goes further and is different from the familiar liberal constitutional position. The conception of civil society, however, is close to what liberalism has come to understand as the core of the term. Konrád calls for a mood of experimentation in order to test the communist regime, and his formulation has a distinct Tocquevillian ring to it: "When I look around I see that everyone is starting something, planning, trying his skills, telling of some small success. It may be an experimental school, an interesting research project, a new orchestra, a publishing opportunity, a screenplay accepted, a little restaurant about to open, an association of mathematicians, an attractive private shop, a private gallery, a trip to the West, cultural undertakings, independent publications, semiunderground journals" (1984, 166–67). Writing during communism, but in the early 1980s when the Kádár government had already moved some distance down the road of liberalization and moderate privatization, it is clear that Konrád perceives the new civil society as an alternative (social, political, and economic) sphere paralleling the official culture and joining forces with the so-called second economy. "Alongside the second economy a second culture is coming into style which may stimulate and enliven the officially accepted culture, whose own boundaries, if not exactly open, are at least not so terribly closed as they once were" (1984, 167).

Throughout his treatment of the Hungarian political situation in *Antipolitics*, it is striking how far Konrád thinks the communist government has shifted in the direction of reform at this particular time. He describes in some detail the laxity in, and opening up of what was once a closed totalitarian system without tolerance for cultural, social, and political deviations. The relative softness of this "post-totalitarian" regime is for Konrád a reflection of the self-confidence of the government, not the beginning of a breakdown. "The essence of the Hungarian road is the emergence of a certain limited pluralism within the confines of the Yalta system. This limited pluralism doesn't reflect any weakness on the part of the system; on the contrary, it is a sign of its strength" (1984, 168). (Seven years later, the system had crumbled.) Lest we forget that we are dealing with a communist one-party state, Konrád is also crystal clear about the limits to the regime's tolerance, the high price citizens have to pay for speaking out, and his support for exercising the small civil free-doms available. In his characteristically ironic style, Konrád captures in two paragraphs the workings of the Hungarian communist system at the time:

> If a young person wants to succeed, it will do him no harm to become active in the Young Communist League, join the party and enroll in one of the evening schools of Marxism-Leninism; he will sacrifice many advantages and incur many disadvantages if he prefers the pleasures of thinking freely to the goods available from the state, the better jobs and higher pay, the house obtainable with government help on favorable terms, the frequent trips abroad at state expense, the chance to play a part in public life.
>
> Naturally, most people want to succeed, and Western observers should be the last to wonder at that. Making good is a chancier business here, and more suspect than in the West. Still, there is a minority—as there always must be—who prefer to be on good terms with themselves rather than with the state. They pay for this singular friendship with their careers. You can't have it all. (1984, 170–71)

Not all individuals who promote activities in civil society pay that high a price, but obviously the risk is there. This reveals the deep antagonism between the communist state and the oppositional civil society, an antagonism that is built into the very purposes of each side of the conflict. The Communist Party state cannot allow uncensored freedom in the realm of civil society, and the purpose of civil society as conceived of by the dissidents is exactly to expand the realm of free social and intellectual activities. This is not the main role of civil society in a liberal democratic society. In the latter, it is the state that provides the guarantees for a robust civil society through the rule of law. The liberal state creates and protects the boundaries of civil society, and even to some degree regulates the rules of that society. In fact, only a strong but limited state can be the protector of a vibrant civil society. In addition, a civil society does not see its *primary* role as opposing the state, even if it quite often plays that role as well. It is always a precarious relationship, but one cannot do without the other; they are interdependent. One could simplify and argue that ideally, under a communist regime, civil society is a clear challenge and alternative to the state, while in a liberal (democratic) system, civil society performs a complementary role that performs functions that enhance freedom for the citizens and, at the same time, limits the role of the state to ruling and decision-making functions that civil society is incapable of carrying out. In the former system, in other words, the state is opposed to civil society and tries to limit its scope and size through various means and actions—for one thing, by making it largely illegal. In the latter, civil society is legally guaranteed by the state and supplements the role of the state. Finally, from the perspective of the Communist Party, civil society makes for less-desirable citizens and is perceived as a threat to the goals of the party, while in a liberal democracy, civil society (hopefully) improves and enhances its citizens from the perspective of both regime maintenance and the public good. As I will argue, this fundamental difference in perspective on civil society gives rise to both strengths and weaknesses in the dissidents' theory of civil society—the weaknesses becoming particularly visible after the fall of communism.[4]

The inference from Konrád's general discussion of his antipolitics is a broad and open-ended definition of civil society: it is virtually any activity—political, cultural, economic—that escapes the meddling of the communist state apparatus. Concretely, however, his treatment is mostly focused on the role played by writers, artists, and intellectuals—not solely, but it is obvious that it is within this segment of the population that Konrád sees the greatest potential for his antipolitics. On the most general, abstract level, antipolitics is about clearing a space for privacy and friendships, where there is no censorship and repression. In that context, the desire for freedom is more social and cultural than explicitly political. To some extent, this is due to his assessment that the Hungarians reveal their strength in what he calls "the art of living." It is an attractive and charming national characteristic that Konrád presents to the reader: "We do better at those intangibles that one might call the art of living: the cultivation of domestic comfort; an easygoing way of life; the art of getting on with one another; a certain worldly wisdom and a certain distance toward things that others consider vitally important; a healthy, pagan cynicism toward dedicated fanatics. It is as rewarding to sit in a well-kept garden at twilight drinking a quiet glass of wine with friends as it is to tear along a crowded eight-lane highway" (1984, 172). Indeed. One could do worse for one's civil society than this, but it borders on the private sphere, away from a traditional understanding of civil society. Still, a generous conception of civil society and civility certainly would have to include this type of life.[5]

Nevertheless, when Konrád begins his more specific description of antipolitics, he homes in on the world of intellectuals and artists. "Of all the aspects of the critique of state society, the intellectuals' program for setting limits to the state is perhaps the most interesting." Here, the emphasis is on separation from the state, paying the price by trying to survive "without the goods that the state takes from the producers and gives to us." It all translates into a kind of declaration of emancipation or independence for the intellectual class. "Greater independence with respect to redistributive centralism; a brisk circulation of freely associating and self-governing intellectual groups in the marketplace of ideas; alternative enterprises dedicated not to maximum profit but to intellectual activity for its own sake, to making a living without any urge to get rich; in short, an amalgam of the second economy and the second culture—that is the road that beckons to the ablest young intellectuals of Eastern Europe" (1984, 175–76).

In this context, Konrád envisions a "match" between the state and "creative intelligence," and paints a picture of an eternal struggle of almost metaphysical quality, and it is not limited to just communist regimes. "The debate between power and creativity has an ontological character; it cannot but exist. It appears in multiparty political systems, too, because the intellectual transcendence of what exists is always essentially the work of a minority" (1984, 176). This is an argument that seems to recur among the dissident intellectuals; they move almost imperceptibly from relatively concrete statements regarding the shortcomings of the communist system to claims related to philosophical issues of the most abstract and indeterminate quality, often with an implicit, if not explicit, stab at Western political systems as well. Even when the arguments against the powers that be in the communist countries appear to shift in a clearly liberal democratic direction, reminding the reader of a typical Western liberal position, the dissidents have a desire to present their own views in a manner that also draws a distinction with the systems of the West. (In Konrád's case, it is present throughout his *Antipolitics*, mostly in the form of a criticism of both the communist and the Western blocs as participating in an unnecessary and unacceptable power struggle for which both are equally to blame.)

The universal struggle between "informal spiritual authority" and "formal worldly authority" does not have to be violent, however, and here we encounter another central theme running through the dissidents' civil-society program: a call for nonviolence. The emphasis on civil society is seen as less confrontational than an explicit political reform program. Across the region, the dissidents stress the need for peaceful and nonviolent action. A program trying to expand civil society seems particularly compatible with this spirit, and also appealing to the intellectual segment. "If we strive for a state of internal détente, a relaxation of spiritual tensions, then we will meet with defeat less often and these will become less terrifying." This cultural lessening of tensions again points away from explicit political actions, towards a protection of a spiritual and informal private space. "I am most likely to cultivate my freedom in the company of those I like. In organizations, too, small is beautiful; there one finds the solidarity of friends. I don't think I would ever want to name my circle of friends the National Association of Friends—much less the Hungarian State Association of Friends. I consider a network of informal circles of friends to be our natural form of organization." And, in conclusion: "There is no need to wait for a distant triumph of our ideas. Friendship is everything; the final goal is a dream" (Konrád 1984, 177–78). Hardly the stuff of political reform, or of a party platform. Nevertheless, this is typical dissident ideology at the time, and has to be seen in light of the intrusive nature of the communist state. The political sphere needs to be reigned in and reduced. "Politics has grown fat; it has to be trimmed down. The political elite has overextended itself; overstepping its proper sphere of influence, it has meddled with things that are not its affair and neglected those tasks that properly fall within its province" (181). Here Konrád's argument becomes explicitly liberal, but it is almost exclusively moral in tone and content. A suspiciousness towards government power permeates the argument, but it expresses itself through a discussion of neither separation of powers nor checks and balances—nor, for that matter, any institutional or constitutional arrangements. Directed as it is against the Communist Party state, the lack of institutional details is understandable, especially since Konrád sees no possibility for democratic reforms within that system. The criticism becomes instead morally and politically abstract, while the proposed alternative action is rather private, friendship- and intellectual-oriented. A political fatalism and a noticeable privileging of the independent intellectual creep into the prose:

> Since the media of communication and the public meeting halls are under the control of the political censorship in Eastern Europe, the network of friends becomes the means of communicating spontaneous public sentiment. The closer you come to the world of the fringe intellectuals, the truer this becomes. The success of this independent ferment cannot be measured by the replacement of one government by another, but by the fact that under the same government society is growing stronger, independent people are multiplying, and the network of conversations uncontrollable from above is becoming denser. Let the government stay on top, we will live our own lives underneath it. (198)

Even though Konrád makes the claim that his notion of antipolitics is not the same as being apolitical, he moves very close to a politically irrelevant argument when he extends his fatalism to include all regime types. "If we didn't know what state socialism was like, we could still have hopes for it. As it is, we have no illusions about either capitalism or existing socialism. We cannot expect much good from politicians and political systems" (199). As a healthy skepticism towards politics, this is of course acceptable from a liberal point of view, and even commendable given the conditions under communism. It is, as we know, also a common attitude towards politics among citizens in a liberal capitalist system—and certainly understandable, if not desirable, there as well—but it does not add up to a politically relevant doctrine or theory. On the contrary, post-transition politics are made more difficult by such an attitude; it is also easily exploited by demagogues who, for various reasons, are interested in whipping up public opinion against the government and politicians. For

Konrád, this logic pushes him towards a preoccupation with private circles of intellectuals talking to each other. "Withdrawal into our huddled private circles enabled us to survive even the grimmest years of the dictatorship. We didn't really live in a state of constant tension because every evening we could be with one another. We talked a great deal; congregating in our lairs, we experienced a kind of campfire warmth" (203).

After a somewhat futuristic, not to say utopian, appeal to "the international intellectual elite" and the world-wide marketplace of ideas, Konrád concludes his discussion by advising intellectuals to serve only themselves and "the cause of independent thinking." "Without disputing the Church's title to the name, it still seems to me that a really catholic universalism—one that holds all particularisms in check—is represented most authentically today by the international intellectual aristocracy" (1984, 223). This aristocrat of the mind is the quintessentially mature adult who is also the antipolitician par excellence. It is he who will "keep the scope of government policy . . . under the control of the civil society" (227). Under communism, this means shrinking the sphere of politics and policies. It means keeping cultural policies to a minimum and reducing the number of cultural politicians. This amounts to a program of "destatification" and depoliticizing the lives of the citizens. Civil society for Konrád is first and foremost a sphere for the intellectual aristocrats in permanent opposition to the power of the state, and this opposition does not end with communism; antipolitics encourages two realms, one for politics and one for the public intellectuals. "In his thinking, the antipolitician is not politic. He doesn't ask himself whether it is a practical, useful, politic thing to express his opinion openly. In contrast with the secrecy of the leadership, antipolitics means publicity; it is a power exercised directly over society, through civil courage, and one that differs by definition from any present or future power of the state" (232).

It is easy to be sympathetic towards Konrád's arguments, formulated as they were under difficult circumstances for independent writers in Hungary at the time, and my intention here is not to take away the importance of the book either for the time in which it was published or for today's ongoing debate on civil society.[6] It remains a landmark contribution to dissident theory, and it continues to provide insights for our understanding of both communism and civil society. Over time, however, Antipolitics has lost a great deal of its earlier persuasiveness. I want to reemphasize a few points of criticism by flagging four aspects of Konrád's theory that now appear particularly problematic, both theoretically and practically.

Firstly, by insisting that antipolitics is a different dimension from politics and government, Konrád draws too stark a demarcation line between civil society and official politics. Appealing as this position is under communism, it cannot be maintained in a principled manner under a liberal regime. Konrád's argument often slides over into a condemnation of all politics—a condemnation, however common, that is incompatible with and unjustified in a liberal democratic order, and certainly misrepresents the role civil society plays in such a system. There are, of course, always reasons to be suspicious of power in all political systems—liberalism certainly teaches as much—but one cannot take a principled stand against politics and ruling as such. (If the claim is merely, however, that a writer/intellectual—or for that matter any other citizen—has the right to opt out of the political realm and devote all his time to writing that has nothing to do with politics, no liberal would object; on the contrary. Konrád, in my view, is saying more than that.)

Secondly, and related to the first point, Konrád never addresses the relationship between the state and society in any other than antagonistic terms. There is no appreciation, needless to say, for the role of the state under the communist regime. Civil society has to define itself not with support and guarantee of the rule of law, but outside of and in opposition to the state. There are obvious limits to that kind of confrontational civil society. It poses serious challenges and dangers for what is even under the best of circumstances a rather precarious relationship. If one starts out with the assumption that there is a mutual hostility between the two realms, the spontaneous and potentially beneficial interdependency will never materialize. Since civil society includes as a central feature the self-organization of all kinds of interests, there has to be an appreciation for the possibilities built into a positive relationship between the organs of the state and the organized interests in civil society. Konrád's discussion shows no signs of such an appreciation.

Thirdly, there is a remarkable and romantic view of the role of the intellectual in Konrád's writing that permeates his treatment of civil society. It is only a slight exaggeration to say that civil society is a realm mostly reserved for the intellectuals. Although Konrád makes enough references to other aspects of civil society as more than merely a space for the creative writer, artist, and professor, he is first and foremost concerned with freedom of speech and expression for "the intellectual aristocracy"—"the authority of the spirit." Not only are these aristocrats of the mind above and beyond all politicians, they are, or at least should be, completely free from the perquisites and temptations of power. "Any intellectuals who choose to compete for central-government advisory or executive posts are already doubtful members of the intellectual aristocracy" (1984, 224–25). This might or might not be true in specific cases, but it does not hold as a broad generalization. For one thing, this is a thin conception of citizenship and participation that belies the potential of civil society under regimes that do not undermine citizen actions, and that allow multiple types of opportunities for voluntary actions and political participation. But the latter forms of active citizenship are apparently not for the intellectuals, according to Konrád: "The intellectual aristocracy is content to push the state administration in the direction of more intelligent, more responsible strategies. Its members do this as a part of the self-governing intellectual community, even though they act individually, independent of the state. This is the spiritual authority that the most significant writers, thinkers, scholars, and artists have exercised for thousands of years" (225). One seriously doubts this romantic metaphysics of the intellectuals. It seems questionable both from an abstract historical perspective and from a concrete empirical point of view. True perhaps for the Thomas Manns and Spinozas, but hardly for the Knut Hamsuns, Sartres, and Heideggers of this world. If anything, (grand) intellectuals seem amazingly prone to fall for illiberal, extreme, and morally and politically suspect ideologies and various other fantasies of salvation.[7] Be that as it may, the point here is again the limited and narrow implications of Konrád's argument for citizenship and public service, as well as the paucity of interactive points between civil society and the state. It is difficult to imagine any generalization that could be true for the intellectuals as a class; each one has to be judged on the basis of his or her conduct as a citizen among all others in civil society. Some will be social activists, some will be apolitical, some will aspire to positions of power, etc. A few will be moral saints (very few), some will be wild as beasts (also very few, but more numerous than the saints), and most will fall somewhere in between. No moral badge comes with the intellectual costumes donned in civil society.

The fourth and final aspect of Konrád's work that I want to draw attention to is not so much a matter of what he writes as much as what he leaves out, and therefore perhaps an unjustified criticism, but it is still symptomatic of a larger problem in his theory. As I have already stated, Konrád's language on civil society is not particularly concrete or specific, and it is tied to the general antipolitical stand; his argument is simply too antagonistic towards practical politics—not merely communist politics, but politics in general—to put forward any concrete institutional discussion or policy analysis. The lack of attention to an institutional and legal framework for civil society is striking. There are hardly any references to the specific institutions—associations, unions, media, intellectual organizations—of civil society; nor is there a discussion of the state institutions—local government, legal tradition, law-and-order professions, constitutional liberties—necessary for guaranteeing and upholding a civil society. If Konrád had limited his comments to the communist state, one would not have expected any of these reflections, but it is exactly because his generalizations span politics as such that his analysis cries out for more specificity and institutional concreteness. All these points of criticism will of course be tested in Konrád's own comments after the transition from communism to a more liberal democratic regime.

Adam Michnik and Poland

My second example of dissident thinking on civil society is from the writings of Adam Michnik, the Polish dissident intellectual who became the editor in chief of *Gazeta Wyborcza*, the most respectable paper in post-communist Poland. Although akin to Konrád's antipolitics, Michnik's writings reveal a very different temperament and perspective, one in which the moral concern remains at the center, as in Konrád, but expressed in a more tentative and conciliatory tone of voice—often with an explicit desire for pragmatic pluralism and compromise solutions on social and political issues, without at all being any less confident or independent. (Michnik is also a political and historical writer, in contrast to Konrád, who is primarily a novelist and essayist.) During communism, the former is preoccupied with the opening up of the few avenues for pluralism that are available, even if this requires compromise with the powers that be and various acts of cooperation with members of the Communist Party. "But we [the dissidents] live and will live among people who think otherwise. We must learn to live with them and teach them to live with us. We must learn the difficult art of compromise, without which authentic pluralism will not be possible. We must observe the norms of political culture vis-à-vis the government, even if the government itself does not observe them. Only then will we manage to confront totalitarian pressure with dignity" (Michnik 1987, 190). Written in 1979, a year before Solidarity would be officially recognized by the communist government, and three years after the founding of the Workers' Defense Committee (KOR), this cautious and conciliatory approach reflects the critical historical moment when the communist regime began negotiations with aspects of Polish civil society. One year after the Solidarity agreement had been signed, Michnik looks back at the momentous event: "For the first time organized authority was signing an accord with an organized society. The agreement marked the creation of labor unions independent of the state which vowed not to attempt to take over political power." And, "For the first time in the history of communist rule in Poland 'civil society' was being restored, and it was reaching a compromise with the state" (1987, 124).

It is beyond the scope of this essay to go into the historical details, but it is obvious that the peculiar circumstances of each country play a crucial role in the way the dissidents perceive the possibilities for the re-creation of civil society. It is sufficient in the context of my argument merely to give Michnik's (romantic) version of how the Polish situation differs from that of its neighboring countries. This is from his famous 1979 essay "Maggots and Angels":

There are various factors that make us different: historical tradition, the Catholic Church and the courageous albeit realistic policies of the episcopate, the countryside that has withstood collectivization, and finally the incessant pressure of the people. This pressure has manifested itself at times in violent explosion (Poznan´–1956, March 1968, December 1970, Radom–1976), but more frequently through silent, dogged, daily resistance. This resistance is exemplified, for instance, in the refusal to make a denunciation. It permeates the mental atmosphere of a good part of our intellectual life: lectures and sem-inars at universities, doctoral research and publication of learned treatises, nov-els, volumes of poetry, essays, meetings of the Union of Writers or the PEN-Club, films and plays, museums, concerts, and art openings. All this is usually the work of people who do not sign protest letters or make spectacular gestures of opposition. But it is also thanks to them that we in Poland have been breathing a different spiritual air. (1987, 188)

Already in 1975–76, in his *The Church and the Left*, Michnik was initiating an important discussion on the relationship between the intellectuals of the Left and the Catholic Church in Poland (Michnik 1993; Falk 2003, 165–77). Ever since, this theme has been a prominent one in his writings, and mirrors the importance of the church in the history and evolution of Polish civil soci-ety. Michnik is highly sensitive to this role, and he realizes early that the tradi-tional hostility between the secular intellectual Left and the church has to be overcome, and instead transform into some kind of cooperative alliance, how-ever fragile. He also early perceives the pivotal position of the church in the budding civil society under the communist regime. As in Hungary, it is a soci-ety of resistance to the communist state, but in Poland this resistance is by 1980 expressing itself primarily through the labor movement of Solidarity, which rapidly was becoming a gigantic social movement that ended up absorb-ing millions of people, representing a multifaceted Polish civil society against the monolithic communist state (Ash 2002). That an important element of the Catholic Church plays a supporting role in this rise of an independent civil society is a factor worthy of emphasis, and shows a unique aspect of the Polish scenario that eventually culminates in the transition.[8]

Michnik identifies three forces within Polish society that can support a civil society in opposition to an intransigent and unreformable communist regime: the workers, the Catholic Church, and the intelligentsia. The stress on building civil society, rather than direct political action, is for Michnik— ironically, in retrospect—a necessity in the face of the absolute power of the communist government, with no hope for political reform. The civil-society option is the only one available in a system that is backed up by the threat of force by both the Soviet military and the Polish government. According to

Michnik, the origins of what he calls "the Polish self-limiting revolution" is to be found outside official institutions, and as a response to the Gierek regime's somewhat soft attitude towards opposition groups. In 1982, he characterized the opposition in the following way:

> For many years now, democratic opposition groups, supported by significant sections of the population and protected by the Catholic Church, have existed and functioned effectively. Taking advantage of relatively tolerant policies of the Gierek team—tolerant policies that resulted from its relations with the West and its own political weakness rather than from liberalism—these groups promoted social self-help and self-defense, organized independent intellectual activities, and worked outside censorship to fashion programs for the fight of freedom. The essence of the programs put forward by opposition groups. . . . lay in the attempt to reconstruct society, to restore social bonds outside official institutions. The most important question was not "how should the system of government be changed?" but "how should we defend ourselves against this system?" This way of thinking left its mark on the August strikes, on the strikers' demands, and on Solidarity's program, strategy, and actions. (1987, 28)

Unlike Konrád who viewed the liberalization tendencies under the Kádár government in Hungary as a sign of strength, Michnik recognizes a certain weakness in the communist system, and he develops the strategy for the opposition on the basis of this perceived vulnerability. He dates the beginning of this social resistance to 1976. The Polish regime does have a common feature with the Hungarian one, however, in that both governments are at this time slowly liberalizing their attitudes toward the dissenting opposition. Across the region, this "post-totalitarian" system expresses itself through what has been called a "new social accord":

> This "accord" was based on the assumption that the authorities would not make life difficult for the people if the people would not make governing difficult for the authorities. So the government did not interfere too brutally in the citizens' private and professional lives, and the citizens did not meddle in the areas reserved for the party *nomenklatura*. Gierek's Poland and Kádár's Hungary were classic examples of this "new social accord," but certain aspects of it could also be seen in other countries, including the USSR. (Michnik 1987, 49)[9]

It is at this moment in the history of "actually existing socialism" that Michnik and his associates perceive the possibilities for the development of a civil society in opposition to the regime. They understand this society in very similar terms as Konrád in Hungary. It is to be nonviolent, pluralistic, underground but non-conspiratorial; Michnik also repeatedly asserts the need for human rights, individual autonomy and independence, and an ethic based on tolerance and personal conscience. Even after Jaruzelski imposes martial law on 13 December 1981, the Polish opposition continues its activities, and Michnik considers this fact a sign of progress towards democracy. From his jail cell in 1985, he remains optimistic: "[E]ven after official liquidation of independent public institutions (trade unions, artists' associations, youth organizations, editorial boards or various journals, etc.), after forty months of repression and provocation, the independent civil society, although pushed outside the official sphere, has not been annihilated. . . . The Poles have traveled a great distance on their journey from totalitarianism to democracy" (1987, 81). The opposition, with the aid of the church, manages even during martial law to create "islands of autonomy" through civil society, thereby furthering pluralism and pockets of civility. Michnik sees this as a struggle for an "open society" against the communist version of a "closed society." In a conversation with Daniel Cohn-Bendit in May of 1987, he clarifies further both his early commitment to civil society, and why he thinks that the communist system has entered a post-totalitarian phase:

> I just want to tell you what KOR represented for me personally. It stood for a philosophy of political activity in a posttotalitarian system. Why posttotalitarian? Because the power is still totalitarian, whereas society isn't anymore, it is already anti-totalitarian, it rebels and sets up its own independent institutions that lead to something we could call a civil society, in Tocqueville's sense. And that is what we tried to do: build a civil society. (Michnik 1998, 58–59)

Throughout his essays in which he lays out the options, programs, and principles of the Polish opposition, Michnik's arguments are liberal, pragmatic, and democratic. He does not rule out political negotiations and compromise with the communist authorities. In fact, he argues forcefully against what he calls the "fundamentalists," those who reject any form of compromise with the powers that be. Given his personal experience with jail, persecution, and intimidation by the regime, this is impressive prudence, not to say wisdom. He is equally opposed to any form of terrorism and violence on the part of the opposition, and doubts that violence can be a successful tool against the communist Polish state (with Soviet backing), not only for reasons of obvious lack of weapons and military strength, but because violence and terrorism seldom produce pluralistic democracy. There is a mix of moral and political concerns as well as strategic calculations that underlie Michnik's self-conscious stance against violent methods. The end does not justify the means; that type of reasoning is discredited and belongs to the ideology of communism. "We should not assume that bloody confrontation is inevitable and, consequently, rule out the possibility of evolutionary bloodless change. This should be avoided all the more inasmuch as democracy is rarely born from bloody upheavals." The leaders of Solidarity must keep the dialogue with the government alive and open. "Their chances of success will be greater if the level of self-organization of independent Polish society increases. For street lynchings, angry crowds are enough; compromise demands an organized society" (Michnik 1987, 95). In several of his essays, Michnik clearly articulates this link between means and ends—between compromise and pragmatism on the one hand, and civil society, pluralism, and democracy on the other. The reader quickly gains the impression that civil society, civility, and civilized society are, if not synonymous, certainly intimately related, and that these concepts can only be realized in a pluralistic, liberal democracy. These links are not worked out in detail, but are repeated and elaborated in so many different contexts that they become, at least in my interpretation, the core of Michnik's theory and political strategy for Poland.[10]

Parallel to his argument against violence, Michnik takes a stand against conspiracies. Using the title of Dostoyevski's novel, he calls this "the specter of *The Possessed*." "The movement of resistance must teach freedom and democracy." A conspiracy is a sect that promotes values that are not conducive to democracy. The issue here is how to prevent an underground movement from becoming a conspiracy that will undermine pluralism and democratic sentiments. The problem: "Every conspiracy demoralizes." It makes it even more difficult to inspire a civil ethos in a population that already has suffered for a generation under a government that itself reveals the conspiratorial mentality. "A spirit of democracy is not the style favored by it. Underground activity isolates people from the taste and smell of everyday life, skews perspective, gives birth to dangerous absolutism and intolerance. Conspiracy requires disobedience to the enemy and obedience to the underground central command. It proclaims equality but within itself calls for hierarchical subordination" (Michnik 1987, 60). Michnik is opposed to any form of paternalism, which he associates with both the totalitarian system and conspiratorial sects. Instead, he affirms a notion of civil society that nurtures individuals who are neither "pupils, soldiers, or slaves; they act as citizens." In a 1988 interview with John Keane, Michnik affirms solidly liberal tenets grounded in the historical tradition: "The basic principle of the anti-feudal movement was human rights, the idea that everyone has rights equal to those of the monarch. That's what we also want. We want everybody to enjoy the same rights as Jaruzelski, secured by the rule of law" (1998, 105). On this score, Michnik is more firmly grounded in Western liberalism than Konrád's attempt to eke out a space somewhere in between Western capitalism and Soviet-style communism. In the same interview with Keane, Michnik argues further that majority rule is not enough for his notion of democracy; it has to be combined with explicit minority rights and individual freedoms, which means the creation of constitutional law and civil society. Too many times, the revolutionary struggle for power has perpetuated violence and ignored human rights and civility. "In our century, the struggle for freedom has been fixed on power, instead of the creation of civil society. It has therefore always ended up in the concentration camp" (1998, 107).

Both violence and conspiracy are contrary to the *modus vivendi* of a civil society. For Michnik, the resistance movement has to reflect the spirit of compromise and tolerance necessary for a well-functioning civil society. Within limits, it demands these same attitudes towards the communist government. Each issue presents the dilemma of determining the line between collaboration and productive negotiation. It is a matter of establishing channels of communication with the regime without giving up the autonomy of civil society and the independence of public opinion. Since the communist government is not about to give up its monopoly of state power, compromise with and acceptance of this monopoly is an unfortunate necessity. In a Lincoln-like formulation, Michnik articulates his principle underlying this balancing act: "Indeed, I am advocating neither a struggle for independence nor for parliamentary democracy, although I have always made it known how much I cherish these things, and I have not given them up today. But I do believe that faith in the feasibility of such demands amounts to a break with common sense and responsibility for the nation" (1987, 115). If this sounds too conciliatory towards a government that denies basic human rights and dignity, Michnik makes sure there is no misunderstanding regarding his attitude: "I am advocating a compromise with the government that I do not like at all—a government whose principles do not appeal to me but which is to us what a plaster is to a person with a broken bone: burdensome but indispensable." And, "One can dislike the people in power, but they have to be accepted as partners in negotiation. It is not easy for me to write this. Nothing I know about them inspires optimism in me" (1987, 115–16). This comment is from 1980. In Keane's interview, a year before the fall of the communist regime, his attitude had hardened. Asked what advice he would give to the Communist Party then, Michnik answered unequivocally: "There could only be one piece of advice. I would repeat some words in *From the History of Honor in Poland*. I wrote this in prison, and I concluded it by quoting the Polish poet Julian Tuwim, whose words are addressed to Communists in all lands: 'Kiss my arse!'" (1998, 113).

Finally, what needs to be briefly reiterated is Michnik's moral discourse. Again, unlike Konrád's abstract moral concern, in my reading of Michnik, there is a very concrete moral preoccupation permeating his writing. Nevertheless, when critically interrogated, as in most moral messages in relation to politics, there remains an indeterminate quality that ultimately might resist a precise formulation. However, its persuasive dimension consists of an appeal to the individual's conscience, without which no civil society could survive. The issue is twofold (at least). Most importantly, Michnik is concerned with the problem of creating a moral ethos in civil society under communism. This is the already-mentioned task of making sure that this ethos is genuinely democratic, tolerant, pluralistic, nonviolent, and liberty-oriented, even though the communist regime makes this virtually impossible. This is a well-known preoccupation of the dissident intellectuals throughout the region. Secondly, and prior to the transition, there is the purely speculative task of envisioning a moral ethos for a democratic Poland of the future. This is the classical dilemma for liberal democracy: how to instill in free citizens sufficient moral cohesiveness to hold society together and, at the same time, to keep freedom and tolerance alive, as well as to maintain democratic majority institutions whose powers are constitutionally checked so they cannot undermine liberty. It is a hallmark of Michnik's writings that he never loses sight of these moral questions, and keeps addressing them from all angles and in relation to a wide variety of specific issues. His emphasis on the role of the Catholic Church in Poland is merely one, and perhaps the most obvious, example of this. As Ken Jowitt perceptively puts it in his "Foreword: In Praise of the Ordinary":

> In sharp contrast to the Western social scientists who believe that rational choices will magically transform egos into individuals, Michnik argues that only a sense of the moral and sacred can infuse democracy with decency and courage. In situations in which it might be rational to run not fight, doubt not believe, punish not forgive, reject not accept or quit; in those situations morality and a sense of the sacred can be a source of courage, confidence, mercy, toleration, and endurance. Democracies with social and moral depth require Don Quixotes irrational enough to fight the odds. Which in turn raises one of life's "immutable dilemmas." Don Quixotes seek perfection, while Michnik has "always believed that a perfect society could be created only in a concentration camp." (Michnik 1998, xxiii–xxiv)

Whether this moral depth and complexity can survive under less-extreme circumstances than a communist regime is an open question, and perhaps even improbable. The more mundane, everyday politics of a liberal democracy hardly encourages this type of self-reflective moral dignity. It is part of Michnik's accomplishment as a dissident writer and activist that he is capable of sustaining and articulating this type of discourse. That his writings still speak to us with persuasive moral force is not the least of his achievements. On this score, his work differs from the rhetorical abstractness and polemical exaggerations of Konrád's prose in *Antipolitics*.

Václav Havel and the Czech Republic

At one point, shortly after the "Velvet Revolution," the reputation of Václav Havel reaches almost mythical heights. His persona is larger than life, and his biography is worthy of a fairy tale—not least in the West.[11] During his presidency, the image fades, especially within the Czech Republic itself. This is not the place to retell this rather astonishing itinerary; but regardless of his current status in the eyes of the Czech public and his fellow intellectuals in Eastern and Central Europe now that he has left the presidential office, Havel remains a formidable political and intellectual figure who will maintain his central status in the large cast of fascinating characters at the core of the dissident movement, the communist breakdown, and the years following the transition. In addition, his writings span several genres—plays, political essays, philosophical ruminations, presidential speeches, moral sermons, etc.—that are difficult to treat under one rubric or one type of analysis, but that nevertheless display a certain coherency and continuity.[12] For the purpose of this essay, however, I will merely focus on a couple of his most famous essays that illuminate aspects of his theory of civil society.

Czechoslovakia in the 1970s and 1980s differed in one important respect from both Poland and Hungary: there was, during this period, little or no liberalization process in the former as opposed to the very limited but nevertheless important tolerance towards the reemerging civil society in the latter two countries. After the failure to reform the Communist Party from within during the Prague Spring in 1968—and after the decision by the Soviet Union (and the Warsaw Pact members) to militarily occupy Czechoslovakia—the political situation deteriorated rapidly, and a long period of "normalization" set in. The Prague Spring and its abrupt demise also ended any hope to reform the communist system from within. The calls for reform among the more progressive leaders of the party in Czechoslovakia ended in a realization among the dissidents that the system was intractable and could not change towards a more humanistic and democratic form of socialism, or however one wants to label these efforts. In retrospect, the reformers of the Prague Spring operated with serious misconceptions concerning the workings of the Soviet-dominated communist regimes. Tismaneanu characterizes this illusion among the Prague reformers as somewhat of a paradox:

> Those who started the struggle for the overhaul of the status quo were themselves the product, the offspring, of the existing conditions. Their revolt against the irrationality and the injustice of Stalinism was not a rebellion against the Marxist pretense to establish "the best society" but rather an effort to correct

what they diagnosed as distortions of an initially humanist and national program. They were the faithful children of the system. Their opposition to the previous leadership did not challenge the moral and theoretical legitimacy of Soviet-style socialism. Even a radical reformer like Ota Sik, the chief economist of the Prague Spring, could not cross the boundaries of the dominant logic and envision the need for a complete renunciation of the central plan. (1993, 105)

That not much good can emerge from such a conjuncture seems self-evident in hindsight, but was not so at the time. However, it dealt the death blow to all efforts among a broad spectrum of "reformers" to operate inside the Marxist-Leninist paradigm and the primacy of the Communist Party organization.[13]

The harsh conditions under "normalization" forced critics underground and abroad, and it was now that Havel became an important voice in the opposition to the communist system as a whole. He formulated his theory of dissent in the shape of a philosophy of "living in truth," and a dedication to the promotion of an alternative in the form of an alternative civil society, based on the moral principles inherent in his "doctrine." Whether one takes to this theory depends, I suspect, on whether Havel's language resonates with one's own temperament, psyche, or soul, since it is highly abstract, moralistic, romantic, and permeated by existential and Heideggerian markers (or jargon).[14] In fact, coming to terms with this vocabulary is not the least of the challenges facing an assessment of Havel's contribution. It is, in addition, especially for the purpose of my argument in this paper, a matter of deciding how and to what extent this vocabulary or discourse helps or hinders a better understanding of politics in general, and the workings of civil society in particular.

Havel—consistently and persistently—presents a rather essentialist, not to say metaphysical, philosophy of modern man and society. It is a view of a world in which life is absurd and the human being is alienated and her authenticity lost, a world in which objective science and rationality have conquered all forms of human subjectivity, and a world from which morality and higher spiritual values have been banished in the name of raw power, impersonal bureaucracy, and destructive technology. In short, it is a dehumanized, inauthentic, and spiritless world. And politicians are merely puppets in this cosmic malaise:

> The professional ruler is an "innocent" tool of an "innocent" anonymous power, legitimized by science, cybernetics, ideology, law, abstraction and objectivity—by everything, that is, except personal responsibility to human beings as persons and neighbours. A modern politician is transparent: behind his or her judicious mask and affected diction there is not a trace of a human being rooted in the natural order by loves, passions, interests, personal opinions, hatred, courage or cruelty. All that he or she locks away in his or her private bathroom. If we glimpse

anything at all behind the mask, it will be only a more or less competent power technician. System, ideology and *apparat* have deprived us—rulers as well as ruled—of our conscience, our natural understanding and natural speech and, with these, of our actual humanity. (Havel in Keane, ed. 1988, 388)[15]

These types of formulations could be multiplied; they occur throughout Havel's texts, and obviously add up to much more than what just a sample quote can reveal. Nevertheless, unless one accepts the basic premises, one is unlikely to be moved.

In common with Konrád—and reminiscent of Heidegger—Havel too directs his criticism against both the East and the West. The communist totalitarian system is merely a distorted mirror image of the West, and if the latter fails to see this and does not change its ways, all is lost. "In the relation of Western Europe to the totalitarian systems, I think that no error could be greater than the one looming largest—that of a failure to understand the totalitarian systems for what they ultimately are: a convex mirror of all modern civilization and a harsh, perhaps final call for a global recasting of that civilization's self-understanding. If we ignore that, then it does not make any essential difference which form Europe's efforts will assume" (Havel in Keane, ed. 1988, 389). Using the spoiled environment as both metaphor and actuality, Havel continues:

> The chimney "soiling the heavens" is not just a technologically corrigible design error, or a tax paid for a better tomorrow, but a symbol of a civilization which has renounced the Absolute, which ignores the natural world and disdains its imperatives. So, too, the totalitarian systems warn of something far more serious than Western rationalism is willing to admit. They are, most of all, a convex mirror of the inevitable consequences of rationalism, a grotesquely magnified image of its own deep tendencies, an extreme outcropping of its own development and an ominous product of its own expansion. They are a deeply informative reflection of its own crisis. Totalitarian regimes are not merely dangerous neighbours and, even less, some kind of an avant-garde of world progress. Alas, just the opposite; they are the avant-garde of a global crisis of this civilization, one which is European, then Euroamerican, and ultimately global. (Keane, ed. 1988, 389–90)

Amen. Here, Havel goes further than Konrád in his conflation of the communist regimes and Western liberal ones. Unless it is treated as merely rhetorical hyperbole, this litany is of some significance for an understanding of Havel's antipolitical attitude as well as his attraction to a notion of civil society. Unlike, for example, Tocqueville and the Scottish Enlightenment writers, Havel does not approach the issue of civil society within or in relation to a liberal tradition.

There is nothing liberal about these broadside attacks on Western civilization, and there is no interest in trying to suggest a pragmatic or practical political solution to whatever is ailing society. Havel's criticism of the communist regime, and his vision for a democratic society are based on very different assumptions from Michnik's perspective, which is very careful and circumspect in its judgments and recommendations.

I suspect that a large part of the explanation for this existential outlook, with the indeterminate marker "authenticity" at its center, is personal and biographical—a claim, of course, that is impossible to verify. However, Havel himself tells a story along these lines in his autobiographical reflections. Just to give one example, here is an excerpt from one of his letters from prison to his wife, Olga. Havel explains that his bourgeois family background, growing up in communist Czechoslovakia, gave him a feeling of "exclusion," and led "in the deepest level of my relationship to the world, to a powerful existential uncertainty: a heightened sensation that there is a barrier between me and those around me, a tendency to suspect others of plotting against me, combined with a fear that such conspiracies are justified, in other words, a sensation of generalized guilt" (Havel 1988, 287). These and other related feelings connect, he claims, to a "tendency" in his writing:

> I have always been intensely aware of matters like the alienation of man from the world, the dehumanization and the incomprehensibility of the "order of things," the emptiness and unintentional cruelty of social mechanisms and their tendency to become ends in themselves, how things get out of control, fall apart or, on the contrary, evolve to the point of absurdity, how human existence tends to get lost in the mechanized contexts of life, how easily absurdity becomes legitimate, the apparent nature of the "real" and the ludicrousness of the "important," etc. This experience of the world (at many points so akin to Kafka's) would obviously show up in my writing no matter what I wrote. (1988, 287–88)[16]

One has to be inherently suspicious of these kinds of autobiographical explanations—a large dose of embellishment is most likely inevitable—but even if only partially on the mark, it needs to be factored in when assessing the existentialist fog emanating from Havel's pages. It is no surprise that a vision of civil society built on this foundation cannot be of the liberal run-of-the-mill variety.

A different and equally partial explanation for this existential despair is possibly the rather extreme conditions in Czechoslovakia at the time. There was simply no reason to hope for or argue about concrete political changes, or strategies for a pragmatic politics. The totalitarian machinery was effectively silencing any attempt to modify the system in a liberal direction. The main public manifestation of dissidence during the 1970s was the signing of Charter 77, a human-rights organization (funded to a large extent by George Soros [Tucker 2000, 128]) that explicitly kept within legal communist bounds, and viewed itself as apolitical and focusing on moral issues. At best capable of drawing national and international attention to various human-rights abuses, and also, in various ways, aiding those dissidents imprisoned by the regime, Charter 77 nevertheless both inspired the opposition and caused debate.

In 1978, Václav Benda, a Czech dissident philosopher and mathematician, wrote a highly influential essay entitled "The Parallel *Polis*" in which he argues in favor of parallel social structures that can exist alongside (and ignoring) the official communist ones. He criticizes the Chartists' emphasis on purely moral issues and suggests a broader and more concrete approach, which amounts to nothing less than a creation of a new, complex civil society, and in fact, an entirely parallel set of political and economic structures (Benda 1991, 35–41; see also Falk 2003, 247–51, and Tucker 2000, 127–34). The proposition is arguably utopian and vague, but it presents a different language and perspective than Havel's despairing and metaphysical approach. But given the oppressive Czechoslovakian government, it is not clear who is more realistic or persuasive. Here is Tucker's summary of the situation at the time of the appearance of Benda's essay:

> In Czechoslovakia, the few existing independent initiatives, most notably Charter 77, had to face the full brunt of state oppression. Consequently, the legally ambiguous space that Benda wished to occupy did not exist in Czechoslovakia. Totalitarian oppression obliterated civic society and effectively isolated the dissidents from the rest of the population. This reality was reflected in the responses of other dissidents to Benda's article. They recognized that, from a practical standpoint, Benda's parallel polis was impossible under the conditions of "normalized" Czechoslovakia. At most, the dissidents were able to maintain their authenticity and develop their culture within their community. Dissidents characterized their independence as personal and communal *authenticity*, free expression of one's self and free association. (Tucker 2000, 129)

According to Tucker, Havel, seeing little possibility in Benda's "parallel polis," sticks to culture and literature as the most promising realms for autonomy and independence from the communist power structure. It is also within these fields, rather than politics, that the existentialist vocabulary seems less out of place. But, as we have seen, Havel does not limit his assertions and claims to the cultural and literary spheres. In addition, his argument, in my interpretation, is not quite as different from Benda's as Tucker claims, although there is a world of difference in style and rhetoric. As we will see, Havel views Benda's parallel structures as the most mature stage of "living in truth," albeit that this stage is only present in an embryonic form.

Arguably, the central exposition of Havel's theory from the post-1968 period is his famous long essay, written in 1978, "The Power of the Powerless" (Havel 1992a, 125–214).[17] The essay begins with a perceptive description and dissection of the communist dictatorship as it imposes its version of "truth" on the people through its ideological hegemony. He also gives the reason why he characterizes the current communist system as "post-totalitarian."[18] Here, Havel weaves a perceptive tapestry of how and why people submit to an ideology that they know is ultimately false, but nevertheless offers them comfort and security. One central feature is a stress on the loss of individuality and personal responsibility, and the deadening of one's own conscience. This argument points towards a desire to restore or defend a robust individualism—a core element of Tocquevillian civil society—but it is so cloaked in existential garb that it is not easy to discern what Havel thinks of individualism in the liberal tradition. He describes the workings of communist ideology in terms of a "secularized religion": "It offers a ready answer to any question whatsoever; it can scarcely be accepted only in part, and accepting it has profound implications for human life. In an era when metaphysical and existential certainties are in a state of crisis, when people are being uprooted and alienated and are losing their sense of what this world means, this ideology inevitably has a certain charm" (1992a, 129). The premise here, as elsewhere in Havel's writings, is the presence of a spiritual and psychological crisis that spans, if not the entire globe, at least the Northern and Western hemispheres. This crisis manifests itself differently, depending on regime type, and it is particularly acute under communism because its ideology presents a false solution in the shape of a dangerous homecoming:

> To wandering humankind it offers an immediately available home: all one has to do is accept it, and suddenly everything becomes clear once more, life takes on new meaning, and all mysteries, unanswered questions, anxiety, and loneliness vanish. Of course, one pays dearly for this low-rent home: the price is abdication of one's own reason, conscience, and responsibility, for an essential aspect of this ideology is the consignment of reason and conscience to a higher authority. The principle involved here is that the center of power is identical with the center of truth. (1992a, 129–30)

This is persuasive as a characterization of how ideology operates in the communist system, but Havel goes further and connects this use of ideology with a value system that is Western in origin. The iron curtain is no longer sealed; the consumer mentality is all-pervasive, even within the communist bloc.

> For some time now this bloc has ceased to be a kind of enclave, isolated from
> the rest of the developed world and immune to processes occurring in it. To the
> contrary, the Soviet bloc is an integral part of that larger world, and it shares and
> shapes the world's destiny. This means in concrete terms that the hierarchy of
> existing in the developed countries of the West has, in essence, appeared in our
> society (the long period of co-existence with the West has only hastened this
> process). In other words, what we have here is simply another form of the con-
> sumer and industrial society, with all its concomitant social, intellectual, and
> psychological consequences. (1992a, 131)

Perhaps, but difficult to determine without further elaboration and
exemplification. Havel leaves it on this rather abstract level, and focuses
instead on the consequences of this system—a communist totalitarian ideology in combination with a mass consumer consciousness. That this is not fertile ground for a civil society, parallel or not, is an understatement.

Without going into the details of Havel's extensive, and no doubt worth-
while, analysis and dissection of the communist ideology and its operation, we
have to ask how all of it relates to his commitment to a (theory of) civil society.
For one thing, the power of the post-totalitarian system with its all-encompassing ideology makes both an independent citizen and an independent social
realm free from the state's ideological and secret-police tentacles impossible.
"By pulling everyone into its power structure, the post-totalitarian system
makes everyone an instrument of a mutual totality, the auto-totality of society"
(1992a, 143). Being a firm believer in absolute but indeterminate dichotomies
like authenticity vs. inauthenticity, living the truth vs. living the lie, fake interests vs. real interests, etc., Havel postulates an inborn authenticity and truth
that is not alienated, and that therefore provides each individual with a criterion for what is the correct way to live. It is this drive or impulse that needs to
assert itself, but that cannot come to realization under the rule of the post-communist system. "Individuals can be alienated from themselves only because
there is something in them to alienate. Living the truth is thus woven directly
into the texture of living a lie. It is the repressed alternative, the authentic aim
to which living a lie is an authentic response." And, "Under the orderly surface
of the life of lies, therefore there slumbers the hidden sphere of life in its real
aims, of its hidden openness to truth" (1992a, 148). For Havel, then, living in
truth is a direct political challenge and threat to the post-totalitarian system.
This authentic and true life can only be lived outside of the existing power
structures—hence the need for an antipolitical and morally pure civil society.

The supporters of Charter 77 are living examples of the authentic life, and
they are committed to living in truth, according to Havel. Although apolitical
in its aims and methods, Charter 77 becomes indirectly politically significant

exactly because it is a moral counter-society that shows the lies of post-totalitarianism. "As a civic initiative that is politically undefined and does not seek to implement a political program of its own, it is—if I may say so—'above' it all, or, to put it more modestly, outside it all" (1992a, 326). Havel also calls this antipolitical realm "pre-political," and rejects any concern with political reforms within the post-communist structures. A movement or dissident action cannot be judged on the basis of its explicitly political content. "The extent to which it is a real political force is due exclusively to its pre-political context" (1992a, 178). On occasion, Havel seems to reject *any* form of conventional politics, regardless of which system we are talking about. In those instances, his contempt for political parties or interest politics comes to light, as in the following sentence: "People who live in the post-totalitarian system know only too well that the question of whether one or several political parties are in power, and how these parties define and label themselves, is of far less importance than the question of whether or not it is possible to live like a human being" (1992a, 161). On some level, this might be true, but it is obviously not very helpful if we want to understand what kind of politics or society would follow from such a generalization. As with Konrád, and unlike Michnik, this assertion moves beyond the concern with communist oppressive rule into an abstract moral realm, which might have philosophical or intellectual appeal, but no practical consequence.

Instead of articulating his conception of an independent civil society in more concrete language, Havel turns his attention to "the limitations of the traditionally political way of looking at things." Like Konrád, he opposes conventional politics and parties, not in the name of an intellectual aristocracy, but in much more metaphysical terms. Havel is not interested in an opposition to communist rule that ends with a change in government; something much more existential is at stake. His exact formulation is revealing in its rhetorical scope: "To oppose [the post-totalitarian system] merely by establishing a different political line and then striving for a change in government would not only be unrealistic, it would be utterly inadequate, for it would never come near to touching the root of the matter. For some time now, the problem has no longer resided in a political line or program: it is a problem of life itself" (1992a, 180).

Havel does, however, concretize to some degree his understanding of civil society. First, he describes what people who live authentic lives in truth actually do with their lives in civil society: they may write and contribute to the growth and circulation of *samizdat* literature; they may be teachers who teach unofficial truths not taught in the state schools; they may be clergymen who manage to practice their religion freely; they may be artists of various kinds who promote and contribute to an independent culture; or they may be defenders of the interests of workers through independent unions, etc. (1992a,

178–79). All this is concrete enough, but when Havel sums it up, he returns to the moral and existential abstractions:

> The first conclusion to be drawn, then, is that the original and most important sphere of activity, one that predetermines all the others, is simply an attempt to create and support the independent life of society as an articulated expression of living within the truth. In other words, serving truth consistently, purposefully, and articulately, and organizing this service. This is only natural, after all: if living within the truth is an elementary starting point for every attempt made by people to oppose the alienating pressure of the system, if it is the only meaningful basis of any independent act of political import, and if, ultimately, it is also the most intrinsic existential source of the "dissident" attitude, then it is difficult to imagine that even manifest "dissent" could have any other basis than the service of truth, the truthful life, and the attempt to make room for the genuine aims of life. (1992a, 179)

The "independent life of society" is not particularly difficult to imagine, but to issue calls for "living within the truth" and in "the service of truth" are not very helpful, except for the already converted. Here Havel fails both to convince and to explain. However, when he discusses Benda's parallel society, he is mostly concerned with cultural activities—literature, art, theater, and music—and seems to think that Benda's expansive vista is premature, although Havel concedes that there will "at a certain stage" be a need for "a certain amount of organization and institutionalization" in the emerging "second" society. "Along with it, a parallel political life will also necessarily evolve, and to a certain extent it exists already in Czechoslovakia." All these mostly "pre-political," parallel structures are for Havel "the most articulated expressions so far of living within the truth" (1992a, 193–94).[19] In spite of the Heideggerian and existentialist language, one can discern, in this treatment of the parallel society, concrete elements that, although not framed in liberal democratic terms, are still compatible with and even close to the idea of a liberal civil society. Havel, for example, insists on the individual's responsibility for all his/her actions, and claims that changes are taking place spontaneously from "below," due to people acting as autonomous human beings without being told what to do; they act on the basis of their conscience and universal moral values, he asserts, without specifying these values any further. He also praises the limited but growing pluralism and diversity of views that are finding outlets in both the parallel and official social structures. This does not add up to a liberal conception of civil society, but at the very least it is reminiscent of one.

Unfortunately, Havel ends his long treatment in "The Power of the Powerless" on a downright illiberal note. He returns to Heidegger's controversial claim that "only a God can save us now," and calls for his favorite and now familiar "existential revolution." Again, he engages in a lamentation on "the crisis of contemporary technological society as a whole." He quickly slips over into an equally broad critique of parliamentary democracy as the desirable alternative to the communist system. "But to cling to the notion of traditional parliamentary democracy as one's political ideal and to succumb to the illusion that only this tried and true form is capable of guaranteeing human beings enduring dignity and an independent role in society would, in my opinion, be at the very least shortsighted" (1992a, 209). Havel wants nothing short of a "moral reconstitution of society, which means a radical renewal of the relationship of human beings to what I have called the 'human order,' which no political order can replace" (1992a, 209–10).

It is downhill from here. In spite of his often-voiced objection to utopian ideas in favor of individual autonomy, Havel develops his own misty and pastoral communitarian utopia opposed to any form of power center and organized institutional order, especially if structured in terms of political parties. It is an ideal that is based on personal relationships, and trust in leaders who do not belong to parties but whose authority is based on their personalities and their impeccable integrity. He even hints that this new society ought to be based on complete consensus: "It is only with the full existential backing of every member of the community that a permanent bulwark against creeping totalitarianism can be established" (1992a, 211). It is a spontaneous order, and not just for civil society, but for politics and economics as well:

> Both political and economic life ought to be founded on the varied and versatile cooperation of such dynamically appearing and disappearing organizations. As far as the economic life of society goes, I believe in the principle of self-management, which is probably the only way of achieving what all the theorists of socialism have dreamed about, that is, the genuine (i.e., informal) participation of workers in economic decision making, leading to a feeling of genuine responsibility for their collective work. The principle of control and discipline ought to be abandoned in favor of self-control and self-discipline. (211)

This is not a theory of civil society in which the state and society exist within a productive and virtuous circle. The ideal moves, according to Havel, "significantly beyond" liberal parliamentary democracy. He calls it a "post-democratic" system, and suggests that the dissident groups and the parallel polis under communism are intimations of this system. Since this vision is left rather open-ended, to put it mildly, one can only conclude that it reveals the intense longing in Havel for an "existential revolution" that transcends and avoids the mundane and everyday bickering of a liberal democracy. It is a longing for a community that is both harmonious and anarchic, both spontaneous and organized, and both free and without vices. In short, it is the very definition of a utopia.

Reading "The Power of the Powerless" next to Michnik's essays, one realizes the profound contrast and difference both in style and content between the two dissidents' perspectives. While Michnik takes a clear stand against utopian thinking, and is constantly checking his thoughts against the practical political reality surrounding him, Havel, as his argument deepens and moves forward, sounds increasingly utopian and, in spite of his claim to be preoccupied with everyday existence, loses touch with anything that could be called concrete, everyday, or practical. I would even argue that Havel's abstract moralism puts him at odds with Konrád's similar tendency. At least the latter's style contains a self-reflective irony and skeptical distance. Unlike his own plays, Havel's long essay is humorless and jargon-ridden. In terms of concrete substance and practical suggestions, it remains indeterminate and vague—and hardly a blueprint for a robust and vibrant civil society. In retrospect, it is surprising that it has been viewed as a seminal and central essay for the dissident movement. What remains valuable, however, is the dissection and exposure of the workings of ideology and practice of the communist system and the *nomenklatura*. On this score alone, the essay deserves attention. But the vision of a "post-democratic" society does not convince, and has little to offer as a guide to understanding how the promotion and creation of a civil society can serve as an important element in the transition from communism to a well-functioning and legitimate democracy.

After the Fall of Communism

It remains to briefly discuss the views of civil society among our three protagonists after the fall of communism. As would be expected, a shift takes place, and in the case of Konrád and Havel, we see a turn to a more realistic assessment of both what can be achieved and how civil society should be understood. Michnik remains true to his prudent and circumspect style of analysis.

The essays in Konrád's *The Melancholy of Rebirth* display the same irony, skepticism, and humor that is found in *Antipolitics*, this time with a noticeable appreciation for the positive changes that have occurred in the wake of the transition (Konrád 1995). In addition, Konrád shows a definite if guarded support for parliamentary democracy and all the cornerstones of liberalism. There is equal emphasis on the importance of institutions and procedures on the one hand, and civil society and individual liberties on the other. In fact, this is, in my reading, one of the main recurrent themes in his essays. He is also observing and promoting a "bourgeois society" and the growth of the middle (or bourgeois) class in Hungary because it is most likely to show tolerance and moderation, and reject revolutionary rhetoric and solutions. Konrád does not want another version of the Communist Party, whether on the right or the left; he is tired of ideologies proclaiming the correct truths.

> Revolutionary dynamics fosters the belief that there is one overriding truth and that it can be represented solely by the ideologically pure—a belief that legitimizes the ever increasing power of the vanguard (that is, the Party), the sole source of ideologically pure thinkers. Consequently, what the ideology labels "correct" its followers must consider positive and its enemies negative. The bourgeois mind is skeptical of such an approach: it posits a variety of truths and interests and is therefore tolerant of, and even curious about, ideas differing from its own basic way of thinking. (1995, 35)

In fact, Konrád puts a lot of hope in the middle class as the main source for moderation, and as a check on the extreme nationalists as well as the communists. Writing in the mid-1990s, he makes an intriguing and encouraging observation, worthy of a Montesquieu or a Tocqueville: "The formation of a middle class was the most interesting social development of the eighties. The change in regime has only intensified the process, and by the end of this decade we shall be a more or less normal bourgeois society. The process of *embourgeoisement* is stronger than any political ideology, stronger than state socialism or state nationalism" (1995, 189). But he is equally devoted to the establishment of a decent civil society capable of respecting the distinction between private and public; this will also temper the urge to punish those who belonged to the Communist Party in the past. Here, too, he endorses a liberal perspective. "If we had to sum up the essence of a civil society in one sentence, we would refer to what might be called the autonomy of the spheres, that is, the fact that in a civil society politics is separate from administration, the economy, science, culture, and religion. Who belongs or belonged to which political party or who professes or professed which political principles is a private affair" (1995, 36). Civil society is separate, but it is not in radical opposition to the state and the regime, as it was under communism. On the contrary, Konrád shows repeatedly that it is now a matter of trying to get a complex machinery moving, in which each part has to perform its appropriate function in order for the whole society to make progress in the direction of a more liberal democracy.

Konrád is no longer showing his earlier contempt for politics in general; he now wants limited government both in terms of power and reach. He has admiration for some of the new politicians in Hungary, but he wants them to keep their distance and show self-control. "All I want from a regime is that it keeps its distance: I don't want it to ban me or uphold me, just to leave me alone. I want it to do its job courteously, like the staff of a fine hotel" (1995, 48). Gone is the claim that all politics are corrupt and contemptible, and gone is the view that politics are irrelevant for the intellectual aristocracy. Konrád himself sounds more like the bourgeois citizen that he is hoping will emerge in a democratic Hungary. He knows that the learning curve is long, and that both civil society and parliamentary democracy take time and experience to function properly; but he is moderately optimistic. "When I observe the way Hungary is developing internally, the first thing I see is the formation of a constitutional state based on the rule of law, a state that has not yet infringed upon its citizens' human rights and seems unlikely to do so in the near future" (1995, 55).

Hungary has continued this development into the twenty-first century, and a moderate optimism regarding the consolidation of democracy and the growth of civil society appears justified. Konrád, of course, is aware of the potentially destructive legacies for liberal democracy in Hungary's past, but he concludes on a prudent and cautiously hopeful note:

> If Hungarian democracy is to make a valid response to the issues facing us at the end of the century, we must call for moderation from our political class. We must take a long, hard look at the two legacies of our century—the Horthy period and the Kádár period, the gentry tradition and the feudal-bureaucratic tradition—which are amazingly similar. (Both, for example, granted the politician a hegemonic position.) And while both have failed, their traditions live on in the personalities—and children—of their followers and are seeking an outlet. (1995, 189)

All of this does not add up to a new theory of civil society and its role in a liberal democracy, but given Konrád's experiences with a communist regime, and his courageous role through difficult times—and given his assessment in *Antipolitics*—what is most striking about these more recent reflections is exactly that he ends up embracing civil society and liberalism. That alone is somewhat of an achievement.

In an interview in 1993, Michnik proclaims that his own dissident cohorts (or, as he calls it, the 1968 generation) are now ending their "historical potential." They consist of a group of activists that span the period from 1968 to the formation of the first government after the Round Table negotiations. He stresses the difference between being an oppositionist under communism and being a politician in an infant democracy. Whatever coherency holds the dissidents together under a communist regime falls apart after the regime change. Michnik gives several examples of former dissidents that he now disagrees deeply with, and he declares the previous war between the dissidents and the communist power structure over. The challenge at hand now is to build a Polish democracy. Nobody appreciates the complexity of this task more than Michnik, and his writings after the collapse of communism often focus on the conflicts and dilemmas in Polish society that the transition continues to generate. As journalist and editor of *Gazeta Wyborcza*, he uses the paper in order to get his message to the public, and unsurprisingly, he views it as a primary tool for the process of democratization: "It's easy to succumb to megalomania, but I don't think I'm mistaken when I say that *Gazeta Wyborcza* is playing a major role in creating a new language in which to discuss and evaluate the world around me. For us, *Gazeta* is not just a newspaper, it's an instrument of civil society, an institution of Polish democracy" (Michnik 1998, 288–89).

In the post-communist world, Michnik plays a different role than under communism, but given his consistent liberal democratic convictions, his anti-utopianism, his commitment to compromise and tolerance—including an amazingly conciliatory attitude towards his former persecutors—and his level-headed realism, there is remarkable continuity in his overall political convictions. Unlike both Konrád and Havel, there is no need for a major repositioning in moral and political outlook. Naturally, the specific issues shift, and new problems appear on the Polish political and economic horizon. The growth of extreme nationalism and xenophobia across the region, for example, is worrisome in Michnik's eyes, and he devotes a great deal of time and effort to this issue (see, for example, Michnik and Habermas 1994, 24–29). Furthermore, his opposition to all moral absolutism makes him highly sensitive to and critical of any attempt to resurrect any form of totalizing ideology, whether on the left or the right on the political spectrum.

These characteristics—all liberal, I should add—of Michnik's political position serve him well in the international debate over the type of democracy that ought to be promoted in the post-communist period. Ira Katznelson, for example, criticizes Michnik for his principled liberal stand and wants him to move his views in a more—if not socialist—certainly social-democratic direction. Katznelson seems to think there is a "middle way" between capitalism of the West and socialism of the East, and he criticizes Michnik for thinking this an illusion, and chalks it up to "the liberal-totalitarian antinomy" in the perspective of the dissidents.

I think this legacy—that is to say, yours—is double-edged. It teaches a deep skepticism of all illiberalisms (including soft illiberalisms that devalue liberal tolerance as potentially oppressive) and demonstrates how communitarian, republican, socialist, Foucauldian, feminist, or other transliberal bases of critique run profound, even dangerous, risks when they seek to go it alone without being embedded within liberal principles and practices. But in showing how an assertively liberal political and moral public philosophy can matter, the dissident legacy, by primarily focusing on negative liberty, also teaches less satisfactory lessons drawn mainly from Popper: that the liberal tradition is so vulnerable it must be guarded uncritically; that liberalism should be closed and autarchic, nervous about alliances with traditions focusing on positive liberties; hence that positive ideologies as normative conceptions should be feared because they are susceptible to being mobilized on behalf of historicist and potentially totalitarian grand narratives. (Katznelson 1996, 41–42)

In the spirit of Michnik, one could answer, "Precisely!" There is a more circumspect response by Michnik himself, however—a response in which he reiterates his liberal democratic ideas. He advocates what he, with Habermas, calls "radical democracy" (without, incidentally, really showing what is radical about it), but gives special attention to the dangers of moral absolutism. He ends up endorsing "gray democracy":

> Democracy is a continuous articulation of particular interests, a diligent search for compromise among them, a marketplace of passions, emotions, hatreds, and hopes; it is eternal imperfection, a mixture of sinfulness, saintliness, and monkey business. This is why the seekers of a moral state and of a perfectly just society do not like democracy. Yet only democracy—having the capacity to question itself—also has the capacity to correct its own mistakes. Dictatorships, whether red or black, destroy the human capacity for creation; they kill the taste for human life, and eventually, life itself. Only gray democracy, with its human rights and institutions of civil society, can replace weapons and arguments. Parliamentarianism became an alternative to civil wars even though a conservative would argue with a liberal and with a social democrat whether that was the result of common sense or the wisdom that comes from misfortune. (Michnik 1998, 326)

This passage can serve as an appropriate summary of Michnik's reflections as a dissident under communism, and as a writer and citizen in a new, hopefully liberal, democracy.

Arguably, none of the former dissidents had to make the kind of radical transformation of his role as did Václav Havel. As president of first Czechoslovakia and then, after the "Velvet Divorce," the Czech Republic, he threw himself into the middle of the political fray, and clearly had to make some serious revisions of his dissident views. His writings during this period consist understandably of speeches and more hastily put-together essays, but civil society features prominently in several of them. But now, it is a more conventional version of civil society, even though the existential, moral vocabulary is liberally sprinkled throughout these reflections as well. He continues to raise his objections to shady party politics, and he remains committed to a moral, honest, and truthful politics based more on a notion of the common good than a variety of interests. As president, Havel certainly set a high moral standard for the office, although his sermon-like qualities work both ways: there has also been a noticeable degree of disillusionment with Havel's type of rhetoric. The gap between the moral discourse and people's everyday concerns is simply too stark for the moral admonitions to have the desired effect.[20]

Havel himself is not unaware of this, and one cannot fail to notice the sobering impact this has had on his speeches and essays. Most of them are concerned with the relatively mundane problems and issues that the Czech Republic faces as a new democracy. I will merely illustrate this tendency via one example, a speech given by Havel to the senate of the Czech Republic in December 1997, in the wake of the resignation of the Klaus government due to allegations of a host of improprieties (Havel 1998, 42–46). It is a kind of "state of the union" speech to the legislature, but instead of discussing achievements and progress, it is the lament of a nation. Here is a sample:

> Many people—and public opinion polls confirm this—are upset, disappointed, or even disgusted with social conditions in our country. Many people believe that once again—democracy or not—there are people in power who cannot be trusted, who are concerned more with their own advantage than they are with the general interest. Many are convinced that honest business people operate at a disadvantage, while dishonest profiteers get the green light. The belief prevails that in this country it pays to lie and steal, that many politicians and civil servants are on the take, and that political parties—though they all, without exceptions, declare their intentions honorable—are secretly manipulated by shady financial cabals. (1998, 42)

A post-communist "debilitation" has set in. After a thorough description of the state of affairs in the republic, Havel moves on to call upon the legislature to pass the appropriate laws, and to attend to their business in a responsible fashion. He addresses a long list of weaknesses and problems, and the actions that have to be taken by the parliament: simplification and clarification of new and existing laws; public administration reforms and local government empowerment; furthering of the integration into the European economic and political structures; improvement of all defense policies, including pushing for application to and integration into NATO; increase in the speed of privatization of the economy; and simplification of the laws for charitable and nonprofit organizations. After this wish list, Havel ends with a plea regarding an issue that he considers "the most important of all, something that deserves to be mentioned at the very conclusion of my remarks. . . . I mean culture in the broadest sense of the word—that is, the culture of human relationships, of human existence, of human work, of human enterprise, of public and political life. I refer to the general level of our culture. I am afraid it is here that we have our greatest debt to pay and therefore have the most work ahead of us" (1998, 45). It turns out that what Havel means by "culture" is a civil society.

Without suggesting any specific measures or laws to create improvement, Havel outlines his own vision of an ideal civil society:

> That means a society that makes room for the richest possible self-structuring and the richest possible participation in public life. In this sense, civil society is important for two reasons: in the first place it enables people to be themselves in all their dimensions, which includes being social creatures who desire, in thousands of ways, to participate in the life of the community in which they live.
>
> In the second place, it functions as a genuine guarantee of political stability. The more developed all the organs, institutions, and instruments of civil society are, the more resistant that society will be to political upheavals or reversals. It was no accident that communism's most brutal attack was aimed precisely against this civil society. It knew very well that its greatest enemy was not an individual non-Communist politician, but a society that was open, structured independently from the bottom up, and therefore very difficult to manipulate. (1998, 45)

Although not the most precise definition, this is still a classical liberal understanding of the role and function of civil society. Here, Havel has left behind the Heideggerian and existentialist language, and found a way of describing civil society that both captures how it ought to function in a mature liberal democracy, and gives the reason why a totalitarian regime fears the mere existence of an independent and free civil society.

There is something very revealing about this juxtaposition: to see civil society as the pinnacle of a free and democratic society, and at the same time, as the number-one enemy of the totalitarian state. This might be one indirect legacy of the dissident movement's preoccupation with civil society. To some extent, all three former dissidents end up with this conclusion, and it is an appropriate way to close what could perhaps be seen as a final chapter in the history of the dissidents of the region.

As most of the chapters in this volume indicate, the politics and economics of the transition are now in a different phase. More concrete nuts-and-bolts issues preoccupy both the politics and the scholarship of the region. For all the pessimism by some of the former dissidents, as well as some scholars, there is now a growing civil society in each and every former communist country, and it is very plausible that at least part of the foundation for this was built by the dissidents in what was an extremely intense and dramatic period. All is not well; but, as Norman Graham shows in his chapter in this volume, when you look at the empirical reality of civil society, the record is encouraging, even if there is a lot more to be done. We are, as he argues, probably somewhere in "stage five" in the evolution of civil society in the countries of my three protagonists.[21] Further progress is not guaranteed, of course—there are too many unknowns ahead—but contrary to the views of some former dissidents, the evolution of civil society is a slow and mostly spontaneous process. At this stage, one should certainly recommend all kinds of measures by both governments and NGOs, but without high expectations, since building civil society through social engineering is, even in the best of circumstances, a difficult process. But there is no reason for fatalism either. The state can and must play an active role for civil society, but mostly in an indirect way, protecting and legally guaranteeing and regulating the sphere, and it has to know when not to interfere and leave it to its own devices.

In terms of the ideology of civil society by the (former) dissidents, one now has to draw the conclusion that once the communist regimes were gone, the ideology of civil society began to lose its intensity for both the intellectuals and the practitioners of the region. That should come as no surprise. There are simply too many other tasks—including (perhaps especially) the building of political institutions and a private economic market—that have to be done, and civil society has to be put on the back burner and maybe even, as I just stated, be left to evolve slowly and spontaneously. The dissidents did not add anything new to the theory of civil society, but they did, under very difficult conditions, practice it, so to speak. They will have a place in history for this reason, if for no other.

Still, they leave a political legacy with regard to civil society that is not without significance. The arguments reviewed in these pages reinforce the central liberal commitment to limited government, since the state is not to interfere in the sphere of civil society, except by guaranteeing its existence and protecting its boundaries through the rule of law. The strong anti-statist stand confirms the importance of leaving areas of society free from state interference and open to the free actions of citizens. In that sense, even the antipolitical attitude teaches a political lesson: the rights of individuals to be left alone. (The downside of this is, of course, that this posture can become an excuse to ignore and even despise practical, messy politics as it has to be practiced in a liberal democracy.)

In addition, there is—at least among the dissidents discussed here—a commitment to individual autonomy and responsibility due to their emphasis on individual freedom in society, especially the freedom of speech and association.

Moral absolutism, especially in Havel, is also tied to the individual in the sense of a Kantian moral imperative. The entire dissident movement shows that individuals can make a huge political difference, even when it appears least likely. The danger on this score is the moralism that can easily creep into the views of those who feel (self-)righteous in their purity and devotion. Michnik is an antidote to Havel here. The former's emphasis on compromise, tolerance, and negotiation is a reminder of the importance of leaving behind moral absolutism and utopian schemes.

Again, there is nothing startling about these insights, but the dissident movement certainly reinforces what we already know, and it even stands out as a historical episode that shows the courage, integrity, and tenacity of individuals who are willing to make gigantic personal sacrifices for the ideals of freedom and democracy. Only time will tell whether this legacy will be long-lasting and will carry over into the new regimes of the region.

NOTES

1. For a comment on the absence of "big new ideas," see Timothy Garton Ash's "Conclusions," in Antohi and Tismaneanu (2000, 397–98). For an opposing view on this topic, see Jeffrey C. Isaac's essay "The Strange Silence of Political Theory" (1998, 41–58).

2. Throughout this article, unless otherwise indicated, I will use "democracy" to mean "liberal democracy," i.e., rule of law, civil and individual rights, free and fair elections, limited government, separation of powers—in short, the type of regime often referred to as "constitutional liberalism." For an interesting recent discussion of liberal vs. illiberal democracy, see Zakaria (2003).

3. Although Garton Ash equivocates on the issue, he does make a different overall evaluation of the ability of the intellectuals to resist the temptations of power and corruption: "The record of intellectuals in power in the twentieth century suggests that they are among the least likely to resist the insidious poison, precisely because they are most able to rationalize, intellectualize, or philosophically justify their own submission or corruption by referring to higher goals or values" (2001, 134).

4. For perspectives on some of these liberal claims, see Rosenblum and Post, especially the "Introduction" (2002, 1–25).

5. After all, even Putnam, in his *Bowling Alone*, includes the frequency of dinner parties with friends and neighbors as a measurement of social capital (2000, 93–115).

6. For a more favorable reading of Konrád than the one I present here, see the impressive and massive study of the dissidents by Barbara J. Falk (2003, esp. 298–309).

7. The bottom line here, from my perspective, is that there seems to be no correlation in an individual between literary, artistic, and intellectual achievements, on the one hand, and moral superior judgment, political prudence, and civil courage, on the other. For two books that reveal this tendency convincingly, see Mark Lilla (2001) and Francois Furet

(1999). Konrád's argument, in *Antipolitics*, in favor of the intellectuals is somewhat surprising in light of his previous critical work on intellectuals under communism. See George Konrád and Iván Szelényi (1995).

8. As Barbara Falk argues, "If the Church was not a powerful ally, then it most certainly was both a shield and a sanctuary for Solidarity and the democratic opposition more generally" (2003, 167).

9. According to Michnik, the term "new social accord" was first coined by the Czech intellectual Antonin Liehm.

10. Even his historical essays are, to some extent, an elaboration of these themes. Michnik looks to Polish history to explicate and exemplify his own thinking and strategy in the present. Although perhaps a bit romantic on occasion, one still realizes that there is a tradition of civil society in Poland that can be tapped into for current purposes, and that might prove important for the post-transition society. See, for example, the long essay "Conversation in the Citadel," written in jail in 1982 (1987, 275–333).

11. For an intriguing biography—with an odd title—of Havel's life, see John Keane (2000).

12. Keane, in his previously mentioned biography, certainly manages to integrate all these writings into a coherent, well-conceived interpretation, albeit a controversial one. For other extensive treatments of Havel's work, see Aviezer Tucker, *The Philosophy of Czech Dissidence from Patoc̆ka to Havel* (2000), and Falk (2003).

13. In the region in general, the moment when the critics of the communist system take leave of the Marxist perspective—when they have become completely disillusioned by this, as it were, metanarrative—is a crucial one for the dissident movement. It is after this disillusionment that we see the rise of a new type of criticism focusing on antipolitics and the building of a civil society.

14. Havel's thinking also has roots in the Czech philosophical tradition of phenomenology and existentialism. For an interesting account of this intellectual influence, see Tucker (2000).

15. A slightly different version is also printed in Václav Havel, *Summer Meditations* (1992b, 249–71), under the title "Politics and Conscience." The original occasion for this essay was an address sent to the University of Toulouse, where Havel received an honorary doctorate. He was not allowed to leave Czechoslovakia and could not attend. The year was 1984.

16. For another (very similar) autobiographical take on his childhood and adolescence, see Václav Havel (1991, 3–33).

17. The essay can also be found in Václav Havel et al. (1985, 23–96). The example Havel uses in the essay is the now infamous greengrocer who hangs a sign in his store window proclaiming "Workers of the world unite," even though he does not believe in the slogan. Throughout the essay, the greengrocer's motives, mentality, and actions are analyzed and discussed.

18. Havel uses this term for a kind of late communism, more cynical and jaded than good old Stalinism.

19. For a more extensive discussion of the second or parallel culture with emphasis on the arts and literature, see Havel's essay "Six Asides About Culture," from 1984, in Havel (1992a, 272–84).

20. For a critical and sober assessment of Havel as president, see Tucker (2000, chap. 7). For the most reflective and philosophical work by Havel after becoming president, see Havel (1992b).

21. See Graham's chapter in this volume, especially note 4. For an impressive and recent study of the problems of post-communist civil society, see Howard (2003). The focus is on former East Germany and Russia, but the study contains discussions and insights applicable to the entire region. It is a first-rate work, both theoretically and empirically.

REFERENCES

Andor, Laszlo, and Martin Summers. 1998. *Market failure: Eastern Europe's "economic miracle."* London: Pluto Press.

Andorka, Rudolf. 1993. Cultural norms and values: The role of the intellectuals in the creation of a new democratic culture in Hungary. *Society and Economy* 15(5): 1–17.

Antohi, Sorin, and Vladimir Tismaneanu, eds. 2000. *Between past and future: The revolutions of 1989 and their aftermath.* Budapest and New York: Central European University Press.

Ash, Timothy Garton. 1999. *The magic lantern: The revolution of '89 witnessed in Warsaw, Budapest, Berlin, and Prague.* New York: Random House/Vintage Books.

———. 2001. *History of the present: Essays, sketches, and dispatches from Europe in the 1990s.* New York: Vintage Books.

———. 2002. *The Polish Revolution: Solidarity.* 3rd ed. New Haven: Yale University Press.

Bartlett, David L. 1997. *The political economy of dual transformations: Market reform and democratization in Hungary.* Ann Arbor: University of Michigan Press.

Benda, Václav. 1991. The parallel *polis.* In *Civic freedom in Central Europe: Voices from Czechoslovakia,* ed. Gordon H. Skilling and Paul Wilson. London: Macmillan.

Berglund, Sten, and Jan Ake Dellenbrant, eds. 1994. *The new democracies in Eastern Europe: Party systems and political cleavages.* 2nd ed. Aldershot: Edward Elgar.

Bhaduri, Amit, and Deepak Nayyar. 1996. *The intelligent person's guide to liberalization.* New Delhi: Penguin Books.

Blanchard, Olivier Jean, Kenneth A. Froot, and Jeffrey D. Sachs. 1994. *The transition in Eastern Europe.* Vol. 1, *Country studies.* Chicago: University of Chicago Press.

Bryant, Christopher G. A., and Edmund Mokrzycki, eds. 1994. *The new great transformation? Change and continuity in East-Central Europe.* London: Routledge.

Csepeli, Gyorgy, Daniel German, Laszlo Keri, and Istvan Stumpf, eds. 1994. *From subject to citizen.* Budapest: Hungarian Center for Political Education.

Diamond, Larry. 1999. *Developing democracy: Toward consolidation.* Baltimore: Johns Hopkins University Press.

———, ed. 1994. *Political culture and democracy in developing countries.* Boulder, CO: Lynne Rienner Publishers.

Diamond, Larry, and Marc F. Plattner, eds. 1996. *The global resurgence of democracy.* 2nd ed. Baltimore: Johns Hopkins University Press.

Falk, Barbara J. 2003. *The dilemma of dissidence in East-Central Europe: Citizen intellectuals and philosopher kings.* Budapest and New York: Central European University Press.

Fuller, Graham E. 1991. *The democracy trap: Perils of the post–cold war world.* New York: Penguin Books.

Furet, Francois. 1999. *The passing of an illusion: The idea of communism in the twentieth century.* Translated by Deborah Furet. Chicago: University of Chicago Press.

Graham, Norman A. 1999. Globalization and civil society in Hungary and the Czech Republic. In *The revival of civil society,* ed. Michael G. Schechter. London: Macmillan.

Gray, John. 1998. *False dawn: The delusions of global capitalism.* New York: New Press.

Habermas, Jürgen. 1991. *The structural transformation of the public sphere: An inquiry into a category of bourgeois society.* Cambridge, MA: MIT Press.

Havel, Václav. 1988. *Letters to Olga: June 1979–September 1982.* Translated by Paul Wilson. New York: Alfred A. Knopf.

———. 1991. *Disturbing the peace: A conversation with Karel Hvizdala.* Translated by Paul Wilson. New York: Vintage Books.

———. 1992a. *Open letters: Selected writings, 1965–1990.* Edited by Paul Wilson. New York: Vintage Books.

———. 1992b. *Summer meditations.* Translated by Paul Wilson. New York: Alfred A. Knopf.

———. 1998. The state of the republic. *New York Review of Books,* 5 March.

———, et al. 1985. *The power of the powerless: Citizens against the state in Central-Eastern Europe.* Edited by John Keane. London: Hutchinson and Co.

Howard, Marc Morjé. 2003. *The weakness of civil society in post-communist Europe.* Cambridge: Cambridge University Press.

Hunt, Louis. 2000. Civil society and the idea of a commercial republic. In *The revival of civil society: Comparative and international cases,* ed. Michael G. Schechter. London: Macmillan.

Huntington, Samuel P. 1991. *The third wave: Democratization in the late twentieth century.* Norman: University of Oklahoma Press.

Isaac, Jeffrey C. 1998. *Democracy in dark times.* Ithaca, NY: Cornell University Press.

Katznelson, Ira. 1996. *Liberalism's crooked circle: Letters to Adam Michnik.* Princeton, NJ: Princeton University Press.

Keane, John. 1988. *Democracy and civil society: On the predicaments of European socialism, the prospects for democracy and the problem of controlling social and political power.* London: Verso.

———. 2000. *Václav Havel: A political tragedy in six acts.* New York: Basic Books.

———, ed. 1988. *Civil society and the state: New European perspectives.* London: Verso.

Kettle, Steve. 1996. The development of the Czech media since the fall of communism. *Journal of Communist Studies and Transition Politics* 12(4): 42–60.

Kofman, Eleonore, and Gillian Youngs. 1996. *Globalization: Theory and practice.* London: Pinter.

Konrád, George. 1984. *Antipolitics: An essay*. Translated by Richard E. Allen. London: Quartet Books.

———. 1995. *The melancholy of rebirth: Essays from post-communist Central Europe, 1989–1994*. Translated by Michael Henry Heim. San Diego and New York: Harcourt Brace & Co.

Konrád, George, and Iván Szelényi. 1995. *The intellectuals on the road to class power*. New York: Harcourt Brace & Jovanovich.

Kornberg, Allan, and Harold D. Clarke. 1992. *Citizens and community: Political support in a representative democracy*. New York: Cambridge University Press.

Lánczi, András, and Patrick H. O'Neil. 1996. Pluralization and the politics of media change in Hungary. *Journal of Communist Studies and Transition Politics* 12(4): 82–101.

Lasch, Christopher. 1995. *The revolt of the elites and the betrayal of democracy*. New York: W. W. Norton.

LeDuc, Lawrence, Richard G. Niemi, and Pippa Norris, eds. 1996. *Comparing democracies: Elections and voting in global perspective*. Thousand Oaks, CA: Sage Publications.

Lewis, Paul G. 1997. Theories of democratization and patterns of regime change in Eastern Europe. *Journal of Communist Studies and Transition Politics* 13(1): 4–26.

Lilla, Mark. 2001. *The reckless mind: Intellectuals in politics*. New York: New York Review of Books.

Lomax, Bill. 1997. The strange death of "civil society" in post-communist Hungary. *Journal of Communist Studies and Transition Politics* 13(1): 41–63.

McGrew, Anthony, ed. 1997. *The transformation of democracy? Globalization and territorial democracy*. London: Polity Press.

Michnik, Adam. 1987. *Letters from prison and other essays*. Translated by Maya Latynski. Berkeley: University of California Press.

———. 1993. *The Church and the Left*. Translated by D. Ost. Chicago: University of Chicago Press.

———. 1998. *Letters from freedom: Post–cold war realities and perspectives*. Edited by Irena Grudzin´ska Gross. Foreword by Ken Jowitt. Berkeley: University of California Press.

Michnik, Adam, and Jürgen Habermas. 1994. More humility, fewer illusions: A talk between Adam Michnik and Jürgen Habermas. *New York Review of Books*, 24 March, 24–29.

Milton, Andrew K. 1996. News media reform in Eastern Europe: A cross-national comparison. *Journal of Communist Studies and Transition Politics* 12(4): 7–23.

Miszlivetz, Ferenc. 1997. Participation and transition: Can the civil society project survive in Hungary? *Journal of Communist Studies and Transition Politics* 13(1): 27–40.

Olson, Mancur. 2000. *Power and prosperity: Outgrowing communist and capitalist dictatorships*. New York: Basic Books.

Orenstein, Mitchell A. 2001. *Out of the red: Building capitalism and democracy in postcommunist Europe*. Ann Arbor: University of Michigan Press.

Putnam, Robert D. 2000. *Bowling alone: The collapse and revival of American community*. New York: Simon and Schuster.

Putnam, Robert D., et al. 1993. *Making democracy work: Civic traditions in modern Italy.* Princeton, NJ: Princeton University Press.

Rosenblum Nancy L., and Robert C. Post, eds. 2002. *Civil society and government.* Princeton, NJ: Princeton University Press.

Sadowski, Christine M. 1994. Autonomous groups as agents of democratic change in communist and post-communist Eastern Europe. In *Political culture and democracy in developing countries,* ed. Larry Diamond. Boulder, CO: Lynne Rienner.

Seligman, Adam B. 1992. *The idea of Civil Society.* Princeton, NJ: Princeton University Press.

Sen, Amartya. 1999. Democracy as a universal value. *Journal of Democracy* 10(3): 3–17.

Smolar, Aleksander. 2002. Civil society after communism. In *Democracy after communism,* ed. Larry Diamond and Marc F. Plattner. Baltimore: Johns Hopkins University Press.

Sorensen, Georg. 1998. Democracy and democratization: Processes and prospects in a changing world. Boulder, CO: Westview.

Szekely, Istvan, and David Newbery. 1993. *Hungary: An economy in transition.* Cambridge: Cambridge University Press.

Tismaneanu, Vladimir. 1993. *Reinventing politics: Eastern Europe from Stalin to Havel.* New York: Free Press.

———. 1998. *Fantasies of salvation: Democracy, nationalism, and myth in post-communist Europe.* Princeton, NJ: Princeton University Press.

Tucker, Aviezer. 2000. *The philosophy of Czech dissidence from Patoc˘ka to Havel.* Pittsburgh: University of Pittsburgh Press.

Weiss, Linda. 1998. *The myth of the powerless state.* Ithaca, NY: Cornell University Press.

World Bank. 2000. *Making transition work for everyone: Poverty and inequality in Europe and Central Asia.* Washington, DC: World Bank.

Zakaria, Fareed. 2003. *The Future of liberty: Illiberal democracy at home and abroad.* New York: W. W. Norton.

5

Nation-Building in East Central Europe: Civic or Ethnic Majorities?

Kathleen M. Dowley

Since the collapse of communist regimes in 1989, the countries of East Central Europe have faced the simultaneous challenge of economic and political liberalization. This double burden has been rendered even more difficult by the threats of ethnic polarization and state disintegration, leading the editor of a special edition of *Slavic Review* to suggest that each state has had to wrestle with a "triple transformation"—national, democratic, and capitalist (Roeder 1999a). Democratic theorists from John Stuart Mill (1861) to Robert Dahl (1971) have long identified the potential problem posed to democratization by subnational pluralism, and more recent studies focusing on the post-communist space seem to reinforce these long-standing concerns (see Roeder 1999b; Snyder 2000). But the fact remains that democratization has been historically possible and relatively successful in some ethnically plural settings (Switzerland, India), and a visible failure in others (Yugoslavia).

Explaining when pluralism threatens the process of democratization and when it is compatible with it has been a challenge to social scientists and practitioners seeking to avoid another Yugoslavia. Ethnic heterogeneity within states is actually declining, as the tendency has been to construct increasingly homogeneous smaller states, as in the former Yugoslavia and Czech and Slovak states. Poland, Hungary, the Czech Republic, Slovenia, Slovakia, and even Russia now contain only small minority populations within their borders; that is, they make up less than 20 percent of the total population. But as Gurr (1993) has pointed out, this often leaves these minorities even more "at risk" if their political preferences diverge significantly from the majority, because of their diminished numbers and political clout.

They appear most at risk when the state in which they reside pursues what Brubaker (1996) refers to as the "nationalizing nationalism" of newly independent or newly reconfigured states. "Nationalizing nationalisms involve claims made in the name of the core nation or nationality, defined in ethnocultural terms, and sharply distinguished from the citizenry as a whole" (Brubaker 1996, 5). Ostensibly, then, the desire to promote the core nation at the expense of non-nationals among their population stems from a previous history of denied or inadequately served interests. The question, in Brubaker's view, is not "whether the new states will be nationalizing, but *how* they will be nationalizing, and *how nationalizing* they will be" (106).

Anthony Smith makes a distinction between *civic* and *ethnic* conceptions of the nation, where civic nations are defined in terms of a shared culture, common laws, and a territorial basis for citizenship. Ethnic understandings of the nation focus on common descent and the popular mobilization of the vernacular culture (Smith 1993, 34). The emergence of the latter, says Smith, is correlated with the appeal of exclusive nationalist movements for self-determination or for the "ethnic purification" of existing states.

Previous nationalizing projects in this region occurred in the interwar era, during which Brubaker saw states like Poland attempting to nationalize differentially, i.e., trying to assimilate ethnic Ukrainians and Lithuanians while trying to dissimilate Jews and Germans. In the current environment, and with smaller minority populations to consider everywhere except the former Soviet states (which in many ways seem closer to the interwar Europe cases), there are alternatives to this differential nationalizing. According to Brubaker (1996), in the civic model, where all citizens are equal, ethnicity has no public significance, policy is governed by the principle of nondiscrimination, and citizenship is territorially based.

The bi- or multinational model explicitly recognizes two or more national groups as "owners" of the state (for example, the state becomes officially bilingual), with much more emphasis in the public sphere on group rights and representation compared to the first model. The final is the hybrid model, where the state is explicitly national or claimed by one national group, but special provisions are made for minority groups to continue nurturing their own culture and language, and there is no attempt to assimilate or dissimilate non-national groups.

In his essay, Brubaker posits that the civic model, ironically, may only be adopted in the most homogeneous states in the region, like Slovenia and the Czech Republic. The bi- or multinational model would be likely from the merger of two currently independent states, as is suggested by the Belarus/Russian confederal arrangements. That leaves the nationalizing state (which seeks to assimilate or dissimilate its minority populations) or the hybrid minority-rights model for the remainder of the region. While all pay formal respect to the latter option, in practice nationalizing tendencies are still visible in the region—in Romania, Slovakia, and the Baltics, for instance, despite recent accession to the European Union (Brubaker 1996, 104–5). EU claims (and written declarations) suggest that the protection of minority rights was an integral part of the criteria for accession, though some observers remain concerned that contested understandings of minority "rights" both within the European Union and new member states will lead to "possible backlashes on the EU" (Wiener and Schwellnus 2004).

There are, therefore, compelling reasons to seek to identify the preferences of majority groups in the region, and ultimately, to be able to predict and explain variation in titular support for particularly exclusive forms of nation-building. It remains the empirical task of this study to understand where in the region ethnic majorities have supported the construction of ethnic nations, as well as to understand what the consequences have been for their minority populations. It is important to look at mass political attitudes about membership in the political community, even though most of these states have now formally adopted minority-rights legislation that conforms to EU expectations. Problems may well eventually develop in states where the preferences of a pro-EU elite diverge significantly from the majorities within these states. For example, Haerpfer et al. (1999) found that among East Central European publics, more people in 1996 and 1998 felt "threatened" by ethnic minorities in their own country than by potential external threats such as Russia or Germany. Outside the former Yugoslavia, Slovakia and Romania recorded the highest percent feeling threatened by national minorities, with 43 and 32 percent respectively (Haerpfer 1999, 1009).

Accession alone does not render these concerns irrelevant. The largely elite-driven process of EU expansion has yet to take mass attitudes seriously, and forthcoming referendums in member states on the new constitutional treaty will surely encounter the gap in mass and elite preferences regarding EU form and substance.

To evaluate the attitudes of majority populations in East Central Europe vis-à-vis their minority populations, I will rely primarily on the International Social Survey Program's (ISSP) 1995 *National Identity* survey, which included data from Latvia, Bulgaria, the Czech Republic, Slovakia, Slovenia, Poland, and the Russian Federation. In measuring the political consequences, I will use data gathered by the Minorities at Risk Project (University of Maryland) for the region from 1996 to 1998.

Measuring Nationalizing Tendencies among Majority Populations

The ISSP survey included a number of questions that allow me to capture majority (and ultimately minority) views of the nation and its membership. A scale of support for a policy of "nationalizing nationalism" was constructed on the basis of responses to the following five questions, each with five-item responses ranging from "very important" to "not very important":

vi5   "How important do you think each of the following is for being truly (*Polish, etc.*)? To have been born in the country?"

vi6   "How important do you think it is for (*R's nationality*) to have citizenship?"

vi8   "How important do you think it is to speak (*R's country's dominant language*)?"

vi9   "How important do you think it is to share (*R's dominant religion*)?"

v45   "How much do you agree with the following statement about minorities in your country: It is impossible for people who don't share (*R's country's*) customs and traditions to become fully (*Polish, etc.*)?"

The more the respondents "agree strongly" with the above, the more they support a model of "nationalizing nationalism," and the more their minorities are potentially at risk. The five items are highly intercorrelated and seem to tap into a single underlying conception of the nation (Cronbach's alpha = 0.65 of the pooled data for the seven East European countries).

The mean responses of majority and minority populations in each of the seven states are depicted in table 5.1, and the difference between the two scores is calculated to estimate the degree of polarization present in that society. Evans (1998) has defined ethnic polarization as the "extent of measurable distance between the positions taken by members of the ethnic majority and members of ethnic minorities on issues concerning citizenship and minority rights" (Evans 1998, 2). The table clearly demonstrates, according to this definition, that majorities and minorities are most polarized in Bulgaria, Latvia, and Slovakia, at least in terms of their understanding of what is required for full membership in the political community.

In Bulgaria, the self-identified majority held the strongest "nationalizing" views on the criteria most important for "full" membership in the community. Bulgarian respondents valued the importance of shared traditions, a shared language, and being born in the country above all other majorities in the region. This was not, however, a visible or apparent response to nationalist attitudes of the minority Turk and Roma populations, who on average expressed

TABLE 5.1 Ethnic Polarization: Mean Score on National Identity Items and Nationalizing Nationalism Scale

		Born in country	Citizenship	Speak language	Share religion	Share Traditions	Scale	N
Czech Republic	Majority	2.00	1.70	1.32	3.16	2.55	10.67	871
	Minority	2.13	1.73	1.33	3.24	2.62	11.09	240
	Difference	0.13	0.03	0.01	0.08	0.07	0.42	
Slovenia	Majority	1.95	1.70	1.33	2.82	2.33	10.11	953
	Minority	2.46	1.82	1.65	2.99	2.51	11.14	83
	Difference	0.51[a]	0.12	0.32[a]	0.17	0.18	1.03[a]	
Poland	Majority	1.80	1.70	1.56	2.42	2.52	9.98	1544
	Minority	2.12	1.83	1.69	2.57	2.60	11.12	54
	Difference	0.32[a]	0.13	0.13	0.15	0.12	1.14[a]	
Bulgaria	Majority	1.56	1.59	1.47	1.82	1.36	7.72	927
	Minority	1.71	1.67	1.92	2.68	2.02	10.10	178
	Difference	0.25[a]	0.12	0.45[a]	0.86[a]	0.66[a]	2.38[a]	
Russia	Majority	1.94	1.79	1.62	2.70	2.38	10.50	1314
	Minority	2.11	1.81	1.96	2.99	3.04	11.85	271
	Difference	0.17[a]	0.02	0.34[a]	0.29[a]	0.66[a]	1.35[a]	
Latvia	Majority	1.95	1.74	1.35	2.72	1.90	9.63	618
	Minority	2.29	2.27	1.84	2.90	2.35	11.61	426
	Difference	0.34[a]	0.53[a]	0.49[a]	0.22[a]	0.45[a]	1.98[a]	
Slovakia	Majority	2.11	1.62	1.33	3.09	3.63	13.03	1216
	Minority	2.29	1.96	1.84	3.22	3.00	11.18	172
	Difference	0.18[a]	0.34[a]	0.51[a]	0.13	0.63[a]	1.85[a]	

(a.) Indicates difference is significant at $p \_ 0.05$

minority nationalism at levels more than one standard deviation below the level of nationalism expressed by other groups in the region (10.1 vs. 11.4).

The questions above capture attitudes about "what it really takes" to feel "Czech" or "Polish." But this need not result in majorities demanding that the state take action to ensure that minorities either blend in or move. Indeed, it is possible that while respondents might feel it would be better for the minority to learn the dominant language and culture, they would not oppose state policies to allow minorities to protect their own culture. In terms of capturing support for the possibility of constructing the "minority rights" state in the post-communist settings, I look next at majority- and minority-group responses designed to capture support for state policies to protect and even promote minority cultures. Table 5.2 compares the mean responses to the following two questions:

v45 How much do you agree or disagree with the following statement? "Ethnic minorities should be given government assistance to preserve their customs and traditions." (*1 is strongly agree, 5 is strongly disagree*)

v46 Some people say it is better for a country if different racial and ethnic groups maintain their distinct customs and traditions. Others say it is better if these groups try to adapt and blend in to the larger society. Which view comes closest to your own? (*1 is maintain traditions, 2 is blend in*)

The results are presented in table 5.2, in order of state majorities most opposed to the state helping minorities preserve their culture. Again, Bulgaria emerges with the most "nationalizing" majority population in terms of state-policy preferences. Ironically, the Czechs are the second most "opposed" to state promotion of minority interests, but this results in no polarization as their minority populations largely agree with that preference. This may well be reflective of Brubaker's observation that the Czech state best approximates the "civic" model of nation-building, and thus opposes state promotion of any group rights at the expense of individual rights, i.e., "difference-blind" public policies.

Have these attitudes held by East European majorities been articulated in the public sphere? Despite the democratization of the region, the transmission of majority preferences into public policy is not automatic. For one thing, we cannot assess from this preliminary work how deeply held the preferences are; that is, is it the one issue our respondent will bring to the polls and determine the manner in which he or she casts a ballot? Or the one that brings her to the streets? And even if it were, we know that in transitioning states where party systems are not yet well defined or consolidated, cleavages within society may not be reflected in the party system, and may not be reflected in the issues ultimately adopted by the political elite. So what have been the consequences in the political sphere, if any? Are the states with the most nationalizing majorities also the ones that, in the years following the surveys, adopted public policies designed to promote the dominant culture and deliberately demote or assimilate minority cultures?

To begin to answer this question, I turn to data gathered by the Minorities at Risk team on political discrimination and cultural restrictions. The Minorities at Risk Project (MAR) identifies salient ethnopolitical minorities in societies, and attempts to measure annually the degree to which they suffer from collective disadvantages, as a result of deliberate policy or from a policy of neglect or past discrimination.

Within the region (but excluding the former Yugoslavia), the MAR identifies the following countries containing salient ethnopolitical minorities in the 1990s: Hungary, Czech Republic, Slovakia, Bulgaria, Romania, Russia,

TABLE 5.2 Support for "Minority Rights" Model of Nation

		State should help minorities preserve traditions	Groups should maintain traditions
Bulgaria	Majority	2.98	1.52
	Minority	1.40	1.08
	Difference	1.58[a]	0.44[a]
Czech Republic	Majority	2.84	1.49
	Minority	2.86	1.55
	Difference	–0.02	–0.06
Slovakia	Majority	2.65	1.42
	Minority	1.50	1.12
	Difference	1.15[a]	0.30[a]
Latvia	Majority	2.43	1.31
	Minority	1.98	1.26
	Difference	0.45[a]	0.05
Poland	Majority	2.27	1.47
	Minority	2.00	1.41
	Difference	0.27	0.06
Slovenia	Majority	2.26	1.46
	Minority	1.99	1.42
	Difference	0.27	0.04
Russia	Majority	2.09	1.20
	Minority	1.87	1.11
	Difference	0.22	0.09

(a.) Indicates difference is significant at $p \_ 0.05$

Estonia, Latvia, and Lithuania. The initial political-discrimination index attempts to measure the degree of minority group underrepresentation in politics, and to assess whether it is the result of a deliberate strategy of exclusion (dissimilation), or results from a failure to redress past restrictions and their consequences.

The index of cultural restrictions measures policy restrictions in seven specific policy categories:[1] the observance of a religion, use of group language, school instruction in minority language, celebration of group holidays or ceremonies, dress or appearance, marriage and/or family life, and the formation and work of organizations that promote the group's cultural interests.

While few states maintain outwardly restrictive political policies (EU pre-accession agreements would work against them), political discrimination and cultural restrictions are more widespread even in the countries usually cited as examples of successful democracies (as opposed to the war-torn region of the former Yugoslavia).

While the sharpest restrictions on cultural organization, language instruction, and language use in general are to be found in the Balkans, informal and formal restrictions are also to be found in Slovakia, Romania, and Lithuania. The precarious position of the Roma in East Central Europe remains, as does the dilemma they pose to policymakers in the region. What is interesting to note here is that the ethnic majority identified most with "nationalizing nationalism" in the 1995 *National Identity* study (ISSP 1995), the Bulgarians, have not sought or received much support to that end. Bulgaria's treatment of its Turkish minority in the years following the survey, in terms of both the formal and informal restrictions measured by the MAR study, does not reflect an overly nationalistic or exclusive agenda. But divisions remain, and the opposition Socialist Party in Bulgaria did seek to exploit popular dissatisfaction with EU-oriented economic as well as social reforms, adopting the slogan "Enough is enough!" in parliamentary election campaigns (Assenova, 2).

The second most polarized society was Latvia, and here the news was also better. While Latvia (along with Estonia) was originally identified as a state seeking to dissimilate its ethnic Russians, in 1998 the measured discrimination was dramatically reduced, as were overt political restrictions on Russian speakers in Latvia. This is a direct result of the amendments to the formerly very restrictive citizenship law, which abolished age and residency requirements and granted anyone born in Latvia after 1992 automatic citizenship—which clearly extended more rights to Russians and dramatically increased the number of Russians able to naturalize after 1998.

Estonia, which had a similarly restrictive citizenship law, has been more guarded in its amendments to those laws, despite considerable external pressure from the European Union and the OSCE. Language restrictions remain in place and make it more difficult to become naturalized; and within the public sphere, restrictions based on language proficiency continue to inhibit Russian representation in the civil service and local/state government offices.[2] The European Parliament's Committee on Foreign Affairs and Human Rights, evaluating pre-accession progress for Estonia and Latvia, notes that both countries meet all basic criteria, even in the area of protection of minority rights. The rapporteur notes, however, that Estonian language laws contain provisions that remain "over zealous" in the attempt to limit use of non-Estonian languages (European Parliament).

The third most polarized society, on the basis of the *National Identity* survey, was Slovakia. Here we note again that the Roma are still subject to socially exclusionary policies that leave them outside the mainstream of society, but

TABLE 5.3 Minorities at Risk Assessments of Political Discrimination and Cultural Restrictions

		Political Discrimination[a]	Cultural Restrictions[b]
Hungary	Roma	1	0
Czech Republic	Roma	4	5
	Slovaks	3	0
Slovakia	Roma	3	5
	Magyars	2	4
Bulgaria	Roma	4	0
	Turks	0	0
Romania	Roma	3	1
	Magyars	1	2
Latvia	Russians	1	1
Estonia	Russians	4	0

(a.) 0 = no discrimination; 1 = past discrimination, some remedial measures taken; 2 = past discrimination, no remedial measures taken; 3 = social exclusion; 4 = deliberate exclusion. (b.) 0–9 count of number of restrictions such as those on the observance of a religion, use of a language, school instruction in a language, or the formation of cultural organizations.

that official restrictions against them, as well as the Magyar (Hungarian)
minority, are less visible. However, in the cultural sphere, we note a restrictive
policy against the Hungarian minority, especially with regard to language use
and instruction in public institutions. After the 1998 elections, however,
progress was made, and the attempts by the previous Meciar regime to restrict
the use of Hungarian were rescinded by the new government as early as 1999,
under pressure especially from the European Union to conform to more inclusive language policies. There is some concern expressed by the Hungarian
community, however, that the redistricting of parliamentary constituencies was
intentionally designed to reduce and dilute Hungarian representation. And the
1998 New Democracies Barometer team also identified Slovakia as the country in the region where over 40 percent of the survey respondents saw ethnic
minorities in their country as a "threat to peace and security" in society
(Haerpfer 1999, 1001).

Predicting Majority Support for Minority Rights

While MAR records progress in the states for which we have survey data on
minority rights, monitoring the potential revival of ethnically based nationalism in the region remains a central policy concern. Recent tensions in Macedonia over the implementation of an agreement on the rights of the ethnic
Albanian minority demonstrate the continued relevance of identity politics for

the post-communist space.[3] It is therefore worth continuing to examine the sources of ethnic nationalism at the individual level. Which individuals are most likely to develop exclusive nationalizing tendencies?

We begin by calculating a score for all members of the majority group in each state on the nationalizing index as our dependent variable, with the highest scores representing support for the most nationalizing projects.

Theoretical Approaches

Economic, political, and psychological *insecurity* have often been seen as the root of past "scapegoating" of ethnic or racial minorities. In his review of the group-psychology literature, Horowitz (1985) suggests that a group's apprehension about survival, swamping, or subordination can result in "anxiety reactions" that appear extreme in response to the actual threat posed by other groups. "There are relationships among self-esteem, anxiety, and prejudice. Prejudice allows a discharge of hostility, thereby reducing anxiety. A correlation has also been found between lack of individual self-esteem and degree of hostility towards out groups, and the same relationship should hold for group self-esteem" (Horowitz 1985, 179).

The relationship between perceived swamping and hostility to the non-titular group has been empirically examined in the region. McIntosh et al. found, for example, that Bulgars living in a mixed Turkish-Bulgarian community voiced "greater intolerance of minority rights," which they measured as support for schooling in a native language, minority representatives in parliament, and the right to form cultural organizations (1995, 962). Majority groups that feel most insecure—economically, politically, or demographically—should be most likely to embark on a nationalizing project to protect and preserve their nation in the face of perceived threats.

Insecurity is operationalized by the following indicators:

ECONOMIC INSECURITY	Country-level: GNP per capita for 1995
	Individual-level: Dummies for unemployed and pensioner status
DEMOGRAPHIC INSECURITY	Whether the respondent lives in a homogeneous majority-populated district, a mixed or split district (10–40 percent minority), or a district populated in the majority by the country's minority population.

A second set of explanations focuses on the emergence of majority nationalizing projects as a function of wide cultural differentials between majority groups and minority populations. According to M. G. Smith, a society characterized by groups with wide cultural differences can only be held together by force, or the domination of one group over all others.[4] When the "moral axioms" of one group differ from one or more other groups in that same society, instability is the result. Domination by one group, the attempt to homogenize the society by assimilation, is a response to cultural differentials that threaten the stability of the state.

Ethnic distinctiveness is thus hypothesized to contribute to the nationalizing tendencies of certain majorities in East Central Europe, and is operationalized using data available from the *Minorities at Risk Dataset*, updated in March 1999.

CULTURAL DIFFERENTIALS   Score on the Ethnic Difference Index (0–11) of the largest minority group

Alternatively, pluralist theorists would argue that tolerance is a product of education and urbanization, which correlate with the adoption of more cosmopolitan views about the world. Individuals from urban areas with higher levels of education have been shown to be more tolerant in studies by McCloskey and Brill (1983), and McIntosh et al. (1995) find indirect support for the thesis in their surveys of Bulgaria and Romania. Jackman (1977, 1978) has countered that while well-educated "liberals" may well express tolerance of minorities in general, in acquiring their liberal education, they may have also developed a strain of individualism that does not permit them to support policies to maintain collective identities. The controversy seems worth exploring in this instance.

COSMOPOLITANISM   Urban, small town, or rural residency level of education (five-category scale from primary through complete higher education)

Finally, majority-group nationalizing tendencies may be seen as a response or reaction to the nationalizing tendencies of their minority populations. If the minority populations in each state have been particularly active and mobilized in demanding special status, autonomy agreements, or preferential political or economic policies designed to increase their visibility in the newly reconfigured state, then counter-nationalizing responses by majorities might be expected. Taking data from the *Minorities at Risk Dataset*, I operationalize minority mobilization as the highest protest score a minority group received in that state in the year before the conduct of this survey, in 1994.

MINORITY MOBILIZATION   Highest score for protest for minority populations in 1994, range (0–5)[5]

Analysis

The technique employed here is OLS regression on the pooled *majority* populations' scores (ranges between 4 and 20) on the nationalizing nationalism scale from the seven countries as our relevant sample. Details on the way in which these indices were constructed are included in table 5.4.

Insecurity was modeled in the first block, followed by cultural differentials, the cosmopolitan indicators, and finally, the minority mobilization measure.

The results are presented in table 5.5. Among the insecurity measures, it seems clear that more economically secure individuals are more civic in their beliefs about who can become a member of the nation. That is, there is a significant relationship between pensioner status and GNP/per capita, which supports the idea that "at risk" individuals are more likely to endorse nationalizing projects. Unemployment status, however, does not significantly predict beliefs about membership in the nation, perhaps because it represents a temporary and more recent phenomenon—unlike pensioner status, which is a more fixed part of an older person's identity and prospects.

The ethnic composition of a respondent's district or administrative unit also influences attitudes about membership in the nation, but not as the insecurity theorists would predict. That is, the larger the minority population in the region, the more civic the views of our majority respondents. Exposure to the "other" has a beneficial impact on the majority, findings more supportive of the liberal cosmopolitan theorists. Similar results were found in a study of pre-independence Estonia. The greater the interaction between Estonians and Russians, the more positive the attitudes towards ethnic integration among the majority Estonians (Anderson, Silver, Titma, and Ponarin 1996).

When we move to consider the cultural differential index, we find that including it does not diminish the significance of the insecurity factors. But the cultural distance between the largest minority and the overall majority group does make a small but significant impact in the expected direction in predicting majority support for ethnic conceptions of the nation.

In the third model, in which we include the measures of cosmopolitanism (education and urban residency), we find strong support for the initial hypothesis. The higher a respondent's level of education, the more urban the area in which they reside, the less likely they are to support nationalizing nationalism. This seems consistent with the notion that support for "multiculturalism" is

TABLE 5.4 Indice Constructtion: Support for Ethnic Nation-Building in Post-Communist Europe

	Majority support for nationalizing project country (million)	Ethnic differences (MAR score)	GNP/Cp 1995 1995 (World Bank)	Minor protest score (MAR set)
Bulgarians	7.72	11	1,330	2
Latvians	9.63	3	2,270	3
Poles	9.98	3	2,790	0
Slovenes	10.11	3	4,600	0
Russians	10.50	9	2,240	4
Czechs	10.67	2	3,870	2
Slovaks	13.30	5	2,950	3

TABLE 5.5 Regression Results: Support for Ethnic Nation-Building in Post-Communist Europe

Dependent Variable: Level of Majority Support for Ethnic Nation-Building

	Model One			Model Two			Model Three		
	B	Std.error	t-ratio	B	Std.error	t-ratio	B	Std.error	t-ratio
Regional ethnic composition	−0.619[a]	0.062	−10.015	−0.566[a]	0.064	−8.909	−0.346[a]	0.063	5.487
GNP per capita	−0.0004[a]	0.000	−11.921	−0.003[a]	0.000	−5.118	−0.0004[a]	0.000	−7.002
Pensioner	1.388[a]	0.091	−15.279	1.382[a]	0.091	15.217	1.041[a]	0.093	11.214
Unemployed	0.107	0.137	0.781	0.009	0.137	0.662	−0.008	0.134	−0.651
Cultural differential index (0–11)				0.006[a]	0.018	3.553	0.142[a]	0.018	7.863
Urban-rural							0.437[a]	0.043	9.363
Education							−0.273[a]	0.040	−6.898
Minority protest scores							−0.377[a]	0.031	−11.970
Constant	16.704	0.169	98.822	15.838	0.296	53.435	16.304	0.321	50.770
Adj.R²	0.070			0.072			0.124		
SEE	3.137			3.133			3.045		
N	6,226								

(a.) Indicates difference is significant at p_.05

more typical in what Bauman (1989) calls "postmodern" societies, while several Central and East European states are still "modernizing" entities.

Finally, we note that support for exclusive ethnic nations does not seem to be related to minority protests or mobilization in that state. Indeed, as minority-group protest scores in 1994 (the year prior to the survey) go up, majority-group respondents' support for exclusive versions of the nation goes down.

Conclusion

While more remains to be specified to better understand the causal factors in the construction and maintenance of ethnic nationalism among majority populations, this study helps to illuminate majority preferences in the region, cataloging cross-national and individual-level variation among these populations. Indeed, the within-country variation is dramatic enough to give us pause the next time we try to paint an entire people with a single national character by aggregating their preferences to a country-level mean.

With this caveat in mind, however, cross-national patterns are observable. While old threats to security in Central Europe seem to be declining, surveys suggest that majorities continue to see ethnic minorities within their borders as a potential threat, to both the nation and its identity. This is true even within relatively homogeneous states like Poland (among the most nationalizing of our majority populations), let alone more plural states like Bulgaria, Slovakia, and Romania. This suggests that while Central European elites may have adopted legislation consistent with the minority-rights regime supported by the European Union, enough in some cases to finally achieve membership, mass attitudes have not uniformly kept apace these efforts.

In those states excluded from the first round of enlargement, like Romania, Bulgaria, Serbia, Croatia, and Macedonia, EU accession rhetoric on the need for decentralized, institutionally pluralistic states with porous, open borders is at odds with an increasingly "hard" external-border regime designed to combat illegal immigration. In the phase-two EU-candidate countries and post-Soviet states living on these hard borders, this incongruity generates insecurity, and "lends credibility to the nationalist insistence" on a hard model of statehood: unitary, centralized, and exclusively protective of the titular nation (Batt 2002). A research agenda that continues to track majority preferences regarding membership in the nation ought to be paired with a broader EU commitment to ensure that elite agreements celebrating minority rights are not so far removed from popular preferences that they lack credibility in practice.

Ethnic Difference Index

Composed of the sum of scores from four separate indicators of ethnocultural distinctiveness from the dominant majority group:

- ▶ Different Language Group (0–3)
- ▶ Different Customs (0–1)
- ▶ Different Belief/Religion (0–3)
- ▶ Different Racial Characteristics (0–3)
- ▶ If all of the above are not coded, then ETHDIFF = 0
- ▶ If Lang is different ETHDIFF = +3
- ▶ If Lang = 2 (bilingual) ETHDIFF = +2
- ▶ If Lang = 3 (group has adopted dom lang) ETHDIFF = +1
- ▶ Add remaining scores from Customs, Belief, Race for a total range from 0–11.

Protest Index

0 No protests by minority group reported

1 Verbal Opposition (letters, petitions, posters, written requests for hearings)

2 Symbolic Resistance (scattered acts of symbolic resistance, sit-ins, marches)

3 Small demonstrations reported (under 10,000)

4 Medium demonstrations (under 100,000)

5 Large-scale demonstrations (riots, strikes, mass rallies, over 100,000)

NOTES

The author would like to acknowledge support from the State University of New York and United University Professions Professional Development Award Committee. I am also grateful to those, including Brian D. Silver and Vicki Hesli, who provided comments on an earlier version of this paper at the Midwest Political Science Association meetings in April 2001, and to the organizers of the "Liberalization and Democratization" Conference sponsored by Michigan State University at Babes-Bolyai University in Cluj, Romania, June 2001.

1. Description of the categories and coding scheme are drawn directly from the Minorities at Risk codebook, downloaded from the website, www.bsos.umd.edu/cidcm/mar.
2. Freedom House website, www.freedomhouse.org, from the *Nations in Transit, 1999–2000* report on Latvia and Estonia; the section entitled "The Rule of Law" deals with minority-rights law.
3. Macedonia is bracing for a November 2004 referendum designed to overturn the principles of the 2001 Ohrid Agreement brokered by the EU, which had staved off civil war between Albanians and Macedonians. Activists pledging to protect "the Macedonian identity" seek to force the plebiscite to overturn a law giving ethnic Albanians a majority voice in 16 of the republic's 80 municipalities (Reuter's, Alertnet.org, 3 September 2004).

4. M. G. Smith, "Some Developments in the Analytic Framework of Pluralism," in Kuper and Smith (1969), cited in Horowitz, *Ethnic Groups in Conflict* (1985).

5. See appendix for exact coding rules.

REFERENCES

Anderson, Barbara A., Brian D. Silver, Mikk Titma, and Eduard D. Ponarin, 1996. Estonian and Russian communities: Ethnic and language relations. *International Journal of Sociology* 26: 25–45.

Assenova, Margarita. 2000. The Schengen list impacts Bulgaria's elections. RFE/RL, Newsline, 22 November.

Batt, Judy. 2002. Fuzzy statehood vs. hard borders: The impact of EU enlargement on Romania and Yugoslavia. ESRC Working Paper 46/02, Sussex European Institute, University of Sussex.

Bauman, Z. 1989. *Modernity and the Holocaust*. Ithaca, NY: Cornell University Press.

Brubaker, Rogers. 1996. *Nationalism reframed: Nationhood and the national question in the New Europe*. Cambridge: Cambridge University Press.

Dahl, Robert. 1971. *Polyarchy*. New Haven: Yale University Press.

Dowley, Kathleen, and Brian D. Silver. Subnational and national loyalty: Cross-national comparisons. *International Journal of Public Opinion Research* 12(4): 357–71.

European Parliament. 2000. Report on Estonia's membership application to the European Union and the state of negotiations. Committee on Foreign Affairs, Human Rights, Common Security and Defence Policy.

Evans, Geoffrey. 1998. Explaining ethnic polarization in Eastern Europe. Paper presented at the Midwest Political Science Association Meeting, 23–25 April.

Evans, Geoffrey, and Stephen Whitefield. 1998. The structuring of political cleavages in post-communist societies: The case of the Czech Republic and Slovakia. *Political Studies* 46: 115–39.

Gurr, Ted Robert. 1993. *Minorities at risk: A global view of ethnopolitical conflict*. Washington, DC: United States Institute for Peace Press.

Haerpfer, Christian, Cezary Milosinski, and Claire Wallace. 1999. Old and new security issues in post-communist Eastern Europe. *Europe-Asia Studies* 51(6): 989–1012.

Hirschman, Albert. 1970. *Exit, voice and loyalty: Responses to decline in firms, organizations, and states*. Cambridge: Harvard University Press.

Horowitz, Donald. 1985. *Ethnic groups in conflict*. Berkeley: University of California Press.

ISSP (International Social Survey Program). 1995. *National Identity 1995*. ICPSR: Study No. 2474.

Jackman, Mary. 1977. Prejudice, tolerance, and attitudes towards ethnic groups. *Social Science Research* 6: 145–69.

———. 1978. General and applied tolerance: Does education increase commitment to racial integration? *American Journal of Political Science* 22: 302–24.

Kaplan, Robert D. 1989. Europe's third world. *Atlantic Monthly*, July.

Kuper, Leo, and M. G. Smith, eds. 1969. *Pluralism in Africa*. Berkeley: University of California Press.

MAR. 1999. *Minorities at Risk Dataset*. Downloaded with permission from the MAR website (http://www.bsos.umd.edu/cidcm/mar).

McClosky, Herbert, and Alida Brill. 1983. *Dimensions of tolerance: What Americans believe about civil liberties*. New York: Praeger Press.

McIntosh, Mary, Martha McIver, Dan Abele, and David Nolle. 1995. Minority rights and majority rule: Ethnic tolerance in Romania and Bulgaria. *Social Forces* 73(3): 939–68.

Mill, John Stuart. [1861] 1951. *Utilitarianism, liberty, and representative government*. New York: E. P. Dutton Press.

Pettai, Vello, and Marcus Kreuzer. 1999. Party politics in the Baltic States: Social bases and institutional context. *East European Politics and Societies* 13(1): 148.

Poolos, Alexandra. 1999. Czech Republic: A wall divides the country. RFE/RL Reports, Feature no. 10 (http://www.rferl.org/reports/).

Popov, Stefan. 1998. Democratic review: Bulgaria and the framework convention on protection of national minorities. *Foreign Policy* (Fall): 153.

Roeder, Philip G. 1999a. The revolution of 1989: Post-communism and the social sciences. *Slavic Review* 58(4):.

———. 1999b. Peoples and states after 1989: The political costs of incomplete national revolutions. *Slavic Review* 58(4).

Silver, Brian D., and Kathleen M. Dowley. 2000. Measuring political culture in multiethnic societies: Reaggregating the world values survey. *Comparative Political Studies* (2).

Smith, Adrian. 2000. Ethnicity, economic polarization, and regional inequality in Southern Slovakia. *Growth and Change* 31: 151–78.

Smith, Anthony. 1993. The ethnic sources of nationalism. In *Ethnic conflict and international security*, ed. Michael Brown. Princeton, NJ: Princeton University Press.

Smith, Tom W., and Lars Jaarko. 1998. National pride: A cross-national analysis. *GSS Cross-National Report*, no. 19, National Opinion Research Center. Chicago: University of Chicago.

Snyder, Jack L. 2000. *From voting to violence: Democratization and nationalist conflict*. New York: Norton.

Wiener, Antje, and Guido Schwellnus. 2004. Contested norms in the process of EU enlargement: Non-discrimination and minority rights. Constitutionalism Web-Papers (CON-Web No. 2/2004).

World Bank. 1996/1997. *World Bank Development Report, 1996/1997*, Washington, D.C.

6

Party Development in Russia

Axel Hadenius

According to an oft-quoted statement by E. E. Schattschneider, "modern democracy is unthinkable save in terms of parties" (1942, 1). As an empirical generalization, this statement is largely true. In the modern world, fairly well-functioning democratic systems without political parties can indeed be found—in a number of island states (Anckar 1997). But these are exceptions, and a result of extremely small scale. In all states of any significant size (with respect to population and territory), democracy is associated with the existence of parties.

There is a simple reason for this. Democracy needs to take the form of representative democracy, wherein elected representatives make decisions on behalf of the citizenry. Other forms of decision making, such as referendums, can be applied as well, but these can only function as a complement to the representative-electoral process (Kitschelt et al. 1999, 5). Electoral competition normally yields a strong incentive for candidates to form parties, or to join parties if such already exist. Parties offer a number of services that are critical for winning elections. By joining forces under a common label, groups of politicians can establish a political "brand name" that is easily recognized among voters. Moreover, parties can offer organizational, economic, and professional resources that are difficult to muster on an individual basis. They furnish candidates with a useful political label; they lower transaction costs for entering the political arena; and, due to the economies of scale they provide, they lower campaign and other costs (Aldrich 1995; Kitschelt 2000; Snyder and Groseclose 2001).

It is no wonder, then, that parties normally exist in democracies. Yet it is one thing to say that parties exist; ascertaining how they actually function is another. Parties operate differently in different democracies. In some, they are the major actors on the political scene; in others, their role is more marginal. Conditions also vary with respect to party cohesion, party organization, and other aspects of party life. Does such variation matter?

Are democracy's fortunes affected, for example, if parties are strongly organized and highly influential—or if they are weakly structured and politically insignificant? In the modern literature on political parties, it is often held that well-developed parties are prerequisite to the maintenance of democratic government. Party "institutionalization" (an oft-used catchword) is seen as a condition for democratic consolidation (Mainwaring and Scully 1995; Mainwaring 1998; Diamond 1999; Miller et al. 2000; Bielasiak 2001; Randall and Svåsand 2002). To my knowledge, however, there is no evidence to support this claim. The link between party development and the survival of democracy, it seems, is mainly taken for granted. There may, of course, be some sort of connection, but this remains to be demonstrated. It is an overstatement, in other words, to say that the "be or not to be" of democracy hinges on the development of a certain type of political party.

So, does the character of political parties really matter for democracy's fortunes? Quite obviously it does. It is not, however, the *survival* of democracy that appears to be the key question. Rather, it is the *nature and quality* of democracy that should be our primary concern. The way parties function affects the way the democratic system works. American parties, for example, diverge from their West European counterparts in several ways. This difference is one important reason for the well-known contrasts in political life between the two sides of the Atlantic (see, e.g., Epstein 1981).

The Elusive Concept of Party Institutionalization

As noted above, it is common to speak of "party institutionalization" in connection with the degree of party development. The expression comes from the work of Samuel Huntington. In his influential book *Political Order in Changing Societies* (1968), Huntington points to the institutionalization of political parties as a core condition for political stability in complex societies. What, then, is institutionalization? According to Huntington, it "is a process by which organizations and procedures acquire *value* and *stability*" (12, my emphasis). Among later researchers, Angelo Panebianco in particular has continued this line of thinking about political parties. Like Huntingdon, Panebianco (1988) talks about institutionalization in two ways. On the one hand, he says, it involves certain values associated with an organization (53). In an institutionalized party, attachment to the party is more than just a matter of applying a means to an end (i.e., to find an instrument to promote certain interests). The party and what it symbolizes has become a value in itself among its members and followers. In effect, the party builds up a reservoir of support based on affection and loyalty. On the other hand, Panebianco considers party institutionalization an indicator of endurance: it denotes "the way the organization solidifies" (49). This aspect of institutionalization, then, bears on the question of party stability.

This way of connecting stability of a party organization and the evolution of certain values associated with it can be traced back to the so-called institutionalist view championed by Philip Selznick. Institutionalization, Selznick (1957) claims, signifies a kind of organizational development that infuses the unit in question with value. This means that the organization has acquired meaning as a way of life for its members and supporters. It is value infusion that permits an organization to endure. Thus there is, in Selznick's view, a causal relationship between the two components: value infusion breeds organizational stability.

The clarity about the character of the relationship (of a causal nature) that is evident in Selznick is lacking, however, in Huntington and Panebianco. The latter two scholars use the two components as dual *definitions* of party institutionalization. This ambiguity has been continued by many of their recent followers, such as Mainwaring and Scully (1995), and Randall and Svåsand (2002). These authors suggest a number of different criteria for party institutionalization. Some of these criteria are largely commonsense in nature; others are extremely vague (as in the case of Randall and Svåsand in particular). Their basic meaning is largely enshrouded in conceptual and methodological fog. Should these criteria be seen as definitions of party institutionalization? Or are they causal conditions (or consequences) of such institutionalization?[1] The reasoning, furthermore, is almost tautological at times. Mainwaring, for example, mentions a connection between institutionalization and party age (1999, 31). Institutionalized parties are likely to have a longer organizational existence behind them. Before reaching this conclusion, however, Mainwaring has already defined institutionalized parties as those that enjoy considerable stability (1999, 26).[2]

An Alternative Approach

As I see it, this way of addressing the problem of party development represents a dead end.[3] On the one hand, the basic concept—that of party institutionalization—is too vague; on the other, it is too limited. Its inherent ambiguity has been demonstrated above. Yet this ambiguity could of course be straightened out: we could simply decide to return to Selznick's approach. We would then focus on party stability, while value infusion would be considered a possible explanatory factor. Yet this, in turn, would be too limited an approach. For it is not just the continued existence of parties that interests us when we set out to ascertain the strength and political significance of parties. (Parties can perfectly well be old and yet weak in certain respects: the extraordinary stability of American parties—notwithstanding their organizational fragility—illustrates the point). It is this basic understanding, I assume, that has motivated Mainwaring and Scully (and others too) to lump together a broad range of characteristics under the party-institutionalization umbrella—which has further added to the vagueness of the concept.

We need, I think, a more general and less confusing concept as our starting point. In the analysis that follows, I will speak broadly of *party development* in various areas (most of which bear on the question of party strength). Taking my cue from the work of V. O. Key (1964), I will consider development in three fields: (1) party in government, (2) party in the citizenry, and (3) party as organization.[4]

However, party development (or party strength) cannot be determined without a context. Some point of reference is necessary. The most interesting point of reference, as I see it, is democracy—namely, how party development affects the functioning of democracy.

Huntington's concern (1968), as we saw, was with the preservation of the existing political order. He had no specific preference for democracy as such. His interest in the maintenance of political order included all kinds of political systems—even plainly authoritarian ones. Panebianco, for his part, does not discuss party development with reference to democracy either. Taking his inspiration from organizational theory, he focuses chiefly on the internal life of parties, while party stability—in itself—appears to be his overriding objective. More recent researchers have followed in Huntington's tracks, but have been oriented more explicitly to the question of democratic stability (i.e., how it is contingent—presumably—on the development of political parties). As noted above, however, this connection has not yet been theoretically specified and empirically verified. Until that has been done, it is premature to argue that party development (in the one respect or the other) facilitates the preservation of democracy.

We do know, however, that the organization and behavior of parties can affect the nature and quality of democracy. To evaluate the development of parties, therefore, we need certain normative democratic criteria to serve as our point of reference.

This may appear to be a useless hassle. We all know, after all, that several normative theories of democracy are available in the academic marketplace. Which criteria shall we choose? Is this essentially an arbitrary choice? It is not,

I would argue, in the case of political parties. The fundamental rationale for political parties is to serve as vehicles of political representation. Parties are the instruments by which citizens delegate authority to the men and women who exercise the power of public decision making. Hence, representation—that is, responsiveness to the views and interests of citizens—stands out as the most relevant criterion. Of course, other democratic values, such as participation or deliberation, might be thought applicable here as well. Where the latter criteria are concerned, however, the natural focal point is by no means political parties. Participation and deliberation, it could be said, are better served by other means than through parties. I would contend, however, that in the case of democratic representation, political parties serve as a vital prerequisite.[5] This may be illustrated by a closer look at the logic of representation.

Democratic representation entails the delegation of political authority. All forms of delegation, in turn, present a principal/agent dilemma. The challenge faced by the principal turns on his/her ability to steer the actions of the agent (and thus to guarantee proper representation by the latter). In general terms, there are three difficulties here. One is to find an agent with the requisite personal qualifications—both morally and in respect of competence (the agent, after all, could turn out to be a complete failure or a crook). Moreover, even if this problem is not present, two other difficulties remain. Asymmetry in preferences and in information between the principal and the agent may impel the latter to act in a manner unrepresentative of the interests of the former. Accordingly, the more the principal knows about the personal qualities and preferences of the agent, and the more the agent shares information with the principal, the better equipped is the principal to select a suitable agent and to hold him or her accountable (Moe 1984; Strom 2000).

In political life, it is parties that have supplied the answer to the principal/agent dilemma. Parties offer the voters a choice among different policy packages. Herein, of course, lies a limitation: there are, normally, only a restricted number of policy packages from which to choose (only certain parties, in other words, stand a chance of being elected). Still, the existence of parties makes the voter's choice easier and more reliable. It increases the ability of the principal (i.e., the voter) to find an agent who holds similar preferences, and who is able—by means of concerted action with fellow party representatives in decision-making bodies—to act effectively in support of such preferences. Coherent parties offering relatively distinct policy alternatives make it easier for the voters to find a policy platform in accord with their own political agenda, and to hold their chosen agents accountable (through upcoming elections). The risk of preference asymmetry can thus be reduced.

Where the screening of candidates' personal attributes is concerned, parties normally have an interest in being able to project a clean and professional image; accordingly, they tend to apply codes of behavior whereby individuals who do not meet certain standards find their career ambitions thwarted. In addition, parties serve as channels of information on policy matters, both during and between elections, as they may have an interest in (and resources for) explaining their position on current questions to their followers.

It is generally to the advantage of voters, then, if the party system is basically stable. This follows from the fact that it takes time to build up a political reputation. A history of policy stands and voting records is required; it is only thus that voters can be furnished with the information requisite to making a well-informed choice. By contrast, a fluid party system—wherein parties quickly come and go—increases the likelihood of preference asymmetry (Mainwaring 1998; Rose et al. 2001). A longer record also makes it easier for voters to make a valid judgment of the personal qualities of candidates, as well as of the accuracy of information provided by parties. Besides, it takes time to set up appropriate procedures for internal screening and information exchange.

Criteria of Party Development

Using a threefold typology drawn largely from the work of V. O. Key (1964), we can distinguish a number of criteria that seem relevant in regard to political representation:

PARTY IN GOVERNMENT

The question here is the extent to which parties serve as agents of representation in the organs of public decision making. In well-developed party systems, the following conditions apply:

1. Persons tied to political parties dominate all representative organs—both parliamentary and executive, and at both national and regional levels (Rose et al. 2001). This is not to say representatives at the regional level must be attached to national parties; regional parties can exist as well. However, a weak presence of national parties at the regional level often indicates a weakly developed party network out in the country. Such weakness may undermine the capacity of the party in question to act vigorously on the national level.

2. Parties operate as unitary actors in representative organs. They form stable party blocs whose members act in concert. There should be no floor-crossing among the deputies—no constant movement between party blocs. Nor should the votes of individual representatives diverge on important political

issues from the party line. In other words, the parties must be able to control the behavior of their representatives (Kiewiet and McCubbins 1991). This presupposes a frequent and effective use of the party whip. The advantage of such practices, from the standpoint of representation, is that unitary parties can more easily be held accountable (Strom 1990).

PARTY IN THE CITIZENRY

The question here concerns the relationship between parties and the citizens. Three aspects will be observed: the stability of parties, party attachment among citizens, and the coherence of party support.

As we saw, a high degree of party-system stability enhances voters' ability to choose rationally among parties, using political platform and past performance as a guide. Stability manifests itself in the magnitude of change between elections.[6] This can be measured in two ways. One is by counting the number and proportion of parties that appear and disappear in elections (Rose et al. 2001).[7] Another is by noting the level of volatility—i.e., the overall change in electoral outcome for different parties from one election to another. This is normally expressed in an index ranging from 0 to 1—with the former extreme indicating no change at all, and the latter indicating total change (Pedersen 1979). A stable party system, accordingly, exhibits a high degree of "frozenness" (cf. Lipset and Rokkan 1967), together with a low magnitude of change (volatility) in elections.

Stability in the party system presupposes stable patterns of voting—that many people vote for the same party in election after election. Such patterns of voting, in turn, presuppose a high degree of attachment between parties and citizens. Attachment of this kind is usually assessed by measuring party identity—a method that taps the mass basis of party support. Studies of party identity seek to measure the proportion of citizens who regard themselves as supporters of a given party (Weisberg 1999). Another way of assessing party attachment is to investigate the magnitude of split voting. If voters select different parties in different elections, this is a token of weak ties between parties and citizens (Aldrich 1995).

If effective representation is to be achieved, it is desirable that people of the same "sort"—in respect of demographic characteristics or policy orientation—cast their vote for the same party. This way, parties can serve as a channel for certain interests and policy demands in society (Kitschelt 2000). If this is the case, we can expect those who vote for party A to be different from those who vote for parties B and C. This is a matter of electoral coherence. People of similar background are able to join forces behind the same party. Their votes, accordingly, are not arbitrary—and the parties can offer a real choice.

PARTY AS ORGANIZATION

A party apparatus is a means for gaining recognition and support (Panebianco 1988). A developed organization provides resources that encourage electoral coherence, party attachment, and party stability. In addition, it can enhance party dominance and party unity in representative organs. However, access to vital resources can also create a troublesome dependence on the external interests providing such resources. From a representation standpoint, moreover, the mode of decision making—i.e., the incidence of internal democracy—should be considered as well.

Where party resources are concerned, a number of parameters play a role. It is normally an important asset to have a sizeable number of members, as well as a core of supporters who can be called upon for party work. Traditionally, a large and committed group of followers was the essential instrument for reaching out and communicating the party agenda. In modern times, by contrast, more direct forms of communication—advertisements, media, etc.—have come to play an ever-greater role. Nonetheless, it is still a plus to have access to party people "on the ground" (Aldrich 1995). It is advantageous, moreover, to have an organizational network—party units and party offices—all over the country. Furthermore, economic resources are critically important. Once upon a time, membership fees could be a major source of revenue (which in turn added to the weight of a large membership). Today, however, party financing relies primarily on external sources, of a public or private nature. Besides contributions in cash, support in kind can be most helpful. Such support can take various forms. Well-organized parties have often developed close ties with strong interest groups in society. A connection of this kind can help to strengthen a party's profile (the party can, so to speak, borrow identity from its support group). In addition, it can serve as a vital source of recruitment—of both leaders and members. Finally, the party can draw on the organization and communication network commanded by the auxiliary group (Crewe 1981).

This brings us to the problem of independence. On the one hand, as we saw above, access to resources strengthens a party's ability to reach out and gain support in elections. This can enhance the party's capacity to serve as an instrument of representation. On the other hand, the way in which these resources are supplied may entail chains of dependency vis-à-vis the interests in society commanding such resources (Panebianco 1988). This can have detrimental consequences from the standpoint of representation, since it builds in a tendency towards structural preference asymmetry between voters and their party representatives. (The risk is that the representatives will come to regard themselves more as agents of those providing external support than of their voters.) This is indeed a tricky balance. The usual ways of coping with the problem include establishing rules for the regulation of support (especially financial support) from private sources, as well as introducing public subsidies for parties in order to make them less dependent on private sponsors.

This final criterion—the use of democratic internal procedures—stands out as the most controversial. From the standpoint of such democratic values as participation and deliberation, the use of such procedures may seem to be quite obviously called for; after all, internal democracy promotes activity and discussion among party members (Scarrow 1999; Teorell 1999). It has been argued, however, that the use of such procedures has unfavorable effects from the standpoint of representation. To cut a long story short, one effect in particular is of concern here: the fact that internal democracy opens the door to highly effectual intervention by party activists. Such activists are prone to hold more extreme political preferences than supporters of the party in general. The system of representation can thus get distorted (May 1973; McKenzie 1982). All the same, I would contend that democratic internal procedures do, overall, promote the ideal of representation. The use of open procedures for decision making provides opportunities for party people to gain insight into, and influence over, the selection of party representatives. An important "filter"—whereby candidates can be screened for their personal qualities—is thus established. In addition, the use of such procedures put constant pressure on the party leadership to give an account of its doings between elections. This lessens the risk of information asymmetry. On both counts, the tendency towards "backroom politics" can be counteracted. At the same time, it becomes possible to curtail any drift towards personalism (whereby the party becomes merely an instrument for a dominant individual).[8] Party activists normally play an important role in these regards. Moreover, it is these activists in particular who tend to lobby for the intensification of the policy platform, thus serving to counteract tendencies towards a political congruence between parties, and a resultant lack of distinctive alternatives in elections. Furthermore, it is this group that puts the greatest pressure on political representatives to stick to party voting (Aldrich 1995; Grofman et al. 1999). Thus, while the group is not necessarily representative with regard to policy preferences, it can contribute in several ways, via democratic procedures of internal decision making, to strengthening the mechanisms of representation.[9]

Russian Parties in Perspective

On the basis of the criteria laid out above, I shall now examine the development of parties in Russia. In an effort to put Russian conditions in perspective, I shall at each point provide a (necessarily brief) description of the standing of parties in Western Europe and in the United States.[10] In certain cases, moreover, I shall compare the development of parties in Russia with that in the new democracies of Central and Eastern Europe, and Latin America as well.

PARTY IN GOVERNMENT

The question here, as we know, concerns the dominance and cohesiveness of parties in representative bodies. Where dominance is concerned, it is well known that the electoral system plays a part. The general rule is that parties are better able to dominate the scene in proportional systems, since the latter feature elections by list in large districts. Such lists require a common designation (indicating that a group of some kind lies behind the electoral effort). Moreover, the list in question must enjoy fairly broad support from the electorate if its candidates are to be elected; this requirement is particularly plain in systems where a party's vote must exceed a fairly high threshold if the party is to enter parliament. Individual (i.e., non-party-affiliated) candidates make their mark more easily in elections from single-member districts (SMD). Elections of this type exhibit a strong local connection. Here, more than in proportional systems, it is a question of serving one's district. A candidate's personal standing in the locality in question can be of great aid in getting elected. Another important factor is whether an absolute majority of votes is needed in order to be elected, or whether a mere plurality is sufficient. The latter type of arrangement increases the chances of election, which favors non-party-affiliated candidates. The manner in which the executive is chosen is important too. Parties have, as a rule, a stronger position in parliamentary than in presidential systems. The former type of system requires more in the way of coordination and cohesion in the legislative body—and it is parties that are able to supply this. Presidential elections may also feature a significant personal element, which renders the candidates less dependent on party backing. This effect is reinforced if the presidential election does not take place on the same date as the legislative one (Epstein 1981; Shugart and Carey 1992).

Where the cohesiveness of parties is concerned, we have seen that (due to necessity) it is more pronounced in parliamentary systems. It is also often greater in unitary than in federal states, inasmuch as strong regional interests are usually present in parties within states of the latter type. The procedures by which elections are conducted have an impact as well. The critical thing here, however, is not whether the elections are proportional or based on single-member districts. An important factor—irrespective of electoral system—is how the nomination of candidates is done. The cohesiveness of a party is affected by whether nominations within it are controlled by the central leadership, or whether instead they take place under local control. In the same way, the degree to which the leadership can control the resources needed for winning elections is important (a matter to which we shall return below). Such resources give the leadership a strong trump card in dealing with recalcitrant party delegates. Similarly, control over career opportunities and access to resources in the parliamentary organs endow the leadership with a weapon for maintaining cohesion (Kitschelt et al. 1999; van Biezen 2000).

Let us now consider conditions in Western Europe and the United States. In both cases, parties exercise a large measure of dominance in the representative organs—and at both national and regional levels. With only occasional exceptions, the members of legislative bodies and the occupants of executive office are associated with parties. Elected representatives are furthermore faithful to their party to a high degree: floor-crossing is unusual. Where voting in legislative assemblies is concerned, however, there is a difference. In votes of a party-dividing kind, cohesion tends to be very strong in West European parties: in many countries, representatives vote with their party in more than 95 percent of such cases. In the United States, party-line voting has certainly increased over recent decades, but it remains lower than in Western Europe: in party-dividing votes, about 80 percent of congressmen toe the party line.

Let us turn our attention now to Russia. Where the dominance of parties is concerned, conditions in that country are undeniably different. In elections to the State Duma, a mixed electoral system is applied. Half the members are chosen through proportional list elections (with a threshold of 5 percent); the other half are elected from single-member districts. Those elected on a proportional basis are, as might be expected, party-connected throughout. In the other category, by contrast, an extremely large number of independent candidates have been elected. (This applies in the case of all three elections to that body: in 1993, 1995, and 1999.) The proportion fell in 1995, but it increased again in 1999. In the latest election, according to the calculations of Rose et al. (2001), a majority (51 percent) of the members elected from single-member districts were independents.[11] This, furthermore, is probably to some extent an underestimate. In a good many cases, those reckoned as associated with a party had an extremely weak connection to it. At times, it was simply a matter whereby a party expressed its support for a local candidate who seemed to have a good chance of winning (Ishiyama 2000). Furthermore, the electoral procedure applied (only a plurality is needed), together with the great number of candidates (on average 10 per district), meant that only a modest measure of support was required in order to get elected. In general, those winning election from single-member districts in 1999 had the support of just 30 percent of the electorate; in some cases, the share of the vote was actually under 20 percent. These conditions have likely made it easier for independent candidates to win. As we know, comparable electoral procedures are applied in many countries— Great Britain and the United States, for example—without comparable effects arising. In these cases, elections are completely party-dominated, notwith-standing the use of single-member districts. The difference is that the parties with a serious chance are substantially fewer, and better equipped in terms of resources.

In the 1999–2003 Duma, only three-quarters of the members can be classified (generously) as elected with a party connection. In addition, the cor-responding proportion in the upper chamber, the Council of Federation (the members of which are chosen by regional organs), is appreciably smaller still. In this chamber, it is only a minority of members who can be said to represent a party, and sometimes only diffusely (Remington 2003). In view of the com-position of corresponding bodies in other federal states—e.g., Germany, the United States, and Brazil—this is a remarkable fact.

The presidential office in Russia is extremely powerful. The striking thing is that the two occupants of this office hitherto (Yeltsin and Putin) have not rep-resented any party. Their mandate, rather, has been a personal one. To be sure, both presidents have had a "party in power" (of a shifting kind) associated with them. But they have not themselves been the leader—or even a member—of the party in question (McFaul 2001). This is, in comparative perspective, an exceptional circumstance. Nowhere else in the democratic world are similar conditions known to prevail. In Latin America, it is true, political "outsiders" have appeared several times over the course of recent decades, and have tri-umphed in presidential elections (as in Brazil, Peru, and Venezuela). All of these leaders, however, have ended up creating a party (or at any rate a politi-cal movement) to serve as a basis for their operations. Yet this has not been the case in Russia. The parties employed by Russian presidents have been dispos-able goods: in no case have they lasted longer than a single term.

Turning now to the regional level, we see that parties tend to have a very weak standing in legislative assemblies. A study of these organs' operations between 1993 and 1997, by Stoner-Weiss (2001), has demonstrated a heavy dominance by independent candidates (see also Golosov 2000). At the end of this period, parties controlled about 17 percent of the positions in such organs—11 percent in the case of national parties, 5 percent in the case of regional ones. Among the national parties, only one could boast representation of any significance—the Communist Party, with 7 percent. Among the other parties that cleared the threshold for representation in the Duma election of 1995, all had a share of less than 1 percent in regional bodies.[12] As expected, parties were best represented in regions applying some kind of parliamentary system.

In gubernatorial elections (which are politically much more important), parties have sought to make their mark as well. Here, too, their efforts have met with but limited success (albeit greater success than in the case of the regional legislatures). Stoner-Weiss reckons that 19 of the 73 governors (or 26 percent) who were elected between 1995 and 1997 were clearly associated with the Communist Party. By contrast, other national parties won just a few governorships here and there, as did the regional parties. In other words, a clear majority of governors had no party affiliation at this time. However, later figures from the same author point to a clear improvement for the parties. In the gubernatorial elections of 2000, independent candidates emerged victorious in just 18 percent of the cases (8 of 44). Candidates associated with national parties won in all the other cases. The elections went best for the Communists, who won 12 gubernatorial posts (27 percent). It bears noting, however, that more than one party often declared itself the winner (since the candidate in such cases had dual—or diffuse—party affiliations). In the more unambiguous cases too, moreover, the winning candidate's party connections have tended to be tenuous. In their actual policies, most governors demonstrate independence; seldom do they follow any clear party line. In this regard, however, they are scarcely unique to the Russian Federation. Governors in the United States, after all, take positions on concrete political questions without reference to the national parties to which they belong.

Turning now to the question of the parties' parliamentary cohesiveness, we may note that the studies that have been done of voting behavior in the State Duma testify to a relatively high degree of party unity. Even in the case of voting patterns in the first Duma (that of 1994–95), studies have demonstrated a surprisingly high degree. In many of the party groups, 80 to 90 percent of members voted with their party on politically controversial questions. Only occasionally did the figure fall to 70 percent or just under (Haspel et al. 1998; Remington 1998). Moreover, studies of the second Duma (that of 1996–99) have indicated a successive improvement in the parliamentary cohesion of the parties (Thames 2001; Belyaev et al. 2002). In view of the fact that the Russian party system has been created practically from scratch (1995), this could be seen as a remarkable development. The level of cohesiveness for most of the Russian parties is now nearly on a par with that in Western Europe (and higher than that in the United States). Perhaps, therefore, we can say with McFaul that "the core of a party system has emerged within the Russian parliament" (2001, 1171). The representative function of parties, we might then conclude, is becoming stronger in Russia.

Unfortunately, however, this appears to be an overstated conclusion. There are two important factors that make for a less palatable impression. The one has to do with the relationship between parties as electoral organizations and as parliamentary units. It is critical, from the standpoint of representation, that the party formations that run in elections find their direct correspondence in parliament (Rose et al. 2001). To a substantial extent, however, this is not the case in Russia.

The party groups in the Duma are of two kinds. First, all parties winning representation in the proportional part of the election have the right to form parliamentary factions. Second, groups consisting of at least 35 deputies can come together and form a deputy group with a certain designation. There are strong incentives to belong to a parliamentary group, since membership yields advantages in terms of administrative resources, influence over the Duma leadership, better opportunities to take part in floor debates, etc. (Haspel et al. 1998; Thames 2001). By such means, the leadership of these groups is often able to exert great influence over the voting patterns of the members. It is this that was shown in the above-mentioned studies. The problem is that these groups correspond only in part with the parties (or party blocs) that ran for election. First, several large parties have split into different factions in the Duma: this took place, for example, at the inauguration of the present Duma in the case of the Communists and Fatherland-All Russia. It is also common for persons who have been elected as party representatives from a single-member district—but whose party did not clear the threshold in the proportional election—to join up with another party's faction. Second, parliamentary groups have been created that do not correspond to any of the parties that ran for election. Often these consist of independent candidates; however, they have also attracted deputies who were chosen as representatives for a party—both in the proportional election, and in the single-member districts. The regrouping that has thus taken place has embraced some 25 percent of the Duma members after the election of 1999. In the present Duma there are, in addition to the party factions, three deputy groups. One of these corresponds to a party that failed to clear the threshold, but that did better in the single-member districts (and that also acquired deputies from another party). The other two may be regarded largely as bodies created ad hoc (Rose et al. 2001).

The other circumstance making for a dispiriting impression is the substantial measure of floor-crossing that has take place. To be sure, deputies have generally been members of a Duma group (and have voted with it); however, there has also been great mobility among the groups. It has been calculated that, in the first Duma, 25 percent of the deputies changed group affiliation at least once over the parliamentary term. The proportion in the second Duma was approximately as large (Haspel et al. 1998; Rose et al. 2001).[13] In comparison with legislative bodies in other countries, the Russian Duma exhibits very high figures in this area. To find anything comparable, we must make our way to Brazil, a country that is conspicuous—even by the standards of Latin America (where parties are generally considered weak)—for its extremely high level of floor-crossing (Mainwaring 1999; Mainwaring and Scully 1995). It is clear, in sum, that the positive picture considered above—which looked attractive as long as we restricted our investigations to voting behavior within the parliamentary groups—proves to be much less attractive when we take into account how these groups have been formed, and still less so when we recall the degree of mobility among them. The establishment of the "core of a party system" in parliament—which, in many countries, has served historically as the basis from which a stable and well-developed party system has emerged (Duverger 1954)—remains for the most part to be accomplished.

PARTY IN THE CITIZENRY

Let us now consider the parties' contacts with their principals—those whom they exist to represent: the voters, and through them the population as a whole. There are three aspects to bear in mind here. The first aspect is the stability of the party system, which is a question of party permanence and of mobility between elections. The second aspect is the intensity of attachment between parties and citizens, which can be measured in two ways: in the level of party identification in the population, and in the incidence of split voting. The third aspect treated here is the degree of political coherence among citizens. The question is whether those who support, or vote for, a given party exhibit any group characteristics—i.e., whether they, in respect of social traits or political attitudes, have anything in common.

Again, we should begin our examination with a look at conditions in Western Europe and the United States. We find several common denominators here. The level of stability in both cases has been extremely high. Where Western Europe is concerned, Lipset and Rokkan (1967) noted that the party structure established at the time of democracy's breakthrough in the early 1920s remained, in all essentials, unchanged at the start of the 1960s. Forty years later, this "freezing" of the party system mainly persists. The old parties—socialists, liberals, conservatives, and Christian democrats—still dominate the scene in the great majority of the countries of Western Europe. Certain changes have indeed occurred. Communist parties have retreated, making way for left socialist parties. Newer arrivals have included green parties, regional parties, and parties of the far right. But on the whole, the changes have been marginal. Generally speaking, the old parties—with roots reaching back 80 years or more—attract close to 90 percent of the vote in Western Europe. The old left/right division remains; indeed, it has come to set the tone of political conflict all the more. More and more clearly, there are two blocs of parties confronting one another. The electoral support accruing to each bloc, furthermore, is almost exactly the same as in the 1950s. In the United States, for its part, political life has been dominated for 150 years by the same two parties: the Democrats and the Republicans. A so-called Progressive Party was established at the end of the nineteenth century, and for a few decades it enjoyed some significant successes. Similarly, a formation known as the Reform Party appeared in the early 1990s. For a short time, it attracted substantial support in opinion polls and among voters. Its story, however, was a brief one, and today it is practically gone. It is the two old parties, once again, that dominate the scene completely.

The normally high degree of party loyalty exhibited by voters is also evident in the degree of volatility—that is, in the changes in party support—taking place from one election to another. In the United States, it has long remained under 10 percent, a sign of great stability. The average figure in Western Europe was for a long time around 10 percent. Recently, however, it has increased to about 15 percent—although this, too, is a low figure in comparative perspective.

In Western Europe, as in the United States, the level of popular attachment to established parties has traditionally been high (which of course is one explanation for the above-noted stability). One common way of measuring the level of attachment is through surveys asking people about their party identification. As we shall see, however, this can be done in a variety of ways. Comparisons are thus not always so easy. It is clear, however, that notwithstanding a certain decline in recent years, the level of party identification remains relatively high. For Western Europe, the level generally lies over 60 percent (and in certain cases, such as Great Britain, it reaches as high as 90 percent). In the United States at present, close to 80 percent normally identify themselves with a party.[14] As for the other aspect—split voting—it is of interest in particular to look at the conditions in the United States, which like Russia bears the mark of strong presidentialism. In the United States, voters have tended, increasingly, to choose one party in congressional elections and another in presidential elections. In recent years, some 30 percent of electors have distributed their votes in such a manner.

The parties of Western Europe have traditionally distinguished themselves by the high degree of political cohesiveness among their voters. Parties have represented relatively distinct groups in the population—groups marked off from each other by fissures of social origin and political orientation. The basis for this firm segmentation has no doubt weakened with the years: social and political mobility among the voters has increased. Yet despite talk about a drift towards so-called catchall parties—parties with a vague political profile that try to gather support in all societal groups—the shape of the party structure remains much the same as ever. In the United States, by contrast, the parties have had a more diffuse electoral foundation. The Democratic Party, in particular, has exhibited features (in respect of social and political heterogeneity) that bring it close to the ideal type of a catchall party. Even so, there are differences in the type of voter attracted by the two parties. The districts typically won by each party do not look the same. They diverge both socially (in respect of average income, for instance)

TABLE 6.1 Parties over 5% in State Duma Elections

PARTY	1993	1995	1999
Agrarian	8.0		
Communist	12.4	22.3	24.3
Democratic	5.5		
Fatherland–All Russia			13.3
Liberal Democratic	22.9	11.2	6.0
Our Home is Russia		10.1	
Right Forces			8.5
Russia's Choice	15.5		
Unity			23.3
Women	8.1		
Yabloko	7.9	6.7	5.9

SOURCE: Biryukov and Gusev 2002.

and in terms of attitudes (liberal vs. conservative). Available data suggest, more-over, that the difference between the parties has become more pronounced in recent decades (Grofman et al. 1999; Fisher 1999).

Let us return now to Russia. We begin with the stability of the party system. Table 6.1 shows the parties that won representation to the State Duma in the proportional elections of 1993, 1995, and 1999. Of the eight parties that won representation in 1993, only three are left in the Duma today: the Communists (CPR), the Liberal Democrats (LDP), and Yabloko. Together, these parties received the support of 36 percent of the electorate in 1999. In the second elec-tion (that of 1995), a new party made its entrance: Our Home is Russia, the new party of power. It disappeared, however, in the next election. In the third election (that of 1999), three new parties won seats in the Duma—among them Unity, the party of power. Taken together, these new parties obtained 45 percent of the vote—substantially more than that achieved by the three "old" parties. This is, of course, an indication of a very high—and furthermore increasing—level of instability.

When we look at volatility, the conclusion is the same. It was 43 percent in the election of 1995. In the next election, it rose to 52 percent. By way of compar-ison, it may be mentioned that volatility in Latin America has tended to lie at around 25 percent on average—with Brazil as an outlier, at an average level of some 40 percent. In the other formerly communist states of Eastern Europe, the average level has been about the same as in Latin America. The highest figures in this region have been those in the most recent elections in Bulgaria and Lithuania: 47 and 50 percent, respectively (Bielasiak 2001). Where individual high figures are concerned, then, Russia is not unique. In respect of its average, however, Russia stands—with 47.5 percent—in a class of its own.[15]

If mobility is so high, the level of attachment between citizens and parties ought to be low. Several studies have been done of the level of party identification among Russians. The trend is an upward one. The level of party identification—which was extremely low at the beginning of the 1990s—has clearly increased (Miller et al. 2000). Where exact figures are concerned, however, the uncertainty is greater. Estimates for the mid-1990s and the years following have yielded mixed results. In this area, it is well known, the answers given depend to a great extent on the questions asked (Weisberg 1999; Sanders et al. 2002). The method of measurement has a heavy impact on the outcome. Colton (2000) asked the respondents if they considered any party to be "my own": as a result, 31 percent of Russians stated a party identification in 1996. Miller et al. (2000) focused instead on opinion representativeness: is there, they asked, any party that "expresses your views better than any other party?" In this way, an identification level of 52 percent was registered for 1995, and a level of 61 percent for 1997. In the Russia Barometer done just after the election of 1999, finally, the focus was also on opinion representativeness: Does any party, respondents were asked, have "policies closer to you than others"? The result was that 49 percent reported a party identification (Rose et al. 2001).

In our own Russian survey, which was carried out in 2000,[16] the following question was asked: "Do you usually think of yourself as a supporter of a particular party or movement?" Those answering "no" were then asked: "Is there still some party or movement that you feel closer to than others?" Those answering "yes" to any of these questions were asked to state which party they had in mind. When asked in this way, 41 percent of respondents reported identifying with a party (and among these, a clear majority said their identification was a strong one).

As we have seen, measuring party identification is not an exact science. Different methods measure partly different things. Our method is part of a "common core" of survey questions being applied in a coordinated fashion in some 10 European countries. It involves asking about support for and closeness to a party (not opinion representativeness), and as such it aims at capturing the kind of value infusion that organizations may acquire. As we know, this is a quality thought to contribute to the durability of organizations.[17] But it bears noting that, for such a quality to be registered, it must be possible to ascertain that the identification is in fact a lasting one—and that it is directed towards one and the same party over a substantial period (Aldrich 1995). This can only be done by means of a panel study, i.e., follow-up interviews with the same respondents.[18] A high level of party identification that flows back and forth among the various parties does not, of course, infuse the party system

TABLE 6.2 Party Identity

PARTY	IDENTITY %	STRONG IDENTITY %[a]
Communist	44.9	51
Fatherland–All Russia	5.6	23
Liberal Democratic	7.1	38
Right Forces	8.9	23
Unity	17.7	21
Yabloko	11.4	30

(a.) Calculated as the share of people indicating party identity who express a strong identity.

with much stability. And there is much to indicate that it is still, in large meas-ure, a fleeting identification of this kind that is to be found among the voters of Russia (Colton 2000; Rose et al. 2001).

Nevertheless, a large number of individuals in Russia state a party identification. What this identification is worth, of course, can be questioned. But it expresses, in any case, support for and closeness to a party. What then sets this group apart? How does it differ from the rest of the population? The investigations of Miller et al. (2000) report little in the way of demographic dif-ferences. The most divergent traits of those who state a party identification are their greater political knowledge and their heavier exposure to the media. In our study, too, both knowledge and exposure to the media yield correlations (r = 0.13 and 0.20 respectively). Another feature marking off this group is a higher-than-average age (r = 0.14).

To a large extent, however, this last-mentioned factor (the age of the group) is an artifact of its party-political composition. As we see in table 6.2, 45 per-cent of those stating a party identification are adherents of the Communist Party. The table also shows the number of respondents—expressed as a per-centage of those reporting identification with a party—who aver that their identification is a strong one. Here, too, the Communists are in a class of their own. It is also worth noting that, much as we might expect, the three "old" par-ties (the Communists, the Liberal Democrats, and Yabloko) have a higher pro-portion of supporters expressing strong identification than do the more recently formed parties (Unity, Fatherland-All Russia, and Right Forces). What is most striking, if anything, is the fact that the difference is not greater (par-ticularly where Yabloko is concerned).[19]

Experience from other countries suggests that party identification is a fac-tor stimulating electoral participation, and thus voter support for the party in question. Russia is no exception. The disposition to vote is clearly higher within this group: the proportion who have voted is a good 10 percent higher than for the population as a whole.[20] A very large proportion also report having voted in elections to the Duma for the party with which they identify. The proportion is highest in the case of the Communists: 98 percent of those identifying with that party voted for it as well. Next come the other two older parties, LD and Y, with 94 and 92 percent respectively; then RF with 89 percent; U with 80 percent; and FA with 80 percent.

Another way of estimating the attachment between parties and citizens is to measure the incidence of split voting. The interesting thing here is to see whether those who supported a given party in the Duma election also supported that party's candidate in the subsequent presidential election. The leaders of three parties—the CP, the LD, and Y—ran against Putin in the presidential race. To what extent did they receive the votes of those who had supported their respective party in the earlier Duma election? In both the LD and Y, there was a heavy preponderance for Putin. Among those who had supported the LD in the Duma, Putin obtained 55 percent of the vote, as against 36 percent for the party leader. The corresponding figures for Yabloko were 61 and 34 percent. Among adherents of the CP, 41 percent supported Putin and 55 percent the party leader. In this last-mentioned case, then, the party's own candidate mobilized a majority; yet the proportion supporting Putin was strikingly large. The proportion supporting the party leader was higher among those stating a party identification; the difference, however, was insignificant. For the CP, the figure was 60 percent (as against 35 for Putin); for the LD it was 42 percent (47 for Putin); and for Y it was 39 percent (57 for Putin). This in turn indicates that the effect of party identification is not particularly strong. In this area too, the Communists diverge from the others: split voting is the least dramatic among them. But it is considerable all the same. The fact that as many as a third of the party's self-proclaimed supporters voted *against* their party's candidate in the presidential election speaks for itself.

Now to the third question: that of the political coherence of the parties' voters and sympathizers. What do we find in Russia? Is it the case that the parties there win support from all the various sections of society (in terms of both social position and political orientation), with the consequence that the parties display considerable similarity in their composition—as in a political landscape characterized by catchall parties? It bears recalling that, in Latin America, the party system in many cases displays such a character. Brazil is a well-documented example (Mainwaring 1999). Or is it rather the case that the parties each function as a community animated by common interests and beliefs? It is of, course, the latter state of affairs—wherein the parties exhibit clear differences—that is to be preferred from a representation standpoint (Kitschelt 2000). In view of the parties' weak position in Russia, however, this is scarcely to be expected.

TABLE 6.3 Social Composition of Parties

Parties	Communist	Liberal Democratic	Unity	Fatherland–All Russia	Yabloko	Right Forces	Pop. Average	Squared eta
Income							2740	
supporters	2330	2830	3730	4540	3060	4920		0.228
voters	2200	2330	3290	4135	2990	3400		0.161
Education							2.1	
supporters	1.9	2.1	2.1	2.4	2.5	2.5		0.289
voters	1.9	2.1	2.1	2.3	2.5	2.4		0.283
Age							43	
supporters	55	40	42	41	42	36		0.435
voters	54	42	44	44	46	37		0.369
% female							55	
supporters	54	32	44	48	58	65		0.223
voters	56	36	51	46	67	66		0.167
Urbanization							2.1	
supporters	2	2.04	2.06	2.42	2.44	2.53		0.27
voters	1.96	2.03	1.94	2.43	2.38	2.44		0.285
Skills							0.24	
supporters	0.25	0.16	0.29	0.45	0.45	0.4		0.212
voters	0.23	0.24	0.24	0.48	0.4	0.39		0.164
Knowledge							2.1	
supporters	2.1	1.8	2.5	2.1	2.6	2.6		0.217
voters	2	1.9	2.3	2.3	2.4	2.5		0.175
Media							3.4	
supporters	3.6	3.7	3.7	3.7	3.8	3.6		0.139
voters	3.5	3.7	3.6	3.7	3.7	3.4		0.152
Organization							0.47	
supporters	0.42	0.66	0.76	0.54	0.77	0.72		0.17
voters	0.36	0.65	0.6	0.53	0.72	0.6		0.141

NOTE: supporters = people expressing party identity; voters = in the 1999 State Duma election.

Let us begin by examining the social composition of the various parties, as seen in table 6.3. The differences between the parties prove, in many cases, to be considerable. In respect of incomes, the CP stands out as the party of the worst-off; the composition of the LD, at the level of the voters, is similar. FA and RF are both a sharp contrast in this regard. The supporters of these parties enjoy incomes clearly above the average for the population as a whole. When it comes to education, it is above all Y that is the outlier, although RF and FA have a clear foothold among the well-educated, too. The CP, on the other hand, is the party of those with little education. Where the age composition of the parties is concerned, we see dramatic differences. The CP has an average age of 55, while the typical follower of RF is almost 20 years younger. The CP diverges sharply from the other parties in this area—its people, generally speaking, are well on in years. The impact of gender is also strong, although it follows a different pattern. RF is strongly overrepresented among women, as is Y (at the level of the voters). The LD, by contrast, is heavily dominated by men. To a much lesser extent, finally, FA displays a masculine predominance, too, as does U (at the level of its supporters).

In addition, place of residence—i.e., in a larger city vs. a smaller center—confers a special character on some of the parties. It is most especially RF, FA, and Y that display an urban character. No party, on the other hand, stands out as clearly centered in the countryside. The next trait we consider has to do with people's organizational contacts. In our interviews, those citizens who were backing Y, U, RF, and the LD reported having relatively extensive organizational contacts. The CP people, once again, diverge in the opposite direction.

We have also investigated the impact of skills in working life, of level of political knowledge, and of exposure to the media. The first-mentioned variable has a heavy impact. People tied to FA, Y, and RF have a clearly professional background, while adherents of the LD, in particular, diverge in the opposite direction. We see a similar pattern in respect of knowledge level: RF and Y, and to a lesser extent FA and U, diverge in a positive direction. The LD, on the other hand, diverges in a negative direction in respect of its adherents' knowledge level. Where exposure to the media is concerned, the LD comes out better. In this area, however, the differences between the parties tend to be small. Without presenting the matter in table form, finally, I can report that the impact of ethnic and religious distinctions is insignificant. In general, Russians and Russian-Orthodox believers are overrepresented (although not very strongly). But the differences between the parties in this regard are marginal.

Up to this point, we have considered the average values for the parties. Such a method of measurement shows, one might say, what the typical voter for (or sympathizer with) a given party possesses in the way of social characteristics. But it says nothing about the range within the group. We also want to know about the homogeneity of the parties—i.e., their degree of cohesiveness in social regards. For this we need another, and statistically more advanced, technique. The method we have chosen is variance analysis. The results are expressed in an overall figure—a squared eta-value—for each variable. The results are shown in table 6.3.[21] If we take an eta-value of higher than 0.15 as a sign that the parties differ significantly in their degree of social cohesiveness, we discover that the differences are indeed significant in most cases. The picture thus proves to be somewhat different from how it appears when we focus on the average values of the parties. Now it is the variables of age, education, and urbanization that have the strongest effect. It is in these areas, we may conclude, that the parties display the greatest social homogeneity.

To summarize the results so far, we can say that parties in Russia clearly vary in their social composition. If we regard the parties' differing composition as a sign that a range of different interests in society are being represented (as is often assumed in the research on parties), then there is no doubt that, to a great extent, this is true in Russia. The CP is the party of the underprivileged: its people tend to be advanced in years, to have low incomes, to reside in medium-sized towns, to have little education, and to enjoy only limited access to organizational networks. The LD people share some of these characteristics; in addition, they display a heavy masculine preponderance. RF and FA are distinguished for their greater backing among professionals, the well-educated, those living in the big cities, and those enjoying access to extensive organizational networks. They also attract the support of a large share of women. RF furthermore stands out as the party of the young, as well as of those earning high incomes. The latter applies to FA as well; this party too seems to attract professional, well-educated urbanites. U, finally, seems to be the party in the middle where social composition is concerned. Its followers enjoy, however, relatively good organizational contacts and incomes clearly above the average.

How do things look at the level of attitudes? Are there differences there as well? There are certain particular issues that have stood at the center of political conflicts in Russia. One dividing line has been that between the forms of government: democrats have confronted those associated with the old order. A subsequent conflict has concerned economic reform: champions of privatization and the market economy have squared off against forces opposing them. This question has recently broadened into a more general division into a Left and a Right. Parallel with this, a nationalistic dimension has been present in Russian political life. A central question here has been how (by what means) the unity of Russia should be preserved. A more general conflict between center and periphery has also emerged: in recent years, the central authorities have sought to strengthen their position vis-à-vis the regions (Urban and Gel'-man 1997; Myagkov and Ordeshook 2001).

A number of questions in our study took up issues corresponding to those adumbrated above. We sought to measure support for democracy with a series of questions, the result of which were combined into an additive index. Attitudes towards economic reform were measured with a question about state ownership. We also asked respondents to place themselves on a left/right scale. To measure nationalism, we asked whether it was justified to use the army to impose order in Chechnya. Finally, we included a question about whether the

TABLE 6.4 Democracy

PARTY	SUPPORTERS [a]	VOTERS [b]
Communist	−2.8	−2.6
Fatherland–All Russia	−0.4	−0.2
Liberal Democratic	−1.6	−0.6
Right Forces	2.0	1.1
Unity	0.9	0.0
Yabloko	1.2	0.8

(a.) people expressing party identity. (b.) in the 1999 State Duma election.
Eta sq.: supporters 0.497; voters 0.377

TABLE 6.5 Public Ownership

PARTY	SUPPORTERS [a]	VOTERS [b]
Communist	3.7	3.7
Fatherland–All Russia	1.6	1.7
Liberal Democratic	2.2	2.0
Right Forces	0.3	0.5
Unity	1.8	2.1
Yabloko	0.0	1.2

(a.) people expressing party identity. (b.) in the 1999 State Duma election.
Eta sq.: supporters 0.426; voters 0.114

central government should have a strong measure of control over how the regions are governed (the aim here being, of course, to measure attitudes towards centralization).

The results are shown in tables 6.4 to 6.8. Here we see the average position on various scales for the parties' sympathizers and voters. The figures furthermore present information on eta-values. If we begin with the scales, we see that there are certain parties that plainly diverge from the others. Communists show a clear preference for nondemocratic alternatives, while adherents of RF in particular take a clearly pro-democratic position. The other parties are scattered between these poles: the LD stands closest to the CP; Y and U are closest to RF.

Much the same pattern emerges in the area of economic reform. The CP people are strongly opposed. Respondents who prefer RF and Y are much more favorable. We see as well that the party distribution has a leftward tilt (expressing a positive attitude towards state ownership). The parties take differing positions, but on the whole they merely vary in the degree of their skepticism towards privatization. The distinctive traits of Communists can also be

TABLE 6.6 Left / Right

PARTY	SUPPORTERS [a]	VOTERS [b]
Communist	2.6	3.1
Fatherland–All Russia	4.9	5.5
Liberal Democratic	5.1	5.5
Right Forces	6.7	6.4
Unity	5.9	5.9
Yabloko	6.1	5.9

(a.) people expressing party identity. (b.) in the 1999 State Duma election.
Eta sq.: supporters 0.598; voters 0.276

TABLE 6.7 Nationalism

PARTY	SUPPORTERS [a]	VOTERS [b]
Communist	3.2	3.1
Fatherland–All Russia	3.2	3.0
Liberal Democratic	3.6	3.2
Right Forces	2.3	2.4
Unity	3.2	3.2
Yabloko	1.7	1.8

(a.) people expressing party identity. (b.) in the 1999 State Duma election.
Eta sq.: supporters 0.206; voters 0.175

TABLE 6.8 Centralism

PARTY	SUPPORTERS [a]	VOTERS [b]
Communist	3.8	3.7
Fatherland–All Russia	3.7	3.6
Liberal Democratic	3.8	3.5
Right Forces	2.4	3.0
Unity	3.7	3.4
Yabloko	3.2	2.8

(a.) people expressing party identity. (b.) in the 1999 State Duma election.
Eta sq.: supporters 0.184; voters 0.170

seen in how respondents place themselves on the left/right scale: those favoring the Communist Party stake out a clear position on the left. The other parties stand relatively close together towards the middle of the scale. As earlier, furthermore, (and as the party name suggests) those preferring RF stand furthest to the right.

The two remaining scales—nationalism and centralism—display substantial similarities, inasmuch as there, all parties cluster towards the one extreme. All favor the use of military means to restore order in Chechnya. The idea of increased federal control over the regions musters even greater support. The Communists do not differ on these issues from the others; rather, they exhibit the same pattern as do adherents of several other parties (if they stand out at all, it is merely as vanguard representatives for a universally embraced nationalism and centralism). The ones who partly deviate here are the adherents of Y and RF: they express a more reserved attitude towards the war in Chechnya, and towards centralization as well.

Up to this point, our focus has been on average findings for the various parties. With regard to democracy, economic reform, and the left/right scale, we find clear differences. The typical voter for each respective party is distinctive in these areas. The variation is less, however, where nationalism and centralism are concerned. Here too, however, we see that at least certain parties deviate to a degree from the others. We have also seen that, generally speaking, those who describe themselves as supporters of a party (i.e., those reporting a party identification) hold opinions of a sharper profile than do those who vote for the party—the span is wider in the former group. This is also what we might expect. Those who stand close to a party (and who constitute the recruiting pool for party activists) tend to have more distinctive political notions than do those who vote for the party.

Where we turn to the eta-values, we find that the impact of the attitude variables is stronger than that of the social variables. In certain cases, the figures are strikingly high. The two questions dividing respondents into party groups most sharply are democracy and the left/right scale. It is on these questions that the parties' sympathizers and voters diverge most pronouncedly. By contrast, the question about reform (for or against state ownership) shows a clear result among the parties' supporters, but not to any great extent among their voters. Nationalism and centralism have a modest yet significant effect within both categories of party followers. We find, furthermore, that the results are generally stronger, and in several cases appreciably stronger, among party supporters than among voters. The opinions held by those belonging to the former group are not just more marked, as we saw earlier; they are also more homogeneous (within each party).

What emerges is a party picture in which a political Left confronts a political Right—a picture that moreover coincides with the distribution of attitudes towards democracy: the Right is favorable, the Left opposed. Furthest left stand the followers of the CP; furthest right are the followers of RF and Y. Between these extremes, the followers of the remaining parties distribute themselves in a somewhat variable pattern. The LD people are closest to the

Communists where attitudes towards democracy are concerned; however, they find themselves in a middle position—together with U and FA—with regard to economic reform and the left/right scale. Where nationalism and centralism are concerned, the situation is different. Here it is the followers of Y and RF who diverge—from the broad concentration of opinion at the activist end of the scale.

It is furthermore interesting to note that the manner according to which the followers of the parties place themselves on the strongest attitude dimensions—those bearing on democracy and the left/right scale—coincides in large measure with the pattern observed in connection with the parties' social base. In social terms too, it was often the followers of the CP who formed the sharpest contrast with those favoring RF and Y, while adherents of the other parties ended up in a middle position (the pattern being particularly pronounced in regard to income, age, skills, knowledge level, and degree of organization). To a great extent, then, attitudes and interests appear to coincide.[22] In both cases, the difference between the parties can be largely explained in terms of class. Have-nots on the left stand against haves on the right. That, of course, is the pattern that traditionally has dominated the party scene in many of the countries of Western Europe. To this extent, Russia is not unique. One difference on the social level, however, is the fact that the followers of the different parties in Russia are more sharply divided by age, and to some extent also by gender, than is usual in Western Europe.

PARTY AS ORGANIZATION

We will now shift focus to the internal life of parties. We begin by examining the parties' access to resources of various kinds. Such an examination raises the question of the parties' independence (or lack thereof) vis-à-vis interest groups in society that command great resources. Finally, we shall review the internal forms of decision making, to examine the state of democracy within the parties.

The parties of Western Europe, for many decades, were the very model of so-called mass parties. In the mid-twentieth century, large portions of the population (in some countries almost 20 percent) were members of a party. Since then, generally speaking, memberships have sharply declined. Today, about 5 percent of citizens are members of a party in Western Europe. This is still a high figure, comparatively speaking. In the United States, on the other hand, membership parties of a corresponding kind have never developed. Citizen participation in American party politics has been of a more short-term kind, taking place largely in connection with electoral campaigns. Notwithstanding these differences in formal structures, however, large groups have taken part in party politics in the United States also. Studies show that about 20 percent of the population has carried out some sort of activity in support of a party (and such activities have been almost wholly restricted to one and the same party). The resource increment furnished by members/activists is probably, in practical terms, about as great in the United States as in Europe. In both cases, the parties can count on substantial efforts by "their people" at the grass-roots level. Conditions are also similar when it comes to the organizational apparatus of the parties; as a rule, it is well-developed. The parties typically dispose of a network of offices and local representatives covering the entire country. This, needless to say, demands economic resources. Still greater resources, moreover, are needed to cover the enormous cost of electoral campaigns. This is a question of great sums of money—in the United States especially, but in Western Europe too. On both continents, the financial resources of the parties have greatly increased over recent decades. The sources of the funding, however, are quite different in the two cases. In Western Europe, public financing is the dominant factor (although membership dues play a role as well—a small one). American parties receive public subsidies, too; private contributions, however, are far more important (Medvic 2001). The dependence that can arise as a result is a hot political issue today. Demands have been made for stricter legislation in this area. In Western Europe, too, private contributions play a role. Secret contributions have come to light in several countries, creating political scandal. As we have seen, however, the proportion accounted for by private contributions is lower in the case of Western Europe. Another important difference is the fact that, in the United States, external financing goes largely to individual candidates, rather than—as in Western Europe—to the parties centrally. This contributes to a higher degree of political fragmentation in the United States.

The mass parties of Western Europe have claimed, as a rule, to be built on democratic foundations. Organs on all levels have applied largely democratic forms of decision making. One line of criticism, dating back to the days of Robert Michels, has held that the leadership has in fact been heavily dominant, notwithstanding the representative framework applied. A similar critique was directed at American parties at an early point. The purpose of the Progressive reform movement that broke through around the turn of the last century was, among other things, to put an end to the boss rule that marked the established parties. As a result, many states introduced legislation requiring that primary elections be held for the nomination of candidates (referendums and so-called recall procedures were also set up at this time). The tendency throughout the twentieth century was in the same direction: towards an increased role for direct elections in the nomination process. The leadership of the parties, for its part, lost control over this process to a corresponding degree. This too has contributed to fragmentation within the parties. In Western Europe as well there is a trend—albeit a modest one as yet—towards the increased use of direct democratic methods. Primaries on the American model have been introduced in some cases, and direct elections are increasingly used to select the party leader. One of the purposes behind this has been to enhance the attractiveness of party membership—and thus to reverse the tendency towards decline in this area (Scarrow 1999; Grabow 2001). The overall aim has thus been—in the United States especially, but to some extent in Western Europe also—to vitalize democracy within the parties.

How are things in Russia in these regards? Few parties, to begin with, have any membership to speak of. The exception is the Communist Party, which claims to have 500,000 members. This puts it nearly on a par with the German Christian Democratic Union (CDU), which boasts some 600,000 members (Ishiyama 2000; Grabow 2001).[23] Otherwise, however, the membership of Russian parties is small, at least as far as can be judged (oftentimes the parties provide no information on the subject). It could perhaps be that, as in the United States, the small size of the formal membership is balanced by the availability of a cadre of faithful activists, ready to enter the fray when the party calls. This does not appear, however, to be the case. In our interviews, we asked about a wide range of party activities (membership, volunteering, meeting attendance, economic contributions, etc.). Fewer than 1 percent of the respondents, *in toto*, reported taking part in any way. Moreover, since half these individuals reported an affiliation with the CP, little public participation was left for the other five Duma parties to share. By contrast, available data from Eastern Europe suggest that many of the parties in that region have been much better able to attract citizen participation (Mair and van Biezen 2001).

Where the organizational presence of the parties is concerned, a similar pattern can be seen. The CP has an organization covering almost the entire country, and reaching out to many of the smaller centers. This, together with its large membership, is for the most part a legacy from the Soviet-era party apparatus that the party inherited. The other parties—which had to begin practically from scratch—have a much less impressive apparatus. Many have tried to make it without "a party on the ground." They have tried, rather, to get their message out through the media, as well as with the help of commercials. During the 1990s, however, the LD did make an ambitious attempt to build an organization across the country; in all essentials, however, the effort was a failure. Yabloko's strategy has been a more cautious one. The idea has been to put down roots in areas where the party enjoys strong support. Yabloko has thus been able to achieve an organizational presence in the big cities, particularly in the western regions of the country (Biryukov and Gusev 2002; Golosov 1999). Some of the parties of power, meanwhile, have sought to create an organization using regional power holders (especially governors) as a base—and thus to do without a party apparatus throughout the country. In general, however, this strategy has only worked on a short-term basis—the local potentates have usually had their own (highly independent) political agenda. The leaders of Russian Unity (the new party of power, formed in the autumn of 2001 through an amalgamation of U and FA) are no doubt conscious of this history; it is likely for this reason that the party is now trying to build up an independent organization throughout the country. It is still too early to say whether or not this effort will succeed. It is however clear that, in many cases, the new party is meeting with active resistance from representatives of the regional power structure (Ledovskoi 2002).

Public party subsidies in Russia are extremely limited. By contrast, the situation faced by parties in the new democracies to the west is for the most part much more favorable in this regard (Toole 2000). Moreover, with the partial exception of the Communist Party, no Russian parties collect membership dues of any significance. The parties also largely lack any pool of volunteers on which to draw; furthermore, they depend heavily on costly media exposure in order to get their message out. External contributions, in cash or in kind, are therefore required. Parties in Western Europe have often had close ties with well-organized popular movements—churches, trade unions, business organizations, cultural and nonprofit associations—which have been able to furnish significant support for the parties' activities. But little in the way of such a support structure exists in Russia. The growth of a free network of organizations—also something that has had to start almost from scratch—has not proceeded very far as yet. The requisite resources have instead been arranged in other ways. All of the parties have established close contacts with moneyed industrial and financial groups. For each party, one or more such groups can be pointed out. Such groups provide economic resources; sometimes, moreover, they are in a position to offer valuable access to the media (such portions as stand under their influence). Parties that control the public sector, on the other hand, have had a complementary source of funding to which to turn. This has been the special privilege of the parties of power (Biryukov and Gusev 2002). In addition to being able to use the public apparatus as an organizational resource (which is a great advantage, given prevailing circumstances), the parties of power have been able to parlay their position into a means for obtaining economic support, access to public media, and valuable business contacts. On the regional level especially, this has proved to be a winning strategy. The rule of regional bosses is based—in classic machine fashion (Hadenius 2001)—on a far-reaching exploitation of the public organs. The parties in power at the national level have applied the same methods, albeit with less success at the beginning. The first such parties enjoyed only weak support in elections, and their existence was brief. However, the new creation for the election of 1999 (Unity) acquired a much larger share of the vote than did its predecessors, and it is now seeking to broaden its base by amalgamating with FA and building up a party apparatus. It remains to be seen whether this party will become anything more than an extension of the public apparatus out in the country (meaning that part of the apparatus under the control of the central government).

It is well known that parties of the machine (or clientelist) type are ill suited to serve as instruments for opinion representation; after all, their policy profile tends to be very unclear. On the other hand, they are quite suitable for the kind of pork-barrel politics that provides people with concrete benefits (Kitschelt 2000). They can thus function as channels for interest representation (of a narrow, particularistic type). From a democratic standpoint, however, parties of this kind have several disadvantages. For one thing, machine politics leads to a systematic imbalance in the political game between insiders and outsiders. For another, it requires for its functioning that strict legal and administrative principles be set aside within the public machinery. It presupposes, that is to say, the existence of a "soft state"—a state that can be exploited politically. States of this kind are typically attended by a low measure of efficiency, as well as (over the longer term) a low measure of legitimacy among citizens. Finally, machine politics has repercussions for internal party life, in the form of hierarchy and elite rule (Hadenius 2001). We shall return to that aspect shortly.

As we have seen, however, dependence on the public sector is just one side of the issue. In addition, there is a far-reaching dependence on financial centers of a more private sort (it bears recalling that the boundary between public and private is fuzzy in Russia). Powerful economic interests are thus able to buy access to the organs of public decision making. It is difficult to determine, of course, just how much the parties are directed by such interests (or how much the different parties may vary in this regard). The problem is not, of course, unique to Russia. Similar conditions prevail in the United States. The difference is that parties in the latter country are not one-sidedly dependent on particular financial and economic centers (Shlapentokh 2004). Corporations have a tendency to spread their favors among the parties. In addition, contributions from private persons and from public sources account for a much greater share (Medvic 2001). In Russia, finally, legislation and oversight are relatively undeveloped in the area of external contributions.

Let us turn, finally, to the question of internal democracy. No Russian party applies any direct-democratic procedures in its internal life. The CP, however, does have a fairly well-developed process of representation. Party programs, the choice of leaders, and the like are recurrently decided by organs chosen from below in the party apparatus (Ishiyama 2000). In this area too, then, the CP is the party that follows the West European model most closely. Yabloko also applies (at least in form) proper democratic procedures for internal decision making. One special factor is the element of personalism. Here the LD stands out. It is a party built in all essentials around its leader (Zhirinovsky). At the beginning of the 1990s, this individual was chosen (typically enough) as party leader for life. The leader of Yabloko (Yavlinskii) also dominates his party, which survives to a great extent on his personal charisma. Right Forces, Fatherland-All Russia, and Unity are all parties created around a small circle of political notables. It is these elite coteries that have dominated party life (Biryukov and Gusev 2001). Centralism has also been a prominent characteristic of the newly formed party of power, Russian Unity. The proposal for its charter was sent out to regional units for approval in November 2001. The proposal was sent with only the briefest of advance notice. A directive was laid down, moreover, that only one decision was possible: approval. According to the charter (which was approved despite certain protests), it is the central party leadership that has the decisive word when it comes to candidate nominations on the regional level. This is also a principle that is evidently practiced. Regional opinion, for example, has been without effect when it has opposed the central leadership (Sarychev 2001; Ledovskoi 2002). Centralism with a democratic polish (in the form of apparent local participation) seems to be the model for the new party of power.

Conclusion

We have examined the Russian parties in three of their roles: in government, in the citizenry, and as organizations. Where the first aspect is concerned, we can say that the parties have as yet but a weak dominance at the national level. The persons who have been elected president of the republic have run for that office in a purely personal capacity. In the upper chamber of the parliament, parties are hardly present at all. In the Duma, of course, their position is much stronger. The proportional procedure employed in elections to that body (whereby the entire country is treated as a single constituency) guarantees the parties control over 50 percent of the seats. However, no more than half the winning candidates (generously reckoned) from single-member districts are affiliated with the parties. In the latest election, moreover, their share of the vote fell in such districts. At the regional level, the standing of the parties in legislative assemblies is extremely weak. On the other hand, they have turned in progressively better performances in gubernatorial elections. Where voting patterns are concerned, the party factions in the Duma have demonstrated a strikingly high (and increasing) level of cohesiveness. The procedures of the Duma have helped in this regard. At the same time, the party factions are extremely fragile units: they do not always correspond with the parties that ran for election, and considerable floor-crossing takes place. Briefly put, the parties have an unusually weak presence in the halls of government, and they continue to display a low degree of cohesiveness. This renders them very weak as instruments for representation.

When it comes to their presence in the citizenry, the parties in Russia are marked by great instability—both in terms of their existence over time, and in terms of electoral volatility. Party identification has increased over time. It seems, however, that it is still of the thin (exchangeable) variety. The high level of split voting in presidential and Duma elections supports such an interpretation. The most divergent finding in this study has to do with the relatively clear party map found among the followers of the parties. This is a fact that had not emerged so clearly in earlier research;[24] nor is it something one might have expected, given the generally weak position of the parties. Parties have come and gone, and their profiles have often been less than clear; despite this, however, Russian voters have proved themselves more than equal to the task of placing themselves in party camps. Voters sort themselves into clearly distinct groups, in respect both of social position and of political orientation. In many cases, moreover, these groups display a high degree of internal homogeneity, particularly at the level of attitudes. Voters are no fools, as V. O. Key has put it in reference to the American electorate (1966, 7–8). The same can certainly be said of voters in Russia.

In organizational terms, finally, the parties in Russia face great difficulties. The membership in most cases is vanishingly small, and the organizational capacity highly limited. Nor do the parties have any surrounding organizational network on which to draw. Dependence on external resources is great. The parties of power are able to utilize the public sector; the others rely on financial centers that provide economic support and media access. It cannot be denied that such dependence is worrisome, from the standpoint of representation. Forms for internal democracy have been developed in some cases. A high degree of personalism infuses certain parties, however. In the other parties, too, the closed rule of an elite prevails, but in a more collective form. In many cases, the channels for ensuring accountability and influence from below are extremely limited.

Russian voters and party supporters orient themselves strikingly well on the party map. This illustrates, at the same time, that Russian parties are functioning well as political labels. However, the ability of the parties to represent the interests and attitudes that are expressed is very limited. There are few signs, moreover, of any imminent improvement in that regard.

NOTES

This article is based on a paper presented at the conference Democracy in Russia, Uppsala University, 12–13 April 2002.

1. Randall and Svåsand try to escape the analytical fuzziness of which they report (and to which they also contribute) by declaring that "most interesting and fruitful concepts in political science are multi-dimensional and riddled with ambiguities and tensions" (2002, 12).

2. We find statements of a similar kind in Huntington (1968).

3. This is not to say that the work by Panebianco, Mainwaring and Scully, and others is without merit. On the contrary, these studies give a useful account of party life in different countries. What I am questioning is the clarity and relevance of their underlying conceptual structure.

4. Where the second category is concerned, Key refers to "party in the electorate." As can be seen, I apply a broader category.

5. For a similar view, see, e.g., Ranney (1962). For a contrasting view—wherein parties are mainly considered as instruments of expression—see Sartori (1976, 27–28).

6. I am focusing here on electoral stability. Another (and somewhat related) aspect is party-system stability. In that case, the formation of governmental coalitions could be used as a prime indicator (Mair 1997). However, this indicator is suitable above all in systems marked by a substantial measure of parliamentary government—which is not, so far, the case in Russia (McFaul 2001).

7. A more indirect indicator of this (i.e., of party fluidity) is the effective number of parties (Bielasiak 2001).

8. Aware of this limitation, personalist leaders tend to surround themselves with organizational networks marked by fuzzy procedures of decision making. It should be noted that personalist (or charismatic) parties are normally considered to provide the least substantial form of political representation (Kitschelt et al. 1999).

9. It bears noting that the party-activist disparity argument has been questioned, on empirical grounds, by Herrera and Taylor (1994) (on the basis of American data). In any case, the danger of preference asymmetry is normally counteracted by a high degree of concord between party leaders and voters (Aldrich 1995).

10. Where no specific reference is given, the account of conditions in Western Europe presented herein is based on Mair (1997) and Gallagher et al. (2001). In the case of the U.S., my sources are Aldrich (1995) and Wattenberg (1998).

11. In 1995, the proportion without any party affiliation was 46 percent. Stoner-Weiss's analysis (2001) of the Duma elections of 1993, 1995, and 1999 gives the same trend over time (and approximately the same figures) for the proportions of successful independent and party-affiliated candidates, respectively.

12. The figures reported by Stoner-Weiss (2001) for later elections do not indicate any improvement on the national parties' part.

13. It is still too early to say in the case of the third Duma (which was elected in 1999).

14. In the U.S., respondents are usually directly asked whether they consider themselves Democrats or Republicans. Surveys in Western Europe typically ask about support for, adherence to, or inclination towards a party (Weisberg 1999).

15. The average for Bulgaria is 25 percent; for Lithuania 40 percent (Bielasiak 2001).

16. The survey was carried out in the fall, in cooperation with VCIOM (All-Russia Centre for Public Opinion Research). It was based on a representative sample of the Russian population.

17. Much the same idea can be found in Hirschman (1970): it is one's loyalty (one's emotional connection) to an organization that dissuades one from leaving it—even when one is unhappy with its actions. Unhappiness is expressed through "voice" instead of "exit."

18. We shall undertake such a study during the fall of 2002.

19. The following abbreviations will henceforth be used: Communist Party: CP; Unity: U; Fatherland-All Russia: FA; Liberal Democrats: LD; Right Forces: RF; Yabloko: Y.

20. A multivariate analysis of the factors explaining participation in the Duma election of 1999 shows that party identification has a significant independent effect. However, the effect of such factors as age, education, life-satisfaction, and exposure to the media is greater (adjusted R sq. = 0.24).

21. The squared eta-coefficient corresponds to explained variance (R sq.) in regression analysis.

22. It may be of interest here to note that the supporters of the two parties that joined together after the 1999 election, FA and U, are close to the other in terms of political attitudes. In their social composition, however, the followers of FA more nearly resemble those of RF and Y.

23. The German SPD has ca. 800,000 members.

24. See, e.g., Myagkov et al. (1997); Moser (1999); Miller et al. (2000). Rose et al. (2001), however, have published findings on voter attitudes (but along other dimensions) that are in line with those presented here. A certain similarity is also evident with the work of Brader and Tucker (2001), who compare the "core voters" of different parties. At the same time, these studies find only weak correlations between voting patterns and social traits. In this regard, the results presented here paint a more structured picture.

REFERENCES

Aldrich, John H. 1995. *Why parties? The origin and transformation of political parties in America.* London: University of Chicago Press.

Anckar, Dag. 1997. Dominating smallness: Big parties in Lilliput systems. *Party Politics* 3: 243–64.

Amorim Neto, Octavio, and Fabiano Santos. 2001. The executive connection: Presidentially defined factions and party discipline in Brazil. *Party Politics* 7: 213–34.

Bielasiak, Jack. 2001. The institutionalisation of party systems in emerging democracies. Paper presented at the American Political Science Convention, San Francisco, CA, 29 August–2 September.

Belyaev, Andrei, Nikolai Biryukov, and Victor Sergeyev. 2002. A major change in the State Duma voting behaviour: Consolidation of parliamentary parties or consolidation of parliamentary elite? Mimeo. Moscow State University.

Biezen van, Ingrid. 2000. On the internal balance of party power: Party organizations in new democracies. *Party Politics* 6: 395–417.

Biryukov, Nikolai, and Leonel Gusev. 2002. Russian parties and political groups represented in the State Duma. Mimeo. Moscow State University.

Brader, Ted, and Joshua A. Tucker. 2001. The emergence of mass partisanship in Russia, 1993–1996. *American Journal of Political Science* 45: 69–83.

Colton, Timothy J. 2000. *Transitional citizens: Voters and what influences them in the new Russia*. Cambridge, MA: Harvard University Press.

Crewe, Ivor. 1981. Electoral participation. In *Democracy at the polls: A comparative study of competitive national elections*, ed. David Butler, Howard R. Penniman, and Austin Ranney. Washington, DC and London: American Enterprise Institute for Public Policy Research.

Diamond, Larry. 1999. *Developing democracy: Toward consolidation*. Baltimore: Johns Hopkins University Press.

Duverger, Maurice. 1954. *Political parties: Their organisation and activity in the modern state*. London: Methuen.

Epstein, Leon D. 1981. Political parties: Organization. In *Democracy at the polls: A comparative study of competitive national elections*, ed. David Butler, Howard R. Penniman, and Austin Ranney. Washington, DC and London: American Enterprise Institute for Public Policy Research.

Fish, Steven M. 1995. *Democracy from scratch: Opposition and regime in the new Russian revolution*. Princeton, NJ: Princeton University Press.

Fisher, Patrick. 1999. The prominence of partisanship in the congressional budget process. *Party Politics* 5: 225–36.

Gallagher, Michael, Michael Laver, and Peter Mair. 2001. *Representative government in modern Europe*. New York: McGraw Hill.

Golosov, Grigorii V. 1999. From Adygeya to Yaroslavl: Factors of party development in the regions of Russia, 1995–1998. *Europe-Asia Studies* 51: 1333–65.

———. 2000. Political parties in the regions of Russia. ESRC Research Seminar: Russia's Regional Transformation. London School of Economics.

Grabow, Karsten. 2001. The re-emergence of the Cadre party? Organizational patterns of Christian and social democrats in unified Germany. *Party Politics* 7: 23–43.

Grofman, Bernard, Samuel Merrill, Thomas F. Brunell, and William Koetzle. 1999. The potential electoral disadvantages of a catchall party: Ideological variance among republicans and democrats in 50 U.S. states. *Party Politics* 5: 199–210.

Hadenius, Axel. 2001. *Institutions and democratic citizenship*. Oxford: Oxford University Press.

Hale, Henry E. 2001. Why not parties? Supply and demand on Russia's electoral market. Paper presented at the American Political Science Convention, San Francisco, CA, 29 August–2 September.

Haspel, Moshe, Thomas F. Remington, and Steven S. Smith. 1998. Electoral institutions and party cohesion in the Russian Duma. *Journal of Politics* 60: 417–39.

Herrera, Richard. 1999. The origins of opinion of American party activists. *Party Politics* 5: 237–52.

Herrera, Richard, and Melanie K. Taylor. 1994. The structure of opinion in American political parties. *Political Studies* 42: 676–89.

Hirschman, Albert. 1970. *Exit, voice, and loyalty: Responses to decline in firms, organizations, and states.* Cambridge, MA: Harvard University Press.

Huntington, Samuel. 1968. *Political Order in Changing Societies.* New Haven: Yale Universtiy Press.

Ishiyama, John T. 2001. Candidate recruitment and development of Russian political parties, 1993–1999. *Party Politics* 4: 387–411.

———. 2000. Candidate recruitment, party organisation and the Communist successor parties: The cases of the MSzP, the KPRF and the LDDP. *Europe-Asia Studies* 52: 875–96.

Josefson, Jim. 2000. An exploration of the stability of partisan stereotypes in the United States. *Party Politics* 6: 285–304.

Key, V. O. 1964. *Politics, parties, and pressure groups.* 5th ed. New York: Thomas Y. Crowell Co.

Kiewiet, D. Roderick, and Mathew D. McCubbins. 1991. *The logic of delegation: Congressional parties and the appropriations process.* Chicago: Chicago University Press.

Kitschelt, Herbert. 2000. Linkages between citizens and politicians in democratic polities. *Comparative Political Studies* 33: 845–79.

Kitschelt, Herbert, Zdenka Mansfeldova, Radoslav Markowski, and Gábor Tóka. 1999. Post-Communist party systems: Competition, representation and inter-party cooperation. Cambridge: Cambridge University Press.

———. 1966. *The responsible electorate. Rationality in presidential voting, 1936–60.* Cambridge, MA: Harvard University Press.

Ledovskoi, Arsenil. 2002. Russian regional report: Party building in the Russian regions. *East West Institute* 7: 1–3.

Levitsky, Steven. 1998. Institutionalism and Peronism: The concept, the case, and the case for unpacking the concept. *Party Politics* 4: 77–92.

Lipset, Seymour M., and Stein Rokkan. 1967. Cleavage structures, party systems, and voter alignments: An introduction. In *Party systems and voter alignments: Cross-national perspectives*, ed. Seymour M. Lipset and Stein Rokkan. New York: Free Press

Mair, Peter. 1997. *Party system change: Approaches and interpretations.* Oxford: Clarendon Press.

Mair, Peter, and Ingrid van Biezen. 2001. Party membership in twenty European democracies, 1998–2000. *Party Politics* 7: 5–21.

Mainwaring, Scott. 1998. Party system in the third wave. *Journal of Democracy* 9: 67–82.

———. 1999. *Rethinking party systems in the third wave of democratization: The case of Brazil.* Stanford, CA: Stanford University Press.

Mainwaring, Scott, and Timothy Scully, eds. 1995. *Building democratic institutions: Party systems in Latin America.* Stanford, CA: Stanford University Press.

May, John D. 1973. Opinion structure of political parties: The special law of curvilinear disparity. *Political Studies* 21: 135–51.

McFaul, Michael. 2001. Explaining party formation and nonformation in Russia: Actors, institutions, and chance. *Comparative Political Studies* 34: 1159–87.

McKenzie, Robert. 1982. Power in the Labour Party: The issues of intra-party democarcy. In Kavanagh, Dennis, ed. *The politics of the Labour Party*. London: G. Allen and Unwin.

Medvic, Stephen K. 2001. The impact of party financial support on the electoral success of U.S. house candidates. *Party Politics* 7: 191–212.

Miller, Arthur H., Gwyn Erb, William M. Reisinger, and Vicki L. Hesli. 2000. Emerging party systems in post-Soviet societies: Fact or fiction? *Journal of Politics* 62: 455–90.

Moe, Terry M. 1984. The new economics of organization. *American Journal of Political Science* 28: 739–77.

Moser, Robert G. 1999. Independents and party formation: Elite partisanship as an intervening variable in Russian politics. *Comparative Politics* 31: 147–65.

Myagkov, Mikhail, and Peter C. Ordeshook. 2001. The trail of votes in Russia's 1999 and 2000 presidential elections. *Communist and post-communist studies* 34: 353–70.

Myagkov, Mikhail, Peter C. Ordeshook, and Alexander Sobyanin. 1997. The Russian electorate, 1991–1996. *Post-Soviet Affairs* 13: 134–66.

Panebianco, Angelo. 1988. *Political parties: Organization and power*. New York: Cambridge University Press.

Pedersen, Mogens. 1979. The dynamics of European party systems: Changing patterns of electoral volatility. *European Journal of Political Research* (7): 1–26.

Randall, Vicky, and Lars Svåsand. 2002. Party institutionalisation in new democracies. *Party Politics* 8: 5–31.

Ranney, Austin. 1962. *The doctrine of party government*. Urbana: University of Illinois Press.

Remington, Thomas F. 1998. Political conflict and institutional design: Paths of party development in Russia. In *Party politics in post-Communist Russia*, ed. John Löwenhardt. London: Frank Cass Publishers.

———. 2003. Majorities without mandates: The Russian federation council since 2000. *Europe-Asia Studies* 55: 66–91.

Robinson, John P., Phillip R. Shaver, and Lawrence S. Wrightsman, eds. 1999. *Measures of political attitudes*. San Diego, CA: Academic Press.

Rose, Richard, Neil Munro, and Stephen White. 2001. Voting in a floating party system: The 1999 Duma election. *Europe-Asia Studies* 53: 419–43.

Sanders, David, Jonathan Burton, and Jack Kneeshaw. 2002. Identifying the true party identifiers: A question wording experiment. *Party Politics* 8: 155–75.

Sarychev, Sergei. 2001. Russian regional report: Kursk activists protest Yedinstvo's centralisation. *East West Institute* 6: 7.

Sartori, Giovanni. 1976. *Parties and party systems: A framework for analysis*. New York: Cambridge University Press.

Scarrow, Susan E. 1999. Parties and the expansion of direct democracy: Who benefits? *Party Politics* 5: 341–62.

Schattschneider, E. E. 1942. *Party government*. New York: Farrar and Rinehart.

Scully, Roger, and Samuel C. Patterson. 2001. Ideology, partisanship, and decision making in a contemporary American legislature. *Party Politics* 7: 131–55.

Selznick, Philip. 1957. *Leadership in administration.* New York: Harper and Row.

Shlapentokh, Vladimir. 2004. Wealth versus political power: The Russian case. *Communist and Post-Communist Studies* 37: 135–60.

Snyder, James M., Jr., and Tim Groseclose. 2001. Estimating party influence on roll-call voting: Regression coefficients versus classification success. *American Political Science Review* 95: 689–99.

Shugart, Matthew Soberg, and John M. Carey. 1992. *Presidents and assemblies: Constitutional design and electoral dynamics.* Cambridge: Cambridge University Press

Stoner-Weiss, Kathryn. 2001. The limited reach of Russia's party system: Under-institutionalization in dual transitions. *Politics and Society* (September).

Strom, Kaare. 1990. A behavioral theory of competitive political parties. *American Journal of Political Science* 34: 565–98.

———. 2000. Delegation and accountability in parliamentary democracies. *European Journal of Political Research* 37: 261–89.

Teorell, Jan. 1999. A deliberative defence of intra-party democracy. *Party Politics* 5: 363–82.

Thames, Frank C., Jr., 2001. Legislative voting behaviour in the Russian Duma: Understanding the effect of mandate. *Europe-Asia Studies* 53: 869–84.

Toole, James. 2000. Government formation and party-system stabilization in East Central Europe. *Party Politics* 6: 441–61.

Urban, Michael, and Vladimir Gel'man. 1997. The development of political parties in Russia. In *Democratic changes and authoritarian reactions in Russia, Ukraine, Belarus, and Moldova,* ed. Karen Dawisha and Bruce Parrott. Cambridge: Cambridge University Press.

Wattenberg, Martin P. 1998. *The decline of American political parties, 1952–1996.* Cambridge and London: Cambridge University Press.

Weisberg, Herbert F. 1999. Political partinsanship. In John P. Robinson, Phillip R. Shaver, Lawrence S. Wrightsman, eds. *Measures of political attitudes.* San Diego: Academic Press.

7

The Political Elite in Hungary Through Transition

Jiří Lach

Conditions for Change

The development of the Hungarian political elite, as well as of the whole society, was significantly influenced by the timing of the greatest political crisis in this Central European country. It was the year 1956 that raised hopes for a change in the political climate of the communist regime, as in the case of Poland and later Czechoslovakia. There were multiple visions, political programs, and vague ideas at this time, ranging from moderate reform of the socialist state up to radical requests for a pluralist democratic system. Although the Hungarian events were accelerated by Nikita Khrushchev's critique of Stalinist repression earlier in 1956, the Soviet leader of this time did not wish to tolerate political liberalization in Central Europe.

Hungarian prime minister Imré Nagy's declaration of his intention of leaving the Warsaw Pact provoked the savage military suppression of the Hungarian Revolution in November 1956.[1] In contradiction to the later Czechoslovak reform attempt of 1968, the Hungarian revolution was restrained solely by a military campaign on the part of the USSR, although several communist states, including Yugoslavia, offered military support.[2] The number of victims and methods of repression also differed from the situation in Czechoslovakia after the invasion of 21 August. The period from 1956 to 1958 in particular brought a violent revenge of the regime against many active revolutionaries, including capital punishment and long terms of imprisonment. Estimates of the number of civilian victims of actual military operations in November 1956 vary from several thousand up to one hundred thousand people killed in the streets of Budapest and by the Soviet and Hungarian secret services.

János Kádár was the main actor in the process of Hungary's communist consolidation after 1956. After the period of persecution, which also generated around 200,000 emigrants,[3] Kádár sought for societal compromise. This compromise was to be based on the social and economic satisfaction of the population. In 1968 Hungary started the so-called "New Economic Mechanism" (NEM), which was agreed on by the Central Committee of the Hungarian Socialist Workers' Party[4] as early as 1965 (Kontler 2001, 402). The NEM was mainly expected to introduce the decentralization of economic decision making, increased production efficiency, and higher participation of the population in the economic life of the country in the form of limited and directed private ownership. Kádár's strategy really brought about a relative improvement of living standards in the 1970s and early 1980s, according to some authors (e.g., Goldman 1997, 184).

The different chronology of communist regimes made the Hungarian system easier to live under than Czechoslovakia during "normalization," East Germany, or Poland after the introduction of martial law in December 1981. Nevertheless, Hungarian communism had to face a crisis again in the 1980s, the one that led to the final failure of the system in 1989–90. There were four main factors in this process: (1) the revision of Soviet foreign policy after Gorbachev's accession; (2) the economic decay of the country, followed by the worsening of the social conditions of the population; (3) the formation of civil society; and (4) the assurance of the Communist Party that no concession should erode the political monopoly of the party (see Király 1995, 4).

Crisis and Change

The form of the Hungarian political elite after 1989 was, to a large extent, influenced by processes in internal politics in the second half of the 1980s. A more intensive resonance of disagreement with the political leadership of the Communist Party can be seen after 1985. However, it was mainly the economic failure of the system that, together with other factors, nourished popular discontent from as early as 1980.

Kádár's economic "liberalization" met its limits in this period, despite the MSZMP's facade of being the leading reforming force of the Communist bloc in Europe (Cottey 1995, 93). The average citizen opposed the threat of pauperization by seeking two, sometimes even three occupations at once. The housing situation contributed to social unrest in Hungary (Goldman 1997, 185). As in other communist countries, declining living standards brought about the increasing alienation of the masses from the system.

The disintegration of communist rule in Hungary passed through several stages. Serious expressions of popular discontent define the first period (from June 1985 to September 1987). Kádár's policy of "speeding up," announced at a party rally in 1985, only increased the foreign debt of the country, and caused chaos in the economic leadership too. Political disagreement spread from above, on the part of the political elite, as well as from below. Professional groups, especially economic reformers, represented the "from above" group. Their disillusionment sprang from the ignorance displayed by political decision-makers towards attempts for economic reform. The pressure from below was far more diversified as regards the social origin of the critics, as well as in terms of the variety of reforming visions. Nevertheless, reformed communists and dissident groups represented the mainstream of popular criticism. The division of power between the Communist Party and the nation was their chief motive. The party's reformers and the dissidents, however, differed in their long-term aims. The first sought a semi-constitutional system that would improve the position of the individual in society; however, the Communist Party should not lose its substantial influence on political decision making. The long-term vision of the opposition was democratic government. However, the opposition did not act as a compact and party-based power factor in the first period. The political elite was still represented by the communists, although divided into reformers and "hard-liners" (Bozóki, Körösényi, and Schöpflin 1992, 1).

The formation of an opposition was the key phenomenon of the second phase (September 1987–May 1988). The differences between opposition groups laid the foundations of political pluralism in Hungary. The Hungarian Democratic Forum (MDF), established in autumn 1987, attempted to mediate dialogue between other opposition groupings and the Communist Party, in which Kádár's wing started to lose its position.

The clash of hard-liners with Communists seeking a compromise took place at the party's convention in May 1988. It also opened the third phase (May 1988–January 1989, dominated by Kádár's replacement in the position of general secretary of the party, when Károly Grósz became party leader. Although the basic structure of the Communist monopoly on power was not significantly affected as yet—neither the MDF nor the Alliance of Free Democrats (SZDSZ) represented a profiled opposition—its position as the political elite, established as a consequence of post-1956 consolidation, was already corrupted.[5]

The crisis of legitimization of political power from above in Hungary in this period is crucial. This legitimization was not typical only of Kádár's leadership, but had been present in the communist system since Lenin's era. It particularly emphasized the following aspects: (1) the justification of political means by momentary needs and the degradation of legislation to the level of an administrative tool, (2) a monopoly of decision making based on the assumption of holding the absolute truth, (3) the fact that popular opinion is not essential for confirmation of this truth, and (4) the vitality of the relationship between the center of power and administration for the functioning of the system, rather than the relationship between the government and people (Palma 1999, 57).

Two important factors of nascent democratization can be observed in Hungarian developments in summer 1988—a free press and the process of formation of new political parties. The party system grew, with the exception of the Communist Party, from reform-oriented groups, which ranged from small circles, through social initiatives, up to the nuclei of political parties. However, these cores, represented mostly by intellectuals (Tőkés 1997, 127), were still debate clubs, rather than structured and organized political parties. Subsequently, intellectuals also took a substantial role in the formation of the Hungarian post-communist elite.

The future development of Hungary was not decided during Grósz's era. Kádár's successor only represented a different clique of the hard core of the Hungarian Communist Party, which had already accepted the need for certain reforms, but was undermined by the political monopoly of the leading party. This notion of "democratic socialism" is also known from late-1980s Czechoslovakia; however, neither the public nor the crystallizing opposition in Hungary expressed appreciation for this policy. The third period thus brought about a situation in which the MSZMP adopted a defensive political strategy, while the opposition was not yet prepared to take over power.

The year 1989 was politically hectic for Hungarians too, despite the fact that the Hungarian path towards political pluralism and democracy represented a rather smooth change, at least in comparison with Czechoslovakia, East Germany, or Romania. Imré Pozsgay, the leading figure of reform communism as early as the late Kádár era, made a remarkable impact on the political situation at the beginning of the fourth period (January 1989–16 June 1989). Pozsgay departed from the traditional explanation of 1956 as a counter-revolution, and called it a "national uprising." Such a statement was in sharp contradiction to the traditional communist interpretation of 1956. Despite the immediate summoning of a Central Committee session, political and social groupings received Pozsgay's characterization of the most sensitive event in Hungarian postwar history positively. The Communist Party approached a clearly defensive position at this time, which was proven by the Central Committee's redefinition of 1956, but mainly by its acceptance of the existence of a multiparty system (Körösényi 1992, 7).

In spite of differences in timing, it was a typical feature of all the Communist parties in Hungary, Poland, the GDR, and Czechoslovakia that deeper reform attempts were made only at the time when opposition had developed to such a level that it could aspire to direct confrontation with the leading party. Of course, the stage of the opposition's evolution was different in all these countries, and Hungary is given as the example of the most established opposition structures. The reaction of the MSZMP to popular and opposition voices was given by a deepening split, into a reform wing on one hand and hard-liners on the other. While Imré Pozsgay was already talking openly about pluralist democracy, Károly Grosz's group refused to even begin roundtable talks.

Important historical anniversaries played significant roles in the end of communist regimes in Central Europe. Their evocations and celebrations often signaled the outbreak of political changes. This was the case with the 150th jubilee of the 1848 revolution in Hungary, which turned into a massive demonstration blaming the communist government, which had lasted 40 years, for the pulverization of the country.

The fourth period spanned the differentiation between die-hard communists on one hand, and reformers and technocrats on the other. MSZMP members who were open to change, like Gyula Horn[6] or Miklós Németh, did not search for a collective guarantee of the whole party's position in power; rather, they were trying to secure individual membership of the new political elite, which they correctly saw in the growing opposition. A similar situation also occurred in other communist countries, for example in the case of Milan Kuc̆an in Slovenia. The erosion of the communist elite deepened, thus making it easier for the opposition to crystallize (Parrot 1997, 13).

Opposition groups began to work as real political parties from this moment. Their alliance was established in March 1989 under the title of the Opposition Round Table (EKA). Single-party rule virtually finished at this time, and Hungary faced nascent party pluralism. The EKA very soon expressed its readiness for direct confrontation with the Communist Party. The EKA assumed that the political and economic crisis could not be solved by any sharing of power between the old government and the nation. The organization of absolutely free and valid elections was the only way for the legitimization of power to be carried out, according to the opposition. Anybody rejecting this principle supported the Communists, in the EKA's view (Bruszt and Stark 1998, 31–32).

Historical reminiscences began to excite the political situation and the public even more with the commencement of the fifth phase (16 June–October 1989). Hungarian politics and society were entirely captivated by questions about the personality of Imré Nagy, particularly his rehabilitation and the reburial of his remains after 31 years. The communists' declining power was not proven only by the actual ceremony, but also by the fact that public opinion favored the participation of representatives of the MSZMP at the funeral of the 1956 prime minister.

The Communists did not recover from this attack on their position of power and finally accepted roundtable discussions (Körösényi 1992, 8). It was at the so-called National Round Table where the EKA, representatives of the MSZMP, and also leaders of the social organization met. The talks brought a number of decisions on 18 September 1989, witnessing further democratization. A request for a change of constitution and modification of the financing and activities of all parties were the most important legislative proposals (Benda 1998, 366). It is peculiar that the EKA, as well as the Communists, was represented mostly by its moderate wing: the Hungarian Democratic Forum (MDF) was the counterpart of the reform communists, because the Alliance of Young Democrats (SZDSZ) declared its independence from the communists as well as from the opposition.

The unity of the opposition was already broken before the first free elections in Hungary, unlike the situation in any other country of the region. The leaders of the SZDSZ and Alliance of Young Democrats (FIDESZ) refused to sign the 18 September agreement. Conflict broke out over the presidential elections when the parties signing the 18 September protocol suggested the realization of the presidential election before parliamentary elections, which was in contradiction of the constitution then, while the radical opposition perceived parliamentary elections as its highest priority.

The clashes of autumn 1989 over the presidential office provided the basis for the problematic position of the Hungarian presidency, both with respect to government and the legislature, and this difficult situation was typical of post-authoritarian Hungarian politics for a long time (O'Neil 1997, 202). The presidential election was part of the referendum initiated by the radical opposition.

During this "year of wonders," the changes in Hungarian political life were further confirmed by the affairs that took place at an international level, such as the then-anticipated visit of George Bush, president of the United States of America, and most importantly, the massive movement of East Germans to Western Europe via Hungary (Bozóki 1995, 63). A new political class had started to form even before the beginning of the sixth, and final, phase of the fall of communist power in Hungary (October 1989–March 1990), that is, during the National Round Table talks held behind closed doors, where both parties[7] gave up the idea of mobilization. This process concerned changes not only in legislation and external affairs, but also in the political rituals and the conduct of the negotiating representatives (Bruszt and Stark 1992, 47).

In this period, the presidential election was included in the referendum initiated by the radical opposition. The alliance of the Free Democrats and Young Democrats (also supported by the renovated Independent Small Farmers' Party [the FKGP] and the Social Democratic Party of Hungary [the MSZDP]) managed in a short time to get many more signatures than the one hundred thousand needed for the referendum, which included some other fundamental issues such as the disbanding of the Workers' Militia, a ban on the activity of the Communist Party in the workplace, and the already mentioned date of the presidential election (Körösényi 1997, 9).

The decision of the Hungarian communists to agree to the holding of a free election was essential if the political system were to undergo a radical change (Kuran 1991, 38). The MSZMP was split within, and the idea of a free election was being pushed through by the reform communists. Their attitude was not a consequence of an effort to liberalize the political system, but of a conviction that direct competition in the election would stabilize their power or possibly bring them closer to the future political elite. Although the end of the communist system in Hungary has been compared to how Wojciech Jaruzelski handed over power in Poland, Solidarity, structured differently both in terms of organization and institutions, represented a stronger opposition than that in Hungary. This led the Hungarian reform communists to underrate the election prospects of the opposition (Bruszt and Stark 1998, 20).

This attitude seems principally to have been influenced by a deep crisis within the MSZMP. One of the most sensitive issues of systems in transition is how much the old elite transforms into the new elite. Such a transformation did not take place only at the end of the 1980s and 1990s, but is also a typical feature of all important changes of political regimes in the twentieth century. We can trace it back to the process of building up a new Germany after 1945, and we also find it during the years after the Bolshevik coup of October 1917. Despite declarations about developing a brand new system, Soviet Russia founded the new organization of the state on the basis of the administration and other structures of the tsar's era.[8]

A possible method to analyze the "flow" of the old elite into the new regime is to take a close look at the development of institutions within a communist system. The degree of change and conservation in such institutions reveals how profound the transformation was. A major role in the transformation of Hungarian politics was played by the collapse of the party then in power, which, de facto, ceased to exist at the extraordinary congress summoned as a result of the pressure from the reformists and held in October 1989. Consequently, the reform communists, as in Poland but unlike in Czechoslovakia (this only applies to the Czech KSČM [Communist Party of Bohemia and Moravia], and not to the Slovak SDL [Party of democratic Left]), founded a new political party that would grow into the shape of the West European model of a social democratic party (Barany and Volgyes 1995, 179). The new Hungarian Socialist Party (MSZP), however, was not a huge monolith like the MSZMP a short time before. Most of the 700,000 members left the Hungarian Socialist Workers' Party without signing up to its successor, with its stress on reform.

After the foundation of the MSZP, the membership was about 20,000. The collapse of the Communist Party, along with the October referendum—which pushed through, among other things, the postponement of the presidential election—meant the ultimate end of communism in Hungary. Moreover, the preparations for the upcoming general election to be held in March 1990 were definitely over, too. The critical impact of the referendum on the election was that it brought publicity for the Free Democrats, who had been barely recognized in the public's awareness before that moment (Körösényi 1992, 10).

What was surprising about the profound changes in the Central and East European countries at the end of the 1980s was the absence of violence (apart from Romania), which can be accounted for by the passivity of the masses during the transfer of power (the public had been mobilized several times, but only for short periods of time that did not last long enough to have a long-term impact on the political decision-making process), then by a reluctance to persecute the representatives of the communist system, and the opportunities that opened for involving those representatives in the new political structures. The last two facts are particularly striking in relation to Hungary, as it was this country that had experienced the most violent ways of dealing with internal crises of the communist system in the Soviet satellite states in the post-Stalinist period (Poznanski 1999, 329).

The new elite that was forming saw the persecution of the former political representatives as the worst possible choice to make at the beginning of revolutionary changes. The fact that it was impossible to predict future developments gave rise to fears about possible revenge that might be taken in case of failure (Haraszti 1999, 288).

The way power was transferred in the Central European countries, from which we derive the way in which the new elites were established, would be called, after the case of Hungary, "the negotiated revolution."[9] Using this term, Rudolf Tökés does not imply that the launch of liberalization in political, economic, social, or cultural terms was the result of a priori agreements between the opposition and the communist *nomenklatura*. The theory of a previously-arranged transfer of power is rather popular (especially with people of lower educational attainment and the right-wing extremist electorate), although the trouble in the case of Hungary is the degree of polarization of both the opposition and the *nomenklatura* at the end of the eighties.

Major structural changes did not take place until the democratic political forces of the public had appeared as stabilized representatives of the new elite. Comparing the opinions and concepts of the leading dissidents, symbolizing the future elite, in Hungary, Poland, and Czechoslovakia from the beginning of 1989 with the political situation at the end of this period, we find that a number of radical changes took place. The leading opponents of the communist regimes, such as Ferenc Fehér, Agnes Heller, János Kis, Adam Michnik, or Václav Havel, did not, in January 1989, doubt the future collapse, or at least humanization, of communist rule, but saw their dissident activities as an act of long-term penetration into the then-existing structures, and an ongoing process of restoring public life, without expecting any sudden or major changes (Tismaneanu 1999, 70).

The Hungarian Political Elite in the Period of Democratic Changes

At the beginning of transformation, the small size of the original revolutionary elite, recruiting chiefly from the intelligentsia, made it necessary to form "large coalitions" with other various segments of civic society. These coalitions, quite hybrid ones when seen through the perspective of a developed democratic political system, did not last long, and ceased to exist with the approaching differentiation of the political system (Highley and Pakulski 1992, 110–11).

In Hungary, though, this differentiation took place earlier than in the neighboring countries. The first free election was not a referendum against the Communist Party, but a real choice of a new system of political representation; and the self-dissolution in October 1989 of the Hungarian Socialist Workers' Party, a party symbolizing the 40-year-long oppression, made its contribution to this. As a result, the opposition parties, unlike the Civic Forum, found themselves without an enemy. An enemy would have allowed the new parties to shape its political platform just through a negative program.

The formation of a new system of democratic representation in the Hungarian National Assembly was carried out on the basis of a rather complex electoral system, which underwent some changes in 1994. There were 386 members of the single-chamber parliament to be elected, using three kinds of tickets: 176 members of parliament were elected from single-mandate constituencies, 152 on the regional ticket of the political party, and 58 seats on the national ticket. In the Hungarian system, each voter has two votes, one for a single-mandate constituency and the other for the regional ticket of the bodies standing for election (Körösényi 1992, 74).

The 1990 election, with its two rounds held in March and April respectively, resulted in a right-center government under Prime Minister József Antall, consisting of a coalition including the Hungarian Democratic Forum (MDF), Christian-Democratic People's Party (KDNP), and Independent Small Farmers' Party (FKGP).[10] In this coalition, the leading role was played by Antall's MDF, which ran for election with the slogan "Calm Force," which quite reflected the mood of the Hungarian people. They would prefer a smooth transition to a democratic system rather than the shock therapies being offered by the SZDSZ and FIDESZ. The unacceptability of these programs was under-lined by an almost militant anti-communism. Its relatively mild approach earned the MDF the largest electoral support (Goldman 1997, 193).

One of the critical points of all the transformations was to ensure the con-tinuity of the legislative process. In Hungary, this was to be secured through a document known as the "Pact," signed by the MDF and the opposition SZDSZ in April 1990 and suggesting a number of constitutional changes (the Alliance of Free Democrats had received second place in the election, winning a total of 94 seats). The purpose of the changes was to provide a smooth transition to democracy. The "Pact" also resulted in the presidency of Arpád Göncz, stand-ing as the SZDSZ candidate. A prototype of the "opposition agreement," how-ever, did not serve long, as the alliance began to lose the credit it had had as an opposition in the eyes of its electorate, and their support started migrating in favor of the FIDESZ (Benda 1998, 369).

What kind of a legacy was it that the right-center government had to cope with? Hungary, along with Poland and Czechoslovakia, could benefit from the fact that the country had experienced a reform attempt before. The three crises in Central Europe—the year 1956 in Hungary, the Prague Spring, and the rise of Solidarity—had helped to establish the core of civic society. In addition, some participants in those dramatic moments became dissidents who contem-plated the reforms necessary for the overthrow of communism. This is related to the restoration of nationhood and patriotism, severely suppressed during the Soviet era, and also to the renaissance of cultural awareness, which is (as are politics and the economy) influenced by the external world from the point at which changes are launched.

One of the worst consequences of a totalitarian system, and perhaps the most critical point in the process of restoration and development, was the destruction or major restriction of private entrepreneurship, resulting in the absence of a middle class, which is absolutely indispensable for building up a market system (Rupnik 1999, 59–60). This factor seems to be crucial. Where was the middle class to be recruited? The same question must be asked as far as the genesis of the political elite is concerned. Observing the development of Western democracies as well as the transitional regimes at the end of the twen-tieth century, we discover that the concept of the political elite is too narrow. Defining the concept of the elite by means of power, we have to conclude that the sources of such power are not just of a political, but also an economic (if not some other) nature.

In the 1990s, the Hungarian elite was gathered from three groups that had been constituted as early as during the previous regime: (1) late technocrats around Kádár, (2) persons who appeared in public life outside the established structures and did not wish to be associated with them (i.e., the opposition), and

(3) the opposition and reform intellectuals appearing in public life, but within the structures of power. The reform intelligentsia was split into two groups: the first one was affiliated with the democratic opposition, and the other group, the populist writers, was concentrated around the national ideology.

These platforms played the role of external political structures only until the collapse of the communist system. Then competition took over, with the winner the Hungarian Democratic Forum, a party established around populist writers. This result was accounted for by social empathy on the part of the writing intelligentsia, who had managed to anticipate the moods and expectations of the people (Szalai 1995, 162). However, the transformation's requirements put a stop to an immediate fulfillment of those expectations concerning, above all, a rapid achievement of the standard of living common in the Western European democracies.

The political elite was not confined only to the national government; it also involved the opposition. The opposition SZDSZ, as well as the ruling MDF, were hoping that a bipartisanism would be constituted, which would allow an alternating distribution of power between these political bodies (Benda 1998, 370). The declining electoral support of both parties, conflicts inside the national government, and, most importantly, increasing suspicion among party members prevented that scenario from being implemented.

The then high-profile technocrats enjoyed a much sounder position. These people succeeded in putting down roots, especially in the banking sector, thus founding their positions on increasing economic strength (Szalai 1995, 162).

Sustaining credit in the eyes of the nation was a fundamental problem of all the countries under transformation. In Hungary, apathy came very early, and later on there was even a deterioration of affinity for the new system's politics. Low membership in the new political bodies outside the center, especially in small towns and rural areas, was a contributing factor (Stumpf 1995, 109). Some sources state that in 1990, 20 percent of the population lived in poverty (Goldman 1997, 203), which might be the reason why József Antall was promoting a slower rate of transformation than recommended by the noted economist Jeffrey Sachs, an advisor to the Polish government and also to the Free Democrats and FIDESZ in Hungary.

Despite the declarations of the national-conservative government in favor of the social market economy, the influence of the state administration on the economy significantly decreased in 1990–94. The results, with the plunge into much more modest social conditions being the most politically sensitive, called for major intervention later on. At the same time, Václav Klaus, in order to gain support from the public, meticulously followed the line of social peace by pursuing a far milder economic policy, although his neoliberal rhetoric played the most radical note among all of the transforming post-Soviet European states

(Bruszt and Stark 1998, 156–57). The starting position of Hungary was much worse than that of Czechoslovakia. In the latter, the Czech national government benefited for some time from the split of the federal state, which among other things lifted the harshest social burdens from the responsibility of the cabinet in Prague.

For the future development of the Hungarian Republic, it was important that, despite political controversies and the economic and social downturn, the major political forces accepted a form of competition based on democratic rules and institutions (Highley and Pakulski 1992, 111). In those countries that had failed to find such a consensus, or where the consensus had been largely upset, the formation of a representative democracy and a free-market economy was jeopardized and threatened by possible evolution into an authoritarian regime (Slovakia under Mr. Mečiar or Belarus are examples).

Hungary, like the Czech Republic, Poland, and Slovenia, adopted a model of legitimizing the political elite from below, elections being of primary importance. In Hungary, the electorate's preferences have fluctuated between the right- and left-center since 1990. What is symptomatic is the declining support for extremist groups, which, when applied to Hungary, resulted in the rejection of the right-wing extremist István Czurka (Rose 1999, 52).

Because of this circulation of the elite, there occurred a radical change of political representation in 1994. The MDF, which received less than half the number of votes compared to the 1990 election, bore the brunt of the election defeat. Immediately after the election, the victory of the post-communist Hungarian Socialist Party (under the leadership of Gyula Horn) was accounted for (1) by the party's being in opposition during the previous electoral term, which had seen the transformation's social and economic impact and revived the myth of the stable Kádár era; (2) by good organization within the party; and (3) by the effects of anti-communist attacks by the media under the government's influence. In addition, the party elite's alleged ability to lead was presented as one of the fundamental factors that had caused the victory of the socialists (Szabó 1994, 96).

Taking a close look at how the media impacted the structure of a society undergoing transformation, we find that the electronic media (television, radio) played a negative role in the Hungary of the first half of the 1990s. Not only had they acted as the loudspeaker for the government until the new mass-media bill was passed in 1995, but they also discouraged the common people from being interested in politics by concentrating on the negative aspects of the contemporary political scene (Tökés 1996, 126).

Shortly after the election, the victorious MSZP tried to convince both the public and its political opponents that the party was no successor of the monolithic communist body—by proposing a coalition with the union office Democrats

forming a coalition (Király 1995, 29). The MSZP did so despite enjoying a parliamentary majority of 54 percent. What also contributed to the MSZP's success
was the fact that there had been a revival of extremism, whose chief spokesman,
István Czurka, was fond of the dangerous sport of refreshing memories of the
notorious rule of the Arrow Cross during World War II. In 1994, the electorate
opted for a safe development of the political system, and there is no doubt that
the MSZP benefited from fears of right-wing extremism.

Horn's cabinet had to adopt an economic policy that was not in accordance
with the MSZP's ideological profile. However, a similar approach is typical of
Central European governments during the transformation process, and was
applied by Hungarian cabinets in 1990–98 as well as their Czech counterparts
in 1992–97 (here with the opposite polarity) and in Poland, too.

The position of the then-communist minister of foreign affairs was at first
supported by the deterioration among the opposition after the election, when
the MDF and FIDESZ fell below the eligibility rate for some time. However,
the cabinet struggled for a long time to shape an economic policy, which
resulted in the increase of the national debt to US$30 billion. In early 1995, the
government defined its economic policy—which, despite Horn's declarations
about its social nature, would have a harsh impact in the social field, and which
economists now call an "orthodox liberalism" (Bruszt and Stark 1998, 173).

Then came a restoration of right-wing opposition caused by contradiction
between the original promises of Horn's government and the reality of its political steps. The popularity of Horn's cabinet was significantly declining from
1995 to 1997. But the crisis of the MSZP ceased in 1997, and it was clear that
only a coalition could elbow the party out of power. Emerging were two right-
wing political bodies that might attract the opposition towards Horn's left-center cabinet. One was the FKGP, with electoral preferences fluctuating in
1994–98 between 6 and 34 percent and ending up amounting to 13.2 percent
in the election (Cabada and Dvořáková 2000, 114). The alternative was the
Union of Young Democrats, which had received pathetically few votes in the
1994 election. However, in 1995 the FIDESZ started its efforts to create a right-
wing coalition, which would take its final shape after many complications
(mainly because of the KDNP) at the end of 1997. When the party changed its
name to the Union of Young Democrats–Hungarian Civic Party (FIDESZ-
MPP), and its policy shifted from liberalism to a more conservative position, it
formed a coalition with the MDF (Benda 1998, 376).

Unlike in the 1994 election, when Antall's unsuccessful policy had pre-
saged a change in the elite in power, the 1998 election results were difficult to
predict, and the first round showed oncoming troubles due to the low
turnout.[11] The first round featured careful campaigning by the greatest rivals
(FIDESZ-MPP and MSZP), but the second round turned dramatic because of

the ultranationalist Czurka, who had made it through the first round, and brought about a significant change in the electoral rhetoric towards a radical note on both sides. The socialists were warning of a possible after-election coalition of the Union of Young Democrats and Czurka's Party of Hungarian Justice and Life (MIEP), while the FIDESZ-MPP retaliated by reminding voters of the unfulfilled promises of Horn's cabinet (Lomax 1999, 120).

Negotiations about the coalition began after the second round, which had seen a close victory for the FIDESZ-MPP. As far as the MDF was concerned, they found a consensus very soon, but negotiations with the Small Farmers' Party were not launched until an extraordinary party conference. The coalition agreement was much more complex, and included a promise that the FKGP would propose a candidate for the 2000 presidential election.

Orbán's FIDESZ won the election of 1998, even though the MSZP obtained more votes.[12] The electoral coalition of FIDESZ and MDF established before the elections could create stable government only due to the support of FKGP. However, it was FIDESZ that became the leading force of the 1998–2002 government.

Conclusion: The Hungarian Political Elite since 1998 in the Context of Central European Politics

Hungarian politics since 1990 is probably the most visible example of voter support oscillating between the Left and Right. This tendency was proven again in the 1998 elections. FIDESZ's government of Viktor Orbán followed some general tendencies of the political elite in Central Europe, such as an increased effort to control the media, rearrangement of the administrative divisions of the state in favor of the governing elite, and coalition building or cooperation with nontraditional political forces. Some of these aspects can be observed in more established democracies: Silvio Berlusconi's dominance over the media in Italy, or the presence of the extreme right-wing Austrian Freedom Party in the Austrian government.

Soon after its composition, Orbán's government sought to establish guarantees for political dominance beyond one electoral term. There were a number of such attempts in Central Europe in the late 1990s—for example, the Slovak electoral law of 1998, which was designed by Mečiar's ruling party to achieve victory in the September elections (Dürr 2000, 14), or the so-called "Oppositional Treaty" between the Social Democrats and Klaus's Civic Democratic Party in the Czech Republic, which was designed to create an equal distribution of power between these two parties by a set of constitutional changes. These attempts, especially their complexity, kept Central European regimes in the category of transition countries (this was often perceived as a negative label by the leaders of the region, such as Klaus). Existing opposition and the media criticized such a policy in all the countries. Furthermore, the public became increasingly sensitive to the monopolization of power and the subsequent undermining of democratic institutions and practices. However, FIDESZ's government widely ignored public concerns about the monopolization of power. Orbán's cabinet was the only post-communist one of that time bolstering its position by unspoken but existing support of an extremist party. This party, István Czurka's MIEP, represented one of the most anti-Semitic and xenophobic forces in the whole region, and the vast majority of Hungarian society perceived MIEP as a direct threat to democracy. This was not the only sign of FIDESZ's change from a very progressive democratization force of 1990 into a rather extreme right-wing party by the late 1990s. FIDESZ very soon attempted to "weaken the legislature and the autonomy of local governments and thus decrease the checks and limits on the executive power" (Kiss 2002, 745), which was very unique even for a transforming country. Despite a pledge by the government to represent all 15 million Hungarians inside and outside the country, Orbán divided the society with attempts to increase governmental control over the media, and efforts to scandalize the opposition. The split between the "left-wing Budapest and pro-right-wing countryside was so deep that some authors describe it as 'cold civil war'" (Chmel 2002, 5).

In the late 1990s, international issues once again became important for Central European elites. The end of the 1980s brought the collapse of external threats, which largely shaped the Central and Eastern European political elite after World War II. At the dawn of the twenty-first century, the governments of Poland, Hungary, and the Czech Republic were looking to incorporate their states into NATO and the European Union. As Viktor Orbán turned into a very populist leader, his government welcomed Hungary's admittance to NATO in 1999 based on a 1997 referendum that Orbán could not ignore. However, FIDESZ became known for a rather nationalist foreign policy, which criticized neighbors and EU officials as well as domestic left-centrist forces and their supporters. Orbán's government repeatedly talked about the 15 million members of a Hungarian nation, which raised fears about a rising nationalism. These fears appeared to be confirmed by the so-called "Status Law" that extended social-security benefits for Hungarians living outside the country. This troubled not only countries with a Hungarian minority, especially Slovakia, but Brussels too. Orbán also commented on postwar Czechoslovak presidential decrees, and he did not prevent MIEP from making openly anti-Semitic statements.

What is the recent structure of the Hungarian political elite? It is definitely more polarized than any other nation in the region. There could be some parallel with Slovak politics, although former prime minister Mečiar's movement has been withdrawing from the political scene since the 2002 elections. Hungarian politics continues to have the left–right division of political forces. There is still a clear discrepancy between action and propaganda, particularly in the economic sphere.[13] Transitional political elites in Central Europe continue their attempts to establish long-lasting political influence, but Orbán's FIDESZ went furthest in its methods, rhetoric, and reliance on extreme political forces (MIEP). Only the future will answer the question of whether or not the behavior of FIDESZ from 1998 to 2002 was the exception to an already largely democratized political elite in the region, or if the post-communist political elite still needs to complete the democratization process.

NOTES

1. The Soviet leadership was divided on the question of a military response to a revolution in a member state of the Warsaw Pact. Part of the Soviet elite suggested a very careful policy after the October decision to bring Soviet troops into the streets of Budapest as guards. However, Nagy's speech on 1 November caused the Soviet armies to change from patrol activity to offensive military action.

2. The Yugoslav leader Josip Broz Tito was afraid of possible Hungarian revisionism in case of the successful withdrawal of Hungary from the socialist camp. The threatening vision of a territorial dispute with a new Hungarian leadership enabled Tito to forget about the Soviet-Yugoslav split for a moment.

3. The relatively smooth emigration was caused by the Soviet agreement to open the Hungarian-Austrian border to refugees during the first months after the invasion. The U.S. authorities also granted asylum to a large group of Hungarians, and urged the Austrian side to organize the quick processing of asylum applications to the United States (Nálevka 2000, 37).

4. The Hungarian Communist Party was originally called the Hungarian Workers' Party. It was renamed the Hungarian Socialist Workers' Party in 1956, and finally changed its title to the Hungarian Socialist Party in 1989. Henceforth Communist Party or MSZMP.

5. David Stark and László Bruszt, "Remaking the Political Field in Hungary: From the Politics of Confrontation to the Politics of Competition," in Banac (1992, 30). MDF had fewer than 10,000 members, and SZDSZ around 1,500.

6. Gyula Horn was minister of foreign affairs at this time, and later prime minister of Hungary (1994–98).

7. The representatives of social organizations had been, de facto, forced to step aside.

8. For details, see Pipes (1990).

9. Rudolf Tökés, a Hungarian political scientist, used this term with respect to the situation in Hungary. However, it is also applied to other countries in the transitional process towards democracy (i.e., Poland, and more rarely the former German Democratic Republic and the Czech Republic).

10. See Cabada and Dvor̆áková (2000), 99 and 114. MFD won 164, FKGP 44, and KDNP 21 seats.

11. Under the electoral law, results are invalid in those constituencies where less than 50 percent of eligible voters came to cast their ballot.

12. For the results and the distribution of the seats see http://www.election.hu/en/13/13_3.html.

13. Large domestic private enterprises as well as foreign investors and the EU were threatened by Orbán's statement announcing possible renationalization of the oil and gas company MOL. They were rather satisfied with the perspective of electoral victory of the more credible MSZP. See Christopher Condon, "Hungary Makes a Surprise Left Turn," *Business Week On-line 4*, no. 23 (2002).

REFERENCES

Banac, Ivo, ed. 1992. *Eastern Europe in revolution.* Ithaca, NY: Cornell University Press.

Barany, Zoltan, and Ivan Volgyes, eds. 1995. *The legacies of Communism in Eastern Europe.* Baltimore: Johns Hopkins University Press.

Benda, Lukás̆. 1998. Systém politicky´ch stran v Mad̆arské republice. *Politologicky´ c̆asopis* 5(4): 366–91.

Bova, Russell. 1991. Political dynamics of the post-Communist transition: A comparative perspective. *World Politics* 44(1): 113–38.

Bozóki, András. 1995. Hungary's road to systemic change. In *Lawful revolution in Hungary, 1989–94,* ed. Béla K. Király. New York: Columbia University Press.

Bozóki, András, András Körösényi, and George Schöpflin, eds. 1992. *Post-Communist transition: Emerging pluralism in Hungary.* London: Pinter Publishers.

Bruszt, László, and David Stark. 1998. *Postsocialist pathways: Transforming politics and property in East Central Europe.* New York: Cambridge University Press.

Bunce, Valerie. 1999. Lessons of the first postsocialist decade. *East European Politics and Societies* 13(2): 236–43.

Bútora, Martin, and Zora Bútorová. 1999. Slovakia's democratic awakening. *Journal of Democracy* 10(1): 80–95.

Cabada, Ladislav, Vladimíra Dvor̆áková, eds. 2000. Komparace politicky´ch systému˚ III. Prague: VSE.

Chmel, Rudolf. 2002. Volby nielen mad̆arské. *OS–Fórum obc̆ianskéj spoloc̆nosti* 6(6): 2–7.

Cottey, Andrew. 1995. *East-Central Europe after the cold war: Poland, the Czech Republic, Slovakia and Hungary in search of security.* London: Macmillan.

Dawisha, Karen, and Bruce Parrott, eds. 1997. *The consolidation of democracy in East-Central Europe.* Cambridge: Cambridge University Press.

Dunay, Pál. 1995. New friends instead of old foes: Hungary's relation with the West. In *Lawful revolution in Hungary, 1989–94,* ed. Béla K. Király. New York: Columbia University Press.

Dürr, Jakub. 2000. Political elite in Slovakia. Unpublished manuscript.

Furet, François. 1998. Democracy and Utopia. *Journal of Democracy* 9(1): 65–79.

Geremek, Bronislaw. 1999. The transformation of Central Europe. *Journal of Democracy* 10(3): 113–20.

Glatz, Ferenc. 1995. Multiparty system in Hungary, 1989–1990. In *Lawful revolution in Hungary, 1989–94*, ed. Béla K. Király. New York: Columbia University Press.

Goldman, Minton F. 1997. *Revolution and change in Central and Eastern Europe: Political, economic, and social challenges*. Armonk, NY: M. E. Sharpe.

Haraszti, Miklós. 1999. Decade of the handshake transition. *East European Politics and Societies* 13(2): 288–92.

Hashim, Mohsin. 2002. Shadows of the past: Successor parties in the Polish, Hungarian, and Russian transitions. *Problems of Post-Communism* 49(3): 42–58.

Highley, John, and Jan Pakulski. 1992. Revolution and elite transformation in Eastern Europe. *Australian Journal of Political Science* 2: 104–19.

Irmamová, Eva. 1999. Kadárismus. Vzestup a pád jedné iluze. Prague: Karolinum.

Hollander, Paul. 2002. Hungary ten years later. *Society* 39(6): 66–72.

Kende, Péter. 1995. The Trianon syndrome: Hungarians and their neighbors. In *Lawful revolution in Hungary, 1989–94*, ed. Béla K. Király. New York: Columbia University Press.

Kennez, Peter. 2002. Hungary on the road to democracy. *New Leader* 85(5): 8–10.

Király, Béla K. 1995. Soft dictatorship, lawful revolution, and the Socialists' return to power. In *Lawful revolution in Hungary, 1989–94*, ed. Béla K. Király. New York: Columbia University Press.

Király, Béla K., ed. 1995. *Lawful revolution in Hungary, 1989–94*. New York: Columbia University Press.

Kiss, Csilla. 2002. From liberalism to conservatism: The federation of young Democrats in post-Communist Hungary. *East European Politics and Societies* 16: 739–63.

Kontler, László. 2001. Dějiny Maďarska. Prague: NLN.

Kopeček, Lubomír. 2001. Transformace středoevropských komunistických stran. Polský a maďarský příklad. *Central European Political Studies Review* 3(2). (Available at http://www.iips.cz/seps.html).

Körösényi, András. 1992. The decay of Communist rule in Hungary. In *Post-Communist transition: Emerging pluralism in Hungary*, ed. András Bozóki, András Körösényi, and George Schöpflin. London: Pinter Publishers.

Kuran, Timur. 1991. Now out of never: The element of surprise in the East European revolution of 1989. *World Politics* 44(1): 7–48.

Lomax, Bill. 1999. The 1998 elections in Hungary: Third time lucky for young democrats. *Journal of Communist Studies and Transition Politics* 15(2): 111–25.

Nálevka, Vladimír. 2000. Světová politika ve 20. století II. Prague: Nakladatelství Aleš Skřival ml.

Palma, Giuseppe di. 1999. Legitimation from the top to civil society. *World Politics* 44(1): 49–80.

Parrott, Bruce. 1997. Perspectives on post-communist democratization. In *The consolidation of democracy in East-Central Europe*, ed. Karen Dawisha and Bruce Parrott. Cambridge: Cambridge University Press.

Rose, Richard. 1999. Another great transformation. *Journal of Democracy* 10(1): 51–56.

Poznanski, Kazimerz. 1999. Recounting transition. *East European Politics and Societies* 13(2): 328–44.

Rupnik, Jacques. 1999. The post-communist divide. *Journal of Democracy* 10(1): 57–62.

Seda, Jakub. 2000. Parlamentní volby v Maďarsku 2002. *Central European Political Studies Review* 4(4). (Available at http://www.iips.cz/seps.html)

Stumpf, István. 1995. Evolution of political parties and the 1990 parliamentary elections. In *Lawful revolution in Hungary, 1989–94*, ed. Béla K. Király. New York: Columbia University Press.

Szabó, Máté. 1994. Volby v Mad'arsku (8.-29.5. 1994). *Politologický časopis* 1(2): 96–99.

Szalai, Erzsébet. 1995. The metamorphosis of the elites. In *Lawful revolution in Hungary, 1989–94*, ed. Béla K. Király. New York: Columbia University Press.

Tamás, G. M. 1999. Victory defeated. *Journal of Democracy* 10(1): 63–68.

Taras, Ray, ed. 1997. *Post-communist presidents*. Cambridge: Cambridge University Press.

Tismaneanu, Vladimir. 1999. Reassessing the revolutions of 1989. *Journal of Democracy* 10(1): 69–73.

———, ed. 1999. *Revolutions of 1989*. London and New York: Routledge.

Tóka, Gábor. 1998. Hungary. In *The handbook of political change in Central Europe*, ed. Sten Berglund, Tomas Hellén, and Frank H. Aarebot, 231–74. Northampton, MA: E. Elgar.

Tökés, Rudolf L. 1996. Hungary's negotiated revolution: Economic reform, social change, and political succession, 1957–1990. Cambridge: Cambridge University Press.

———. 1997. Party politics and political participation in post-communist Hungary. In *The consolidation of democracy in East-Central Europe*, ed. Karen Dawisha and Bruce Parrott. Cambridge: Cambridge University Press.

Tong, Yanqi. 1997. *Transition from state socialism: Economic and political change in Hungary and China*. Lanham, MD: Rowman and Littlefield.

Whitehead, Laurence. 1999. Geography and democratic destiny. *Journal of Democracy* 10(1): 74–79.

INTERNET SOURCES

http://www.mfa.gov.hu/NATO/joint-EN.htm
http://www.mfa.gov.hu/euint/huneu_chr.html
http://www.election.hu/en/index.html

8

A Post-Communist Landscape: Social and Moral Costs of the Regime Change in Post-Communist Hungary

András Lánczi

ast European political developments have been out of focus as a result of the completion of democratic transition in most of these countries in the late 1990s. Many criteria are applied to measure the level of the completion; the least demanding one suggests that if at least two free, fair election cycles have been finished, the particular new democracy can be declared to be consolidated. Bruce Parrott puts it in this way: "To say that democracy has been consolidated in a country suggests, at a minimum, that the introduction of fully competitive elections has been completed and that the new political system has become stable. . . . Whether any of the postcommunist states have achieved democratic consolidation is a complex issue" (Parrott 1997, 6). This minimal requirement is certainly silent about the type, quality, output, and relevant social and cultural dimensions of a democratic regime other than mere procedural aspects. "Complexity" of post-communist transition entails all these variables. All things considered, Hungary can be declared to be a stable democracy, with democratic institutions and with four free elections. The specificity of the systemic change in Hungary and in Eastern Europe in general was detected in its peaceful character, and the chief means of restructuring the political institutions were the roundtable negotiations first applied successfully in Poland. Founding a new polity, however, requires both legal and moral grounds—a sort of common sentiment and faith in the evolving constitutional frameworks.

When East European states were reestablished as democracies, these were purely acts of political construction, without overt reference to such standards as natural law or justice. Instead, the new political elite derived its legitimacy from a vision of following Western-type democratic arrangements and procedures, with substantial and intellectual support from the United States and other Western societies, and based all its activities on legal positivism. Good was automatically identified with the West, which made debates over fundamental political notions into side issues—hence the lack of authentic political philosophy in the post-communist world (cf. Faragó 1986, 49; Lánczi 2000, 200–201). Instead, such immediate political goals were set as turning a command economy into a free-market one, redrawing the whole constitutional framework, and demolishing the iron curtain in terms of social, cultural, and spiritual development.

Acknowledgement of the adoption of Western political patterns and procedures was expressed by admitting several post-communist countries into both NATO and the European Union in the past few years. Unfortunately, one is less inclined to ponder over the real conditions and costs of these achievements. Does it matter, for example, that during the past 14 years, the post-communist political parties and movements have often managed to return to power in several post-communist ountries, for example, Poland, Hungary, and Romania? By post-communists, I mean all those politicians and successor parties that served the communist regime in various ranks, and that pride themselves on dismantling communism by undermining it from within—also known as "reform communists." This line of argument has gone so far as to practically deny communism as a vicious and politically corrupt form of government. Similarly, moral relativism has become a predominant worldview and form of judgment, still regarding history as the only source and reference point of moral standards. Historicism has hardly even been questioned, together with other diluted Marxian tenets such as exploitation, historical necessity, atheism, etc. Communism as a form of government may be dead, but as morality and political judgment, it is just as virulent as ever. I claim that communism as a political culture, mentality, and attitude is not dead at all, and even where it is dead, nihilism is always at hand.

The return of the communist vote was first observed in the mid-1990s, when—with the exception of the Czech Republic—post-communists returned to power in ex-Soviet satellite countries. And it was repeated in the early 2000s. While voters in the European Union have been shifting right, they seem to be turning left in post-communist countries. James Geary writes of the possible reasons as follows: "The Central European left has often been more successful in implementing 'right-wing' policies—like privatization and other market-focused reforms—than the right itself. In Hungary, for example, it was the Socialists who in the mid-1990s began privatizing the banking and utility sectors, reforming the pension system and introducing unpopular budget cuts" (Geary 2002). The author also cites Jiri Pehe, a Czech political analyst, in his piece: "In Central Europe, people are voting Socialist because they feel these parties are more competent to lead them into the European Union." Such views keep moving within the boundaries fixed by the intentions of the founders in 1989, but tend to forget about the complexity of the reasons leading up to the political tendencies in Central Europe, which are almost the opposite experienced in the European Union. To date, no one has analyzed the interplay of social, cultural, and intellectual trends resulting in what we call a "post-communist" society.

Below, I try to give a rough sketch of the social and moral costs of the systemic change started in 1989. The aspects treated here include issues like standards of life, trends in employment policy, gender gap, and their economic background. As for the moral aspects, I wish to point out that the political arena is still divided along the communist/anti-communist cleavage, although with diminishing fervor. It is also a point of concern to analyze the relative weakness of conservative political parties in Central Europe, and the underdeveloped condition of conservative thought and policies.

The Meaning of Regime Changes in Eastern Europe

A considerable amount of ink has been used to interpret the nature of political transition or systemic change or regime change in the post-communist world. Timothy Garton Ash coined the term "refolution," trying to come as close as possible to the essence of political developments in Central and Eastern Europe in 1989 and the ensuing decade. The neologism implies that what happened was more than mere implementation of a set of reforms, but also less than a brand-new beginning. Some prefer to use the term "systemic change," referring to the social-engineering nature of the political transition from communist to democratic political arrangements, also implying that changes penetrated the deeper tissues of the society. This interpretation is voiced mainly by reform communists, whose interest is to get themselves accepted as thoroughbred democrats. Others tend to apply the concept of "regime change," by which they want to convey the idea that the system of government was restructured, but deeper layers of societal life and attitudes resist changes. No wonder that among the main cleavages the communist/anti-communist cleavage has remained strong next to urban-rural and religious-secular dichotomies, and is now being reproduced by the emerging-nationalism/European-integration cleavage. This latter one could also be interpreted in terms of particularism and universalism, or in another dimension as the conflict of the nation-state and globalization imperatives.

Without raising the issue of legitimacy of a post-communist polity, it is impossible to interpret current developments of a post-communist society. Those participating in the roundtable negotiations in 1989 to frame a new constitution, which put an end to the communist rule, tacitly acted under the assumptions of legal positivism often related to the conception of Hans Kelsen. Prior to legal positivism, power needed some ethical justification to survive. In the age of legal positivism, a power is legitimate if it is effective. Norberto Bobbio writes: "On the basis of the principle of effectiveness a regime remains legitimate until its effectiveness has reached the point of making probable or foreseeable the effectiveness of an alternative regime" (Bobbio 1989, 87). This alternative regime was foreseeable in 1989, and by placing the representatives of the ruling Communist Party, of the opposition movements and parties, and those of the so-called "third side" (trade unions, youth organizations, etc.) at a table, they posited themselves as a quasi-national assembly (for more details, see Tökés 1996). There was no appeal to natural law or natural justice, as if founding a new regime was nothing else than replacing an old and worn machine by a new one, making good use of the working parts of the old machine and building them into the new. No wonder that any moral issue appearing afterwards has been either hushed up, or treated inadequately. The most relevant example is the case of lustration, which was applied in a few post-communist countries and haunts these societies even today. There have been three routes taken in this respect. The first option was taken by the Czechs and the Germans, who passed laws of incompatibility, thus excluding the most notorious representatives of communism from political life. Another option was to make public all the names involved in the secret agencies of the previous regime. The third one was followed by Hungary, where a lustration procedure was conducted, and the possible outcome was either forcing someone to resign from his/her position due to incompatibility, or, because of the individual's unwillingness to resign, to make the name in question public. The Hungarian practice can be regarded as a mixed method, but at the same time, the least effective one. No one has had to leave the public field because of his/her earlier communist background.

The mixed and morally ungrounded character of the Hungarian political institutions, not only the institution of lustration, precisely reflects the dubious and undecided nature of the transition, and the unbalanced situation of power relations during the time of the roundtable talks and the following years. It is enough to take a look, for instance, at the Hungarian electoral system, which is one of the most complicated ones in Europe, to get a rough idea of what is meant by the above statement. The 386 seats in the Hungarian unicameral parliament are allocated on the basis of single-member districts (176), territorial party lists (152, calculated by the Hagenbach-Bishoff formula), and national lists (58, calculated by the d'Hondt formula). Also, other institutions have been struggling with earlier unbroken practices inherited from the communist past. A good example is the impoverished conditions of health care and public education preserved from the old regime; the most scandalous is perhaps the tipping system in health care where, irrespective of one's social-security payments, every medical treatment has its own price—paid by the patient by means of an envelope slipped into the doctor's pocket. Such practices mar not only public morality, but the effectiveness of the state through an unjust taxation system.

The media is also one of the most unbalanced areas of political competition. After five years of parliamentary debates and extraparliamentary clashes, a new media bill was passed by the Hungarian parliament in 1995 (cf. Lánczi and O'Neil 1997). This law, which is a prime example of constructivist reasoning, had fallen into disfavor even in the eyes of its framers by 2002. Its failure is partly due to the constant financial crises of public media, the importance of which is traditionally high and has symbolic significance, and partly due to the breaching of the various provisions of the media law sanctioning programs that do not comply with "the spirit of the law." Again, we have proof of the inadequacy of a law that is too detailed, and despite its explicit intention to keep politics away from the media, because of the bureaucratic and paternalistic supervising council established to guard the proper functioning of the media, political agents can interfere with the media relatively easily. Media policy offers a reliable insight into the low level of trust cementing post-communist Hungary, as well as other countries sharing the same plight.

More and more signs show that the peaceful character of the regime change has left untouched various segments of social life, with the exception of the economic field. Whereas in the economy there was a strong and mandatory pressure to restructure both ownership relationships and macroeconomic policymaking, fields like interest representation, lobby activities, the media, education, and culture in general have been dominated by networks established during the communist period. More and more people have come to realize that among interest groups both in economic life and emerging civil society, the old ties have proved to be more virulent and effective than any other new formations. There is enough evidence to point out that the one-time communist functionaries managed to convert their political power to economic might through the yet-unknown story of privatization throughout the post-communist countries.

In studying the meaning of regime change in a post-communist country like Hungary, it is necessary to give a short description of the economic transition, which is indispensable to understanding the issue of social costs, and its impact on political elections between 1989 and 2002. Economic transition from a planned economy to a market economy required three macro-level political changes and their realizations: first, privatization (i.e., changing the ownership structure based on roughly 90–93 percent public ownership to a more market-friendly ratio of 75 percent private ownership by means of privatization devices); second, introducing a new taxation system to make production expenses visible (i.e., every single economic decision should be made accountable, and the costs calculable); third, restructuring the whole economy by getting rid of unprofitable forms of production, transforming the banking system, and reforming the public sector. By and large, these were the urgent imperatives for every former command economy: to restructure the whole economic system with the stipulation that the size of the state and its power to interfere should be minimized.

In Hungary, paradoxically but predictably, the goal of minimizing state intervention in the economic sphere even gained impetus while the state was conducting privatization and restructuring the economy. It was a state agency, the State Privatization and Assets Agency (it has been renamed several times) that carried out one of the most liberal and fastest privatization projects in Eastern Europe, the essence of which was to sell public assets to the highest bidders without any discrimination. Foreign investors, therefore, were welcome and even preferred. A second feature of the Hungarian economic policy was a challenge posed by an almost unmanageable amount of foreign loans (ca. US$20–22 billion in 1989) accumulated and misspent by the communist governments. And a little over 14 percent of the annual public budget of 2000 still had to be spent on clearing foreign debts. A third feature was a dilemma that had to be decided in every post-communist society: the speed and resultant political risks of restructuring. It was obvious from the outset that a highly centralized economy cannot be changed without pain and tears—that is, without paying the costs of economic transformation. Poland opted for a quick and painful restructuring policy, also known as "shock therapy." The currency was devalued, unprofitable factories were closed, and public spending was drastically reduced. In other countries, for example Hungary, explicit shock therapy was not implemented, but in March 1995 an economic-austerity package was introduced (also known as the "Bokros package" after the name of the finance minister then in office), and public spending was radically cut back. Although people understood that they needed to tighten their belts, the goal was to shift public resources from the public sphere to the private, thus beefing up an ailing economy. As a result, the most demanding areas of public expenditure— like health care, education, and pensions—have had to pay the price, thus creating grave tensions between the government and diverse social groups. In short, the initial political consensus about the role and significance of the above-mentioned macroeconomic policy goals became fragile, or even ceased to exist by 2000. Needless to say, the political and social consequences must be understood within this framework.

Social Costs

Social trends and tendencies can be measured in various contexts. What I wish to do here is simply to point out statistically how economic and political developments may have influenced the length and quality of life under conditions of a peaceful regime change in Hungary. I have no intention to provide exhaustive data, only facets of what I call the social costs of a regime change, thus grounding arguments about the outcomes of the general political elections taking place in Hungary in 2002, and explaining the return of the communist vote after 1989.

A natural starting point is to study the demographic charts in a broader time context. Thomas M. Kando writes in his article about demographic and public health-care trends in Hungary:

> Like the other former Communist countries of Eastern Europe, Hungary faces challenges on the demographic, public health and family life front. It would be an exaggeration to say that the country is facing a public health and demographic crisis. . . . Nevertheless, the country's demographic and public health statistics are unhealthy, showing population decline, short life expectancy, high suicide rates, low fertility and low marriage rates. These, in turn, are caused by economic factors such as unemployment and housing shortage, and by a *cultural malaise.* (Kando 2001)

It is hardly possible to describe a case more succinctly than above. Let us look at each item in a somewhat more detailed breakdown. As for life expectancy, data for men in the population between 20 and 49 years of age reflect a serious decline, the nadir of which occurred in the mid-1990s. Average Hungarian male life expectancy was 64.5 (1995), which was eight years less than comparable European figures. By 2000 it had changed a little, climbing a bit above 66 years—still well below similar figures in other European countries. Women have been less hard-hit in this respect, but they were a lot more affected by rising unemployment throughout the 1990s. Roughly one-third of the Hungarian female population is unemployed (the European average is 32.6 percent), so seemingly there is nothing to worry about. The problem is that before the regime change, the proportion of the inactive population was 24.5 percent, and this figure jumped up to 46.1 percent by 1998. It was mainly women who were forced from the active into the inactive category. This is due to shrinking job opportunities, especially in age cohorts over 40. There has been a very strong tendency to devalue the expertise of those over 40 who, even if they have college or university degrees, lose their jobs. Statistics show that among the potential workforce, the proportion of those in jobs is 57 percent in Hungary, whereas the same figures are 73 percent in the United States, 82 in Japan, and 69 in the European Union, respectively. And it is mainly rural women who are discriminated against in the job market.

It is always difficult to name actual reasons for social and political changes, but there is an outstanding correlation that is observed between abortion rates and political commitment in Hungary. Abortion has always been very high in Hungary; the peak was in the 1960s, 1970s, and 1980s. The highest figure was 206,817 in 1969 (Hungary's total population has oscillated between 10.80 million and 10.13 million), and ever since there has been a slow decline, until now it stands at about 70,000 annually. The picture was still very dim in the 1990s, despite all efforts to reduce the number of abortion cases. The 1993 Abortion Law was liberal in judging who could apply for a legal abortion, and the relatively high number of abortion cases annually was partly responsible for the population decline, causing many headaches for the politicians. Table 8.1 shows Hungary's declining population, and table 8.2 the age distribution of Hungarian and U.S. populations with predictions.

Despite soaring abortion figures earlier, actual population decline began only in the 1980s, but seems to be constant in subsequent decades as well. Fewer than 10 million people were predicted to be living in Hungary in 2000, but according to the latest census, this has not yet happened. The last column indicates that Hungary has been slipping further back among the nations of the world.

Kando (2001) adds as an explanation that Hungary's population is older than that of the United States, and what is more, Hungary's population pyramid is one of the most inverted ones, i.e., "top-heavy with elderly and with a small base of young, tax-paying workers." Now it is understandable why the previous prime minister, Viktor Orbán, had wanted to facilitate the immigration of ethnic Hungarians from neighboring countries, making himself politically vulnerable to the opposition's accusation that "millions of Rumanians will flood the Hungarian job market." It was a strong message to the Hungarian electorate, despite the government's constant denial of this possibility (now that the "Status Law" regulating foreigners' job applications is in effect, only a few hundred (!) such applications have been submitted to the Hungarian authorities through 2002—but the elections are over, and the opposition won).

Returning to the point of the observable relationship between political commitments and the number of abortion cases, it was shocking to see that the counties in Hungary (there are 19 of them in addition to the capital,

TABLE 8.1 Hungary's Population, Selected Years, 1970 to 2010 (projected)

YEAR	POPULATION (THOUSANDS)	GROWTH RATE	RANK
1970	10,337	4.0	49th
1980	10,711	3.0	54th
1984	10,681	–1.0	58th
1999	10,569	–0.3	63rd
2000	10,139	–0.2	75th
2010 (projected)	9,831	–0.3	—

SOURCE: Kando 2001.

TABLE 8.2 Age Distribution of Hungarian and U.S. Populations

COUNTRY	2000		2010 (PROJECTED)	
Hungary	<15: 16.9%	>65: 14.6%	<15: 13.9%	>65: 15.6%
United States	<15: 21.2%	>65: 12.6%	<15: 21.6%	>65: 14.4%

SOURCE: Kando 2001.

TABLE 8.3 Number of Divorces in Hungary

YEAR	DIVORCES
1960	16,590
1980	27,797
1990	24,888
1999	25,605

SOURCE: *Nők és férfiak Magyarországon* [Men and Women in Hungary] 2000.

Budapest) where abortion rates are extremely high (Budapest is traditionally the leader in this list) are almost identical with those constituencies where the post-communist Hungarian Socialist Party achieved a landslide victory in the first round of the elections. These areas used to be the strongholds of enforced heavy industrialization projects of the communists, or places where the mining industry prevailed, or agricultural areas hard-hit by the economic restructuring in the 1990s. I would not venture to call this visible relationship a correlation, but perhaps this observation is enough evidence to detect one of the reasons for the return of the communist vote.

The number of divorces grew from year to year throughout the 1990s, as can be seen in table 8.3.

TABLE 8.4 Number of Suicides in Hungary

YEAR	MEN	WOMEN
1980	3,344	1,465
1995	2,478	891
1999	2,550	778

SOURCE: *Nők és férfiak Magyarországon* [Men and Women in Hungary] 2000.

TABLE 8.5 Death Rates in Four Countries from Three Sources, 1994 (per 100,000)

COUNTRY	HEART/VASCULAR DISEASE	LUNG CANCER	LIVER DISEASE
Hungary	411.2	65.9	81.3
Poland	189.1	52.1	12.8
Russia	706.0	44.7	n.a.
United States	221.7	57.3	10.5

SOURCE: Kando 2001.

Suicide rates have always been very high in Hungary, too; the roots proba-bly go back to the Habsburg-Hungarian monarchy, when suicide was a rela-tively widespread social means of private conflict management. It is true that the number of completed suicide cases decreased after the political changes of 1989, but in absolute figures and on a comparative basis with similar figures of other nations, this is still a vital problem in Hungary. Table 8.4 depicts the changes.

Hungary was the first among all nations in the 1980s in terms of the num-ber of completed suicide attempts compared to the total population. Consider-able changes have been registered only among women. Table 8.5 presents morbidity figures in Hungary from three main causes. Hungary does not com-pare favorably, especially with Poland and the United States.

Kando has a point in saying that "Hungary's astronomically high rates of morbidity due to heart disease and liver disease reflect its poor dietary habits and its extremely high alcohol consumption. The contrast with Poland is espe-cially instructive" (2001, 17). One would like to know if the reasons for these differences between the post-communist countries are mainly due to different cultural features determined by historical development, or if they reflect the different courses of transition already taken by sovereign and freely elected national governments. It is widely known that varied privatization schemes have been applied in the post-communist countries, and diverse public policies have been pursued, but the objectives were roughly the same: restructuring their command economies, introducing new constitutional arrangements, and joining the West in terms of social and cultural developments. It is not very likely that differences in implementation have led to different social and moral costs of the transition. An economic shock remains a shock, just as a pill does not lose its bitterness if you take it in cachet form. Post-communist transitions have been an expensive endeavor, and the expenses have been paid by the people. The psychological and material burdens had to be borne by everyone, and only a few could instantly benefit from the transition. Especially the elderly and/or inactive segments of the society, and children—as well as people living in old strongholds of communist industrialization and in some rural areas— can be called the losers of the transition.

The social impacts can be observed in the distorted social structure in Hungary as well. What is striking is the lack of a massive middle class, not only in Hungary but in post-communist societies in general. You have a very thin but extremely rich upper segment, the nouveau riche, a weak and narrow middle class, and an enormously large pool of people (45.7 percent in 1999) whose incomes fluctuate from year to year, sometimes living just above the poverty level, from hand to mouth (cf. Kolosi 2000, 114). This lower segment of the society amounts to 50 percent of the electorate who constitute the core of the post-communist parties. If the post-communist Socialist Party did not do anything in an election campaign, they would still get around 30–33 percent of the eligible votes. This, however, cannot simply be explained by the widening winners/losers gap. A lot of people, especially above the ages of 45–50, have been educated and indoctrinated by communist-controlled media and education systems, which are still dominated by post-communists (hence the bitter and constant struggle for controlling public media, the only possibility of the Right to counterbalance the weight of leftist-oriented private print and electronic media). Their worldview is certainly dominated by leftover ideologies of communist history books and other sources of ideological clichés that reflect post-communist ways of thinking. What is more, most of these people, understandably, would not accept any alternative political views offering a complete refusal of communism, because they would feel that their earlier life was also being devalued. Due to psychological reasons, one cannot expect people to turn against their own personal experiences and emotions that constitute their lives: most men and women were in love with each other, laughed, made trips, had fun of various sorts, lost their passed-away relatives and friends, etc., under communism, too. This is an important reason for the reemergence of the communist vote, and the opposite political trends in Western and Eastern Europe, despite policies of leftist governments between 1990 and 2002 that are more akin to right-wing policies in the West—a paradox that should be heeded by all analysts.

Hungary during the Kádár regime—roughly between the late 1960s and mid-1980s—was praised even by Western governments and political analysts because of its apparently more lenient political line and higher consumption ("goulash communism"). This attitude backfired after the collapse of communism. The so-called communist-reform elite could preserve its image as political reformers who are to be thanked for their political flexibility. As a consequence of their Western approval and political emancipation, they could become the champions of not only the economic transition but of political development as well. They preserved a sense of exceptionality and regard themselves as superior to non-communists. These two major factors combined—i.e., the masses of losers of the transition from communism to democracy, and the survival of some of the political elite rooted in the previous regime—are enough to explain why post-communists were able to return to power in 2002.

Elections of 2002: A Moral Divide in Post-Communist Hungary

The American reader is sometimes informed about Hungary by the *New York Times*, and may get the impression that there is a sound Left—including the successor party of the communist Hungarian Socialist Workers' Party, now called the Hungarian Socialist Party (MSZP), and the Alliance of Free Democrats (SZDSZ)—dedicated to liberal values. About the right-wing parties, the most denigrating views have been published describing the ex–prime minister, Viktor Orbán (aged 42), as flirting with an extreme, xenophobic, anti-Semitic radical right-wing party (which, by the way, failed to be reelected to the Hungarian legislature), and being an initiator of an authoritarian and nationalistic policy. It seems that post-communist rhetoric is still vivid and influential. One of the distinguishing features of surviving communism is its insistence that what is politically to the right cannot be anything but nationalistic. Post-communists usually turn a deaf ear to such insights like the one expressed by Ralph Dahrendorf (2001) that in Eastern Europe, nation-state "embodies not just sovereignty but freedom." It is, however, true that the meaning of concepts like national identity, national interest, order, self-assurance, family, and community values in general are vague, due to 40-odd years of communism that desperately worked to mop up every bit of national and intellectual traditions, which they had doomed to oblivion. What post-communist countries badly need is a modern conservatism based on a careful analysis of post-communist reality. Since post-communist politicians and their concerned journalists do their best to preserve this previous status and ready to use any means, however morally questionable, the price of the so-called and often celebrated "peaceful

TABLE 8.6 Allocation of Parliamentary Seats

Party	Single-member Districts	Regional Lists	National List	Overall	Proportion of Mandates in Parliament
FIDESZ					
MDF	95	67	26	188	48.70%
MSZP					
SZDSZ	1			1	0.26%
MSZP	78	69	31	178	46.11%
SZDSZ	2	4	13	19	4.92%
Total	176	140	70	386	100.00%[a]

SOURCE: Official Results of Hungarian Elections 2002 ().

(a.) Tabular numbers do not add to 100 due to rounding error.

transition" would be utmost moral and political relativism that sinfully mixes up the perpetrator and the victim, the powerful and the defenseless, the controller and the controlled—ultimately, good and evil.

Let me elaborate what it is like in everyday post-communist politics in terms of the last parliamentary elections. In Hungary, as we have seen, there is a mixed electoral system of single-member majoritarian constituencies and two lists securing proportionality, with two rounds sending 386 members to the unicameral Hungarian parliament. The president is elected by the parliament every five years. After a stormy campaign, the Socialists (MSZP) won the elections in coalition with the Free Democrats (SZDSZ) by a narrow margin, having only 10 seats more than the previous right-wing coalition led by Viktor Orbán (FIDESZ and MDF). Table 8.6 shows the allocation of seats in the Hungarian parliament as of 2002.

The FIDESZ and MDF formed a right-wing coalition government between 1998 and 2002. The MSZP and SZDSZ were already coalition partners between 1994 and 1998, and are considered a left-wing marriage between the post-communist Hungarian Socialist Party and the liberals (SZDSZ), whose original leaders had been hard-core dissidents under communism. The irony lies in the fact that one-time communists and persecuted political dissidents now sit side by side in the parliament and join their efforts to contain the political Right. The Socialists would not be able to govern the country by themselves, therefore the liberals' assistance is vital in maintaining the incumbent coalition government.

In many ways, the Hungarian elections resembled the last American presidential elections, for in a few constituencies only a couple of votes decided the contest, there were recounts, and the main cleavage was between the leftist capital, Budapest (with almost two million inhabitants), and the rural areas with their definitely conservative bent. Despite rumors about the Socialists' dubious maneuvers, Orbán's party (FIDESZ) finally admitted their failure. The new prime minister, Péter Medgyessy, who once held a high-ranking position in the very last communist government, seemed to be the only option to balance between the various socialist platforms in the party, and was also acceptable to the Free Democrats. After a month as a prime minister, documents were published in the only conservative Hungarian daily newspaper (the other three nationwide dailies are openly siding with the Left), proving that the newly elected prime minister worked for the Hungarian counterintelligence agency between 1977 and 1982—i.e., ultimately for the KGB. Under the weight of evidence, Péter Medgyessy admitted that he was an organized agent for one of the secret agencies in communism. And he is not the only one in the public administration of the new government. The new chief of the Hungarian Police was also obliged to admit that he reported about the activities of fellow citizens, but resignation is the last thing on his mind.

As a response, rather than retaliation, a well-known ex-communist journalist casually mentioned in a TV talk that he knows that the father of a prominent opposition political leader was also an agent. The politician referred to, Zoltán Pokorni—the ex-president of FIDESZ and the then leader of the parliamentary faction of FIDESZ—immediately resigned because "penetrated with anger and passion," one cannot lead a party. He was personally affected; a public man was struggling with his private fate and tears on live TV. No doubt there was an element in his resignation that appealed to the responsibility of the prime minister, who is still unwilling to resign. For Zoltán Pokorni, it was a tragedy to uncover the past, to understand why his parents split up in the early 1970s after his mother came to know what her husband had been involved in since 1956, after the crushing defeat of the Hungarian Revolution. One has also to bear in mind that Pokorni's father was a political prisoner between 1953 and 1956, and he could only survive by signing up for the communist secret police after the revolution.

In response to the political attacks, the government set up to two parallel parliamentary committees—one to investigate the past of the incumbent prime minister, and another to investigate the past of all public administrators (ministers and deputy ministers) serving in any government since 1990. After months of futile attempts to find out anything relevant about the activities of Péter Medgyessy, who appeared in front of the committee but confessed only trivialities, he could even benefit from these proceedings, and according to recent polls he is the most popular politician of the country. As a result of the activity of the other committee, however, several names were made public of people who had been "involved in secret-service activities"—irrespective of whether they were informed on, or it was they who spied on fellow citizens. The working of both committees turned out to be mockery, and only the post-communists could benefit from it.

Negation of Communism

Now we come to what I call the "negation of communism," and the almost complete moral nihilism that is implicit in phrases like "historical necessity" and the "you cannot understand because you are too young" type of paternalistic condescension. Péter Medgyessy defended himself by calling himself a patriot who, as a counterintelligence agent, fought against the KGB during Hungary's negotiations with the IMF in the early 1980s, when the country was seeking loans. Needless to say, nothing happened under communism without the consent of the KGB in a satellite country. Popular talk now calls the new government "the cabinet of networks," thus referring not only to the communist background of the new political leadership, but to their vicious and unpardonable past. There were serious concerns about whether an ex-agent is capable of representing Hungary during the final stage of negotiations with the European Union, and justifiable worries as to whether Péter Medgyessy would be able to represent Hungary's national interests under the burden of his past. Another imminent danger stemming from Medgyessy's election as prime minister is the potential radicalization of the Right, signs of which are already visible.

But there are more indirect and long-term impacts of this policy of self-preservation. The ex-communists and their journalist counterparts are now trying to save themselves by relativizing everything connected to the communist past. Their efforts are not hopeless, because they can make the elder citizens believe that nobody could do anything against the communist regime—meaning that against the Soviet coercive mechanism, one could only fight from inside. It is a sheer lie. One has to distinguish between the two cases: Péter Medgyessy had a choice, for nobody coerced him to be involved in the most vicious communist practices, i.e., spying on his fellow citizens, whereas Pokorni's father was coerced into complying to save his life. Medgyessy was a perpetrator, and Pokorni's father was a victim. Medgyessy is the prime minister, Pokorni's father is a 75-year-old man humiliated throughout his life, and now through his son as well. Communism as a form of government is over, but its moral consequences are just as vital as 20 years ago. Communism as an ideology may be dead (although I am not convinced), but communism as an illusion is very much alive: if you look at the Eastern European electoral results in the past 12 years, you will realize that communism is the only living political tradition in the widest sense of the word. The post-communist elite now denies the practices and essentials of communism by relativizing their previous deeds and trying to persuade the rank and file that they were also victims of that regime. As if a regime could function without operators. As a by-product of recent embittered political fights in Hungary, one can understand that morally, there is no difference between what is sometimes called a "soft" versus a "hard" dictatorship. Soft dictatorships, like the one in Hungary under the Kádár regime of its last phase in the 1980s, put a greater emphasis on falsifying the language to keep the inner structure more intact. But the case of Pokorni's father and his politician son uncovers the futility of distinguishing between various forms of communist dictatorships morally.

Twelve years of political struggles concluded with two opposing conceptions of democracy in Hungary. Ex- and/or post-communists regard democracy as a neutral instrument by which you can preserve peace and handle political and social perils. Democracy's morality is derived from the belief that it was the reform communists who destabilized communism from inside; thus they have a right to set democratic rules and oversee their implementation. They regard their own past—i.e., communism—as a source of endless and useless debates similar to religious controversies in early modern ages. In opposition to this vision, the anti-communists, whose concerns are extremely varied, wish to push aside the post-communists, which they deem a precondition for a morally grounded democracy.

Relativism of any sort is a modern phenomenon, thus becoming a philosophical issue. Bernard Williams writes: "The aim of relativism is to *explain away* a conflict, and this involves two tasks. It has to say why there is no conflict and also why it looked as if there were one" (Williams 1993, 156–57). In politics, this simple, although difficult, application of relational relativism is very common. The question is whether there are any limits to political relativism, or is it merely a desperate intellectual endeavor? The question is whether present anti-communism can be dismissed along the Jeffersonian line—i.e., transcribing "It does me no injury for my neighbor to say there are twenty Gods or no God" into "It does me no injury for my neighbor to say I was a communist and now I am your prime minister." Post-communist argument claims that everyone living under communism, including every single member of today's political elite on both sides, unavoidably participated in, and thus maintained, communism—therefore there is no conflict between political roles assumed under communism and those of today. Conflict is only seeming, because although communism was a vicious political arrangement, it was capable of self-improvement—the proof being 1989, when communists accepted the new democratic rules. They learned from the past and transformed into ardent democrats. So it really does no injury if my neighbor was a communist and now he is my prime minister. Roughly half of the population seems to accept this argument, whereas the other half does not. This division is reflected by the 2002 election results.

The only flaw in this argument is the issue of political responsibility. Who is to take responsibility for communism? Or should anyone take responsibility for it at all? Liberals and post-communists refuse even to raise the issue, for it has no relevance for the future. The debate is full of empty slogans or sophistry about the "pinko" image of the European Union. Nobody likes to see his or her life devalued: the communist government failed, but we, including previous leaders and party functionaries, have a rightful claim to be looked upon as brand-new men. Communism is treated as an unhappy detour, a sort of East-European *Sonderweg* following the German pattern applied to the Nazi period between 1933 and 1945. Once post-communists, with Western assistance, manage to survive, communism will not be evaluated at its real cost. What is more, it seems that the problem of "political responsibility" under post-communist conditions is not a moral one per se, but a political one: does politics have any meaning at all? Many thinkers in Eastern Europe have a growing conviction that it is not democratic politics that returned, but instead that a new set of rules has been imposed on these new societies without any explicit need for substantial popular consent. If my judgment is correct, then the actual source of the present resentment against joining the European Union and globalization in general can also be detected. The so-called Europeanization project is connected with leftist orientation, which is to be understood as "post-communist." In the spring of 2002, there was a referendum about Hungary joining the European Union. The turnout was the lowest among the 10 new accession countries (45.62 percent), and only 37 percent of all eligible voters said "yes" to the EU accession.

No one wants to deny that in the post-communist Right, there are unacceptable political forces by liberal democratic standards. East and Central European new conservatism is thus confronted with post-communist opponents, and the social losers of the transition represented by radical right-wing forces. To many, therefore, it seems that new conservativism in Eastern Europe is being crushed before its actual birth. Its nature is distorted in the very beginning, and would yield an utterly unbalanced political spectrum—you have a democracy without internal political alternatives.

What ex-communists offer is pure amnesia—forget about the past, since it might yield unwanted fruits, more poisonous than the biblical apple. One of the first administrative attacks against the achievements of the previous government is more than symbolic. In Budapest, there is a museum ("House of Terror") founded to commemorate the victims of terror in Hungary in the twentieth century. The building used to serve as the headquarters of the Hungarian counterpart of the soviet KGB, called ÁVH (Államvédelmi Hatóság, or "State Protection Authority"), the activities of which had a significant role in the national uprising of 1956. Many of the perpetrators are still alive, and their names are indicated in the museum. The museum was built and has been maintained ever since by public funds, so it is vulnerable to the will of the incumbent government. Instead of turning it into a place of common memory, they offer reconciliation in the name of "presentism"—i.e., what matters are only our present decisions and our present deeds. In practical terms it might mean, for instance, that nobody should prepare a resumé from now on, since it is (a) unreliable and full of sheer lies, and (b) it does not matter where you come from, the only thing that matters is what you are saying and doing today (cf. Gorka, 2002). The past is a field with hidden landmines. Being aware of its dangers, the newly emerging and handicapped Eastern European conservatism intends to refuse this view because a new democracy needs moral grounds. Getting rid of communism through amnesia, or through denying or relativizing its deeds leads nowhere. All that mainstream conservatism would like to achieve in Hungary is to draw practical conclusions about the very nature of communism that people can attempt to deny, as they have attempted to deny the Holocaust; yet it is still around us, and in those of us who were doomed to live in such a regime. Because of the nature of the regime change, the post-communist political forces have been privileged from day one; they had infrastructure, networks, and an organized civil society. The weakness of post-communist conservative parties is to be attributed to the broken traditions in terms of intellectual development and organizational skills. And when anti-communist words are uttered on the political right, the opponents are ready to call the right "fascist." Communism has developed into a tradition that seems to survive well beyond its actual death, and it is likely that the evaluation of communism cannot be declared finished.

Conclusion

Economic and social-psychological factors have contributed to the reemergence of the communist vote in Hungary (1994 and 2002). With the tacit and some-times overt support of the Western governments, post-communists managed to survive in a pro-capitalist and market-oriented democratic society (a project mainly initiated by them) and became the main beneficiaries of the new regime. They could convert their skills and experience gathered during communist management into economic and political positions. They were able to preserve old networks of political and social power, let alone the undisclosed world of intelligence services. They also managed to identify themselves with notions of social justice and pro-Western attitudes. Meanwhile, making use of the pre-political, inexperienced state of the society (still characteristic of most middle-aged and elderly people) and their deep-seated psychological, economic, and social frustrations, post-communists can harvest their votes. On the other hand, the rising and also inexperienced right-wing political parties and movements are forced to step up to a form of more radicalized political activity, trying to fight back from their handicapped position stemming from the period of communism. As a result, conservatism in Central Europe often looks radical, and post-communists look like conservatives since, due to the uninterrupted nature of the regime change, they have something to conserve—"the developments of communism." This phenomenon has been labeled "the communist paradox" (Lánczi 2002, 11–12). Post-communists and liberals have succeeded in denigrating the emerging Right as "fascist" and strengthening old fears of "conservatism" indoctrinated by communist education and media. But the past cannot be waved aside by will. The Hungarian prime minister, Péter Medgyessy, had failed to disclose his involvement as an officer in the communist counterintelligence, serving as an officer. After the revelation of his past, he kept saying that he served his country against the KGB, which was a very poor excuse, but it fit the post-communist tactics to relativize everything belonging to the communist past. The resultant moral chaos has divided society partly along the lines of the post-communist/anti-communist cleavage, and partly along the dimensions of social losers vs. winners, younger vs. older generations, and the more affluent Western areas of Hungary vs. the more underdeveloped Eastern territories, roughly divided by the river Danube.

Alasdair McIntyre has a point in describing the situation under modern moral conditions: "We cannot expect to find in our society a single set of moral concepts, a shared interpretation of the vocabulary. Conceptual conflict is endemic in our situation, because of the depth of our moral conflicts" (McIntyre 1966, 268). Whether a young democracy can handle the diversification of moral concepts is open to contest. What we can safely say is that a post-communist society has been undergoing a process of making sense of what McIntyre had described as producing a peculiar body of experience called "post-communist society." One cannot but agree with Vladimir Tismaneanu, who began his essay on Eastern Europe as "Left, Right, Center: All these notions have strange and elusive meanings under post-Communism" (Tismaneanu 2001, 209). The attempt above is meant to be a contribution to the clarification of these notions.

REFERENCES

Bobbio, Norberto. 1989 [1980]. *Democracy and dictatorship*. Cambridge: Polity Press.

Dahrendorf, Ralph. 2001. Can European democracy survive globalization? *The National Interest*. Fall (65): 17–22.

Dóra, Ilona, Ildikó Nagy, and Katalin Polónyi, eds. 2001. *Nők és férfiak Magyarországon, 2000* [Men and women in Hungary, 2000]. Budapest: Szociális és Családügyi Minisztérium.

Faragó, Béla. 1986. *Nyugati liberális szemmel* [By Western liberal eyes]. Párizs: Magyar Füzetek Könyvei

Geary, James. 2002. When East meets West. *Time Europe Magazine* 159(26).

Gorka, Sebestyén L v. 2002. Questions to ask yourself. *Budapest Sun* 10(37).

Kando, Thomas M. 2001. Demographic and public health trends in Hungary in the first post-communist decade. *Society and Economy in Central and Eastern Europe* 23(1–2): 7–27.

Kolosi, Tamás. 2000. *A terhes babapiskóta* [The pregnant cake]. Budapest: Osiris Kiadó.

Lánczi, András. 2000. *A XX. század politikai filozófiája.* [The Political philosophy of the 20th century]. Budapest: Pallas Stúdió/Attraktor Kft.

———. 2002. *Konzervatív Kiáltvány.* [Conservative manifesto] Máriabesnyo"-Gödöllo": Attraktor.

Lánczi, András, and Patrick O'Neil. 1997. Pluralization and the politics of media in Hungary. In *Post-communism and the media in Eastern Europe,* ed. Patrick O'Neil. London: Frank Cass and Co.

McIntyre, Alasdair. 1966. *A short history of ethics.* New York: Macmillan.

Parrott, Bruce. 1997. Perspectives on postcommunist democratization. In *The consolidation of democracy in East-Central Europe,* ed. Karen Dawisha and Bruce Parrott. Cambridge: Cambridge University Press.

Tismaneanu, Vladimir. 2001. The Leninist debris; or, Waiting for Perón. In *Politics at the turn of the century,* ed. Arthur M. Melzer, Jerry Weinberger, and M. Richard Zinman. Lanham, MD: Rowman and Littlefield.

Tőkés, Rudolf L. 1996. *Hungary's negotiated revolution: Economic reform, social change and political succession.* Cambridge: Cambridge University Press.

Williams, Bernard. [1985] 1993. *Ethics and the limits of philosophy.* London: Fontana Press.

9

Why is Romania Different? A Perspective on the Economic Transition

Mircea T. Maniu

R omania presented a rather peculiar "getting rid of its communist past" pattern after the return to democracy in 1989, a pattern that proved to be considerably slower than in the neighboring countries of the region. The explanations for this situation could be traced to the distinguishing features of Romanian communism, notably of Ceausescu's regime in the late 1980s. The existence of a highly developed and highly repressive police state hindered dramatically the development of an operational "underground" opposition that could have come out into the light in the 1990s with a coherent strategy for political and economic transformation. Moreover, at the outset of transition, the country had no previous experience whatsoever of democratic or economic reform during communism.

Back in 1989, the Romanian economy was almost entirely state-owned (only 12.8 percent of GDP came from private sources). The overcentralized planning system was extremely remote from rationality criteria and instead created a very rigid economic structure. Economic inefficiency had been accentuated by the concentration of production in giant plants, mostly energy-intensive and lagging behind international technological progress. The alleged "fully employed" labor force lacked motivation for on-the-job training and increased productivity, given the complete absence of credible links between productivity and compensation packages and the nonexistence of true property rights. The communist conception of property, understood at the same time as nobody's and everybody's property, has induced over time a clear case of free riding (in terms of labor input) and depletion (in terms of repartition of output).

In the early transition stages, the country also presented features that could have constituted a comparative advantage with respect to other countries in the region. Romania demonstrated the least dependence on the Council for Mutual Economic Assistance (CMEA—a.k.a. COMECON Treaty—the Soviet designed counterpart to the European Common Market), and the absence of previous hesitant reform measures prevented the emergence of obscure "quasi-property" rights. Moreover, an obedient population, disciplined by the experience of a police state and the severe recession previous to 1989, could have shown an increased resistance to the old regime and a strong will to undertake the difficulties of the reform process.

The dismantling of the command economy after 1989 and the creation of a sustainable economy in the long run had to accommodate more than inherited macroeconomic disequilibria. While the sluggishness of economic reform can be largely attributed to unfavorable economic initial conditions, it cannot be denied that the insufficient competence of the political leaders and economic management, as well as a population lacking democratic experience, also represented delaying factors or even braking forces to reform. This paper is an attempt to unveil the main reasons why Romania could be branded as a specific case of transition in Central and Eastern Europe.

In the first pages of his 1937 book *Prosperity and Depression*, Gottfried von Haberler contrasted the idea of less-developed countries as opposed to the developed Western European model through an illustration (Haberler 1937). He used two countries that were comparable in terms of economic performance at that time, Romania and New Zealand. Evidently, the world has changed a lot since those days. Both countries have evolved according to completely different patterns, specifically developed and eventually evolving into clear examples of the assets and liabilities that characterized the two major political and economic systems that confronted each other during most of the twentieth century: capitalism and socialism.

Most observers of the contemporary Romanian situation since 1989 agree on the fact that the country has peculiarities setting it apart from the other Central and Eastern European countries. This fact has shaped Romania's evolution both positively and negatively, and though the country is not itself a transition "case," a clear impression can only be sketched by combining within a coherent analysis several broader assumptions and contexts. Such essential issues to be accounted for are Romania's modern history, the specificity of domestic communism during the 1970s and 1980s, particular strategies adopted for modernization prior to 1989, and the puzzling transition course followed by the country during the democratization process and establishment of a free market in the 1990s.

However difficult such an approach might be, it should nonetheless be undertaken because beyond the observable "institutional mimesis" currently dragging all European countries in transition towards the European Union's structures,[1] in the case of Romania we are dealing with a large country by regional standards. It is second only to Poland among the former communist satellites, generously endowed with natural resources,[2] possessing a large stock of skilled labor, and having a reasonably large market potential.

The Constitution of 1923 created the basis for almost two decades of interwar democracy, and facilitated economic growth to the extent that by 1938, the peak pre–World War II year, income per capita amounted to US$76—comparable to Greece (US$80), or nearby Poland (US$104), these two countries being reasonable European benchmarks for Romania. This was still only one-third of the US$222 European average, and a fraction of the US$521 income in the United States (Dobre 1996, 138). The interwar progress made by Romania has been seen in Western Europe as an "interesting evolution" (Saizu and Tacu 1997, 87–89), especially when compared with neighboring countries that remained agricultural to a larger extent. In 1934 the English historian R. W. Seton-Watson wrote that "two generations of peace and clean government might make of Romania an earthly paradise" (Seton-Watson 1934). Unfortunately, neither peace nor clean government followed. All the progress of the interwar years came to a halt during the Second World War and the early years of the communist regime.

The burden of war was particularly heavy on Romania, this being paradoxically due to its natural gifts, oil and agricultural potential, that were needed by both warring sides. At the end of the war, though it was the fourth largest contributor among the Allied Nations in terms of human and material effort (Muresan 1995, 10–16), Romania was to a large extent materially and structurally destroyed. The oil output in 1944 (3.3 million tons) was only half its prewar total, railroad infrastructure represented only 30 percent of the previous network, agricultural output amounted to about half the average prewar output, and to sum up, the income per capita halved during the period 1939 to 1945 (Manescu 1984, 254).

The Background of the Romanian Transition

Communism had practically no domestic political support apart from the Soviet tanks (if one might call them that) present in early postwar Romania. Thus, in order to create a socialist form of society, several crucial anti-capitalist laws were enforced: land reform in 1945, the monetary law of 1947, and especially the switch towards national ownership of the capital means of production (1948). This last measure ensured that at the end of 1948, three-quarters of Romanian industry and 100 percent of the transport and telecommunication systems were owned by the state. Foreign trade became a state monopoly in 1949 and was soon followed by the nationalization of small and medium enterprises. The destruction of Romania's interwar economy was accomplished when a Soviet-model planning body was empowered to regulate all the aspects of economic life.

The story of the Romanian five-year plans[3] is similar to that of the five-year plans imposed in all the countries of the region that came under Soviet influence. It is about forced, artificial industrialization for the sake of industrialization as such—that is, the creation of an industry able to manufacture the means of production. The sacrificed industrial area was the sector responsible for the production of consumer goods to the extent that it had developed during the period of industrial growth between the two world wars. If we add the fact that socialist industry was conceived in terms of manpower at the expense of agriculture, we can account for the imposition of a decreasing standard of living for most citizens. Actually, this was a deliberate political tool, more evident during the first years when the memories of prewar capitalism had to be destroyed, and less evident during the last decades of communism when prestige considerations became important in the face of an ever more opulent West.

Romanian socialism evolved in two distinct sequences. From the early postwar period until the early and mid-1970s, it evolved as naturally as was feasible given political circumstances. Under Ceausescu, it then switched to the most unnatural approach possible; it became more and more alienated from both available reference systems, European socialism (including the Soviet model seen during glasnost and perestroika) and European and world capitalism. The only possible benchmark for Romania's evolution from the mid-1970s to the late 1980s could be, in our opinion, the fanatical communism seen in East Asia.

The first years of communism could be branded as typical Stalinist years. The only European socialist country not to have any borders with capitalist countries, Romania was still an occupied country. Soviet troops were not stationed for the purpose of facing external enemies, but rather to secure the stability for an extremely unpopular regime, and to stand guard during the looting of the country under the name of war reparations. Special joint ventures, the so-called *Sovroms*, once established, were responsible for the shipment of as many valuables as possible to the USSR. Formally it was a barter trade, but the overvalued price of Soviet goods compared to Romanian commodities ensured that the system was essentially a rip-off.

Moreover, the USSR badly wanted and tried to impose during the mid- and late 1950s some sort of international division of labor that represented the internationalization of the regional development framework applied within the Soviet Union from the early 1930s. This attempt to segregate socialist countries into industrial and agricultural ones, which suited Soviet interests while going against the very communist principle of self-determination, was the triggering element for Romania's first moves towards relative independence in the early 1960s.[4]

The second factor in this process is very specific and consists in the accession to power in 1965 of Nicolae Ceausescu as first secretary of the Romanian Communist Party (RCP). He was a less-educated communist activist, though quite intelligent overall, and evidently bore anti-Soviet resentments and consequently pursued a policy that was first branded as "national communism." However, due to its main feature of anti-Sovietism, this position was highly popular during the mid-1960s for a number of reasons. When Romania refused to join the invasion of reformist Czechoslovakia, in opposition to the rest of the Warsaw Pact countries in the summer of 1968, Romanian national janus-faced communism was demonstrated for the first time (and as it was soon to be proven, for the last) in its history. The regime received popular support for this policy and, even more importantly, was henceforth perceived internationally as the maverick in the Soviet camp, worthy of support as a means to weaken the system as a whole.

The year 1968 inaugurated almost a decade of erratic practice in terms of economic policy in Romania. The regime's perceived independence[5] triggered an inflow of foreign money. Since the domestic laws, deeply rooted in the communist doctrine, did not favor foreign direct investment, money was lent to the Romanian government in order to buy Western technology—this again in order to escape a Soviet monopoly in several critical areas.[6] The scheme rolled on during the 1970s.

Romanian industry benefited most from these funds, though agriculture was also helped. In the early and mid-1970s, the outlook of the economy was reasonably optimistic. Ties with the developed countries were stronger than ever, and the markets of the developing countries also seemed fully open to Romanian industrial commodities. This was important given the search for hard currency to pay for raw materials and compensate for the already increasing foreign debt generated by the import of Western technology. More than 50 percent of the working force was in the industrial sector, and the figure for the agricultural sector decreased to less than 30 percent.

Two factors undermined this positive trend after the mid-1970s. The first was exogenous and relates to the impact of the oil crisis. Being a traditional oil producer, but with drastically reduced domestic outputs, Romania acted offensively towards the Middle Eastern producers (especially in doing business with Iran and Iraq) during the early 1970s, and created an extensive domestic refining capacity. In total, this was three times the domestic-oil output level (at that time approximately 10 million tons). This larger capacity was designed for processing and reexporting oil products all over the world. The oil crisis hit Romania exclusively among the communist countries, as the others were insulated by preferential CMEA-type subsidized prices. These were not available for Romania due to the obvious political constraints.

The second factor, the endogenous one, became more and more evident with time and hit even harder. It was a purely political factor, but with huge and eventually disastrous economic consequences. This can be described as a return to a Stalinist approach to the management of the economy and society, due to the progressive alienation of the top leadership of the Romanian Communist Party. The cult of the personality of Nicolae Ceausescu started shortly after several visits to China and North Korea, and was rooted in fertile soil. Soon, the basics of business and economics were replaced by self-imposed will, rationality by voluntarism, and common sense by impulsive decisions. No other European country experienced this kind of nightmare. In conjunction with these developments, the Western World acknowledged its strategic political mistake with respect to Romania and took steps accordingly. A political blockade emerged, and all sorts of economic liabilities followed.

These two factors were the most important in terms of the exogenous and endogenous causes that underpinned Romania's idiosyncratic course after the mid-1970s, though not the only ones. The aggregate effect of these developments was devastating to the Romanian economy (and society as a whole) during the 1980s. Another new feature, uncommon to any rationally managed economy during peacetime, was the extent of autarchic economic policy. A secondary feature of Romania's alienated economics might be described as the propensity to start enormous projects and pyramid-like monuments.[7] These infrastructural investments[8] deprived the country of its very last resources.

During a time when other economies became more and more integrated, regardless of the ideology they reflected, Romania became insulated from both the socialist and capitalist camps. The attempt to disguise the absence of partnership with foreign countries by manufacturing all the necessities of a fairly big market resulted in huge costs, a major misallocation of resources, and a general pattern of industry first, agriculture second,[9] followed lastly by trade and other sectors of activity.

Though statistics indicate that in 1989 Romania had foreign trade with 59 international partners, the bulk of it went to less competitive, technologically backward markets. The Romanian economy by this time was on course for self-sufficiency, regardless of the costs and the overall lack of efficiency. This absurd economic approach, along with the pursuit of large-scale projects and—the ultimate self-inflicted pain—the forced repayment of the foreign debt, caused extreme economic strain on the population and paved the way for the overthrow of the regime in December 1989.

When analyzing the initial conditions for economic growth after 1989, or the so-called socialist intensive-development phase, at least two methodological aspects should be clarified. The first concerns the time scale required for a balanced analysis. The second concerns the accuracy of statistical data, both before 1989 and after.

Many foreign sources in the area argue that explanations should start with the distinguishing features of Ceausescu's regime during the late 1980s. Romanian sources (Daianu 1997; Daianu 2000a; Negucioiu 1999) underline the necessity of going back at least a decade, and point to the fact that in the case of Romania, the relevant processes occurred in the late 1970s and early 1980s. In this sense, the alienated economy and society of the late 1980s were only the visible peak of the iceberg as seen from the West. I concur with this view.

The falseness of Romanian communist statistics has been depicted both as humorous and tragic. After 1989, Western statistical methodology[10] was adopted, and much of the communist-era data was reinterpreted. Studying the available figures, it is simply the best option to take into consideration the pre-1989 data "as it becomes available," because no relevant mechanism of computing the presumed intentional error has been devised. Therefore, taking into consideration the fact that both Romanian and international sources point to a decline in the traditionally ascending communist-style indicators (Maniu 1998, 193; OECD 1993, 10–13), we simply must assume the presumed errors are acceptable. Actually, by comparing sources of data published before 1989 (Negucioiu 1987) with sources published after 1989 (Constantinescu 1992), we cannot sustain a substantial rejection of the pre-1989 data.

It must be also stressed that the initial constraints, including the distortions induced by deliberately falsified statistics, had a significant impact on the accuracy of forecasting during the early stage of transition.[11] This consequently triggered a change within the forecasting horizons: no relevant Cartesian-like statement was to be issued during the early and mid-1990s. Romanian economic assessments became much more descriptive during this decade. The reign of the "figure" was once again present center-stage a couple of years later, along with EU accession benchmarks.

The Evil Heritage of Communism

The extensive growth that fueled the economy of the 1960s and early 1970s came to a halt after the oil crisis. All over Central and Eastern Europe, the problems of stagnating industries, declining output, and accumulating foreign debt were highly visible. Many, if not all, of these countries responded with more or less partial liberalization: economic incentives were introduced, rigid planning was dropped, and decentralization occurred in several fields. Only Romania experienced a rather peculiar, erratic progression.

In my opinion, there are four sets of issues concerning the initial preconditions that properly highlight Romania's transition towards a market economy. These are: political and politically generated factors, demographic and social factors, output and investment factors, and the foreign-debt issue. The following section tries to investigate these most important issues of the communist heritage that shaped, through their cumulative impact, the outlook of the transition process during the 1990s.

Ceausescu's regime managed to generate most of the bad publicity that was associated with Romania's history in recent times. The myth of Romania as Dracula's country was apparent throughout the world media in the mid-1980s. Tough domestic policy, the repression of basic human rights, and the explicit rupture with millennium-old traditions were the features of the last European Stalinist regime. Obviously enough, some issues were exaggerated abroad in order to paint a darker picture of Ceausescu. The bloody revolution of December 1989 also damaged the public image of a country badly in need of investment and growth. Immediately after the fall of communism, the new regime was again perceived, both internally and abroad, as a softened extension of the former dictatorship, a product of the country's relative poverty and collective social mentality.

The aggregated effect of all these factors was a heavy burden faced by the entire society during the late 1980s and in the early transition years. The international perception of Romanian realities, a vital factor for development, was heavily distorted. Not a single country out of the Central and Eastern European transition group could have made successful progress on its own without at least a reasonable level of foreign aid, and in this context, Romania also lost the opportunity to project a convincing image on the international capital markets.

A very important Romanian feature that heavily contributed to the lack of interest and the absence of investment incentives derived from the extensive state ownership of essentially all the relevant productive capacity. Property and wealth that theoretically belonged to the whole nation in fact practically belonged to nobody. It was cared for accordingly. This, among other things, created a huge deficit within the specific institutions. This institutional fragility was to be replaced by more and more rigid planning. The lack of property and related institutional structures induced a strong sentiment of alienation within the work force that was to be manifested more clearly in the future.

Even more important was the fact that the legacy of the most orthodox communist regime in Europe consisted, among other things, of a deliberately induced lack of experience among the population concerning the basics of market economy. Despite the fact that liberal measures were undertaken all over the communist world in the early 1970s,[12] quite the opposite happened in Romania. Though not rooted in the country's history, the evil of overpowerful state control of the economy and the whole society induced unnatural behavior (Schoepflin 1993, 16–34). State-controlled media channels promoted propaganda about the adoption of market reforms and related incentives as a source of inflation, unemployment, and unfair social polarization for most citizens.

What could be described as the major liability in this area was the complete lack of markets of any sort, with the unfortunate exception of the unavoidable black market.[13] Rigid planning completely failed to provide an adequate tool for producing even the bare necessities in Romania. During the late 1980s, only 14 percent of the currency available in the market had an equivalent in corresponding goods and services (Serbanescu 2000), and this scarcity of goods and services induced a profound individual and social crisis. The main damage that communism could (intentionally) do was to pervert human minds. It succeeded to a large extent.

Probably the most significant self-induced benchmark for Romanian hypercentralization was demographic policy. In 1980 Romania had a population of 22.2 million, which had increased by one million 10 years later to be followed by a decline immediately afterwards.[14] The amplitude of the increase can only be judged in connection with the halving[15] of output and implicitly the standard of living: from US$2,446 per capita in 1980, GDP fell to US$1,257 in 1990 (OECD 1993). Under these draconian conditions, demographic laws (comparable from a reversed perspective only to present-day China) were enforced.

Abortion was outlawed in 1966, and meager incentives were provided for motherhood. The marriage age for women was legally reduced to 15, along with compulsory monthly medical examinations of women of childbearing age. The real infant-mortality rate rose dramatically. As a consequence, births were registered only after four weeks. The cynical, industrially patterned approach to demographics in a society deeply attached to Christian values and traditions induced an unbridgeable gap between the elite communist leadership and common citizens. The increased size of the student population also generated a lowering of standards within an educational system that was traditionally of reasonable quality. Vocational education was given priority during this period.

It is also a reality that notwithstanding the medieval demographic policy, the health system was overall better and the mortality index smaller than in any previous time. Unfortunately, the country had its worst-ever environmental record. Extensive industrialization caused pollution levels that were particularly high by European standards.

Some specialists emphasize the fact that the extent of the decline in standards of living during the 1980s, if observed through an empirical rather than scientific lens, was not as bad as appearances suggest: a fair purchasing-power parity (PPP) computation[16] would show a more than doubling of GDP (see also Weidenfeld 1997). Our assessment is that, when grounded exclusively on empirical domestic research, one could draw such a conclusion. But it should be added that a pertinent PPP investigation (as well as consumer price index [CPI] basic research) was not conducted prior to the early 1990s.

Output dramatically decreased during the 1980s as a consequence of the diminishing share of the international market held by Romania. From a rate of growth of 12.9 percent during the early 1970s to 9.5 percent during the late 1970s, and to an average of 3.3 percent during the 1980s, the industry shrank constantly along with exports. This led to a search for alternatives beyond the domestic market as the issue of the balance of payments became critical. The only affordable solution emerging from the communist planners' desks was the dramatic compression of imports: virtually all the imports except raw materials were eliminated.

Romanian exports were rapidly reduced, with the exception of agricultural products to the USSR and "dumping" types of exports (consumer goods and steel being the most notable Romanian exports at the time) traded for the sake of acquiring hard currency at any cost. The industrially manufactured goods of the 1970s were no longer selling abroad. The tourist trade that had flourished in the 1970s also collapsed. By the late 1980s, Romania had entered a virtually self-sustainable, semi-autarchic economic system.

One should add that Romanian industry consisted of two distinct tiers: one grounded on domestic and CMEA[17] technology, and another grounded on Western technology—this latter factor being the one that actually generated most of the foreign debt. These tiers were designed from scratch as respectively domestic- and export-bound. When technology from the second tier became older,[18] imports had already been reduced. In addition, even the second tier soon lost competitiveness, including within the developing-countries market. All through the 1980s, a huge domestic potential for production and export was lost, in many cases due to the lack of inexpensive imported replacements. Import policy was so tight that it often offended common sense. Also, at that time, giant infrastructural projects guzzled most of the Romanian investment funds.

Because zero unemployment was an untouchable dogma of the system, soft budget constraints were the norm rather than the exception. Production had to be sustained in the face of declining productivity by inputs into obsolete areas, such as manpower-hungry fields like metal and heavy industry, thermal energy, and other related sectors. Applying this policy at a time when most of these sectors had entered recession throughout the world eventually deepened the overall inefficiency of the Romanian economy, affecting even the agricultural sector, where competitive advantage had been long unchallenged. In addition, the propensity to export whatever agricultural output was exportable led to the near starvation of the Romanian people. Blatant, irrational resource misallocation (Daianu 2000b) could be detected, not to mention the exclusively politically grounded regional and departmental allocations.

Some economists would argue that despite everything, a major positive event of the late 1980s places Romania in a major league compared to other Central and East European countries: the full reimbursement of the foreign debt (US$10.2 billion in 1980—zero in 1988) within a decade. Actually, Romania was the only example of this kind within an area where massive borrowers (Poland, Hungary) did their best to postpone repayments. The country entered into democracy and the free market in January 1990 debtless, and even in the position of being an international lender,[19] apparently a major asset.

I share the view of those economists assessing the repayment of foreign debt as one of the major initial setbacks of transition in Romania. All the neighboring countries (Hungary being the most notable case) obtained not only favorable terms for repayment but also trade incentives. These countries managed to channel the available investment for boosting the economy exactly to those export-sensitive areas that took off after 1990. Poland performed even better in convincing the Western lenders, through the Paris and London clubs, to act quickly.

Obviously Romania, more exactly Ceausescu, committed a huge mistake in repaying (in advance!) the country's foreign debt. At the time this occurred, the country was squeezed by massively inefficient export dumping and very low-level imports (trade surpluses of US$2.5 billion were the rule during the late 1980s, with an almost double figure peak in 1988). Actually, from the mid-1970s onwards, negative trade balances were the norm until the tendency was reversed in 1981. From then until 1989, only positive trade balances occurred.

Peculiar Transition

As relevant sources covering the transition process indicate (Hajek 2000, 56–73), the starting point in all the former communist countries consisted of a policy mix of privatization and market liberalization, notably in the area of price deregulation and foreign-trade de-monopolization. This being also the case in Romania, one should start the analysis of the early 1990s by keeping in mind that at the outset of the transition, but ultimately during the entire decade of the 1990s, the Romanian political arena displayed the chronic inability of its main forces (presidency, government, parliament, trade unions) to agree on the timing and sequencing of economic and specific institutional reforms.

Privatization, the ignition point of any restructuring "the capitalist way," was delayed, and the limited results have been unconvincing. All the government's goals seemed to be oriented rather to ensure further electoral support from the working class (the most likely to bear the social costs of restructuring) than towards medium- and long-term macroeconomic stabilization and growth of the Romanian economy. Cautious, and in many respects contradictory, economic measures gave way to more serious attempts at macroeconomic stabilization only after 1994, a change mostly due to the contractual pressures induced by the international financial organizations, notably the International Monetary Fund (IMF).

Economic policy has been largely and decisively influenced by current political constraints. The succession to power of social democrats who were arguably former communists (1990–96), a center-right coalition (1996–2000), followed again by social democrats (since 2000) has also induced a succession of conflicting economic policies. This could be interpreted as a negative political cycle, which has undoubtedly influenced the economic performance of the country. A note of caution is in order, nevertheless. As was the case in most of the transition countries, each government coming to power had to set its own policy and make adjustments in accordance with the legacy left by the previous one and the "path dependency" generated by communist development. But unlike Romania, and maybe Bulgaria, the rest of them started the switch towards market economy, with radical policymakers in power, ideologically closer to the Right—or at least willing to adopt appropriate shock therapies and sacrifice political tactics for this purpose.

It might be assessed that no significant restructuring and institutional change were realized until 1993 (Kallai, Maniu, and Popa 2001). The first democratic governments adopted a gradual macroeconomic program of stabilization and price liberalization. Failure to sequentially implement the needed structural changes of the economy (due to the resistance of the state bureaucracy, managers of large state-owned enterprises, and trade unions) gradually led to fundamental macroeconomic imbalances. State subsidies to unprofitable industries resulted in fiscal deficits and a low external competitiveness of goods. This gave way rapidly to inflationary pressures and current account deficits. In 1994, as a result of the IMF condition, Romania introduced more drastic economic measures in the form of tightened monetary and fiscal policy and accelerated privatization. Nevertheless, these measures came later than in other transition countries, reinforcing the idea of a "loss of momentum."

During the very early years of transition, Romania faced a dramatic situation: emigration occurred on a large scale, since it was the first time in postwar history that borders were relatively open. It is, of course, difficult to assess the ratio of skilled labor, affecting the sustainability of economic development, in the total of emigrants to all destinations. However, for Canada and the United States—favorite destinations for Romanians, and where sufficient data on immigrants' education is available—it is estimated that the ratio of university-degree holders in the total of emigrants amounted to one-third in Canada (in 1996) and one-fifth in the United States (in the whole decade of the 1990s). These results are above average when compared with other transition countries of the region, and indicate that the "brain drain" in Romania is more than a peripheral concern: it is a significant social phenomenon with strong economic impact, and should be taken more into consideration by governmental strategic policies.

Beyond emigration, the collapse of communism resulted in major changes in the structure of the labor force. Total employment fell by over two million, from 10,840,000 in 1990 to 8,629,000 in 2000. The labor force participation rate was 63.2 percent in 2000, compared with a reported 80 percent in 1989. Several factors could explain this decline in the labor-force statistics: the inaccuracy of labor statistics previous to 1989 (Romania being a country "proud" to systematically report a zero unemployment rate), the withdrawal of population from the "official" labor force and migration towards the underground economy, emigration, and longer time spans out of the labor force (mainly due to prolonged time spent in education, a sector that expanded significantly in the 1990s). Unemployment, with all its consequences, could be assessed in a comparative frame (European transition countries being the benchmark in this case) as a less lethal factor than in other countries.

The largest amount of job losses can be seen in industry as a result of privatization, as much as it occurred, and the return of many workers (rather forcefully urbanized during communism) to family-owned agricultural properties in the countryside. The return to the rural areas was mainly due to the restitution of land, an ongoing process initiated in 1990. According to the 1999 data, the largest proportion of the labor force (over 40 percent) is working in agriculture and forestry. The cumulated industry and construction workers, as well as the service workers, each account for around 30 percent of the labor force. This share of services in the labor force is extremely low, even by East European standards.

Romania was basically the only country where employment in agriculture increased during the 1990s. While the role of agriculture as socioeconomic "buffer" was to some extent predictable for the initial phase of transition, it becomes extremely dangerous to have an economy relying to such a large extent on agriculture as an absorber of the excess labor force. This is a clear sign of highly fragmented agricultural properties, where economies of scale are not functional and where the inefficiency of resource allocation is perpetuated. Since the onset of land restitution, more than 90 percent of people working in agriculture are self-employed or non-salaried family workers. It is highly unlikely that this form of low productivity subsistence agriculture could survive in the competitive environment of the European Union.[20]

As a result of this environment, both industry and agriculture have sharply contracted (as percentages of GDP) during the transition years. The share of industry in GDP has almost halved, from 46.2 percent of GDP in 1989 to 25.2 percent in 2000. Agriculture and forestry also declined to 11.1 percent of GDP in 2000, after a slight increase of its share in the mid-nineties. However, the share of agriculture in GDP remains significantly high, indicating a strong resistance to change and a slow adjustment to market mechanisms. Moreover, the dominance of extensive agriculture is also detrimental to the expansion of the services sector, in particular trade. Development of trade, as a principal component of the services sector, is hindered by the fact that without a competitive agricultural sector (due to its fragmented nature), there is little prospect for a large contribution from agricultural and food products.

An additional factor explaining the contraction of output between 1997 and 1999 was the relentless reduction of investment from 23 percent of GDP in 1996 to 18 percent in 1999, and the persistence of a negative current account balance. (The average negative current account balance during the period of expansion 1992 to 1996, 5.9 percent of GDP, has been smaller than the average negative current account balance during 1997 to 1999, 6.7 percent of GDP). The country still depends on credits from the international financial institutions as well as on the international capital markets, which it reentered in 1995 with satisfactory credit ratings. However, as a result of economic and political instability and because of the successive governments' loss of external credibility, the ratings have been consistently lower than expected, and the flow of foreign direct investment (FDI) has diminished in recent years.

Romania is struggling nowadays to recover and make up for the lag separating it from the forerunners among the transition countries of EU integration. Though it fully complies with the political criteria, when it comes to economics and to the assessed ability to face competition within the European Union's single market, the country still has far to go. Most observers of Romania consider that this target, a second national obsession (the first one, belonging to NATO, being accomplished), will constitute a true engine for a more coherent and consistent present-day transition. In December 2002 the EU Copenhagen Summit acknowledged 2007 as the integration benchmark for Romania. That long-awaited moment will end a truly peculiar transition.

NOTES

The author is indebted to Miss Dana Popa, Ph.D. student at Central European University in Budapest, for her insights concerning the political assessment of the transition in Romania.

1. It is interesting to note that recent polls, both domestic and EU based, place Romania as the most enthusiastic country among the accession group, as opposed to those countries with much better prospects for early joining. The TNS Factum Poll conducted in 11 countries in September 2001 indicates a 81 percent pro-EU rate in Romania, compared to 63 percent in Slovenia, 60 percent in Hungary, 49 percent in Poland, and only 38 percent in Estonia. This outcome could be assessed from a dual perspective: the emotional one, specific to a Latin country, on the one hand, and the factual one, derived from the lack of information about specific negative consequences of joining, on the other hand.

2. IMF's World Economic Outlook 2000, Focus on Transition Economies considers that only Poland and Romania are moderately (!) endowed with natural resources, all the rest of the transition countries being poor in this respect; this is only one of the seven factors to be considered as "initial conditions," the other six being share of industry, liberalization index, repressed inflation, black-market premium, PPP computed GDP and CMEA participation (*IMF World Economic Outlook 2000* [Washington, DC, 2000], 115).

3. The first Soviet-type five-year plan was 1951–55; when communism collapsed in 1989, it was during the eighth five-year plan, 1986–90.

4. The so-called Valev Plan, bearing the name of a prominent Soviet economist of the time, assigned industry as the main economic sector for European communist countries north of Hungary, and agriculture for those south of it; Romania, falling within the southern tier, was obviously supposed to abandon its industrialization plans and concentrate on agriculture. Another issue that allowed a more independent position towards the USSR was the fact that Soviet occupation troops were pulled out of Romania in 1958.

5. Romania was the first communist country to establish diplomatic links with the Federal Republic of Germany in 1967; it was also the only communist country that did not break diplomatic ties with Israel following the Six-Day War. It was also host for the first American presidential visit behind the iron curtain, when Richard Nixon came in 1969. This country was the first Warsaw Pact state to enter GATT (1971), and the World Bank and International Monetary Fund (1972); it was granted European Community Trading preferences (1973), and U.S. Most Favored Nation status (1975). Romania maintained very good political and trade relations with China, a country ostracized at the time by most communist countries; nonaligned countries, such as Yugoslavia, were considered natural allies of Romania, all these policies being assessed domestically and abroad as anti-Soviet actions above all.

6. For instance, Western equipment allowed Romania to develop a competitive weapons industry. During the 1980s, the country became one of the most important suppliers of conventional weaponry for the developing countries, this in spite of the evident displeasure of the USSR. Top industries such as airplane-engines manufacturing (along with

Rolls-Royce) or military jet-aircraft building (a Romanian-Yugoslav joint venture) were established. Romania was the only communist country to escape Soviet monopoly in producing nuclear energy; the reactors, which were Canadian designed, financed, and built (including heavy-water facilities), are now the only safe installations by Western standards within the former communist system. Automobile companies such as Renault, Citroen, and MAN also started manufacturing cars and trucks in Romania.

7. Well-known all over the world are the People's Palace in Bucharest (the largest building in Europe and second largest only to the Pentagon on Earth—this building could hold 500,000 people), the Danube–Black Sea Channel, the remodeling of Bucharest, huge heavy-equipment plants in all major cities, some enormous oil refineries, an extremely costly nuclear program, etc. The planned (fortunately not accomplished) "systematization" of about half of the 13,000 villages in Romania into 558 agro-towns was concocted in order to destroy what was left of peasant traditions.

8. If, back in 1986, 32 percent of the national income was invested, the vicious circle that the Romanian economy entered, through infrastructural madness, reduced the same figure for 1989 to 18.7, only half of it being actually net investment (*Statistical Yearbook of Romania, 1990* [Bucharest, 1990], 240).

9. Between the mid- and late 1980s, Romanian agriculture was export-driven: the huge cereal-output (mostly wheat) deficit in the USSR allowed an important barter trade, reminiscent of the war compensations of the late 1940s and early 1950s; though CMEA did not play an important trading role, the USSR was the largest partner, absorbing 22.6 percent of the Romanian exports.

10. The Western "National Accounts System" replaced the CMEA-wide "Material Production System."

11. Until 1991–92, an optimistic view concerning transition was obvious all over Central and East Europe; the massive liberalization undertaken during the first years, when the general outlook was still that of planned economies, induced major macroeconomic disturbances. For instance, Romania's 1990 GDP was estimated anywhere between US$30 billion and US$42 billion (see *Statistical Yearbook of Romania, 1991* [Bucharest, 1991]).

12. Reforms introducing the so-called "goulash communism" started in Hungary in 1968; Yugoslavia was already experimenting with self-management, and Poland was also a rather liberal economy by communist standards. Romania formally adopted a so-called "New Economic Mechanism" in 1978, allegedly giving more decision power to lower levels of the economy. This was nothing but a propaganda tool, and did not accomplish anything other than to fortify bureaucracy and central planning. The exclusion from the economic-reform debate all over Central and East Europe later took a heavy toll and resulted in a particularly deep transition shock.

13. See note 2 with regard to the "black-market premium" as an initial condition of transition; Romania's index is 728, while Poland's is only 277.

14. The baby boomers of the decade following the Decree on Abortion were called, somewhat pejoratively, "the Decrees." In a quirk of history, the Romanian Revolution was mostly

carried out by teenagers born in the late 1960s and early 1970s as a consequence of the draconian demographic policy enforced in Romania.

15. The World Bank estimates Romania's 1980 GNP as US$57.6 billion, while the foreign trade reached US$25.4 billion; a decade later, these figures roughly halved.

16. It is worth mentioning that there is a not-so-grim view of the situation: the IMF computed the 1989 GDP, in terms of PPP per capita, as 5,798, this generating a 1989 per capita income of 3,470.

17. Only 3.7 percent of Romania's GDP was CMEA-related in 1989, but since the share of the industry within GDP was 59 percent, it was mostly the third world where Romanian industrial output was heading.

18. During the 1980s, the Romanian stock of machinery was on average 20 to 30 years old (average amortization period 21 years); for comparison, the same stock was 13 years old in the USSR and 6 years old in the U.S. (Muresan 1995, 94–95).

19. Romania's debtors were (and unfortunately still are) several developing countries; though diverse reimbursement schemes were aggregated, the bulk of the credits (lowest estimation: US$3 billion) were never repaid to the country. In fact, Iraq owes the lion's share, and the internationally imposed embargo deprived Romania of the possibility of retrieving the fruit of its investment.

20. The case of Poland, which faced huge difficulties in negotiating its agricultural chapter during the EU-accession procedure, bears significance for Romania, where the situation is estimated to be at least twice as serious.

REFERENCES

Constantinescu, N. N. 1992. *Dileme ale tranzitiei la economia de piata* [Puzzles of transition to market economy]. Bucuresti: Editura Economica.

Daianu, Daniel. 1997. *Vitalitate si viabilitate economica* [Economic vitality and viability]. Bucuresti: Clavis.

———. 2000a. *Incotro se indreapta tarile postcomuniste?* [Where are post-communist countries heading?] Iasi: Polirom.

———. 2000b. Structure, strain and macroeconomic dynamic in Romania. In *Romania 2000—Ten years of transition: Past, present, future.* World Bank Conference Proceedings, Bucharest.

Dobre, Gheorghe, ed. 1996. *Economia Romaniei in context European—1938* [Romanian Economy within a European Context—1938]. Bucuresti: Editura Fundatiei Stiintifice "Memoria Oeconomica."

Haberler, Gottfried von. 1937. *Prosperity and depression: A theoretical analysis of cyclical movements.* Geneva: League of Nations.

Hajek, Ladislav. 2000. *Economy and transition in the Czech Republic.* In *Politics and economics in the Czech transition,* ed. C. de Cueta and L. Hajek. Hradek Kralove: Gaudeamus.

Kallai, Ella, Mircea Maniu, and Dana Popa. 2001. Explaining growth. Country report: Romania (1990–2000). Paper presented at the World Bank Conference on the Global Research

Project, Rio de Janeiro, 13–14 December.

Maniu, Mircea. 1998. *Conjunctura economiei mondiale, 1970–1990* [World economic outlook, 1970–1990]. Cluj-Napoca: EFES.

Manescu, Manea, ed. 1984. *Avutia nationala* [National wealth]. Bucuresti: Editura Academiei.

Muresan, Maria. 1995. *Evolutii economice, 1945–1990* [Economic evolutions, 1945–1990]. Bucuresti: Editura Economica.

Negucioiu, Aurel. 1987. *Proprietatea socialista in Romania* [Socialist ownership in Romania]. Bucuresti: Editura Politica.

———. 1999. *Tranzitia rationala* [Rational transition]. Bucuresti: Editura Economica.

OECD. 1993. *Romania, an economic assessment.* Paris: OECD.

Saizu, I., and Al Tacu. 1997. *Europa economica interbelica* [Interwar economic Europe]. Iasi: Institutul European.

Schoepflin, George. 1993. Culture and identity in post-communist Europe. In *Developments in East European politics*, ed. S. White, J. Batt, and P. Lewis. London: Basingstoke.

Serbanescu, Ilie. 2000. Can the vicious circle be broken? In *Romania 2000—Ten Years of Transition: Past, Present, Future.* World Bank Conference Proceedings, Bucharest.

Seton-Watson, R. W. 1934. *A history of the Romanians.* Cambridge: Cambridge University Press.

Weidenfeld, Werner, ed. 1997. *Central and Eastern Europe on the way into the European Union.* Bucuresti: EURISC.

10

On the Question of European-ness in Romania: Between an Institutional Construction and an Imagological Perception

Marius Jucan

Political and Cultural Premises of European-ness in Romania

European-ness in Romania, perceived as Romanians' affiliation to European culture within an organic relation, has been one of the main and most intensely debated sources of political and cultural capital in modern Romania (Johnson 2000, 19).[1] A recurrent theme in present-day international-relations approaches regarding Romanians and their country, European-ness in Romania may be regarded as a foundational trait of Romanian modernity, engendering the general framework within which Romanian political culture became manifest. The organic relation between the notion of European-ness and the growth of the Romanian political culture has obviously been dealt with more often since the fall of communism, as a recent chapter inscribed in the history of the twentieth century. The controversial and often heated national debates over Romania's allegiances to European cultural space met not only with the expectation of an ongoing social and political transformation in Romania, but also with the necessity of sorting out the intricate web of political and cultural relations that came into being in the years of totalitarian dictatorship. Romania's expected integration into NATO and the European Union could be seen as a major attempt to reassert, and at the same time to rebuild, Romania's image in the actual world, leaving behind the two separate versions of Romanian imagology commonly used in the past—namely, one for the outside world and one for Romanians themselves (Pleşu 2002, 13).

Within this notable effort to modernize Romania, the imagological construction of Romania cannot ignore the existing realities of the country, nor can it embellish or reduce them only to a given purpose fleshed out by imagological effects. European-ness in Romania can be accounted for as a constitutive trait of Romanian culture generally, although as I intend to show, due to internal developments and international events taking place in the twentieth century, the Romanian political and cultural stage was also a place of confrontation between trends favoring modernization (thus upholding Romania's allegiances to Europe), and anti-European currents (both political and cultural). It is worth mentioning that too often, the anti-European drives were directed against realities existing in the Western world, so that westernization of Romania was viewed as doubtful, or it simply came under attack from the declared enemies (censors) of a free political and cultural life in Romania, especially under the communist regime. The indelible cultural marks of Eastern Europe—as, for instance, the religious experience of Orthodoxy—were interpreted as a natural barrier resisting or withholding the process of modernization in Romania, or enabling a different civilizational background for it. It is quite understandable why the concern to define and redefine Romania's belonging to Europe has become an important imagological instrument to pave the way toward actual modernization, as the weight of its symbolic capital became a token of political power.

The political opportunity to examine and debate European-ness in Romania—its traditional roots and actual rebirth—under present circumstances demands a complex approach to realities in Romania. It constitutes not only the favorite field of Romanian politicians, but also of Romanian intellectuals, either in universities or centers for applied political studies, and last but not least of foreign journalists, ever since the period before World War II (Waldeck 2000, 302–3). It is important to underscore that the debate over the right to sustain European-ness in Romania through specific cultural and political means turned too often to the question of whether it would be feasible or not to westernize Romania, or on the contrary, to consider Romania and this part of the world as being definitely severed from the main European context and influence. The latter option gave a supplementary reason for the supporters of the nationalist communist discourse to oppose Romanian traditional cultural values to the European ones.

European-ness in Romania should for practical purposes, therefore, be seen from two distinct perspectives—namely, the cultural and political ones—though such a separation may overlook the common ground of culture and politics in the modern age, often insisted upon by artists, writers, and philosophers. Actually, I would like to note the relative independence of Romanian culture from politics, a phenomenon that held true mostly before the coming to power of the communist regime, and then of course the complete subordination of Romanian culture to communist political ideology and practices, which lasted for almost half a century. At the same time, it should be mentioned that the line of demarcation between culture and politics should not be drawn so sharply that Romanian culture could be regarded as being politically innocent, or object to the candid idea that Romanian culture overlooked political issues. It is nevertheless true that due to the long period of political censorship in Romania, the ideal of an independent culture acted as a coherent endeavor to depart from the political ideology of the communist system, unfortunately not immediately reaching the longed-for liberal cultural foundation.

Yet we should acknowledge that within the same process of constituting cultural and political symbols, we may meet with the same rhetoric, structuring potentially different discourses (Edelman 1999, 12–29, 111–24). The birth of a common rhetoric used in the cultural discourse bears on the most profound levels the meaning of modernity, as for instance the experience of secularization. Due to the limits of this article, I can only mention the importance of secularization in shaping the actual meanings of modernization in Romania. Secularization displayed a sense of deep change in Romania's modernization by its two interrelated phases, the "dis-enchantment" and "re-enchantment" of the world. By "re-enchantment," one may understand the string of political and cultural events that brought about the rebirth of Christian faith, especially with the younger generation after 1989, the year of the upheaval of the communist regime.

I have resorted to a genealogical approach to uphold the idea according to which politics and culture are currently intertwined in their general goals (as, for instance, the presence of Romantic organicism in European and Romanian modern culture and politics in the nineteenth century). It forms the necessary standards to qualify the meaning of European-ness itself, as well as the Romanian institutional and cultural experience, considered as kindred to the European one. Once again, I would not credit the idea that the political and the cultural merge at some point. Although, when one reviews the challenging ways that cultural and political strategies are used in (post-)modernist cultural theories, it is remarkable how the strong dissimilarities between the political and the cultural tend to soften, and how at some point, the political issues of culture and the political culture of the artistic milieu are to be viewed on a common basis.

Reflection on the contents of European-ness in Romania were naturally different, for instance, under the communist regime, when one could trace a division line between the artists, writers, and (quite rarely) philosophers who strove to assert their independence, and the representatives of the official censorship ("apparatchiks") who officially imposed and supervised obedience to the cultural propaganda of the communist party. European-ness in Romania was regarded at that time mostly as an optional cultural policy, rather than a functional component of Romanian tradition. European-ness was perceived and used as a political weapon in the hands of the communist leaders according to the political interests of the communist party, especially during the period of liberalization, when the traditional links of Romanian modern culture to Europe were revalued, and the works of such writers as Blaga, Eliade, Ionescu, Cioran (to mention only the ones most referred to) were thought to reinforce the prestige and legitimacy of the communist leadership. European-ness became, as Romanian modern history may prove, the foundation of the Romanian state, of modern political, administrative, and cultural institutions, as well as being at the core of the Romanian concept of identity. The "European idea" was soon rediscovered after 1989, but the strategies put into practice to uphold the cherished European idea often spoke about the existence of a reserve, if not a certain distrust of entirely following the European way. The anti-European policies of the communist regime meant isolation and a long period of cultural stagnation. In those years, manifest allegiances to European culture were tagged as cosmopolitanism or disregard for national values. Nevertheless, no one could actually deny the core element of European-ness in Romanian culture, starting with its initial stages rooted in the Enlightenment and Romanticism.

In the following pages, I do not intend to discuss the whole course of the issue of European-ness in Romania, choosing to deal only with some developments that may mirror the modalities according to which various aspects of Romania's modernity and modernization implemented European-ness and its imagological reflections. It is also relevant to note that the question of European-ness in Romania has been contested from both directions—from the outside and from the inside of the Romanian cultural community. The recent appearance of a critical viewpoint held by an American professor of European studies, Tony Judt, rekindled the polemical argument, which actually had never died out (2002). Professor Judt's arguments on the thesis of Romania's European-ness are correctly interrelated with the social and political transformation process going on in Romania. Nevertheless, his viewpoint does contain a specific analysis of details concerning the Romanian cultural model, which led the author to use a number of cutting remarks, rather discordant with the whole tone of the essay. But even if the exactness of the historical data is rather foggy, the interpretation of our imagology, as shown in Tony Judt's essay, cannot be either belittled or simply ignored. The critical accents revealing the faked aspects of European-ness in Romania are reminiscent of the surprising remarks of Herman Keyserling made in the 1920s (1993, 275–82). The echo provoked by Tony Judt's essay on the issue of Romanian European-ness is comparable, to some extent, to the one created by Samuel Huntington's thesis regarding the clash of civilizations, and is chiefly positioning Eastern European countries on a map divided by cultural frontiers rather than state borders. This move clearly reveals the necessity of reexamining the issue of European-ness in Romania—considering, for instance, whether culturally speaking, it may be reduced to the opposition of different religious denominations. The very case of the map of Romania being torn apart by the cultural-religious scissors of the "clash" between Orthodoxy and Catholicism in this part of the world naturally provoked a wave of emotional reactions. But when the emotions subsided, the imagological projections (representing the result of a symbolical process through which the political or cultural reality was legitimized) again outstepped reality.

Beyond the cultural implications of any political symbolism employed in political discourse or in the assessment of international strategies, as for instance the case of Romania's capacity to cope with modern European standards, the crux of the issue consists in making legitimacy consistent with historical reality. Putting Romania outside the borders of European-ness may not only be misleading, but is also unrealistic. This may suit some restrictive patterns of European-ness, or the redrawing of some cultural frontiers, as was and still is the case in Central Europe [*Mitteleuropa*]. In spite of all this, placing Romania on the "edge" of Europe, according to the words of Tony Judt, shows the degree of importance given to Romanians' options—namely, whether they would act to become Europeans or not, although they already claimed their allegiance to Europe on the basis of the cultural and political transformation of present-day Romania. Tony Judt's essay might also echo the mixed feelings of a foreign observer when comparing Romanians' attachment to European values with the elections of the fall of 2000, when thousands of Romanians voted for a far-right nationalist party.

The premises of European-ness in Romania were set by the bourgeois-democratic revolution of 1848, the achievement of Romanian statehood (1918), the cultural modernist experience of the 1930s, the repercussions of World War II and the rise to power of communism, and finally, the return to Europe no earlier than 1989. In all the above-mentioned sequences, one could note without much difficulty that the stream of the liberal democratic tradition was in fact endangered, being considered as a foreign implant into the so-called organic structure of Romanian culture. European-ness in Romania seemed to have remained an ideal, or rather an unfinished political and institutional construction. Reflecting on the different approaches of Tony Judt, Samuel Huntington, or Gustav Molnar Tamas (Tamas 2001, 7–21), all dealing more or less with the idea of European-ness in Romania, one may agree that European-ness in Romania is probably more of an unattained goal rather than a fleshed-out reality. Still, present-day Europe is multifaceted, and its philosophy expresses far more differences today than in the times of the birth of what became the European Union. However, no matter how optimistic political provisions in Romania may sound, economic stagnation, political and cultural conformism, the rejection of radical reforms, the practice of the nationalist discourse, and the absence of a liberal cultural vision are weak points of European-ness in Romania. The next stage of approaching European-ness will possibly be one starting from an imagological perception of Europe, and contributing to the consolidation of the institutional process in Romania.

Romanian Imagology: the Expression of a Belated Secularization

The attack on the inconsistency of European-ness in Romania, appearing in numerous critiques made by Romanian intellectuals or by foreigners on the state of things and the course of the social and political transformation after the fall of communism, ultimately leads to what an outstanding nineteenth-century Romanian literary and political man, Titu Maiorescu, called "the form without content." According to his anti-liberal views, modern reforms in Romania were creating only an imitation of European institutions and habits, and thus considering the differences distancing Romania from the Western countries, one should judge them as unsurmountable. Admitting even half-heartedly that today Romania may find itself in almost the same quandary, one could nevertheless note the advancement of various non-European countries that borrowed new forms from the experience of the West, importing novel cultural and political values that did not exist previously in their cultural and political traditions. Deliberate access to modern cultural or political technologies depends on the political will of those who contemplate the risks and the benefits of reform in a changing world.

The ambiguity of the alleged inconsistency of European-ness in Romania lies in the delay of a firm commitment to radical reform, rather than in the existence of an alternative to modernization. Romanian critics of the political and social transformation after 1989 often expressed their skeptical views regarding the chances left to catch up with European standards, but in spite of their sometimes gloomy prophecies, European-ness was brought back, at least in the context of new modernizing efforts to improve the institutional construction.

Wondering about the causes that repeatedly impeded the accomplishment of European-ness in Romania, one must reconsider the expression of a still-functional nucleus of organic Romanticism in modern Romanian culture and politics. The origins of Romanticism both in culture and politics are not to be found elsewhere but in Europe, yet Romanticism developed differently in the

Eastern part of Europe, coalescing the cultural and political experiences into an ideal of unity that the ensuing modernist cultural experiences in Western Europe did not hesitate to alter, and eventually to invalidate. The speed with which cultural and political experimentalism developed in Western Europe— the common ground of European policies chiefly after 1989—turned the spotlight on the belatedness of reforms in Romania. It is relevant for our topic of imagology and institutional construction to remember here that the practically old-fashioned model of "Middle Europe" (*Mitteleuropa*) was consistently favored in Hungary, the Czech Republic, and Poland, with the clear intention to create a distinct cultural and political advantage—a premise to further develop their status according to European standards, on the basis of a common background that was lacking in other regional competitors (Pollak 1998, 11–35). This imagological initiative merged with a strong political will manifested in these countries in order to emphasize the differences rather than the similarities enclosed under the gray label of "post-communist countries."

I think that this could be an eloquent instance proving that imagology cannot be separated from its pragmatic character, in the sense that political will manifests itself in the desire to implement modernizing policies, and needs to coalesce with the political and cultural experiences stored in the vague consensus of the community. It is relevant to remark that in communist times, imagology produced in the propaganda offices of the single, all-powerful party was not only contrary to reality, but it attempted to fabricate an alternative that controlled the perception of reality, strictly following the political decisions of the leading political group in the party. As an aftermath to this long practice, imagology is still considered as a weapon in the hands of the powers that be to correct reality or to excite the population in order to attain the proposed political targets, rather than as a true representation of the state of things. This was the case of the communist cultural ideology, as in the example of "socialist realism," demanding the sacrifice of the individual to the common benefit of the collectivity in order to safeguard national values, in the defense of which stood the autocratic discourse as an omnipresent ideological guide and guardian at the same time. The success of such an imagological practice was guaranteed by the existence of a double standard, a practice that actually subverted modernization by raising a European façade, behind which the grim reality of totalitarianism was hidden. Political and cultural imagology in the years of communism mystified the past and created a utopia of the future instead of the certitude of the present. The deep cleavage between the inner reality of the Romanian community and official propaganda was accepted tacitly and wrongly, due to this strategy to embellish, transform, or idealize reality. The long-term sources for the reception of this type of imagology may be looked for in Romania's belated secularization, and as I already hinted, in the survival of the political and cultural core of organic Romanticism. The specific cultural context of the Byzantine-Orthodox region allowed for the stigmatization of the West, which was considered for a number of reasons the moral author of the prolonged political crises in the region. In speaking about the belated secularization in Romania, one should comprehend the rather superficial impact of Enlightenment values, as for instance in matters concerning the separation of powers, the status of the citizen, and the importance of an urban culture based on the existence of the middle class.

The projection of a local Arcadian world as of a model of native culture refusing to interfere with the world (including, in our own day, with the effects of globalization) caused an excessive appraisal of national values. Even if modern European identity underwent a dramatic process of change starting from the times of religious reform and of Romantic national discourse, one could not deny that the "lesson" of the spirit of the people (*Volksgeist*) did not remain deeply imprinted in the mind of either the intellectual elite or the people. I am not implying that European Romanticism was simply promoting the structure of a collectivistic thinking. On the contrary, it ascertained the development of modern individualism and egoism, mostly expressed in literature, arts, and politics, leading the way to the appearance of a new type of cultural hero. The end of the Romantic revolutions of 1848 coincided with Marxian social prophecies, the general critique of systemic philosophy, Christian existentialism, new political theories about the state (including the foundation of a Jewish state), anarchist movements, the restructuring of political liberal thinking, and especially with the appearance of a new cultural hermeneutics no longer accountable to theology. Regarding the Romanian political model, all these major events found their match in the optimistic and rather fragile attempts to articulate a modern identity, responding to a longed-for political and cultural unity.

The first Romanian state—constituted before 1918, resulting from the union of two Romanian provinces—succeeded in complying with the requirements of the European powers, and paved the way for the introduction of the modernizing reforms the country needed so badly. The Romanian cultural lag, about which most of the Romanian intellectuals complained, should not be regarded as a specter of Romanian society's inability to modernize itself; on the contrary, taking into consideration the Romanian thesis of synchronization put forth by Eugen Lovinescu, European-ness was never a more attainable goal than in the period between the two world wars. If Romanian exceptionalism found a permanent outlet in sustaining the unique drama of our civilization as an outpost of the Western world, facing invasions at the crossroads between East and West, it was due to the absence of a middle class, the lack of an urban civilization, and the prevailing Orthodox disregard for the very idea of modernity.

Romanian imagology became the expression of a belated secularization. Undoubtedly, the much talked-about delay does not signal simply the deficiencies and the imperfections of our political and cultural past, but points to the different *rhythm* of the Romanian model of society (Barbu 1990). Comparing the different cultural and political sequences of Romanian modernity with other instances in the region, one is aware of the diffidence with which novelty was implemented at all levels of society, but also the absence of modernizing policies and the indulgence in triumphant Romantic appraisal of the past. All these difficulties of modern Romania have developed a double status, being on the one hand weaknesses of the present, but on the other, virtues of the so-called "eternal" Romania, a mythical entity fabricated by traditionalists and nationalists. This, however, is not meant to underestimate the traditional discourse about the Romanian cultural model, as it provided the first cohesive attempt to draw a sketch of Romanian identity under circumstances that encouraged the bridging of political divisions and factions.

The creation of cultural and political consent in the process of forging national identity was enabled by the transformation of the Romantic essentialist symbols of nature, nation, and blood into political symbols. The making of this political consent on the basis of an overestimation of Romanian cultural and religious realities—for instance, Orthodoxy in the 1930s—led to a political exclusivism and reduced the cultural vistas to an ideological scheme. The belated secularization affecting Romanian imagology may be recognized in various instances. For example, the birth of the fascist organization called the "Iron Guard" promoted the model of a militant Christian life merging with politically violent actions directed against democratic or liberal policies. The same type of militant, ideological terrorism—but one that had a completely different tone—was exerted by the communists, who before the occupation of Romania by the Soviet troops were just a handful of people, whose leaders were often recruited by the Soviet secret police (Tismaneanu 1995). The Christian model of the far-right movement was not common in Germany or Italy at that time, and also not recurrent in the other fascist parties or movements disseminated in Europe before World War II. During the years of the communist regime, the cult of personality was imported from an Eastern cultural model that was obviously non-secularized. All efforts made by some of the second-rank communist leaders to prevent the disastrous effects of the cult of personality were in vain, and the case of Romania in the 1980s may be a unique and extreme example.

The return to the religious Orthodox tradition once the communist regime was thrown down after 1989, when protesters shouted anti-communist slogans and prayed in groups in public places, offers another illustration that post-communist popular consent needed the traditional imagery in order to be functional. One should also consider the fact that during communism, the Orthodox Church did not react against the gross violations of the rights of man or the arbitrariness of the despotic regime inaugurated by Ceausescu, as was the case in Poland, Hungary, and the Czech Republic. The religious rebirth enlivening a large majority of people in Romania was an appeal for the necessity to reform the Orthodox clergy, as well as to prevent the national church from reiterating conformist and obedient conduct. Lay intellectuals as well as average people advocated openly for radical changes within the high clergy of the Orthodox Church, as they fought to reestablish the Greek-Catholic Church, condemned by communism to prison and oblivion. It is relevant to mention that the Greek-Catholic Church has initiated and supported modernizing policies in Transylvania since 1700. It is interesting to note that after 1989, an impressive willingness was shown by Romanians to reform the national church rather than to opt for new political parties, nongovernmental organizations, and political clubs. This fact demonstrates not only a certain nostalgia for the ideal of national unity ensured by the prestigious authority of the church, but also the narrow space used for actual reformation. The same emblematic idea of unity was underscored by the founding of a National Front of Salvation that took the helm of power after 1989—a political umbrella hosting at the time different wings of the single party. But during the tumultuous decade that followed, the Orthodox Church revealed a clear tendency toward modernization, building a moderate but quite convincing message to its people and also to the world, undertaking the tasks of a participatory policy within the present-day society.

The Present-Day Sources of the Nationalist Discourse

It is not at all likely that the nationalist discourse will lose its preeminent attraction for Romanian politicians. At the same time, it is worth mentioning that the slowness of modernization in Romania, not only in the last years of the past millennium but also in other key moments of Romanian history, instilled in the people's minds the idea of the nationalist discourse as being the only defender of the "national being." For a brief illustration of the appeals of the nationalist discourse, it might be sufficient to mention that between 1990 and 1996, the great majority of the political parties kept in their names the word "national."

Due to some causes I am briefly going to look into, I am of the opinion that the nationalist discourse in Romania, though declaredly belonging to the past, may well return in the future as an alternative discourse for those feeling deprived of any other political symbols. This fact gives us additional ground to believe that the goals and the means of the nationalist discourse will recapture popular attention and acceptance, as both the latest developments on the international political stage after 9/11 and the resurgence of nationalism in Western Europe may attest to.

The popular hypothesis animating both politicians and researchers during the cold war, according to which the landmarks of the nationalist discourse in Europe could have been transgressed by the consent of some great political actors, did not prove to be at all functional, as the balance of the political system shifted in favor of a single hegemonic model. In a number of Western European countries, the nationalist discourse was a means to manifest opposition to the American politics of cultural hegemonism. It was, in fact, a piece of wishful thinking to believe that major cultural differences in Eastern Europe kept silent under the glacier of communism would not eventually surface and gain credit. Beyond the unchanging populist message of the nationalist discourse, the huge popular support for this type of discourse is being motivated by the accentuated fear of failure in the face of globalized economic competitiveness. The high standards of efficiency promoted from within the tradition of a federalist democracy do not seem accessible to other cultural models that followed their latently or explosively conflicting tendencies. The nationalist discourse should not, however, be seen only as a permanent source of dissension and conflict, though it may eventually lead to them. Far from being an "inferior" mode of organizing political culture, the national discourse proved to be rather flexible in adapting itself to the new circumstances of the post-communist political stage. Not being oriented toward democratization and the idea of a state of rights, the national discourse was openly encouraged and supported by important segments of the political class, as well as by the Romanian voters, at least in the period 1990–96.

Looking, no matter how briefly, at the roots of the recent history of ideas in Europe, it is worth showing how the national—and then in a more secular way, the nationalist—discourse during Victorianism in Great Britain, nineteenth-century France, Italy, Germany, Austro-Hungary, and Poland, for instance, created in these countries the symbols of a national mission. The legitimacy of the mission was nevertheless differently cloaked in countries having a long democratic tradition than in other parts of Europe. After all, legitimizing the sense of a national mission in Central and Eastern Europe did not mean to counterbalance the perils of totalitarianism; in fact, it created a "revolutionary situation" that brought along political premises to implement totalitarianism. In order to comprehend the large expansion of the nationalist discourse often tinctured by fascist propaganda, one should recall the increase of the communist sphere of influence before World War II, followed by the brutal Stalinist repression of any national policies in the sovietized Eastern European countries. The economic and political realities of a divided Europe, the iron curtain, and the cold-war legacy did not mellow the national and nationalist claims, no matter how dif-ferent they were from country to country. Not surprisingly, surviving in the test tubes of the Soviet nationalist experiments, Eastern European nationalism returned triumphantly to its natural condition, adding to its gamut of policies the communist experiences (for instance, national communism in Romania) as well.

The nationalist discourse has thus known a strong revival, especially after the identification of its common imminent danger, globalization and cultural hegemonism, as well as after the failure to find the most suitable methods to counteract economic stagnation and poverty in Eastern Europe. The national-ist discourse may be described as *reactive*, putting a special emphasis on the necessity of a united national action, but also constructing the legitimacy of aggressive cultural policies to specify who can be entrusted to act in the name of the national interests. Time and again, political capitalization took over cul-tural tradition. The tradition of the nationalist discourse in Europe—and in Romania as well—as it was developed mostly in the nineteenth century demo-nized the Other, depriving it of any human rights or merits. Out of an impres-sive legacy of common European nationalist policies and practices, it is important to review critically the vocabulary of the nationalist discourse, pay-ing special attention to the artificial impression of its novelty, as it is perceived nowadays. The same resurgent appeal to national union in the face of so-called imminent danger, supposedly binding individuals to collectivistic principles, resounds clearly against economic migration and redistribution of European communitary wealth. The signal of an artificially created danger enhances the impression of novelty, though the enemy may be actually the same victim, embodied by the old and new: racial, ethnic, religious, or political minorities. The invention and then the recognition of the Other as either a friend or a foe depended on political interests thought to be right for the community as well as central to the resources of the imaginary of the community, or its collective mythology. Generally, we can assert that the Romanian nationalist discourse was not basically different from the mainstream of nationalism in Europe between 1880 and 1945.

Nevertheless, the Romanian nationalist discourse, with its extremist mani-festations recorded during the acme of totalitarianism, both fascist and commu-nist, was a cradle of rampant exaggerations regarding national values, paradoxically impoverishing them rather than providing them an additional symbolic space through political instrumentalization, according to which national values became pillars justifying nationalist propaganda. The common enemy was identified with cosmopolitanism, aestheticism, and generally the Western different, more critical view of the past. Within this discourse, an important place was held by the figure of the non-national element, the foreigner who often played the role of a scapegoat, paying indiscriminately for all the misfortunes or failures that distressed the community. This symbolically mortifying treatment applied to the foreigner (as the recurrent image of the Other) speaks clearly about the closed nature of the Romanian rural type of society that evidently prevailed over the urban one. The metaphorical vocabulary of the nationalist discourse, overpraising the qualities of the majority community, proves the underlying connections between the national discourse and the religious one, especially the one supported by the Romanian Orthodox cultural experience in the 1930s.

According to this comparison, one could perceive the allegorical figures of the national vs. religious discourse—as, for instance, in the figure of the "savior" embodied in the "father" of the nation. The Romanian nationalist discourse exalted at its beginnings the uniqueness of the community, distinguishable by the respect paid to the norms of Christianity—thought to be an authentic, harmonious community dedicated to a peaceful life—rather than extolling different performances of power as expressed by military conquests or political regional maneuvers. Such a discourse rejected from the very beginning the idea of a critical analysis in respect to Romanian reality, preferring to invoke the harmony of the traditional (rural) society rather than attempting to determine what was necessary to build a new one and to face the discordant differences leading to political instability, corruption, and poverty. The disparity between the idealistic finality of the national discourse and the economic and political reality of Romania created in the long run a discrediting attitude among voters. The hope for a concrete change—especially in the 1980s, when proletarian urban masses expected a better standard of living—was completely shattered by severe repressive and anti-popular measures taken by the dictatorship regime, ranging from food shortages and cuts in the distribution of electricity and central heating, to the worsening of the political climate and persecutions of the ethnic, religious, and political minorities. From this perspective, the communist nationalist discourse continued and expanded to an unknown extent the demagoguery of the period comprised between the two world wars.

It is, however, interesting to note that the nationalist discourse succeeded in counterbalancing the lack of social consent in the community by the artificially imposed constraint of the "national danger." But when danger actually approached the borders of Romania, as in the case of the rebellion of the Iron Guard, and then by the Soviet invasion in World War II, the nationalist discourse could not provide any sustainable issue to circumvent civil disorders, as well as the occupation of the country with its long-lasting consequences. Other sequences of the nationalist discourse reiterated from time to time the perils of losing the independence of the nation-state, or the "glorious" development toward a socialist economy, putting the blame on scapegoats at hand in the communist regime—usually members of a diluted civil society who did not even have the right to defend themselves. In spite of the differences occurring in the various stages of the nationalist discourse, I note a general feature: the pretense of ignoring the contextual developments in a changing world around Romania. In other words, the nationalist discourse seems to speak to Romanians in all epochs, defying historic time for the sake of the national essence. I find here the particularly essentialist traits of the nationalist discourse of modern Romania—namely, the tendency to credit the vision of a rather small group of people to which the great majority is eventually subjected. The credibility of the nationalist discourse is contradicted by its claim to bridge the organic vision of the role of the nation and the demands of the individuals in a supposedly free, democratic, civil society.

The renewed spirit of the nationalist discourse took by storm the propoganda departments of different parties that have had a say on the issues of Romanian identity, the need for modernization, and the practical policies undertaken to promote democratization and critical transparency. Political capitalization asked a high price for the so-called survival of national values. The necessity to reconsider critically the nationalist discourse is shared by all the actors on the political and cultural stage, including the political class, the press, and the trade unions, but implementation measures vary widely. The sources of the nationalist discourse may be identified not only in the impediments and resistances to modernization and a more profound democratization (including the completion of decentralization), though these appear to be the most important ones. The main source of the nationalist discourse sits in the reductive stereotypes of the community, lightly upgraded by present-day current affairs, transferring the responsibility from individuals to an abstract community—in the name of which a group of people would take decisions without being held accountable for their involvement in the decision-making process. To go on in this manner might seem less costly than doing away with the nationalist stereotypes that provide the flimsy appearance of national consent.

Claiming to defend the eternal values of the community, the nationalist discourse would not promote modernizing issues for fear that the solutions could eventually bring radical changes in the very decision-making process itself. Paradoxically, being the political discourse that promises the most, the nationalist discourse invests the least in order to bring up real change; or if it pretends to follow this path, it is only an allegorical change. It has often been demonstrated that the nationalist discourse is nostalgic, in the sense that it contains a Romantic attempt to return to an idealized, abstract, allegorical reality that would replace the present-day unacceptable state of things. From this perspective, political nationalism exploited the diffuse but permanent feeling of alienation of the ex-rural masses, or, in more recent times, the increasing

mass of the unemployed with its disbelief in institutions and institutional policies. The much-cherished ideal of a strong hand leading the fate of the many
remains an alternative to democracy, and under these circumstances the
nationalist discourse undercuts the continuity of the reform efforts.

Being a discourse that articulates efficiently the illusion of a universal justice and equality, especially after the experience of the national-communism
days, the nationalist discourse deftly exploits the mistakes of weak democracies, especially the image of the deficiencies in democratic power changes.
This fact stands as a significant trait of the appeal of the discourse to the
masses. As for Romania, the nationalist discourse stems from three main
areas: the belated process of secularization, the imagery of failure and isolation
present in the collective imaginary of the Romanians, and the organic Romantic symbolism of the discourse as compared to the liberal democratic type of
discourse. In the first case, one sees not only in Romania, but in the whole
world that secularization is not a completed phenomenon, and even if it were,
it could be proved reversible, at least in Eastern Europe. In addition, the
absence of an assertive liberal tradition in Romania and, consequently, the lack
of an alternative culture to the official one are conducive to extremist political
perceptions in which political compromises are discarded from the beginning.
The fear of failure and isolation may be attested to by the skepticism of the
average man regarding reforms and civic responsibility. As for the organic
Romantic symbolism, one may remark on its content of enhanced protest,
since the economic situation of the population could not match the promised
standards. Generous promises were each time doomed to oblivion, especially
when they were formulated in terms of modern standards of efficiency.

The underestimation of the potentialities of the nationalist discourse could
open the way for false optimism regarding the results of the necessary reforms,
thus discrediting democratic values. On the other hand, we need to look critically at the fact that European political standards regarding nationalism and
the nationalist discourse are not always perfectly cohesive. In recent years, the
perspectives of a flux of working populations migrating temporarily from Eastern to Western Europe pushed into political actuality a number of political
movements brandishing a nationalist message. Under the circumstances, the
study of the nationalist discourse proves to be a cultural and political endeavor
of immediate use.

The Role of Intellectuals

The role of the intellectuals in modern Romanian society has been a fertile
theme for debating the notion of European-ness in this country. At the same

time, it has been an opportunity to identify a cultural hero who could shape the prospects of the age according to personal ideals, not overlooking the task of defining the modern national identity (Neuman 2002). The intellectual was traditionally regarded in Romania as being responsible to the community and thus a kind of "responsive conscience." Intellectuals under communism, however, did not have at all an enviable fate, as they were marginalized. Unless they were part of the newly born technocracy summoned to build the inefficiently grandiose system of communist industrialization, the so-called responsive consciences were severely controlled and repressed. The role of the intellectual was authored by the party activist, who was envisioned as having the mission to explain, convince, and eventually act decisively in all matters of importance for communist society. From the activist's perspective, the intellectual was always seen as lacking in political firmness, always unaware of the efforts needed for social and political historical changes, if not subversive to them.

Even from a brief description attempting to render the disqualifying portrait imposed by communist authorities on intellectuals, one can see that intellectuals were identified with the petty bourgeoisie, unless they were siding officially with the *nomenklatura*. Later on, the "new intellectuals," completely loyal to the communist party, constituted the ranks of communist leaders. Intellectuals were considered as either temporarily needed allies or potential political targets, as in the years of Romanian totalitarianism. Even if their role was perhaps magnified by popular hopes or fears, intellectuals appeared to be an important segment to account for the dimensions of European-ness in Romanian society. Being regarded as the "lights" of the nation, intellectuals were expected to foresee and prevent the perils of the people, a task overburdening an elite that was striving more for personal independence and authority rather than for representing all compartments of society. Intellectuals stood as living examples for what could have been called the nucleus of a middle class, depending on an urban culture and striving to implement civic values. The Romanian intellectual was perceived as a sort of national hero, struggling to make audible the voice of the community as it attempted to modernize itself into civil society. Intellectuals have constantly been considered cultural and political actors, called upon to give a fresh account of the conscience of the nation. But even if the tradition of the Romanian intellectuals was initially a liberal one, a great many of the Romanian intellectuals between the two wars, and especially afterwards, gave away their political independence and willfully enrolled themselves first under the fascist and then later on under the communist banners. In other words, the myth of the independent intellectual ended in the confusion between the perception of the intellectual as a freelance person, the intellectual as a member of the intelligentsia, and the intellectual as politically engaged.

Before looking into the differences between the two sorts of intellectuals, namely the freelance intellectual and the intellectual as a member of the intelligentsia, it would perhaps be relevant to distinguish between the intellectuals' independence and their servitude. The intellectual was perceived—from the perspective of the radical humanistic renewal in the Enlightenment—as an independent, autonomous person who could establish through personally attested options professional standards in all fields of human activities, under an all-encompassing Reason. The modern individual seemed to have recognized this model for the autonomy of individualistic conduct and social practice, within the guidelines of civil society. The fact that the intellectual relied on a universal, abstract conscience, and presumably not on fiduciary conduct, did not mean that the importance of belief was belittled or simply denied. For many years, the intellectual turned out to be the torch-bearer of a secular "light," encouraging mankind through education to oppose religious life in the name of reason and reflection. The intellectual, however, cannot be imagined as a robot of rationality, and besides, after the Holocaust and the Gulag, it was hard to sustain social and political rationality as a shining example. In the case of the politically (ideologically) engaged intellectual, so-called free conscience is supported by a strong and active belief in political or religious ideals, and the portrait of the neutral intellectual changes into the portrait of the self-declared militant.

Intellectuals distinguished themselves in Romania, as well as elsewhere, through articulation of new types of discourses, generally making the public space more transparent and accessible to other citizens. The need to redefine the moral status and the activist dimensions of the intellectual's mission became permanent, which meant that intellectuals considered themselves as following the model of Western intellectuals. They acted less bound by the national community, and more inclined to respect the general ideas of modernist cultural reforms. Intellectuals in Romania actually did not differ substantially from the European model, attempting to build their personal legitimacy and their resistance to tyrannical policies.

The existing difference between the Western type of the intellectual and the Eastern intellectual advocating and defending the interests of the community, the people's needs for cultural elevation, political guidance, and moral exemplarity was clearly demonstrated in the opinions of Pierre Bourdieu or George Hoskins, for instance, who dealt from different angles with the issues of the birth and typology of the intellectual (Bourdieu 1999; Hosking 2001). One can maintain that traditionally, the Romanian intellectual is to be found closer to the definition of the member of the intelligentsia, feeling obliged to sacrifice his/her questionable independence to the ideals of the community. Leaving aside the patriotic motivation of acting for the good of the community, one can notice the utopian idea of evading the political issue, showing disinterest for power to the extent of considering all political activities as corrupt and mendacious. Such an attitude shows the traditional diffident attitude of the Romanian intellectual to politics, which would affect his/her pretense of pure rationality, or of morality, always placed above time and place. The relations of the Romanian intellectuals with the community, in which one could perceive the sense of a mission, are described to be more intense in the period between the two world wars, when a large number of Romanian intellectuals extolled the Romanian village as the place of a cultural matrix that remained untouched by the modern era—an idealized Arcadian island. The intellectuals' split attitudes towards being instrumental in the process of modernization, at least in the first phase at the end of the nineteenth century, was not a singular phenomenon occurring only in Romania. In time, however, the attitude of the intellectuals toward modernization was completely altered, and many representative Romanian intellectuals expressed and supported ideas to accelerate reforms and integrate Romania in accord with the civilizational standards of Europe. The role of the intellectual turned out to be different according to the cultural context, as overt opposition to communism was more manifest in countries of Central Europe than in the ones of Eastern Europe.

The present-day status of the intellectual should be made distinct from the status of the expert or of the bureaucrat. In our view, the intellectual wishes to enhance his/her availability to convert general humanistic ideals into concrete measurable actions, striving to increase the awareness of his fellow citizens of the necessity for a greater transparency in the public discourse. Yet the everyday reality regarding the average Romanian intellectual is far from reaching a common ground, so perhaps the most prestigious feature characterizing the intellectual refers to his/her leading role in civil society, a characteristic relying on the intellectual's capacity to express the identity of the group or national identity through artistic works, theories, and analytical comments. Nevertheless, the Socratic type of intellectual—dominant between the two world wars—directing the conscience of the young and attempting to respond to universal issues is no longer compatible with the present-day world. Actually, in the period following World War II and during the cold war, intellectuals as a social group grew skeptical about their modeling influence upon society.

Without attempting to formulate definitive statements concerning the mission of the intellectuals in the present circumstances of Romania's development, I think that two main tendencies can be observed as being influential in shaping the intellectuals' minds and prestige. As long as intellectuals continue to constitute a social group sharing specific features, apart from experts and bureaucrats, we can think of intellectuals as falling into two types, the *reformed* intellectual and the *nostalgic* one. The reformed intellectual could be pictured as being more inclined to accept rapid changes both in him/herself and in society, being convinced of the general benefits implied in the transformations. In this respect, the reformed intellectual works to create a new identity for the intellectual, giving a new sense to the mission of institutions, organizations, and party system. Being oriented toward the European standards, this type of intellectual may be an active player in the modernization process. The other symbolic type, the nostalgic intellectual, may stand for the conservative, nationalist segment of intellectuals, or simply for those for whom the practice of modernization is but a simple, intuitive imitation of European standards, devoid of real chances to be implemented into our local or regional reality. For the nostalgic intellectual, westernization means a wrongly chosen alternative, since the national developmental potential would be in this manner neglected or wasted, alienating our cultural model from its own tradition.

On the Issues of Transition and Reform in Romania

Defining the specific and complex period Romania is now going through requires a comprehensive, analytical cultural and political basis. The sustaining economic effort of the nation, the accurate expression of the political discourse, the democratic change taking place in the political class and on various levels of civil society, and the congruity of the planned reforms with European and international standards should all contribute to the shaping of the new society. Yet in the recent past, there has been a certain confusion, to say the least, regarding the proper choice for transformation, transition, and reform in terms of their inevitability, means, and political demands (Sandu 1999). Furthermore, in the early 1990s, when important decisions were taken concerning Romania's pro-NATO attitude, there was a certain delay with respect to the support of European policies in the Balkans, especially in the case of the European intervention in the former Yugoslavia. Though it is beyond the scope of this paper to comment here on this traumatic moment of the post-communist transition, it could be suggested that the nationalist discourse gathered many voices in defense of the totalitarian regime in former Yugoslavia. The issue of the intervention proved that Romanian society was not fully prepared at that time to comply with the philosophy of European-ness.

Ever since 1989, concrete steps toward a new course in favor of a liberal democratic society and a market economy were threatened by the inertia of administration and hesitant economic measures, so that the speed of reforms had to be revamped from outside the country. The delay in responding to pro-NATO and European standards of integration was interpreted by a number of Romanian politicians as being part of the natural process of transition, as if the transformation of a communist country into a free market did not depend on the political will of the whole political class. But beyond the dodging of the burning question, namely reform, a good number of our political representatives refused to understand the seriousness of the options of the day, especially in comparison with the more advanced Central European countries, which obviously benefited from their former political reform experiments even during communism. It was particularly on this point that Romanian society needed the cohesion of civil society and its actual reconstruction, which proved to be difficult for various cultural and political reasons—as, for instance, in the ongoing dispute over the presence of the former members of the political police in official state, governmental, or political positions.

The sense of reform belongs to a new type of cultural and political thinking that brings in the necessity of democratic cultural and political experiments, educating and modeling the citizens' will to experience responsibility for their choices. One of the still-unsurpassed difficulties of the period was the building of legitimacy in the years of the new democratic power, which led to giving up the authoritarian discourse and decentralizing political and economic power. For a society existing for centuries in the shade of the single, all-powerful leader, who symbolized "the father of the nation," the challenge of pluralism was often interpreted as an undermining deviation in comparison to the steadfast traditional political experience.

Generally, one knows that religious reforms opened the way to political experiments in European society. Political reformism based on the heritage of the Enlightenment and classical liberalism opened the gate to bourgeois democratic reforms in the revolutions of 1848, but few of the points mentioned in the programmatic declarations were carried out completely. After the outbreak of the 1848 revolutions, there was a new perception of modernity in Romanian society, corresponding in many regards to the European standards; yet the discrepancies between the West and East inevitably expanded. This is why reviewing the inherent difference between transition and reform could explain at least the general context of the present-day necessity of reformism in Romania. After 1990, there was a general agreement that Romania was orienting itself toward a democratic, free-market society, though national realities did not sustain such optimistic official views. Transition was thought to be a normal and quite peaceful process, a sort of well-controlled string of events that would not unexpectedly change the habits and the ways of either the population or the political class. There were only a few signs signaling the unpredictable inner developments that were causing ruptures and divisions inside society, but soon the symptoms of political unrest and economic inertia turned into facts. Hence, one may acknowledge that transition after communism was thought in the beginning to be a sort of popular liberalization, satisfying quite paradoxically the needs both of egalitarianism and of the free-market policies. Nevertheless, part of Romanian society grew aware of the necessity to step onto the path of reform and curtail the generous span of time accorded to a sluggish transition that did not reach its final stage. For this part of society, as for many Romanians today, reforms differ from transition by their declared radical goals, as well as by the supportive political and cultural instruments required to achieve the desired transformation within a reasonable time span. The shadowy presence of the single, all-powerful party remained in these years a constant menace, though the political competition among parties went on, changing the balance of political forces. The economic stagnation of the last years pointed to the necessity for reforms, but they failed to materialize, mostly due to the absence of political courage among the politicians: implementation of reforms demanded too high a price for them to act. In other words, resorting to drastic economic measures to cut out inefficiency might send thousands of unemployed into the arms of the opposition, presumably a nationalist one.

It is due to this rather narrow display of political choices that the political and social transformation would necessitate an agreed feasible program that could ensure progress on the way to democratization. This, however, could not occur without paying a high social cost. Between a desire for reformist activism and the actual lengthy transition, Romanian society did not seek a definite course to sustain its decisive transformation. The crucial weight of the social transformation cannot be thought to depend any longer on the change of the image of Romanian society, without being part of the process of flexible adaptation to European standards.

NOTES

1. About the different perception existing between European countries or states, see Grosser (1999). On the condition of Eastern Europe as a cultural and political invention, see Wolff (2000).

REFERENCES

Barbu Daniel, ed. 1990. *The mind of Romanians* [*Firea românilor*], 39–130. Bucharest: Nemira.

Bourdieu, Pierre. *Les règles de l'art* [Romanian version], 161–86. Bucharest: Univers.

Edelman, Murray. 1999. *The symbolic uses of politics* [Romanian version]. Iasi: Polirom, 12–29, 111–24.

Grosser, Alfred. 1999. *The Westerners* [Romanian version], 5–19. Bucharest: DUStyle, Ceu.

Johnson, William M. 2000. *The Spirit of Vienna: An Intellectual and Social History, 1848–1938* [Romanian version]. Iasi: Polirom.

Hosking, George. 2001. *Russia, People and Empire, 1552–1917* [Romanian version], 180–204. Iasi: Polirom.

Judt, Tony. 2002. *Romania: The bottom of the heap. Polemics, Controversies, Pamphlets* [*România la fundul grămezii, polemici, controverse, pamflete*]. Edited by Mircea Mihăieş. Iasi: Polirom.

Keyserling, Herman. 1993. *Das Spektrum Europas* [Romanian version], 275–82. : Iasi: Institutul European.

Neuman, Victor. 2002. *Ideologie şi fantasmagorie: Perspective comparative asuopra istoriei gândrii politice în Europa Est-Centrală* [Ideology and phantasmagoria: Comparative perspectives on political thinking in Eastern-Central Europe], 108–21. Iasi: Polirom.

Ples̗u, Andrei. 2002. Europe, the critical spirit and the imaginary [*Europa, spiritul critic şi imaginarul*] *Dilema* (477): 13.

Pollak, Michael. 1998. *Vienne, 1900: Une identité blessée* [Romanian version], 11–35. Iasi: Polirom.

Sandu, Dumitru. 1999. *Spaţiul social al tranziţiei* [The social space of transition], 9–17. Iasi: Polirom.

Tamas, G. M. 2001. *Idola tribus* [Romanian version], 7–21. Cluj: Dacia.

Tismaneanu, Vladimir. 1995. *Gheorghiu Dej's Ghost* [*Fantoma lui Gheorghiu-Dej*], 75–105. Bucharest: Univers.

Wolff, Larry. 2000. *Inventing Eastern Europe: The map of civilization on the mind of the enlightenment* [Romanian version], 466–87. Bucharest: Humanitas.

11

Conclusion

Norman A. Graham and Folke Lindahl

t is clearly possible to look at the progress in democratization and economic liberalization of the 27 post-communist countries of Eurasia with some guarded optimism. Belarus, Tajikistan, Turkmenistan, and Uzbekistan are clearly unabashed authoritarian regimes with only sporadic ventures toward political accountability, and very limited effort to liberalize economically. Azerbaijan, Kazakhstan, Kyrgyzstan, and Russia have made more substantial moves, particularly on the economic side, but the regimes seem to be undergoing political retrenchment. Hungary, Poland, the Czech Republic, Slovenia, and the three Baltic States clearly have competitive democracies with effective political institutions and processes and functioning market economies. But, as some of the foregoing chapters suggest, there remain some very serious challenges and unmet expectations. It is clear that the "dual transition" of democratization and economic liberalization has been a challenge for all the regimes that have seriously attempted it. Even the most successful ones in Central Europe and the Baltics find themselves in search of more rewarding strategies for managing tough economic and social measures in an environment of financial constraint and political stress. Indeed, the entire Eurasian region offers a fruitful field for further study.

Erik Herron's analysis of electoral engineering in post-communist states offers insight on the challenges of institutional design in emerging democracies. It is commonly argued that the large number of political parties in transition systems is problematic, particularly if there are no large and mature ones among them. Herron finds that electoral rules do influence the size of the party system and could mitigate the level of multipartism. Noting that some post-communist states suffer more from the lack of strong, independent parties, he stresses that the key in such cases is less the character of electoral laws in existence (now in all 27 states) than the progress toward effective democratization and rule of law more generally. Herron concludes with a list of reform proposals based on his comparative research—flowing from his concern that "the presence of 'too few' or 'too many' parties may undermine democratic stability."

Axel Hadenius's analysis of the Russian case stresses the crucial connection between democracy and the vitality of parties. He finds weakness in their three main roles—in government, in the citizenry, and as organizations—noting the low degree of cohesiveness even in the Duma, the instability more generally, and the challenges they face in formal membership, finance, and personalism. The recent turn back toward authoritarianism would seem to confirm his warnings, as would the somewhat unexpected realignment evident in the December 2003 elections—unexpected perhaps principally in the weak showing of the Communist Party and the apparent large payoff to the pro-presidential United Russia Party from substantial "official" administrative and media support. How strong the president will become in relation to opposition in the Duma and the oligarchs remains an open question, as does the extent to which Putin's personal popularity will transcend concerns about institutional weaknesses in Russian democracy. The anti-terrorism campaign launched with urgency (anew) in the wake of the September 2004 Beslan school massacre seemed to strengthen his popularity even as it promised new restrictions on political freedom and the media.

Kathleen Dowley's assessment of subnational pluralism and ethnic polarization in transition societies offers similarly mixed messages. Her inventory of cross-national differences notes that even in Central Europe, where legislation is more commonly developed to be consistent with the minority-rights positions proffered by the European Union, mass attitudes remain problematic. Ethnic nationalism is a serious challenge in many transition countries, with complex and deep roots that require considerable attention and intensive study. Indeed, beyond Central Europe the tendency toward ethnic conflict clearly threatens the prospect for democratization, particularly in the Caucasus and Central Asia.

The numerous and complex issues connected to the role and health of civil society in the region will no doubt continue to occupy scholars and writers for some time. Although the intensity of the debate regarding questions surrounding civil society and social capital is abating, it will not disappear. Both theoretical and empirical question marks remain, and they will not be removed in the foreseeable future. One looks forward to what will hopefully be a rich and illuminating body of knowledge as the empirical evidence accumulates on the growth of civil society in the post-transition countries. Possibly, this knowledge will shed further light on what role civil society can and should play in the liberalization and democratization process. There is no shortage of speculation regarding this topic, but there are few solid studies of the actual birth, rise, and function of civil society in the new democracies—or studies, for that matter, that address the failure of civil society to either emerge or to perform its supposedly positive role in the process.

On the theoretical level, Louis Hunt's essay reminds us of the necessity to take the classical philosophical investigations on the subject very seriously, and to engage in a reflection on both the moral and the political foundations of civil society. Hunt's chapter shows the importance of maintaining a theoretical separation between the state and civil society, but also its interdependence. To be an active participant in civil society is something different from being a citizen of a state, and the latter might demand a commitment that moves beyond "comfortable self-preservation," if for no other reason than the fact that this very self-preservation might be threatened and undermined unless citizens are morally attached to the state in ways very different from their involvement in civil society. This raises the issue of the role of patriotism in the newly formed democracies, and points in at least two problematic directions: on the one hand, it raises the problem of nationalism, which in its extreme form can turn both illiberal and anti-democratic; on the other hand, moral and emotional commitment or attachment to the state is reminiscent of the communist past and in no need of resurrection. At the same time, no liberal democracy is likely to stabilize and survive without an element of moral patriotism; the problem is how to keep it within moderate bounds and prevent it from developing into forms of political extremism.

Equally important, especially for the post-transition countries, is of course the opposite side of the argument—namely, the danger of individuals becoming "excessively preoccupied with their private well-being." It is not impossible that the widespread cynicism towards the state that communism unintentionally instilled in the citizens will remain and thus make people solely concerned with private gains and money. As Hunt concludes: "In Hegel's view, such preoccupation will lead in the end to an enervation of the energies on which the flourishing of civil society depends. The health of civil society depends on the cultivation of habits of mind that are not automatically produced by civil society itself." At the very least, Hunt clearly reveals the precarious balancing act involved in the relationship between civil society and the state, and the danger when this balance is upset in either direction.

The dissidents under communism who were instrumental in bringing the civil-society debate to center stage viewed civil society in moral terms, partly because patriotism in the form of an emotional attachment to the state was not an option. They were also often openly skeptical of what they perceived as the excessive materialism of the West. Havel, for one, certainly addressed what he judged as a spiritual and psychological crisis of the West, as well as of communism. But, as Lindahl argues in his chapter on the dissidents, the persuasiveness of this lament is limited at best, especially if it is not formulated within a liberal framework or in concrete and practical terms. If Hunt addresses the relationship between civil society and the state in classical *liberal* terms—and thereby gives us the necessary context and vocabulary for a liberal perspective—Lindahl shows the fuzziness and lack of clarity when this vocabulary is absent or lost. Any discussion of civil society has to be open-ended and sensitive to local conditions and history, but it also has to remain liberal, and therefore particularly skeptical of both escapism into civil society as a refuge from politics, and of excessive claims as to the moral superiority of a civil society completely separated from the state. From this angle, the ideology of civil society as it was formulated by the dissidents of the region has limited applicability in the current situation. The evolution of civil society needs to remain in focus, but now only in relation to other efforts at reforms: economic liberalization, the building of political institutions, and the development of a proper, functioning party system. Civil society can no longer be the dominant preoccupation, but it nevertheless has an important role to play for the post-transition societies, and there is ample room for both further theoretical and empirical studies.

The four case studies raise a series of issues for transition in Hungary and Romania. Jiří Lach analyzes "The Political Elite in Hungary," tracing its roots to 1956 and noting concern about the polarization of the leadership today, and the attendant "discrepancy between action and propaganda, particularly in the economic sphere." In his discussion of the new political elite in Hungary in the 1980s and 1990s, he shows the difficulty in getting the democratic house in order after the communist collapse. There are simply too many economic and political pieces that have to fall into place for a smooth transition to take place. Nevertheless, as Lach's chapter illustrates, the overall picture after two decades of reforms—both before and after the transition—is quite impressive, and gives us reason to approach the near future with cautious confidence rather than despair and cynicism. Although most transitional reforms cannot be judged completed, new political elites have emerged and solidified, including the sometimes questionable transformation of "reformed communists" (former members of the *nomenklatura*) into a new social-democratic elite. Lach flags this latter change as a critical question for the new regimes: "One of the most sensitive issues of systems in transition is how much the old elite transforms into a new elite." On this score, the jury is still out, and a serious answer cannot be provided for at least another decade or two. Over the short term, rigorous and careful studies of the growth and evolution of the various political elites in individual countries will make important contributions to our under-standing of this crucial element in the democratization process.

Equally critical is the quality and size of the newly emerging entrepreneur-ial middle class. One major issue for Lach is the recruitment base for both the economic and political elite, and he seems to waffle on the success of the trans-formation regarding its ability to secure this base in an orderly and acceptable fashion. We can hardly be surprised at this, since the establishment of such a recruitment process requires long-term economic, political, and educational changes that can only be judged after a generation or more. It is probably fair to argue that the transitional regimes have entered a stage in their develop-ment that calls for patience and a wait-and-see attitude—without, for that rea-son, accepting an overly fatalistic or deterministic position. The choice of policies, the prudence of political judgments and decisions, the behavior of elites and electorates alike, and the quality of further economic reforms will be decisive factors in the years to come. As Lach is clearly indicating, the most important external factor determining the future of the region is the enlarge-ment of the European Union to include several of the former communist coun-tries, including Hungary itself.

András Lánczi provides a different slant on the critical evaluation of Hun-gary and its neighboring transition states, concerned that "Communism" has not been fully negated. He picks up on the polarization concerns expressed by Lach, and warns of complacency about the widely perceived "progress" of democratization and economic liberalization in Central Europe. He criticizes the policy of self-preservation of Prime Minister Péter Medgyessy, and in par-ticular, he stresses the extent to which the (orchestrated?) indifference evident in Hungarian media and civil society is symptomatic of longer-term dangers.

As Louis Hunt argues in his chapter, Lánczi reminds us of the necessity for something more than merely an economic attachment to a new regime or soci-ety. "Founding a new polity, however, requires both legal and moral grounds, a sort of common sentiment and faith in the evolving constitutional frame-works." Lánczi strongly asserts the lack of attentiveness to this moral dimen-sion and to the issue of constitutional faith. His is a conservative perspective—rather distinctive in the region—that calls for a clearer confronta-tion with and evaluation of the past communist system. He combines a criti-cism of the slackness vis-à-vis former communists with a deep skepticism of what he perceives as a rise of moral relativism and even nihilism in the transi-tional systems.

Lánczi's attack is especially directed against the so-called reform commu-nists who claim that they contributed to the dismantling of the old system by undermining it from within. As he forcefully puts it: "This line of argument has gone so far as to practically denying Communism as a vicious and politically corrupt form of government. Similarly, moral relativism has become a predominant worldview and form of judgment still regarding history as the only source and reference point of moral standards." Unlike so many other observers of the region, Lánczi doubts that the old communist mentality has disappeared from the scene. On the contrary, he asserts: "Communism as a form of government may be dead, but as morality and political judgment it is just as virulent as ever. I claim that communism as a political culture, mentality, and attitude is not dead at all, and even where it is dead, nihilism is always at hand." This concern, together with the "underdeveloped conditions of conservative thought and policies," form the core of the argument in Lánczi's chapter. Ultimately at issue for Lánczi is the complex process of lustration as an unfinished policy in the former communist countries.

There is, in Lánczi's argument, also the suggestion that due to the peaceful nature of the transition, there are "various segments of social life" that have kept their communist form and content, and thus remain to be transformed. Only in the economic sphere was the transformation relatively successful. But the economic transition came with high social costs and negative political consequences, as Lánczi persuasively documents, and provides one reason why the former communists were returned to power in the 2002 election.

Although his claim that the ex- and post-communist strength in Hungary has encouraged a moral and political relativism needs further elaboration and clarification, Lánczi makes a compelling, albeit controversial, case for opening up a thorough moral discussion regarding the legacy of communism and its survival in post-communist regimes. That this debate needs to continue is undeniable; that it will aid, as Lánczi hopes, in the establishment of a moral and political conservative movement is an open question. Regardless, Lánczi's chapter certainly reveals the seriousness of the moral issue involved in and at the center of the entire cluster of questions surrounding the survival of (post-) communism in the new regimes. One of many virtues of his argument is to bring to the forefront this much neglected topic in the post-communist discussion, and to call for an honest and no-nonsense approach to an issue that is often permeated by ideological considerations and shallow political motives.

Mircea Maniu explores the continuing impact today of the economic and political precursors to the onset of transition, stressing the distinctiveness of the Romanian case. He ascribes the "slower" transition in Romania, compared with most of its neighbors, to the lingering effects of repression under Ceausescu and the lack of previous experience with democratic reform and economic liberalization. Maniu also shows the negative results of Romania's unique nationalist communism encouraged by Ceausescu, as well as the devastating consequences of the latter's irrational cult of personality. In addition, Romania's situation was further weakened by bad (exaggerated?) publicity abroad. As a result, Romania became by the early 1980s an isolated, insulated, and impoverished country. No wonder that Romania has faced serious political and economic difficulties during the first decade and a half of the transition.

Given this uphill struggle, Maniu ends his article on a relatively optimistic note, particularly on the maturation of democratic institutions. As with many analysts and politicians in the region, this cautious optimism, especially on the economic side, may depend too much on Romania's prospect for eventual membership in the European Union. Trade growth and regional development aid will help to reduce the lag in progress, he posits. This, of course, raises the crucial question of how much difference EU membership will make for transition countries. Is it, in fact, the final salvation, or simply the beginning of a difficult marriage likely to disappoint the suitors? Why does Poland now seem to view the benefits from its EU membership less positively than most of its Central European and Baltic neighbors? Is the neglect of more focused and limited integration efforts (e.g., through the Visegrad group in Central Europe or through the Economic Cooperation Organization [ECO] in Central Asia) shortsighted? What is the most viable strategy toward economic prosperity and independence?

Marius Jucan finds in the end that Romania can be integrated fully into the new Europe, but he notes several sociocultural factors that will continue to make this problematic and that help to explain the lag that Maniu described economically and politically. Nationalism and limitations on the "European-ness" of Romanians remain strong, as does bureaucratic inertia and a lack of commitment to serious reform. This tension between an introspective emphasis on Romania—often with nationalist and essentialist overtones, and a more cosmopolitan, pro-Western attitude—is, as Jucan shows, deeply rooted in Romanian history and culture, and thus unlikely to be resolved in the near future. However, that much depends on the working through of this profound division is clear from the argument presented by Jucan. Both a possible future within the European Union and a successful outcome of current reform efforts are bound up in this thorny and potentially explosive conflict.

Almost as a confirmation of Lánczi's main thesis, Jucan's chapter illustrates not only the debilitating continuity between the communist and post-communist regimes but also the absence of an explicit process for coming to terms with the communist past. On both these points, Romania is arguably worse off than most of the Central European countries—especially Hungary, Poland, and the Czech Republic—but nevertheless, probably better off than a host of eastern Eurasian countries—for example, Belarus, Tajikistan, and Uzbekistan. Wherever Romania should be placed on such a hypothetical scale, Jucan's narrative reveals the complex interaction and hidden interdependency between cultural, political, and historical factors rooted in a pre-communist past, in the communist era, and in the short post-communist reform period.

Jucan's essay is a fitting end to the studies in this volume, as it underlines the importance of clear and sustained commitment to transformation. The debates over shock therapy vs. gradualism, and on the appropriate mix and sequencing of reforms may seem largely settled for the economies of Central Europe and the Baltics. But the dreams of prosperity and social development remain unrealized for large numbers of the populations in even the most advanced of the transition states. Much remains to be learned on what will work best to advance to the next level, and as to whether this will be largely in the hands of national public officials, or increasingly in those of regional associations and business elites.

The quality of the political leadership in the transition states of Eurasia will also remain a focus of inquiry for some time to come. This includes the impact and challenges associated with the "alternating administrations" experienced in several of the most successful and maturing democracies in Central Europe, as well as the question of what can be done to replace the "elections without democracy" systems evident in Central Asia and other successor republics to the former Soviet Union. If replacement is not in the cards, are there more successful strategies to get the authoritarian regimes more engaged in the project of broadening political participation that is more inclusive for ethnic minorities and disaffected religious opposition groups? Economic liberalization can be a useful point of focus, given the potential for spinoff effects on associational activity.

If replacement is not out of the question, what are the best strategies for influence? While Russia has retrenched since 2000, democratization efforts in other CIS republics may suggest a cautious opening. Most startling is the apparent impact of the condemnation of the November 2004 presidential elections in the Ukraine by a wide range of international observers, accompanied by a well-orchestrated campaign by the opposition for defiance and civil disobedience. It remains to be seen whether this will result in a permanent openly competitive and tolerant democratic system in the Ukraine, but there may well be lessons to be learned by opposition leaders in some of the post-Soviet regimes in Central Asia and the Caucasus. One should not be wildly optimistic, however; elections in 2003–05 were mixed elsewhere in the CIS, with some promise in the Saakashvili presidency in Georgia, but decided bias and corruption in Azerbaijan and Kazakhstan, and no real competition in the Belarus elections. Condemnation by external observers and internal protest seemed to have little effect.

Interesting questions for future research and policy development remain on how effective external observers and foreign-assistance providers have been and may be in the future, after they reflect on both their own work of the past 15 years and the possible lessons of Ukraine 2004. Cutting U.S. foreign assistance—as, for example, occurred in the case of Uzbekistan in July 2004 through a mandated scheme provided in congressional legislation and in 2005 more broadly after the Andijon violence—seems only to have an effect at the margins, and may in fact be counterproductive in limiting civil-society development and opening the country to alternative support from Russia and other interested competitors. A deft touch is required, as is more coordination with UN, EU, and EBRD efforts.

The other side of the research and policy-development challenge here is the question of the posture of a more authoritarian Russia. President Putin has shown clear interest in collaboration with the West to shore up post-communist regimes in the Caucasus and Central Asia against possible external Islamic-fundamentalist influence. But he has also been less than subtle in his interest in the outcomes of regime change in the Ukraine and of regional unrest in Georgia. Are we seeing the beginning of a reassertive Russia, seeking renewed dominance in its old sphere of interest, or simply discrete interventions that will only temporarily perturb the long-term prospects for economic liberalization and democratization (and independence) in Eurasia?

About the Contributors

Kathleen Dowley, Department of Political Science, SUNY-New Paltz

Norman A. Graham, Center for European and Russian/Eurasian Studies and James Madison College, Michigan State University

Axel Hadenius, Department of Political Science, Uppsala University, Sweden

Erik S. Herron, Department of Political Science, University of Kansas

Louis Hunt, James Madison College, Michigan State University

Marius Jucan, Faculty of European Studies, Babes-Bolyai University, Cluj, Romania

Jiří Lach, Department of Politics and European Studies, Palacky University, Olomouc, Czech Republic

András Lánczi, Department of Political Science, Corvinus University, Budapest, Hungary

Folke Lindahl, James Madison College, Michigan State University

Mircea T. Maniu, Faculty of European Studies, Babes-Bolyai University, Cluj, Romania